Contributions to Management Science

The series *Contributions to Management Science* contains research publications in all fields of business and management science. These publications are primarily monographs and multiple author works containing new research results, and also feature selected conference-based publications are also considered. The focus of the series lies in presenting the development of latest theoretical and empirical research across different viewpoints.

This book series is indexed in Scopus.

More information about this series at http://www.springer.com/series/1505

Andrea Caputo • Massimiliano M. Pellegrini •
Marina Dabić • Léo-Paul Dana
Editors

The International Dimension of Entrepreneurial Decision-Making

Cultures, Contexts, and Behaviours

Springer

Editors
Andrea Caputo
University of Trento
Trento, Italy

University of Lincoln
Lincoln, UK

Massimiliano M. Pellegrini
University of Rome "Tor Vergata"
Roma, Italy

Marina Dabić
Faculty of Economics and Business
University of Zagreb
Zagreb, Croatia

Nottingham Trent University
Nottingham, UK

Léo-Paul Dana
Dalhousie University
Halifax, Canada

ISSN 1431-1941 ISSN 2197-716X (electronic)
Contributions to Management Science
ISBN 978-3-030-85949-7 ISBN 978-3-030-85950-3 (eBook)
https://doi.org/10.1007/978-3-030-85950-3

This Springer imprint is published by the registered company Springer Nature Switzerland AG.
The registered company address is: Gewerbestrasse 11, 6330 Cham, Switzerland

To my family, who always supported my "international dimension."
Andrea Caputo

To my life partner, who always withstood my "international dimension."
Massimiliano Matteo Pellegrini

To my family, who always accepted my "international dimension."
Marina Dabic

To Michelle, with thanks for having encouraged my "international dimension."
Léo-Paul Dana

Foreword

It is a privilege for me to welcome you to the new book *The International Dimension of Entrepreneurial Decision-Making: Cultures, Contexts, and Behaviours*, edited by Dr Andrea Caputo, Dr Massimiliano M. Pellegrini, Prof Marina Dabić, and Prof Léo-Paul Dana. Each of the chapters provides a valuable contribution to developing the field of international entrepreneurship.

During the past 30 years, increasingly more attention has been paid to internationalization of small business and international entrepreneurship. Policy makers have been observing on the economic growth potential (job creation, etc.), while researchers have been grappling with analyzing the convoluted border crossing phenomena. Indeed, international entrepreneurship and internationalization of SMEs can take on many forms and develop in a diverse context but common to these activities is that they involve human decision-making, cross-cultural contexts, and risk as well as opportunities.

Research has shown the importance of SMEs and international entrepreneurship in relation to acting on emerging opportunities and developing innovative products and services. Accordingly, a major part of the SME and IE research literature draws the attention to the innovativeness of technology-based firms. However, recently and following global trends, we have seen an increased research attention toward the "innovativeness" in a broader sense. Hence, there has been a rise in literature on the interplay between the potential impact of SME and IE activities on broad-based global issues such as sustainability, social equality, migration, and emerging economies. This research indicates that SME and IE might be a key ingredient in solving these vital issues that we are confronted with.

I believe that this volume offers state-of-the-art insight on the IE phenomenon as it continues a synergic evolution with broader global trends such as migration, digitalization, and increased focus on sustainability.

Enjoy your read

International Business &
Entrepreneurship, University of
Southern Denmark, Odense, Denmark

Martin Hannibal

Acknowledgments

We would like to deeply thank all the friends and colleagues who were involved in the production of this edited book. In particular, special thanks go to all the contributing authors for being interested in participating in this ambitious project and for delivering such high-quality manuscripts in a timely fashion and despite the challenges the COVID-19 pandemic brought to all of us. We would also like to explicitly thank all the reviewers who assisted us and took part in reviewing the manuscripts published in this book. Moreover, we would like to express our gratitude to the European Academy of Management community and the SIG of Entrepreneurship's scholars, who supported this project during its development.

Contents

Editors and Contributors

About the Editors

Andrea Caputo is Associate Professor in Management at the University of Trento (Italy) and at the University of Lincoln (UK). He received his PhD in Management from the University of Rome "Tor Vergata" in 2013. Previously, he was Assistant Professor at Princess Sumaya University. He has also held visiting positions at several universities, like the University of Queensland, George Washington University, and University of Seville, Alicante, Pisa, Macerata, and Naples Parthenope. His main research expertise is related to entrepreneurship, strategic management, innovation, negotiation, and decision-making. He has authored more than 60 international publications, including *Journal of Business Research*, *International Journal of Entrepreneurial Behaviour & Research*, *International Journal of Entrepreneurship and Small Business*, and *Business Process Management Journal*. He is Associate Editor of the *Journal of Management & Organization* and editor of the book series *Entrepreneurial Behaviour* for Emerald, and co-chair of the track Entrepreneurial Behaviour and Decision-Making at EURAM.

Massimiliano M. Pellegrini is an Associate Professor of Organizational Studies and Entrepreneurial Behaviour at the University of Rome "Tor Vergata," from which he also received his PhD in 2011. Previously, he worked at Roehampton University Business School and University of West London. He is currently coordinating two tracks at European Academy of Management (EURAM), one in entrepreneurial decision-making and behaviors and the other in philosophy for business ethics, and he also chaired until 2018 the Strategic Interest Group of Entrepreneurship (E-ship SIG). His research interests and publications are focused on entrepreneurial, ethical, and organizational decision-making and behaviors, also in the light of recent technological evolutions such as the advent of the 4.0 era. These interests led him to be book series editor of *Entrepreneurial Behaviour* with Emerald Publishing and to publish more than 50 contributions, especially in highly ranked journals, e.g., *Journal of Business Research, Journal of Business Ethics, Small Business Economics, Journal of Small Business Management, IEEE Transactions on Engineering Management*, and *Journal of Managerial Psychology*.

Marina Dabić is Full Professor of Entrepreneurship and International Business at the University of Zagreb, Faculty of Economics and Business, Croatia, and Nottingham Business School, NTU, UK. She received her PhD degree in economics, focusing on transfer technology in international business from the University of Zagreb, Faculty of Economics and Business, Zagreb, Croatia, in 2000. Her research appears in a wide variety of international journals, including the *Journal of International Business Studies, Journal of World Business, Journal of Business Research, Technological Forecasting and Social Change, Small Business Economics, Organizational Dynamics, International Journal of Human Resource Management, IEEE Transactions on Engineering Management, Journal of Small Business Management, Technovation*, and *Organizational Dynamics*, among many others. Prof Dabić is an Associate Editor of the *Technological Forecasting and Social Change* listed as CABS 3*, Technology in Society and Department editor of *IEEE Transactions on Engineering Management*, listed as CABS 3*. Prof Dabic was grant holder of EC project and she is reviewer and partner for Horizon 2020 projects. Prof Dabic received the "Highly Commended Award" at the Emerald Literati Network Awards for Excellence in 2017 and 2018 and TOP HOT 25 in the *Journal of World Business* for the period 2000–2007 and WAIB best paper award at AIB 2021.

Léo-Paul Dana is Professor at Dalhousie University and holds titles of Professor at Montpellier Business School and Visiting Professor at Kingston University. He is associated with the Chaire ETI at Sorbonne Business School. A graduate of McGill University and HEC Montreal, he has served as Marie Curie Fellow at Princeton University and Visiting Professor at INSEAD. He has published extensively in a variety of journals including *Entrepreneurship: Theory and Practice, International Business Review, International Small Business Journal, Journal of Business Research, Journal of Small Business Management, Journal of World Business, Small Business Economics,* and *Technological Forecasting and Social Change*.

Contributors

Aldo Alvarez-Risco Universidad de Lima, Lima, Peru

Bob Bastian University of Bergamo, Bergamo, Italy

Lowell W. Busenitz University of Oklahoma, Norman, OK, USA

Andrea Caputo University of Trento, Trento, Italy
University of Lincoln, Lincoln, UK

Arturo Charris-Fontanilla Instituto Nacional de Formación Técnica Profesional Humberto Velásquez García, Ciénaga, Colombia

Naïma Cherchem Entrepreneurship & Strategy Department, Ted Rogers School of Management, Ryerson University, Toronto, ON, Canada

Daniel R. Clark Ivey Business School - Western University, London, ON, Canada

Emilio Costales School of Business and Management, Royal Holloway University of London, Egham, UK

Marina Dabić Faculty of Economics and Business, University of Zagreb, Zagreb, Croatia
Nottingham Trent University, Nottingham, UK

Léo-Paul Dana Dalhousie University, Halifax, NS, Canada

Shyla Del-Aguila-Arcentales Escuela Nacional de Marina Mercante "Almirante Miguel Grau", Callao, Peru

Javier Viloria Escobar Instituto Nacional de Formación Técnica Profesional Humberto Velásquez García, Ciénaga, Colombia

Paul Agu Igwe Lincoln International Business School, University of Lincoln, Lincoln, UK

Christian Keen Entrepreneurship and International Business, Faculty of Business Administration, Laval University, Québec, QC, Canada

Mauri Laukkanen University of Eastern Finland, Business School, Kuopio Campus, Finland

Simona Leonelli Department of Economics and Management, University of Padova, Padua, Italy

Francisco Liñán Universidad de Sevilla, Facultad de CC, Económicas y Empresariales, Seville, Spain

Filippo Marchesani Department of Business Administration, University of "G. d'Annunzio" Chieti, Pescara, Italy

Francesca Masciarelli Department of Business Administration, University of "G. d'Annunzio" Chieti, Pescara, Italy

John Mendy University of Lincoln, Lincoln International Business School, Lincoln, UK

Luis Francisco Miranda Innovscience Research Group—IVS, Santa Marta, Colombia

Claudio Multari University 'Mediterranea' of Reggio Calabria, Reggio Calabria, Italy

Massimiliano M. Pellegrini University of Rome "Tor Vergata", Roma, Italy

Vanessa Pertuz Universidad Nacional Abierta y a Distancia, Escuela de Ciencias Básicas, Tecnología e Ingeniería, Grupo de Investigación Gestindustriales EOCA, Atlántico, Colombia

Robert J. Pidduck Old Dominion University, Norfolk, VA, USA

Franco Ernesto Rubino University of Calabria, Rende, Italy

Giuseppe Valenza University of Palermo, Palermo, Italy

Anica Zeyen School of Business and Management, Royal Holloway University of London, Egham, UK
Department of Psychology, Faculty of Humanities, University of Johannesburg, Johannesburg, South Africa

Antonella Zucchella University of Pavia, Pavia, Italy

Introduction to The International Dimension of Entrepreneurial Decision-Making: Cultures, Contexts, and Behaviours

Andrea Caputo, Massimiliano M. Pellegrini, Marina Dabić, and Léo-Paul Dana

Abstract This chapter introduces the content of the book, presenting the key insights from the contributed chapters. The book comprises 11 diverse and insightful contributions from nine different countries.

Keywords Entrepreneurship · Internationalisation · Decision-making · Culture · Entrepreneurial decisions

Entrepreneurial characteristics have been studied extensively around the globe (Litzky et al., 2020), and entrepreneurship research has recognised several personal characteristics considered to be contributory in stimulating entrepreneurial behaviour (Paul & Shrivatava, 2016). Two commonly cited characteristics connected with the entrepreneurial orientation are an internal locus of control and innovativeness (Mueller & Thomas, 2001). One of the most inquired psychological features in entrepreneurship research is internal locus of control, while innovative action is

A. Caputo (✉)
University of Trento, Trento, Italy

University of Lincoln, Lincoln, UK
e-mail: andrea.caputo@unitn.it

M. M. Pellegrini
University of Rome "Tor Vergata", Roma, Italy
e-mail: massimiliano.pellegrini@uniroma2.it

M. Dabić
Faculty of Economics and Business, University of Zagreb, Zagreb, Croatia

Nottingham Trent University, Nottingham, UK
e-mail: mdabic@net.efzg.hr

L.-P. Dana
Dalhousie University, Halifax, NS, Canada
e-mail: lp762359@dal.ca

A. Caputo et al. (eds.), *The International Dimension of Entrepreneurial Decision-Making*, Contributions to Management Science,
https://doi.org/10.1007/978-3-030-85950-3_1

specific in Schumpeter's explanation of the entrepreneur. However, decision-making in cross-cultural studies and the significance of culture and cognition are rare and, in most occurrences, inadequate to deep understanding and possible comparisons between countries and cultures (Muzychenko, 2008). Thus, the questions are raised behind rationality for this book: *do entrepreneurial habits in the decision process vary systematically across cultures, context and behaviours and if so, why?*

Understanding the international behaviours of SMEs, entrepreneurial ventures, and entrepreneurs have long been of interest by management scholars. Several studies, tend to focalise on firm-level characteristics to unveil the strategic pathways of internationalisation of SMEs (Caputo et al., 2016; Dabić et al., 2020; Dana, 2009).

To achieve a comprehensive understanding of decision-making and behaviour, the augmentation of cognitive sciences is highly relevant (Zucchella, 2021). An up-to-date review about the cognitive grounds of firm internationalisation explores the key role of this view to describe the phenomenon (Niittymies & Pajunen, 2020), and pointed out that 'existing research addressing cognition is fragmented and under-specified'. Zahra et al. (2005) recommend leveraging cognitive science to advance theoretical bases in international entrepreneurship by adding rationality, the role of national and international institutional environments mental models and sensemaking.

Dabić et al. (2020), reviewing the literature on internationalisation of SMEs, have identified a number of future research directions aimed at filling the research gaps in the field. This edited collection of chapters is aimed at contributing to fill such gaps, by presenting contributions from international business and entrepreneurship scholars interested in investigating the decision-making and behavioural aspect of internationalisation of SMEs and entrepreneurial ventures.

Indeed, decision-making processes affect all aspects of business at every stage of their development. Making decisions are well-established topics of interest in many fields, including management, marketing (Crick & Crick, 2018), psychology, sociology, sustainability (DiVito & Bohnsack, 2017), ethics (McVea, 2009), methodology (Lohrke et al., 2018), and political science, to name a few. However, entrepreneurs and their counterparts in international settings, compared to non-entrepreneurial roles, face conditions of high uncertainty, ambiguity, time pressure, emotional intensity, and high risk when making decisions (Caputo & Pellegrini, 2019, 2020; Townsend et al., 2018).

This book was initially born from ideas based on our joint research interests in entrepreneurship and long-term friendship and collaboration (e.g., Caputo et al., 2016; Dabić et al., 2020), which evolved in the development of a successful standing track at the European Academy of Management Annual Conference, within the SIG of Entrepreneurship, titled 'Entrepreneurial Decision Making and Behaviour'.

However, having opened the call or chapters to several audiences beyond the EURAM Conference, we were able to receive many high-quality and cutting-edge scientific contributions from all over the world, making this book a truly international project. We present here 11 contributions from nine different nations: Canada,

Colombia, Finland, Italy, Perù, South Africa, Spain, the United Kingdom and the United States.

In the call for chapters of this edited book, we called for scholars to submit empirical, theoretical, and review chapters, which try to bridge the literature on entrepreneurship, entrepreneurial, and innovative behaviours with decision-making and negotiation. To the best of our knowledge, this edited book is among the first to combine those streams of research thereby offering a new and insightful addition to the entrepreneurship field.

Every chapter that the reader will read in this book has undergone a thorough double-blind peer-review process. It started with authors submitting a chapter proposal in October 2020, which was reviewed and then authors were invited to submit a full chapter by February 2021. Chapters were then reviewed and finalised during 2021. Offering the reader with contemporary and high-quality research investigating the international dimension of entrepreneurial decision-making in terms of cultures, contexts and behaviours.

1 Structure of the Book

Following this introduction, the book starts with Chap. 2, titled *Revitalizing the 'International' In International Entrepreneurship: The Promise of Culture and Cognition*, where Robert J. Pidduck, Daniel Clark, and Lowell Busenitz discuss the fusion of international business and entrepreneurship research to form the field of IE, and how this has provided substantial added value for one half of its coparent disciplines, international business. IE helped extend the traditional phenomenological focus beyond large corporations to include new ventures. The value-add for IE's other coparent discipline, entrepreneurship, though, remains unclear. In this chapter, we build the case that this may be partly due to an unnecessarily restrictive interpretation of what 'international' can represent to be framed as an IE study and to usefully build on and integrate related works in adjacent fields. Our analyses reveal that the 'international' elements in most IE studies are chiefly interpreted to mean geographic contexts for firm outcomes. While useful to an extent, this niche has and continues to limit us from drawing on international dynamics to meaningfully probe the many foundational questions in entrepreneurship; that IE has still left mostly untouched. We argue that a shift in the directional focus of IE is required: to include intercultural dynamics as antecedents to entrepreneurial action, both international and domestic. We discuss how adopting a broader international lens, used through the social sciences, can foster valuable insights from domains such as cross-cultural psychology and international organisational behaviour. Finally, we lay out a research agenda for investigating how intercultural constructs underpinning cross-border dynamics influence the discovery, enactment, evaluation and exploitation of opportunities in general.

In Chap. 3, Mauri Laukkanen and Francisco Liñán present their work titled *Uncovering Entrepreneurial Belief Systems through cognitive causal mapping.*

The chapter illuminates the basic issues of human cognition and the preconditions of disclosing and studying entrepreneurial actors' subjective knowledge or beliefs (aka cognitive maps, mental models, schemas), which underlie their reasoning, intentions, and decision-making. To demonstrate such research in practice, the chapter presents in some detail an established, yet accessible cognitive method, comparative causal mapping (CCM) using the freely downloadable CMAP3 software, for revealing and analysing the belief systems of micro-entrepreneurs and small business advisors. Particularly useful in international studies, this methodology supports research that uses raw data in different languages but a standard language like English for coding the data and reporting the findings. Thus, the CCM-CMAP3 approach can facilitate, for instance, studies that compare cross-cultural or cross-national belief systems or those of specific entrepreneur categories, or which track the cognitive evolution of entrepreneurs or key stakeholders during internationalisation.

Chapter 4 follows and is titled *International Entrepreneurial Ecosystem, Knowledge Exploitation and Innovation: Case of International Biotech Pharmaceutical SME*, authored by Naima Cherchem and Christian Keen. The chapter investigates how innovation and internationalisation are key elements of knowledge-intensive industries such as the biotech pharmaceutical sector. Small- and medium-sized enterprises in this highly competitive and global sector are under significant pressure to innovate and commercialise their product in a short period of time. Given the lack of resources when compared to the big pharmaceutical firms, these SMEs tend to be part of several international entrepreneurial ecosystems. As members of these ecosystems, the biotechnological SMEs collaborate with other members in almost all the different phases of product development. From the first step of working together to develop a new molecule, to form an alliance with a foreign firm to enter a new market. The biotechnological sector has the distinctiveness that technical expertise and reputation are the most important resources. Internationalisation, either to develop or to commercialise a product, is not an option but a day-to-day occurrence.

Bob Bastian and Antonella Zucchella follow with Chap. 5, titled *Ignorance and international entrepreneurship. Two sides of a blade in the decision to enter a foreign market.* This chapter takes an unusual perspective on International Entrepreneurship, namely, how entrepreneurs, when deciding to enter a foreign market, 'don't know'. While a lot has been said about knowledge, scholars rather avoid the other side of the coin: ignorance. Throughout the chapter, we discuss the influence of ignorance on entrepreneurship cognition, when it may be beneficial, and when instead it is detrimental. Practical tools to recognise and unmake ignorance are provided.

In Chap. 6, *Risk or opportunity? Exploring the relationship between entrepreneurial decision and the use of equity crowdfunding campaigns in less- and well-developed regions in Italy,* Simona Leonelli, Filippo Marchesani, and Francesca Masciarelli investigate decisions around crowdfunding in Italy. The democratising role of crowdfunding has had a substantial impact on SMEs development and opportunities. Crowdfunding enables entrepreneurs to fund their firms by drawing on small contributions from many individuals without the help of financial intermediaries. Crowdfunding impacts firms' strategic and financial development and entrepreneurs' decision-making processes because of geographical contexts not offering the same economic and financial opportunities. Mainly, in Italy, characterised by heterogeneity in the regional economic development, crowdfunding may allow entrepreneurs to break out of the traditional linkage between the SME and urban area. The chapter analyses how the entrepreneurial decision-making process differs across Italian regions considering entrepreneurial choices about using equity crowdfunding campaigns and shows that the gap between less- and well-developed regions is reduced thanks to crowdfunding itself.

With Chap. 7, *The Internationalization of Family SMEs: A Literature Review and Research Agenda*, Franco Ernesto Rubino, Claudio Multari, and Giuseppe Valenza discuss the internationalisation process of family Small and Medium Enterprises (SMEs). Although several studies have dealt with overseas expansion strategies, it seems that only a few of them have focused on family SMEs. By a Systematic Literature Review (SLR), based on a sample of 29 articles, the research work intends to investigate the ways that family SMEs undertake to internationalise their businesses. The originality of the study concerns the lack of an SLR about the internationalisation process of family SMEs. The findings highlight that there are some theories supported by most of the academics, while others revealed conflicted opinions. Moreover, there are interesting theories that should be better investigated by future research. Furthermore, it was found out that business literature interest for the topic has been grown in the last two decades. The chapter aims to stimulate the debate about family SMEs' internationalisation strategies.

The following chapter, Chap. 8, is titled *Internationalising HRM Framework for SMEs: Transcending High Performance Organisation Theory's Economic Utilitarianism towards Humanism* by John Mendy. The work rests on the premise that people and economic barriers constitute fundamental challenges to SMEs' performance internationally. SMEs' internationalisation studies have relied on an economic utilitarian approach to resolve this conundrum with limited success. This chapter examines and critiques High-Performance Organisation Theory's five characteristics and highlights both a theory and practice gap in SMEs' internationalisation and how staff's performance is managed humanely. By using a conceptual abstraction methodology based on over eighty referred articles from the Web of Science, this chapter develops an 'Internationalising HRM Framework'. There are four characteristics and principles centring on competency, R & TD, social and resilience capacity. This chapter contributes not only to filling the dual theory-practice gap in SMEs' internationalisation research but also helps in addressing the problem of how managers, entrepreneurs and HRM professionals can manage people humanely way whilst addressing the performativity lag when SMEs operate internationally.

Chapter 9 is authored by Paul AguIgwe and is titled *Cross-cultural tribes, Community and Indigenous entrepreneurship*. This chapter review important concepts of indigenous entrepreneurship including clan entrepreneurship, kindred entrepreneurship, tribal entrepreneurship, community entrepreneurship and nomadic entrepreneurship.

Examining West African popular tribes of Igbo, Fulani, Hausa and Yoruba, the findings reveal that indigenous people have motives for entrepreneurship, as well as exhibit modern entrepreneurial behaviours such as risk-taking, wealth-seeking and entrepreneurial learning.

Besides institutional factors, culture, family and community are the three most important determinants of forces that influence indigenous entrepreneurial behaviour. Among the four Nigerian indigenous tribes examined in this chapter, Igbos are the most enterprising and have a high entrepreneurial passion and they dominate several commercial clusters throughout Nigeria and West Africa. Igbos in the Southeastern region of Nigeria have an established informal apprenticeship system (Nwa-boyi) often regarded as the 'Igbo Traditional Business School' that provides a safe environment for learning the business, starting the business, marketing, risk-taking and innovation.

In Chap. 10, Aldo Alvarez-Risco and Shyla Del-Aguila-Arcentales author the work *Sustainable initiatives in international markets*. This chapter presents a novel contribution on the education gaps that need to be covered to ensure that professionals can successfully develop sustainability initiatives in entrepreneurship and at the corporate level. Various practical examples are shown in various industrial sectors such as hospitality and all its aspects related to its impact on the SDGs. The sustainable approach to supply chains and its link with Industry 4.0, so changing in times of COVID-19, are also presented; Likewise, evidence is shown of the efforts to achieve an eco-efficient management of plastic from the regulatory and practical spheres. Finally, the progress of the increasing implementation of sustainable transport is shown.

Chapter 11, titled *Social Capital and the Morphogenesis of Actors: Lessons from International Social Entrepreneurs*, authored by Emilio Costales and Anica Zeyen utilises empirical examples from international social entrepreneurs in the Netherlands to illustrate the role of social capital in navigating new environments. Particularly, the authors analyse the role of three dimensions of social capital—relational, cognitive and structural social capital—in the decision-making process of international social entrepreneurs. In so doing, this chapter develops a Social-Capital-Morphogenetic model of social entrepreneurship which serves to highlight how each stage of the entrepreneurial process is affected as different types of social capital are accumulated.

The book is concluded with Chap. 12, titled *Determinants of the internationalisation process of Colombian* firms, where Vanessa Pertuz, Luis Francisco Miranda, Arturo Charris-Fontanilla and Javier Viloria Escobar analyse the main determinants of the internationalisation process of Colombian firms. Their study is based on the 2015 GEM Adult Population Survey. The APS explores the role of the individual in the life cycle of the business process. The focus is not only on the characteristics of the company, but also on the motivation of people to start a company, the actions taken to start and manage a company, as well as the attitudes related to the spirit business.

Simultaneously with publishing this book, we combine ideas about the next book since the shared ideas tend to contribute to the synergy that results in this book. Therefore, I send a heartfelt welcome to the network and invite your feedback and opinions. This publication effort would not have been possible without the people participating directly or indirectly in the compilation of this book (authors, reviewers, Springer as publisher, academic, business owners and managers). They all have contributed and collaborated solidly by providing the examples, the realities that help the future growth of the firms and help to prepare entrepreneurs, managers and our students for the realities they will face: challenges and opportunities, confidence and compassion, awareness strength and courage, failures through crises and success stories and most skills, experience, knowledge, wisdom and motivations that will help them to prove the most critical real-life concepts in the business world.

References

Caputo, A., & Pellegrini, M. M. (2019). *The anatomy of entrepreneurial decisions: Past, present and future research directions*. Springer.

Caputo, A., & Pellegrini, M. M. (2020). *The entrepreneurial behaviour: Unveiling the cognitive and emotional aspect of entrepreneurship*. Emerald.

Caputo, A., Pellegrini, M. M., Dabic, M., & Dana, L.-P. (2016). Internationalisation of firms from Central and Eastern Europe. *European Business Review, 28*(6), 630–651. https://doi.org/10.1108/EBR-01-2016-0004

Crick, J. M., & Crick, D. (2018). Angel investors' predictive and control funding criteria: The importance of evolving business models. *Journal of Research in Marketing and Entrepreneurship, 20*(1), 34–56. https://doi.org/10.1108/JRME-11-2016-0043

Dabić, M., Maley, J., Dana, L.-P., Novak, I., Pellegrini, M. M., & Caputo, A. (2020). Pathways of SME internationalization: A bibliometric and systematic review. *Small Business Economics, 55* (3), 705–725. https://doi.org/10.1007/s11187-019-00181-6

Dana, L. P. (2009). Religion as an explanatory variable for entrepreneurship. *The International Journal of Entrepreneurship and Innovation, 10*(2), 87–99.

DiVito, L., & Bohnsack, R. (2017). Entrepreneurial orientation and its effect on sustainability decision tradeoffs: The case of sustainable fashion firms. *Journal of Business Venturing, 32*(5), 569–587.

Litzky, B., Winkel, D., Hance, J., & Howell, R. (2020). Entrepreneurial intentions: Personal and cultural variations. *Journal of Small Business and Enterprise Development, 27*(7), 1029–1047.

Lohrke, F. T., Carson, C. M., & Lockamy, A. (2018). Bayesian analysis in entrepreneurship decision-making research: Review and future directions. *Management Decision, 56*(5), 972–986.

McVea, J. F. (2009). A field study of entrepreneurial decision-making and moral imagination. *Journal of Business Venturing, 24*(5), 491–504.

Mueller, S. L., & Thomas, A. S. (2001). Culture and entrepreneurial potential: A nine country study of locus of control and innovativeness. *Journal of Business Venturing, 16*(1), 51–75.

Muzychenko, O. (2008). Cross-cultural entrepreneurial competence in identifying international business opportunities. *European Management Journal, 26*(6), 366–377.

Niittymies, A., & Pajunen, K. (2020). Cognitive foundations of firm internationalization: A systematic review and agenda for future research. *International Business Review, 29*(4), 101654.

Paul, J., & Shrivatava, A. (2016). Do young managers in a developing country have stronger entrepreneurial intentions? Theory and debate. *International Business Review, 25*(6), 1197–1210.

Townsend, D. M., Hunt, R. A., McMullen, J. S., & Sarasvathy, S. D. (2018). Uncertainty, knowledge problems, and entrepreneurial action. *Academy of Management Annals, 12*(2), 659–687.

Zahra, S. A., Korri, J. S., & Yu, J. (2005). Cognition and international entrepreneurship: Implications for research on international opportunity recognition and exploitation. *International Business Review, 14*(2), 129–146.

Zucchella, A. (2021). International entrepreneurship and the internationalization phenomenon: Taking stock, looking ahead. *International Business Review, 30*(2), 101800.

Dr. Andrea Caputo is Associate Professor in Management at the University of Trento (Italy) and at the University of Lincoln (UK). He received his PhD in Management from the University of Rome "Tor Vergata" in 2013. Previously, he was Assistant Professor at Princess Sumaya University. He has also held visiting positions at several universities, like University of Queensland, George Washington University, University of Seville, Alicante, Pisa, Macerata and Naples Parthenope. His main research expertise is related to entrepreneurship, strategic management, innovation, negotiation, and decision-making. He has authored more than 60 international publications, including *Journal of Business Research, International Journal of Entrepreneurial Behaviours & Research, International Journal of Entrepreneurship & Small Business, and Business Process Management Journal*. He is Associate Editor of the *Journal of Management & Organization* and editor of the book series "*Entrepreneurial Behaviour*" for Emerald, and co-chair of the track Entrepreneurial Behaviour and Decision-Making at EURAM.

Massimiliano M. Pellegrini is an Associate Professor of Organizational Studies and Entrepreneurial behaviour at University of Rome "Tor Vergata", from which he also received his Ph.D. in 2011. Previously, worked at Roehampton University Business School and University of West-London. He is currently coordinating two tracks at European Academy of Management (EURAM), one in entrepreneurial decision making and behaviours and the other on philosophy for business ethics, and he also chaired until 2018 the Strategic Interest Group of Entrepreneurship (E-ship SIG). His research interests and publications are focused on entrepreneurial, ethical and organizational decision making and behaviours, also in the light of recent technological evolutions as the 4.0 era advent. These interests led him to be book series editor of "Entrepreneurial Behaviour" with the Emerald publishing and to publish more than 50 contributions, especially in highly-ranked journals e.g., *Journal of Business Research, Journal of Business Ethics, Small Business Economics, Journal of Small Business Management, IEEE Transaction on Engineering Management, and Journal of Managerial Psychology*.

Prof. Marina Dabić is Full Professor of Entrepreneurship and International Business at University of Zagreb, Faculty of Economics and Business, Croatia, and Nottingham Business School, NTU, U.K. She received her Ph.D. degree in Economics, focus on transfer technology in international business from the University of Zagreb, Faculty of Economics and Business, Zagreb, Croatia in 2000. Her research appears in a wide variety of international journals, including the *Journal of International Business Studies, Journal of World Business, Journal of Business Research, Technological Forecasting and Social Change, Small Business Economics, Organizational Dynamics, International Journal of Human Resource Management, IEEE- Transactions on Engineering Management, Journal of Small Business Management, Technovation, Organizational Dynamics*, among many others. Prof. Dabić is an Associate Editor of the Technological Forecasting and Social Change listed as CABS 3*, Technology in Society and Department editor of IEEE- Transactions on Engineering Management, listed as CABS 3*. Professor Dabic was grantholder if EC project and she is reviewer and partner for Horizon 2020 projects. Prof Dabic received the "Highly Commended

Award" at the Emerald Literati Network Awards for Excellence in 2017 and 2018 and TOP HOT 25 in the Journal of World Business for period 2000–2007 and WAIB best paper award at AIB 2021.

Prof. Léo-Paul Dana is Professor at Dalhousie University and holds titles of Professor at Montpellier Business School and Visiting Professor at Kingston University. He is associated with the Chaire ETI at Sorbonne Business School. A graduate of McGill University and HEC-Montreal, he has served as Marie Curie Fellow at Princeton University and Visiting Professor at INSEAD. He has published extensively in a variety of journals including: *Entrepreneurship: Theory & Practice, International Business Review, International Small Business Journal, Journal of Business Research, Journal of Small Business Management, Journal of World Business, Small Business Economics,* and *Technological Forecasting & Social Change*.

Revitalizing the 'International' in International Entrepreneurship: The Promise of Culture and Cognition

Robert J. Pidduck, Daniel R. Clark, and Lowell W. Busenitz

Abstract International entrepreneurship (IE) has emerged as its own domain—born out of the intersection of international business and entrepreneurship research. This fusion of disciplines has provided considerable value for international business by expanding its traditional focus beyond corporations to include new ventures. However, following an early period of rapid growth, evidence herein suggests that IEs impact and contributions have begun to wane. Through our analysis, we contend that there is a restrictive interpretation of what 'international' represents: cross-border dynamics are chiefly interpreted to mean geographic contexts for new venture outcomes. While valuable, this niche is limiting and leaves many of the foundational questions in entrepreneurship untouched. We argue that a shift in the directional focus of IE is required: to include inter*cultural* dynamics as *antecedents* to entrepreneurial action, both international and domestic. Further, we discuss how adopting a broader international lens, used through management, can foster valuable insights from domains such as cross-cultural psychology and international organizational behaviour. This chapter outlines a research agenda for investigating how intercultural constructs underpinning cross-border dynamics influence the discovery, enactment, evaluation, and exploitation of opportunities at large.

Keywords International entrepreneurship · Cross-cultural · Entrepreneurial opportunity · Cognition · Multicultural experience · Intercultural

---

R. J. Pidduck (✉)
Old Dominion University, Norfolk, VA, USA
e-mail: rpidduck@odu.edu

D. R. Clark
Ivey Business School - Western University, London, ON, Canada
e-mail: dclark@ivey.ca

L. W. Busenitz
University of Oklahoma, Norman, OK, USA
e-mail: busenitz@ou.edu

A. Caputo et al. (eds.), *The International Dimension of Entrepreneurial Decision-Making*, Contributions to Management Science,
https://doi.org/10.1007/978-3-030-85950-3_2

1 Introduction

International entrepreneurship (IE) emerged as a research domain examining issues at the intersection of international business (IB) and entrepreneurship (McDougall & Oviatt, 2000). One phenomenon in particular, the rapid internationalization of new entrepreneurial ventures, demanded compelling explanations, (Reuber et al., 2018), that traditional IB theories alone such as the Uppsala model could not satisfy (Johanson & Vahlne, 2009). With that, a burgeoning subfield of conceptual and empirical work has since developed (Baier-Fuentes et al., 2019). This phenomenon-driven emphasis gave rise to seminal work on international new ventures (Oviatt & McDougall, 1994), born globals (Knight & Cavusgil, 2004), and more recently, born regional ventures (Lopez et al., 2009). All of which have enriched understanding of how and why new ventures grow and develop across borders (McDougall et al., 2014). This focus originated from a desire to extend understanding of multinational corporations to include small and nascent ventures (Verbeke & Ciravegna, 2018); ultimately benefitting the study of IB at large by advancing knowledge into processes and dynamics of early internationalization, such as speed, performance, and timing (Coviello et al., 2011; Prashantham & Dhanaraj, 2010). Further, the entrepreneurship in IE 'contributed back' to IB's foundations by also advancing research into entrepreneurial dynamics of MNCs (Cavusgil & Knight, 2015). As such, to date, much of the work from IE research has benefited IB theory. However, the impact into mainstream entrepreneurship theory, to date, remains very limited.

McDougall and Oviatt (2000, p. 540) developed the primary definition of IE: 'the discovery, enactment, evaluation, and exploitation of opportunities—across national borders—to create future goods and services'. To account for the full remit of the opportunity-centric entrepreneurship phenomenon (Shane & Venkataraman, 2000), and be more in line with the fundamentals of the entrepreneurial process (Reuber et al., 2017). That is, discovering, enacting, evaluating, and exploiting opportunities (Zahra et al., 2005). Given this focus, it would seem likely that by systematically seeking to advance insights into these four central aspects of entrepreneurial opportunities that IE would be growing in representation among leading entrepreneurship outlets. However, this chapter reveals that this is not the case; indeed, while IE's productivity is indeed growing, its presence in the top entrepreneurship outlets is instead falling. The purpose of this chapter is to probe *what is limiting IEs relevance to premier entrepreneurship outlets*. Furthermore, we ask, *where can IE research make significant contributions and offer important insights for mainstream entrepreneurship?* In addressing this, we seek to start a meaningful conversations surrounding how IE can realize its potential and contribute back to entrepreneurship to the same extent as it has to IB.

Our central premise is that the 'across national borders' part of IE's definition is being interpreted far too narrowly. Consequently, we build the case that this narrow focus may be limiting IE's full potential to contribute to core entrepreneurship questions in general. Specifically, we show that 'across national borders' has largely been construed to mean geographic outcomes of firm-level activity. While internationalization of new ventures remains an important phenomenon for continued investigation (Clark et al., 2018; Katz et al., 2021), it is an unnecessarily limiting focus for a field that exists at the intersection of IB and entrepreneurship and has potential to further understanding of how international dynamics influence much wider aspects of entrepreneurial decision-making and opportunities (Caputo & Pellegrini, 2019, 2020). Addressing the contention that IE suffers from a 'theoretical paucity' (Keupp & Gassmann, 2009) and is 'fragmented' (Jones et al., 2011), we provide a constructive path forward. We propose an expansion of IEs directional foci to include the full breadth of cross-*cultural* phenomena that also *antecedes* the discovery, enactment, evaluation, and exploitation of entrepreneurial opportunities *in general*. Stated differently, we argue that the call for 'more cross-fertilization is needed if international entrepreneurship is to fully develop' (Oviatt & McDougall, 2005, p. 6) has not gone far enough—the other side of the 'international' coin in IE has yet to be fully unleashed.

After drawing insights from our review of IE research, we look at some emerging trends within the literature and how our proposed directional pivot on 'international' enhances the relevance of both intercultural and individual-level constructs (over IB-centric emphasis on international and firm-level constructs). We provide illustrative examples of valuable cross-fertilizations and insights from fields such as cross-cultural psychology (e.g., Lu et al., 2017b; Tadmor et al., 2012) and international organizational behaviour (e.g., Gelfand et al., 2007, 2017) that have been overlooked as important for IE research. We select some key constructs, for illustration, within these domains that are gaining traction and illuminate how they—among related others—can greatly inform future IE research questions in each of the four pillars of entrepreneurial opportunity central to IE's definition. Our core aim is that this should bring to light among mainstream entrepreneurship scholars why IE research is important and a much needed subfield for shedding light on core entrepreneurship questions. Furthermore, we hope to stimulate a reinvigorated interest in IE-focused high impact entrepreneurship research.

2 Taking Stock of the Trajectory of IE Research in Entrepreneurship

Since the emergence of IE as a distinctive domain, several comprehensive reviews have been conducted (*see* Coombs et al., 2009; Gamboa & Brouthers, 2008; Jones et al., 2011; Keupp & Gassmann, 2009). Unlike these reviews that sought throughout various periods of IE's development to take general stock of key constructs, theories, and findings—or to delineate subfields within the field such as emerging market-IE (Caputo et al., 2016; Kiss et al., 2012), comparative-IE (Terjesen et al., 2016), IE-methods (Coviello & Jones, 2004), or SME-IE (Dabić et al., 2020)—we conducted a review to critically explore IE-contributions and their implications to mainstream entrepreneurship. Our purpose is twofold. First, we seek to map the publication of IE research and categorize the outlets. Second, we seek to categorize the focus of these papers to contextualize our findings. In so doing, we explore growing trends that are embryonic in IE literature, yet hold promise for further research in providing a deeper understanding of the discovery, enactment, evaluation, and exploitation of opportunities. Based on our observations, we contend that the terms cross-border or international are narrowly interpreted. We then explore some growing constructs within these themes in light of our proposed pivot in the scope of cross-border dynamics that influence entrepreneurial opportunities.

We conducted a review using the following search keywords: *'International entrepreneur*' OR 'Transnational Entrepreneur*' OR 'Entrepreneur*' OR 'Migrant entrepreneur*' OR 'Immigrant entrepreneur*' OR 'New venture' OR 'Startup' OR 'International new venture' OR 'Born global' AND 'Cross-Border' OR 'Cross-Cultural' OR 'Global' OR 'Cross-national' OR 'International' OR 'multicultural' OR 'Cultural' OR 'bicultural' OR 'intercultural' OR 'trans-cultural' IN (Abstract).*

These keywords were entered into the ABI/INFORM Global database, which initially returned a total of over 5000 articles. Refining these results, we sought to include only articles published in journals classified by the CABS (Chartered Association of Business Schools) Journal Guide as $\geq$3 in their quality/impact scale.[1] Following recent review studies (e.g., Nielsen et al., 2017), this approach allows us to consider not only elite outlets but also journals widely considered to be publishing high quality research and thus influential to scholarly conversations. Furthermore, we included those articles which had been published in the 2011-present time period. This period was chosen to reflect recent trends and topics in the development of research in the IE field. These two methodological choices, to include only articles published in $\geq$3 rated journals and to focus on the publication time period over 2011-present, allowed us to capture the current state of IE research. From there, we removed articles that were not directly related to IE, keeping those that specifically mentioned the topic in their title and/or abstract. Accordingly, this process provided a set of 349 articles which formed the basis of the data used to answer our research questions.[2]

In order to analyse the data gathered from the literature review, we first broke down the collected articles based on a categorization of the journals in which they were published. The first category we named 'Premier Entrepreneurship' journals, defined by McMullen (2019) as the wider entrepreneurship fields' elite journals—also those journals which hold a rating of 4 from CABS (specifically,

[1] Although we acknowledge and appreciate that there is fierce debate over how various journal quality ranking systems align (e.g., Australian Business School Deans List, The Rotterdam List, JCR-based lists etc.), $\geq$3 in CABS generally align with outlets considered to be from a "B" to a "A-A*" in many North American Business Schools, and thus 'count' in tenure decisions as 'influential' or 'quality' outlets.

[2] To capture influential articles that can also garner substantial citations yet lie outside of journals (e.g., Venkataraman, 1997)—we also supplemented this with research from within leading research-based book series.

Entrepreneurship Theory and Practice, *Journal of Business Venturing*, and *Strategic Entrepreneurship Journal*). The second category was 'Non-Premier Entrepreneurship' journals, which we defined as those entrepreneurship journals that have a rating of 3. The third category was 'Management and Strategy' journals (which were defined as 3–4 rated journals from the Management/Strategy field). The fourth category was 'International Business' journals (defined as 3–4 rated journals from the IB field). The fifth category was 'Other' journals (defined as 3–4 rated journals not belonging to the previously mentioned fields). From this, we find that the majority of IE papers published during this time period were featured in 'Non-Premier Entrepreneurship' journals. During this time period, there has been an increase in the overall quantity of IE articles published, in all types of journals reviewed. However, while the number of IE articles published overall has *increased*, the number of articles published in premier entrepreneurship journals has *decreased*. Despite this decline in publications appearing in premier entrepreneurship journals, publication of IE articles in non-premier entrepreneurship journals has continued to grow.

Focusing on the content of the IE publications discussed in this review, we see that while articles focused on variants of international entrepreneurial *outcomes* continue to constitute the majority of articles published (relative to antecedent-focused articles), articles that focused on some form of international or cross-border related *antecedent* to entrepreneurial activity have been steadily increasing.

In addition, when comparing IE articles that focus on the individual level or the firm level, we see that both types of articles have continued to increase. In the earlier years of our review time frame, firm-level articles formed the majority of IE articles published, yet individual-level analyses have increased significantly in recent years, highlighting their growing importance for the field. Further, when comparing the incidence of IE articles focusing on cultural aspects of IE, as opposed to geographic aspects, we see initially that the majority of published articles focus on geographic aspects of IE. In recent years, however, there has been an increase in the number of articles focusing on cultural aspects of IE, also suggesting a growing influence in the field.

To summarize, IE articles continue to be published in rising numbers, albeit in non-premier entrepreneurship journals, as publishing in premier journals has decreased. Further, key emerging trends are a growing emphasis on the *antecedent* (over outcome), *cultural* (over geographic), and *individual-level/cognitive* (over firm-level) aspects under the IE thematic umbrella. We turn to addressing the implications of these findings next.

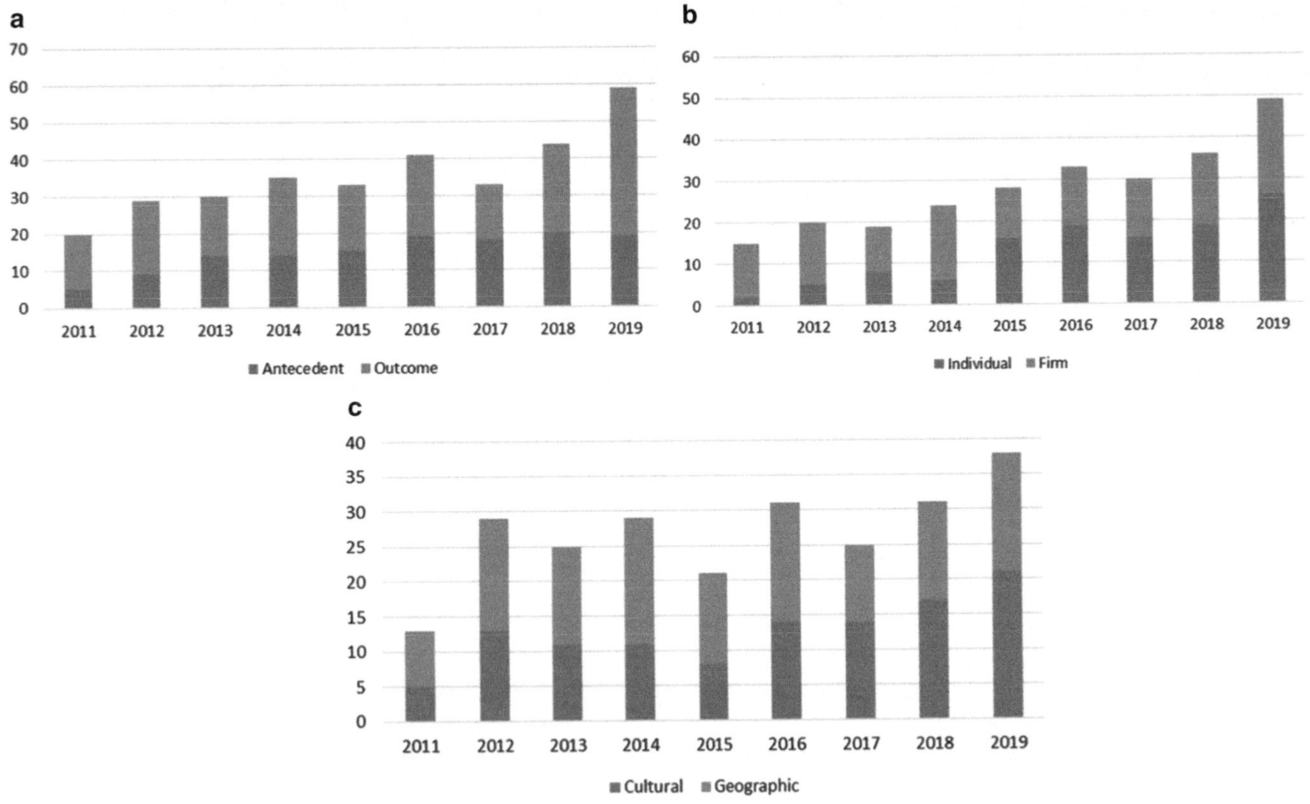

Fig. 1 (**a–c**) Focus of IE Publications: Antecedent vs. Outcome, Individual vs. Firm, Cultural vs. Geographic

3 Broadening the Scope of 'International': International *and* Intercultural Dynamics

The growing trend for individual-level studies—particularly cognition focused (e.g., Bolzani & Der Foo, 2017; Laskovaia et al., 2017); the emphasis on cultural dynamics over geography (e.g., Audretsch et al., 2017; Dheer & Lenartowicz, 2018; Pidduck et al., 2020a); and, examinations centred on antecedent mechanisms rather than outcomes (e.g., Fuentelsaz et al., 2018; Pidduck et al., 2020c; Spigel & Harrison, 2018) are three factors that we posit, together, point to valuable insights. For IE to contribute to entrepreneurship as it has to IB (Coviello et al., 2011), an explicit pivot is required as to what fits under the nomological net of IE constructs and research. Specifically, we argue that the answer lies in how 'international' is interpreted. In the following sections we elaborate on why these three trends open up the relevance and potential for integrating highly illuminating research in adjacent fields.

First, individual-level or cognitive-focused studies that investigate cross-border dynamics as they pertain to antecedent aspects of entrepreneurial opportunities tend to be marginalized (i.e., not explicitly framed as or considered an IE study) if the dependent variable does not directly relate to some aspect of internationalization. For example, Vandor and Franke (2016) made valuable advancements to our understanding of how a key form of cross-border phenomena (cross-cultural experience) influences opportunity recognition—the first pillar of IE's definition. However, as the root contribution was based on understanding opportunity recognition capabilities in general rather than purely opportunities across national borders, they drew directly from a thriving body of individual-level experimental designs in mainstream entrepreneurship (e.g., Hsu et al., 2017; Grégoire et al., 2019; Stevenson & Josefy, 2019)—an approach almost entirely absent in IB research (Zellmer-Bruhn et al., 2016) and perhaps reflective of the lack of IE studies drawing on such research streams. This is a great example of a study that investigated an ostensibly important IE construct but framed it as primarily intercultural, not 'international'. As a result, it is often not cited by IE studies. Yet, by framing the study as intercultural they were able to speak to a much *deeper* question for entrepreneurship theory: 'what influences people to recognize entrepreneurial opportunities?' Had it been 'what influences people to recognize *international* opportunities?', while an equally valid question (*see* Mainela et al., 2014), the theoretical impact for entrepreneurship in general is substantially diminished. Second, there are numerous examples of studies that probe antecedent mechanisms to general entrepreneurial outcomes (e.g., intention or forms of entrepreneurial self-efficacy) and chiefly focus on international or intercultural variables. Such research includes Dheer and Lenartowicz (2018) who probed the role of another prominent construct in international research; multiculturalism (Vora et al., 2019), and how it precedes general entrepreneurial pursuits. Pidduck et al. (2020a) also examined how multicultural experiences stimulate enhanced general entrepreneurial alertness schemata. Such examples of these trends; individual-level focus (over firm-level) and international-focused antecedents (over international-focused outcomes), hint at how IE stands to gain from more research in these streams.

In terms of emphasizing the third theme of cultural dynamics in IE (over geography-based performance outcomes), national cultural comparisons of entrepreneurial pursuits have been informative (e.g., Baker et al., 2005; Hayton et al., 2002; Stephan & Uhlaner, 2010; Tiessen, 1997). But describing or detailing differences in the discovery, enactment, evaluation, and exploitation of opportunities around the world may also hold limited value for stimulating on-going research into the deeper aspects of why/how something 'cross-border' would fundamentally change or advance what we know about entrepreneurial opportunities per se. For example, numerous studies have followed national cultural frameworks such as Hofstede (1984) and GLOBE (House et al., 1999) to make arguments that cultural dimensions influence entrepreneurship outcomes around the world (Steensma et al., 2000). However, akin to concerns that IB research was running out of steam (Buckley, 2002; Peng, 2004), cross-cultural entrepreneurship alone may suffer (or perhaps already has) from the same plight. The 'low-hanging fruit' of describing or comparing differences in new venture activity across nations has been plucked if comparisons alone are the primary focus or intended contribution.

In drawing on these three themes (highlighted above and illustrated in Figs. 1a–c), we propose that the IE research domain is not actually a declining niche, but rather very much at the centre of important opportunity development issues in entrepreneurship—with many of the potential contributions to core entrepreneurship questions lying dormant, waiting to be explored. Our core argument is that the current 'across national borders' part of McDougall and Oviatt's (2000) definition is unnecessarily constraining and it would be very well served by an adjustment. This definition as it currently stands restricts IE 'contributing back' to entrepreneurship through an over-emphasis of research on firm internationalization issues. Even though it has led to valuable insights examining the influence of other international/culture-related variables on entrepreneurial opportunities, it has unduly narrowed perceptions of what IE fully entails and what it can uniquely offer. Consequently, we offer a broadened, modernized perspective by defining IE as *the discovery, enactment, evaluation, and exploitation of opportunities—across cultural boundaries and dynamics—to create future goods and services*. This subtle yet important adjustment from 'cross-border' to 'across cultural boundaries and dynamics' (which includes but is not limited to national borders) has substantial implications for the kinds of research questions and constructs that fit under the IE umbrella to include a much more contemporary and comprehensive range of all things really 'international' in the current entrepreneurial landscape; 'cross-national', 'cross-cultural', 'cross-border', 'intercultural', 'multicultural', 'multinational', 'transcultural', and so on. In essence, IE's core question then meaningfully widens to become: what can we learn about entrepreneurial opportunities in general—domestic or international—by drawing from cross-national *and cultural* dynamics? This of course includes internationalization of firms but is not entirely defined and constrained by this phenomenon alone. Figure 2a and b below conceptually illustrates how this much needed 'cross-fertilization' (Oviatt & McDougall, 2005) helps to stimulate fresh insights from IE.

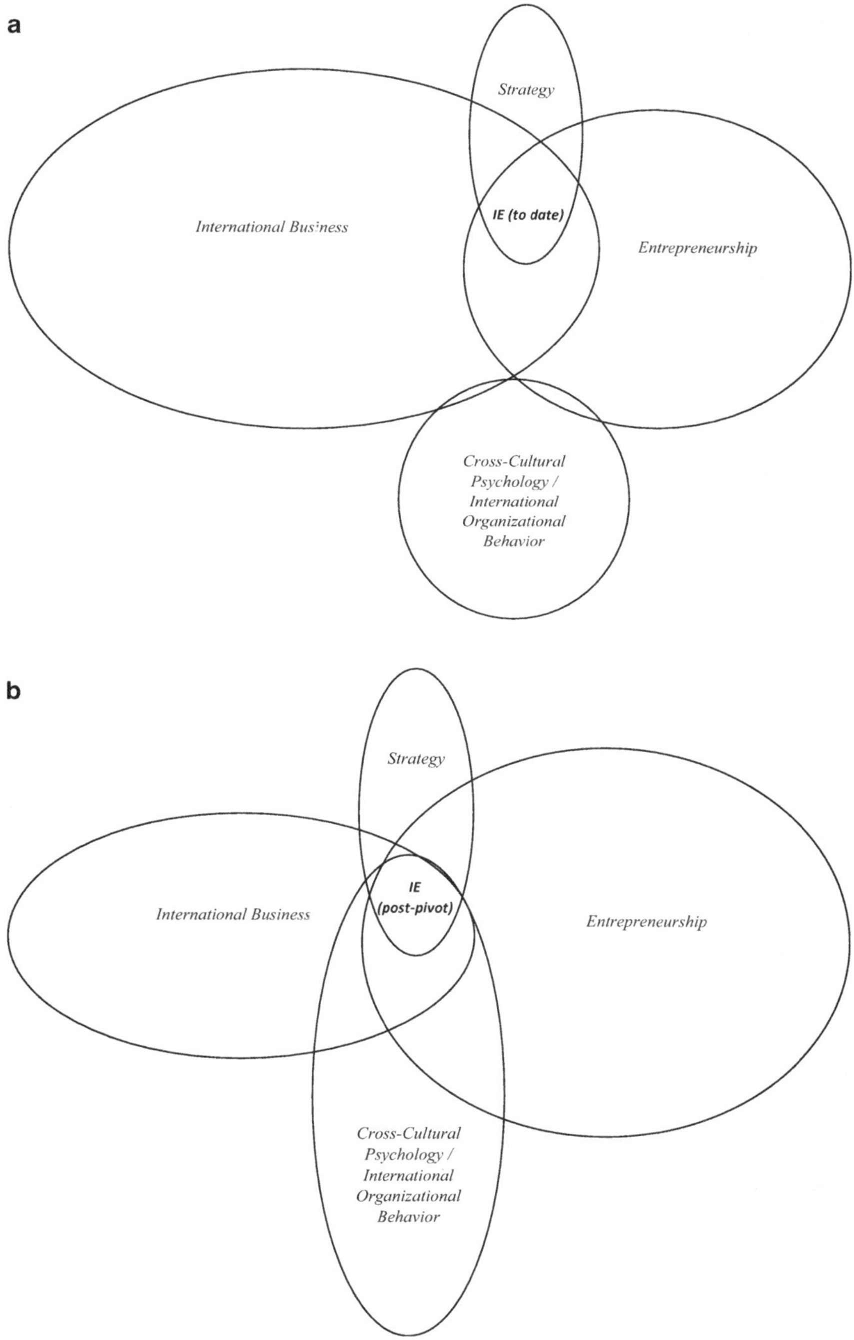

Fig. 2 (**a**) Pivoting the Scope of the International in IE Research. (**b**) Pivoting the Scope of the International in IE Research

4 Out of the Niches and into the Mainstream: The Promise of Intercultural Research

Considering this pivot, we propose building on the emerging trends identified in our review by further integrating (now directly relevant) insights from intercultural research in fields such as cross-cultural psychology and international organizational behaviour. Whether the IE studies in our review implicitly or explicitly acknowledge or ground their culture-based variables in these fields, our goal in the following section is to first highlight how the existing intercultural constructs are specifically helpful to each of the four pillars of entrepreneurial opportunities. We select three areas: *cultural intelligence*, *multicultural experience*, and *global entrepreneurial orientation*. Then, we provide some selected examples from recent studies in these adjacent fields (i.e., outside IE, IB, and Entrepreneurship) that illustrate the value to future IE studies in building on these currently overlooked streams of research and their rich history of conceptual and theoretical development on cross-border phenomena. We also demonstrate that while such research may initially appear to be out of IE's remit due to a saturated focus on firm internationalization; in light of our proposed definitional pivot, we can now advance understanding on how, why, and when cultural boundaries and dynamics influence discovering, enacting, evaluating, and exploiting opportunities.

4.1 Discovery of Entrepreneurial Opportunities

Discovering entrepreneurial opportunities involves the pre-launch or most nascent stages of the entrepreneurial process (Companys & McMullen, 2007). For example, discovering an entrepreneurial opportunity may involve examining the types of knowledge resources that help identify or select a viable business idea (Shane & Venkataraman, 2000), unpacking the intentions surrounding why people discover or create certain types of entrepreneurial opportunities over others (Krueger Jr et al., 2000), or explicating the mechanisms for how and when entrepreneurs identify opportunities such as through alertness (Tang et al., 2012), or systematic search (Patel & Fiet, 2009), or necessity due to social marginalization (Pidduck & Clark, 2021) among other factors. This dimension of IE's opportunity-centric definition also overlaps with what Shepherd et al. (2019) recently termed 'initiating endeavour' variables in entrepreneurship—critical for understanding how entrepreneurship emerges. An example from our review is Dheer and Lenartowicz's (2018) study that probed the critical role of cultural intelligence (CQ) in linking multicultural backgrounds with entrepreneurial intentions. Though other studies have examined CQ, or particular facets of CQ in cultivating international opportunity recognition (e.g., Lorenz et al., 2018), Dheer and Lenartowicz's study is notable in that it probed the role of CQ as an antecedent to entrepreneurial intentions in general. Thus, integrating CQ—a cross-border, intercultural phenomenon—helped advance understanding on how individuals develop intentions to enter entrepreneurship more broadly, not *just* internationally. Providing one example of a key area for IE to 'contribute back' to mainstream entrepreneurship.

What knowledge surrounding the discovery pillar of IE's definition can be generated from drawing explicitly on CQ studies in adjacent fields? CQ is generally defined as an individual's capability to function and manage effectively in culturally diverse settings (Ng, 2013). More specifically, it is 'a form of situated intelligence where intelligently adaptive behaviors are culturally bound to the values and beliefs of a given society or culture' (Earley & Ang, 2003, p. 26). Cross-cultural psychology research suggests that people with a high CQ can more easily navigate and understand different cultures, and therefore are more likely to be successful when working with individuals across cultures and both spotting and developing opportunities (Liao & Thomas, 2020; Ng et al., 2019). The four dimensions of CQ, cognitive, motivational, metacognitive, and behavioural (Ang & Van Dyne, 2008), have been examined in international organizational behaviour research and linked to a variety of both individual and firm-level outcomes such as international project effectiveness and performance (Imai & Gelfand, 2010; Kim et al., 2008; Lee & Sukoco, 2010). Further, intercultural interactions play pronounced roles for enhanced negotiation skills (Benetti et al., 2021; Caputo et al., 2019). To date, very little is known about how CQ emerges or is developed by entrepreneurs, or if it influences how opportunities are recognized by entrepreneurs.

Exposure to international experiences has been shown to open entrepreneurs to a wider range of international opportunities (Clark et al., 2018), however research in this area has been limited and somewhat blunt (e.g., without extension into cognition, mechanisms of action, or related constructs). By extension, research probing how entrepreneurs develop and employ CQ, and to what extent the individual dimensions of CQ (and other cognitive culture constructs, like country familiarity; Clark, 2018) may differentially influence aspects of prospective entrepreneurs' opportunity recognition or new venture ideation skills holds substantial potential. Further, if meaningful effects can be identified, do entrepreneurs possess, cultivate, or apply CQ in characteristically different ways than do managers or employees? Just as Busenitz and Barney (1997) identified heuristics as a key distinguisher, CQ may hold answers for the enduring yet still 'black box' links between migration and entrepreneurial pursuits.

One of the three most important enduring questions germane to entrepreneurship is why some entrepreneurs are better at identifying opportunities than others (Baron, 2004). This question assumes that there are variations across a population in terms of individual ability in articulating where new opportunities might lie. However, in pushing this logic further, it seems likely that variation in cultural backgrounds derived from various forms of intercultural experiences and exposures may stimulate different levels and types of entrepreneurial pursuits. Hybridization and cross-fertilization have been seen as something that characterizes creativity and the development of new ideas (Tang et al., 2012). It is often the process of trying to make sense of information that on the surface appear to be disconnected or even paradoxical that can ultimately lead to new insights (Pidduck et al., 2020b). If an individual with an entrepreneurial mindset becomes emersed in international contexts, it seems likely that the discovery of new ideas will become more prolific through the hybridization and juxtapositions from the exposure to different cultural elements. Relatedly and consistent with our revitalized definition of IE, the benefits of thinking more internationally may permeate more extensively than through focusing on national boundaries. In our increasingly pluralistic societies, exposure to internationalization also happens within countries, through multiculturalism, which manifests at multiple levels of analysis (e.g., Vora et al., 2019).

4.2 Enactment of Entrepreneurial Opportunities

Enacting entrepreneurial opportunities addresses the launching period whereby entrepreneurs take action, in various forms, on the opportunities identified (Alvarez & Barney, 2007). For example, this may include studies surrounding how entrepreneurial actors accumulate the social network or social capital required to feasibly launch a venture (McKeever et al., 2014), how ideas may be initially validated or early seed funding raised to develop prototypes or beta-versions of a product through crowdfunding (Anglin & Pidduck, 2021; Mollick & Robb, 2016), or how a prospective entrepreneur cultivates the personal resources that explicitly enable them to pursue entrepreneurial opportunities as a general career path (Dyer Jr, 1995). This dimension of IE's opportunity-centric definition overlaps with what Shepherd et al. (2019) call 'engaging endeavour' variables in entrepreneurship—important for understanding how entrepreneurship functions and evolves.

An example from our review is the Pidduck et al. (2020c) study that examined the emergence of born global founders. In particular, they adopted a vocational psychology lens and drew on multicultural experience as a powerful driver of a variety of cognitive resources (i.e., international entrepreneurial self-efficacy and interest in global opportunities) that stimulate entrepreneurial actors to systematically seek opportunities offering aggressive foreign-market growth—not simplify as serendipitous one-offs. This research was helpful in that while numerous studies also drawing on cognitive factors have been conducted on young internationalizing firms (e.g., Prashantham & Floyd, 2019; Zahra et al., 2005), the psychological literature on multicultural experience helped Pidduck and colleagues explain a deeper root phenomenon. This surrounded why entrepreneurial actors willingly compound the extant liabilities of newness inherent in pursuing a new venture (one form of risk), with the liabilities of foreignness inherent in overseas markets (another form of risk). Providing another example of a key area for IE to 'contribute back' to mainstream entrepreneurship.

What knowledge surrounding the enactment pillar of IE's definition can be generated from drawing explicitly on multicultural experience studies in adjacent fields? First, we use the term multicultural experience as a meta term reflecting the many terms used—such as cross-cultural experience, international experience, living abroad, foreign experience, and intercultural exposure, among others—in cross-cultural psychology and international organizational behaviour literature (*see* Maddux et al., 2020 for a review). The Structure-Appraisal Model of multicultural experience (Maddux et al., 2020) suggests that within the structure aspect, deeper multicultural experiences produce integrative processes that transform *intrapersonal* cognition such as self-concept clarity and creativity (Adam et al., 2018; Tadmor et al., 2012). The Structure-Appraisal Model can also influence empowerment constructs such as international entrepreneurial self-efficacy (Pidduck et al., 2020c), which unlocks entrepreneurial intention.

In terms of the decision to pursue specific opportunities, little is known about the differential role of multicultural experiences, but it is likely that they may influence both one's attitudes towards oneself and those they are working with. Indeed, broader multicultural experiences activate comparative processes that influence interpersonal attitudes and behaviours such as trust formation and reduced intergroup biases (Cao et al., 2014; Cao & Galinsky, 2020), indeed as one group might be marginalized when compared to the other (Pidduck & Clark, 2021). The appraisal part of this model suggests that these intrapersonal and interpersonal effects are only likely to be realized when an individual's multicultural experiences are perceived to be generally positive rather than negative (Maddux et al., 2020).

We suggest that research into forms of 'broad' multicultural experience hold fruitful avenues for future research by unpacking how and when the interpersonal attitudinal and behavioural changes they stimulate may help to systematically alter the way entrepreneurs enact opportunities. For example, though most of the research to date examines physical forms of broad experiences (e.g., business travelling or personal vacations), do virtually broad intercultural experiences across internet platforms with scattered foreign acquaintances also stimulate attitudinal or behaviour changes pertinent to enacting new venture ideas? Can enhanced trust built through interactions with such foreign contacts seep over into enhanced trust in other aspects of nascent venturing, such as which investors to work with or which initial employees to take a risk on? If so, this considerably alters the experimental ideation landscape for all aspiring entrepreneurs, not just 'international' entrepreneurs.

4.3 Evaluation of Entrepreneurial Opportunities

Evaluating entrepreneurial opportunities involves the more integrated and context-based process of assessing whether identified or enacted opportunities are indeed viable, or in the face of resource constraints, desirable for continued pursuit amid competing or alternative opportunities (Haynie et al., 2009). For example, this can involve research examining human capital factors—such as whether entrepreneurial actors process the general and/or specific experience and credentials needed to make qualified judgements (Marvel et al., 2016), investor or third-party dynamics surrounding whether entrepreneurial ventures also command positive feedback from experts (Chen et al., 2009), or the nuanced cognitive or metacognitive mechanisms surrounding how entrepreneurs evaluate potential opportunities (Scheaf et al., 2020).

This dimension of IE's opportunity-centric definition overlaps with what Shepherd et al. (2019) call 'contextualizing endeavour' variables in entrepreneurship—key for understanding when entrepreneurial actions may be enhanced or inhibited. An example from our review is Clark et al. (2018) research on the role of country familiarity (i.e., through international experience) in evaluating which foreign markets to select for internationalization opportunities. This study was particularly insightful as it drew on multicultural experience as an influential antecedent to the entrepreneurial opportunity evaluation process. While the outcome was foreign-market selection, the deeper theoretical contribution lies in understanding the importance of meaningful exposure to foreign cultures and what this does (systematically) to the ways in which entrepreneurs cognitively evaluate which opportunities to pursue—and equally as important, which opportunities not to pursue. This decision-making is particularly taxing on the entrepreneur as it requires them to engage intuitive and analytical processes towards complex decisions (Clark et al., 2019); and the entrepreneur's multicultural experience engaged to prioritize opportunities will likely influence which are pursued. Providing another example of a key area for IE to 'contribute back' to mainstream entrepreneurship.

What knowledge surrounding the evaluation pillar of IE's definition can be generated from also drawing explicitly on multicultural experience studies in adjacent fields? For example, drawing again on the previously mentioned Structure-Appraisal Model of multicultural experience (Maddux et al., 2020), the deeper multicultural experiences are especially salient to informing how entrepreneurs evaluate opportunities. Specifically, living abroad for extended periods, particularly in cultural distant places from one's home country (Ward et al., 2020), can substantially alter integrative processes that hold lasting influence on aspects of intrapersonal cognition (Adam et al., 2018; Tadmor et al., 2012). Thus, aside from the creative-cognition benefits already widely studied in relation to personal innovativeness (e.g., Leung et al., 2008; Maddux et al., 2020), and the 'finding oneself' benefits from backpacking in far flung places prior to big vocational decisions (Adam et al., 2018), what other intrapersonal changes from multicultural experiences can the wider entrepreneurship field benefit from knowing more about? One such stream of research that may greatly inform the evaluation aspect of opportunity development is the 'dark side' of multicultural experiences. For instance, studies show that studying abroad enhances cheating through the role of increased moral relativity (Lu et al., 2017a). Though some recent efforts are starting to probe these dynamics in relation to entrepreneurial rule-breaking (Pidduck, 2020, 2021), we know very little about how the moral relativity overseas experiences tend to arouse may influence *which* opportunities entrepreneurs pursue—however morally dubious the distal outcomes may be (Brenkert, 2009). On the brighter side, deep multicultural experiences in the form of personal romantic relationships also offer novel research opportunities for probing nuanced aspects of opportunity evaluation. Intriguingly, Lu et al. (2017b) found that intercultural dating with foreigners significantly increased creative performance at work. While seemingly unorthodox, connecting this with research on the role of entrepreneur spouses (e.g., Brüderl & Preisendörfer, 1998; Kirkwood, 2009); could multicultural 'swipes' from popular dating apps be a novel source of data to predict forms of entrepreneurial activity in a given metropolitan area? In sum, there are numerous potential contributions for advancing understanding on how multicultural experience informs entrepreneurial decision-making per se.

4.4 Exploitation of Entrepreneurial Opportunities

Exploiting opportunities involves the on-going competitive dynamics surrounding entrepreneurial action (Kirzner, 1979; Alvarez & Barney, 2007). For example, this can include research investigating how efficiently entrepreneurial actors initiate or leverage a new venture idea in a given industry or sector (Frederiks et al., 2019), new venture survival or temporal dynamics related to performance (Delmar & Shane, 2004), or to what extent an individual, team, or firm is entrepreneurially oriented (Covin et al., 2020; Lumpkin & Dess, 1996); that is, an autonomous, proactive, innovative, and competitive risk taker (Lumpkin & Pidduck, 2021). This includes both beliefs and behaviours in each of these dimensions and lies at the heart of exploiting entrepreneurial opportunities (Lumpkin & Pidduck, 2021).

This dimension of IE's opportunity-centric definition overlaps with what Shepherd et al. (2019) call 'performing endeavour' variables in entrepreneurship—vital for understanding what entrepreneurial opportunities create objective value in the marketplace. An example from our review is Clark and Covin's (2021) research on international entrepreneurial orientation disposition (IEOD). Specifically, this study advances a dispositional perspective on a distinctly international-focused form of individual-level entrepreneurial orientation. Again, while the focus is on a form of entrepreneurial orientation designed to predict pursuit of new foreign market entry, the cognitive theoretical foundation taps into a deeper question in entrepreneurship—is there something *about the nature of an opportunity* that pulls actors international or does the actor themselves push the venture international?

Recent research argues that the entrepreneurial mindset to pursue a given opportunity is indeed a product of both the individual and the opportunity (Pidduck et al., 2021). They propose that individuals form an entrepreneurial disposition based on beliefs regarding global entrepreneurial orientation (GEO: Lumpkin & Pidduck, 2021). GEO, an updated form of Lumpkin and Dess's (1996) multidimensional entrepreneurial orientation, incorporates both entrepreneurial beliefs and entrepreneurial behaviours across the various dimensions and emphasizes the multilevel and varied contextual manifestations of different levels and combinations of these dimensions. Indeed, future studies will benefit from a better understanding of how multicultural experience informs the entrepreneurial disposition, GEO, and entrepreneurial mindset, and ultimately address the question of when and how individuals engage in entrepreneurial behaviour. We posit that this provides another example of a key area of future research prospects for IE to 'contribute back' to mainstream entrepreneurship.

What knowledge surrounding the exploitation pillar of IE's definition can be generated from also drawing explicitly on global entrepreneurial orientation? As stated, although GEO is a newly coined term (or reconceptualization) for globally distinct manifestations of 'what it means to be entrepreneurial' (i.e., displaying entrepreneurial beliefs and behaviours), the individual-level aspects of autonomy, innovativeness, proactiveness, competitiveness, and risk taking can be informed considerably from research in cross-cultural psychology. As decisions and actions are influenced by place-bound culture (Shin et al., 2017), there are compelling reasons to suggest that entrepreneurs' own cultural habitus (i.e., the cultural milieu they are socialized into and mostly venture within) will impact both the extent of their involvement in entrepreneurial action (Ghosh Moulick et al., 2019) and the clusters of GEO dimensions most salient to exploiting opportunities in their locale.

Gelfand and colleagues' (2011) noted that theoretical and empirical implications of cultural tightness-looseness on behavioural manifestations of social norms offer numerous insights. Tightness-looseness relates to 'the strength of social norms, or how clear and pervasive norms are within societies, and the strength of sanctioning, or how much tolerance there is for deviance from norms within societies' (Gelfand et al., 2006, p. 7). The single spectrum from highly loose—weak social norms and a high tolerance for deviance (i.e., 'rule breakers'), to highly tight—strong social norms and low tolerance for deviance (i.e., 'rule-makers'), can be applied at multiple levels of analysis (Gelfand et al., 2006; Minkov et al., 2013). While grounded in deep historical socio-anthropological insights such as existential threats to a cultural group creating tight norms, and periods of unrivalled expansion over rival cultures creating loose norms (Realo et al., 2015), recent evidence suggests that loose cultures create more laissez-faire social norms conducive for experimentation and autonomy, yet tighter cultures can inhibit innovativeness (Jackson et al., 2019). These can also vary greatly across states within a nation (Harrington & Gelfand, 2014) and shift fluidly during major national events (Jackson et al., 2019). By extension, drawing on this literature has ostensibly numerous key implications for which configurations of global entrepreneurial orientation dimensions are likely to not only be more prevalent, but also which predict various performance outcomes by country.

Finally, implementing international new ventures requires consideration of the human endowments and dignity of those involved. This invariably involves, to some extent, faith-based or religious considerations. Despite a rise in the 'religiously unaffiliated' in the West and largely secular North-Western Europe, the faith-related convictions of entrepreneurs undoubtedly play roles in the both the venture ideation and development process, yet only recently is this being explicitly articulated and probed in our fields' major outlets (e.g., Busenitz & Lichtenstein, 2019). Moreover, in the developing world and emerging markets faith is oftentimes inseparable from business practices (e.g., Sharia compliance) making it salient for even secular entrepreneurs from, for example, the Nordic region venturing in host markets high in religiosity such as the UAE, Latin America, or parts of Africa. Faith invariably links with ethical factors and has important connections to individual capability development and how resources are exploited or deployed (Busenitz & Lichtenstein, 2019). Such faith or religion-based issues bring to light several important questions for IE and the exploitation of entrepreneurial opportunities. For example, how do adopting faith-based perspectives impact the entrepreneurs' consideration of a regional market place or the nature of the internationalization process? Relatedly, how does an entrepreneur or host-market's faith impact the product and services offered? For example, can we realistically assume-away factors surrounding entrepreneurs from Islamic countries and their consideration of sourcing or selling to markets that are politically hostile to elements of the Islamic faith or ethnic minority enclaves? Faith certainly plays a role in this entrepreneurial opportunity process. While work and organizational efforts are often conceptualized in a separate silo from entrepreneurs' faith-related thinking, the reality is that for most people they are inseparable. Rather than a control variable used in a similar vein to demographic variables, explicit consideration of entrepreneurs' personal faith conviction and the degree of importance they place on it in their lives is likely to illuminate new insights into various interesting aspects of IE, especially cognitive processes in opportunity development and exploitation.

5 Conclusion

As Companys and McMullen (2007) noted, the intellectual underpinnings that inform the nature of entrepreneurial opportunities are generally derived from three schools of thought, the economic, the cultural cognitive, and the sociopolitical. As our review suggests, the economic school, and to a lesser extent, the sociopolitical school, are the dominant foundations behind much of the quality IE research to date. The cultural cognitive school and many of the recently expanding and increasingly sophisticated methodological tools under its fold—such as between-subject, within-subject, priming and the many other derivations of randomized experimental methods in entrepreneurship (e.g., Grégoire et al., 2019; Stevenson & Josefy, 2019; Stevenson et al., 2020)—have much to offer the field of IE. Beyond methodological novelty and rigour, our insights exemplify the substantially deeper 'cross-fertilizations' and integrations that these adjacent fields can offer—with their richer history of drawing on cultural cognitive foundations.

In this chapter we have examined the ostensive decline of IE research contributions to mainstream entrepreneurship relative to international business (to date, IE's dominant co-parent field). Finding evidence that IE is declining in representation in recent years among premier entrepreneurship outlets, we sought to probe why. Drawing on some promising emergent trends, we put forth a recommendation to expand the focus of IE to encompass a richer array of intercultural and individual-level constructs. This challenges the persistent critiques that IE lacks theoretical substance (Jones et al., 2011) by focusing on how cross-border dynamics impact entrepreneurial opportunities *in general*, over purely functioning as geographic outcome contexts of new venture performance and activity. Akin to Howard Aldrich's quip[3] that there are more research papers on IPOs than there are IPOs (Aldrich & Ruef, 2018)—hinting that the vast majority of entrepreneurship phenomena lies outside a niche research focus, we argue that the myopic and continued focus on internationalization of new or small firms in IE has not done justice to the full breadth of cross-border and cross-cultural dynamics that influence entrepreneurship at large. In a post COVID-19 entrepreneurial landscape, for IE to rejuvenate itself and the relevance of its contributions to wider entrepreneurial phenomena, incorporating into its fold the rise of 'Born Office-less' ventures and their rising reliance on digital intercultural interactions (Pidduck et al., 2020a; Pidduck & Zhang, 2022) may be more prescient than continued studies on the minutia of physical operations of born globals or debates surrounding what is or is not a type of international new venture'.[4]

Acknowledgments We would like to thank our colleagues at the Academy of International Business for their feedback on earlier versions of this work. Also, we'd like to thank Sam Wilson for his help in collating and organizing review articles for this chapter during his time as a doctoral student assistant.

References

Adam, H., Obodaru, O., Lu, J. G., Maddux, W. W., & Galinsky, A. D. (2018). The shortest path to oneself leads around the world: Living abroad increases self-concept clarity. *Organizational Behavior and Human Decision Processes, 145*, 16–29.

Aldrich, H. E., & Ruef, M. (2018). Unicorns, gazelles, and other distractions on the way to understanding real entrepreneurship in the United States. *Academy of Management Perspectives, 32*(4), 458–472.

Alvarez, S. A., & Barney, J. B. (2007). Discovery and creation: Alternative theories of entrepreneurial action. *Strategic Entrepreneurship Journal, 1*(1–2), 11–26.

Ang, S., & Inkpen, A. C. (2008). Cultural intelligence and offshore outsourcing success: A framework of firm-level intercultural capability. *Decision Sciences, 39*(3), 337–358.

Ang, S., & Van Dyne, L. (Eds.). (2008). *Handbook on cultural intelligence: Theory, measurement and applications*. M.E. Sharpe.

Anglin, A. H., & Pidduck, R. J. (2021). Choose your words carefully: Harnessing the language of crowdfunding for success. *Business Horizons*. https://doi.org/10.1016/j.bushor.2021.09.004

[3]We use the term 'quip' as Aldrich provides an official Academy of Management article summary video for the Aldrich and Ruef (2018) article and vividly yet humorously (using a piece of paper) explains why incessant research focus on niches are problematic for knowledge creation of much richer, broader fields of study: https://journals.aom.org/doi/abs/10.5465/amp.2017.0123

[4]To put this in perspective, less than 1% of the 30 million registered firms in the USA even export (Trade.Gov). Yet, it is probable that the vast majority of firms and the entrepreneurs that found them are directly influenced by cross-border and cross-cultural phenomena *despite their venture outcomes being domestic*—such as immigration, changing regional demographics and multiculturism within major metropolitan areas, and digital communication interactions with suppliers overseas.

Audretsch, D. B., Obschonka, M., Gosling, S. D., & Potter, J. (2017). A new perspective on entrepreneurial regions: Linking cultural identity with latent and manifest entrepreneurship. *Small Business Economics, 48*(3), 681–697.

Baier-Fuentes, H., Merigó, J. M., Amorós, J. E., & Gaviria-Marín, M. (2019). International entrepreneurship: A bibliometric overview. *International Entrepreneurship and Management Journal, 15*(2), 385–429.

Baker, T., Gedajlovic, E., & Lubatkin, M. (2005). A framework for comparing entrepreneurship processes across nations. *Journal of International Business Studies, 36*(5), 492–504.

Baron, R. A. (2004). The cognitive perspective: A valuable tool for answering entrepreneurship's basic "why" questions. *Journal of Business Venturing, 19*(2), 221–239.

Benetti, S., Ogliastri, E., & Caputo, A. (2021). Distributive/integrative negotiation strategies in cross-cultural contexts: A comparative study of the USA and Italy. *Journal of Management & Organization*, 1–23. https://doi.org/10.1017/jmo.2020.47

Bolzani, D., & Der Foo, M. (2017). The "why" of international entrepreneurship: Uncovering entrepreneurs' personal values. *Small Business Economics, 51*(3), 639–666.

Brenkert, G. G. (2009). Innovation, rule breaking and the ethics of entrepreneurship. *Journal of Business Venturing, 24*(5), 448–464.

Brüderl, J., & Preisendörfer, P. (1998). Network support and the success of newly founded business. *Small Business Economics, 10*(3), 213–225.

Buckley, P. (2002). Is the international business research agenda running out of steam? *Journal of International Business Studies, 33*(2), 365–373.

Busenitz, L. W., & Barney, J. B. (1997). Differences between entrepreneurs and managers in large organizations: Biases and heuristics in strategic decision-making. *Journal of Business Venturing, 12*(1), 9–30.

Busenitz, L. W., & Lichtenstein, B. B. (2019). Faith in research: Forging new ground in entrepreneurship. *Academy of Management Perspectives, 33*(3), 280–291.

Cao, J., & Galinsky, A. D. (2020). The Diversity-Uncertainty-Valence (DUV) model of generalized trust development. *Organizational Behavior and Human Decision Processes, 161*, 49–64.

Cao, J., Galinsky, A. D., & Maddux, W. W. (2014). Does travel broaden the mind? Breadth of foreign experiences increases generalized trust. *Social Psychological and Personality Science, 5*(5), 517–525. https://doi.org/10.1177/1948550613514456

Caputo, A., Ayoko, O. B., Amoo, N., & Menke, C. (2019). The relationship between cultural values, cultural intelligence and negotiation styles. *Journal of Business Research, 99*, 23–36.

Caputo, A., Matteo Pellegrini, M., Dabic, M., & Dana, L. P. (2016). Internationalisation of firms from Central and Eastern Europe: A systematic literature review. *European Business Review, 28*(6), 630–651. https://doi.org/10.1108/EBR-01-2016-0004

Caputo, A., & Pellegrini, M. M. (Eds.). (2019). The anatomy of entrepreneurial decisions: Past, present and future research directions. Springer.

Caputo, A., & Pellegrini, M. M. (Eds.). (2020). Entrepreneurial behaviour: Unveiling the cognitive and emotional aspects of entrepreneurship. Emerald Group Publishing.

Cavusgil, S. T., & Knight, G. (2015). The born global firm: An entrepreneurial and capabilities perspective on early and rapid internationalization. *Journal of International Business Studies, 46*(1), 3–16.

Chen, X. P., Yao, X., & Kotha, S. (2009). Entrepreneur passion and preparedness in business plan presentations: A persuasion analysis of venture capitalists' funding decisions. *Academy of Management Journal, 52*(1), 199–214.

Clark, D. R. (2018). A multi-dimensional perspective on country familiarity, moderated by entrepreneur cognitive styles. *Frontiers of Entrepreneurship Research, 38*, 363.

Clark, D. R., & Covin, J. G. (2021). International entrepreneurial orientation disposition: Insights into venture internationalization. In A. Corbett, P. Kreiser, L. Marino, & W. Wales (Eds.), *Advances in entrepreneurship, firm emergence, and growth, volume 22: Entrepreneurial orientation epistemological, theoretical, and empirical perspectives* (pp. 87–120). Emerald Publishing Group. https://doi.org/10.1108/S1074-754020210000022002

Clark, D. R., Li, D., & Shepherd, D. A. (2018). Country familiarity in the initial stage of foreign market selection. *Journal of International Business Studies, 49*(4), 442–472.

Clark, D. R., Tietz, M. A., & Kumar, M. (2019). Decision making within the individual-opportunity nexus: The drivers of venture attractiveness. In *Academy of Management Proceedings* (2019, 1, p. 15203). Academy of Management.

Companys, Y. E., & McMullen, J. S. (2007). Strategic entrepreneurs at work: The nature, discovery, and exploitation of entrepreneurial opportunities. *Small Business Economics, 28*(4), 301–322.

Coombs, J. E., Sadrieh, F., & Annavarjula, M. (2009). Two decades of international entrepreneurship research: What have we learned-where do we go from here? *International Journal of Entrepreneurship, 13*, 23.

Coviello, N. E., & Jones, M. V. (2004). Methodological issues in international entrepreneurship research. *Journal of Business Venturing, 19*(4), 485–508.

Coviello, N. E., McDougall, P. P., & Oviatt, B. M. (2011). The emergence, advance and future of international entrepreneurship research—an introduction to the special forum. *Journal of Business Venturing, 26*(6), 625–631.

Covin, J. G., Rigtering, J. C., Hughes, M., Kraus, S., Cheng, C. F., & Bouncken, R. B. (2020). Individual and team entrepreneurial orientation: Scale development and configurations for success. *Journal of Business Research, 112*, 1–12.

Dabić, M., Maley, J., Dana, L. P., Novak, I., Pellegrini, M. M., & Caputo, A. (2020). Pathways of SME internationalization: A bibliometric and systematic review. *Small Business Economics, 55* (3), 705–725.

Delmar, F., & Shane, S. (2004). Legitimating first: Organizing activities and the survival of new ventures. *Journal of Business Venturing, 19*, 385–410.

Dheer, R. J., & Lenartowicz, T. (2018). Multiculturalism and entrepreneurial intentions: Understanding the mediating role of cognitions. *Entrepreneurship Theory and Practice, 42*(3), 426–466.

Dyer, W. G., Jr. (1995). Toward a theory of entrepreneurial careers. *Entrepreneurship Theory and Practice, 19*(2), 7–21.

Earley, P. C., & Ang, S. (2003). *Cultural intelligence: Individual interactions across cultures.* Stanford University Press.

Frederiks, A. J., Englis, B. G., Ehrenhard, M. L., & Groen, A. J. (2019). Entrepreneurial cognition and the quality of new venture ideas: An experimental approach to comparing future-oriented cognitive processes. *Journal of Business Venturing, 34*(2), 327–347.

Fuentelsaz, L., Maicas, J. P., & Montero, J. (2018). Entrepreneurs and innovation: The contingent role of institutional factors. *International Small Business Journal, 36*(6), 686–711.

Gamboa, E. C., & Brouthers, L. E. (2008). How international is entrepreneurship? *Entrepreneurship Theory and Practice, 32*(3), 551–558.

Gelfand, M. J., Aycan, Z., Erez, M., & Leung, K. (2017). Cross-cultural industrial organizational psychology and organizational behavior: A hundred-year journey. *Journal of Applied Psychology, 102*(3), 514.

Gelfand, M. J., Erez, M. E., & Aycan, Z. (2007). Cross-cultural organizational behavior. *Annual Review of Psychology, 58*, 479–514.

Gelfand, M. J., Nishii, L. H., & Raver, J. L. (2006). On the nature and importance of cultural tightness-looseness. *Journal of Applied Psychology, 91*(6), 1225.

Gelfand, M. J., Raver, J. L., Nishii, L., Leslie, L. M., Lun, J., Lim, B. C., . . . Yamaguchi, S. (2011). Differences between tight and loose cultures: A 33-nation study. *Science, 332*(6033), 1100–1104.

Ghosh Moulick, A., Pidduck, R. J., & Busenitz, L. W. (2019). Bloom where planted: Entrepreneurial catalyzers amidst weak institutions. *Journal of Business Venturing Insights, 11*, e00127.

Grégoire, D. A., Binder, J. K., & Rauch, A. (2019). Navigating the validity tradeoffs of entrepreneurship research experiments: A systematic review and best-practice suggestions. *Journal of Business Venturing, 34*(2), 284–310.

Harrington, J. R., & Gelfand, M. J. (2014). Tightness–looseness across the 50 united states. *Proceedings of the National Academy of Sciences, 111*(22), 7990–7995.

Haynie, J. M., Shepherd, D. A., & McMullen, J. S. (2009). An opportunity for me? The role of resources in opportunity evaluation decisions. *Journal of Management Studies, 46*(3), 337–361.

Hayton, J. C., George, G., & Zahra, S. A. (2002). National culture and entrepreneurship: A review of behavioral research. *Entrepreneurship Theory and Practice, 26*(4), 33–52.

Hofstede, G. (1984). *Culture's consequences: International differences in work-related values* (Vol. 5). Sage.

House, R. J., Hanges, P. J., Ruiz-Quintanilla, S. A., Dorfman, P. W., Javidan, M., Dickson, M., & Gupta, V. (1999). Cultural influences on leadership and organizations: Project GLOBE. *Advances in Global Leadership, 1*(2), 171–233.

Hsu, D. K., Simmons, S. A., & Wieland, A. M. (2017). Designing entrepreneurship experiments: A review, typology, and research agenda. *Organizational Research Methods, 20*(3), 379–412.

Imai, L., & Gelfand, M. J. (2010). The culturally intelligent negotiator: The impact of cultural intelligence (CQ) on negotiation sequences and outcomes. *Organizational Behavior and Human Decision Processes, 112*(2), 83–98.

Jackson, J. C., Gelfand, M., De, S., & Fox, A. (2019). The loosening of American culture over 200 years is associated with a creativity–order trade-off. *Nature Human Behaviour, 3*(3), 244–250.

Johanson, J., & Vahlne, J. E. (2009). The Uppsala internationalization process model revisited: From liability of foreignness to liability of outsidership. *Journal of International Business Studies, 40*(9), 1411–1431.

Jones, M. V., Coviello, N. E., & Tang, Y. K. (2011). International entrepreneurship research (1989–2009): A domain ontology and thematic analysis. *Journal of Business Venturing, 26*, 632–659.

Katz, J. A., Renko, M., & Kundu, S. K. (2021). How do internationalizing firms emerge? *Journal of Business Venturing Insights, 15*, e00227.

Keupp, M. M., & Gassmann, O. (2009). The past and the future of international entrepreneurship: A review and suggestions for developing the field. *Journal of Management, 35*(3), 600–633.

Kim, K., Kirkman, B., & Chen, G. (2008). Cultural intelligence and international assignment effectiveness: A conceptual model and preliminary findings. In S. Ang & L. Van Dyne (Eds.), *Handbook of cultural intelligence: Theory, measurement, and applications* (pp. 71–90). M. E. Sharpe.

Kirkwood, J. (2009). Spousal roles on motivations for entrepreneurship: A qualitative study in New Zealand. *Journal of Family and Economic Issues, 30*(4), 372.

Kirzner, I. (1979). *Perception, opportunity, and profit*. University of Chicago Press.

Kiss, A. N., Danis, W. M., & Cavusgil, S. T. (2012). International entrepreneurship research in emerging economies: A critical review and research agenda. *Journal of Business Venturing, 27* (2), 266–290.

Knight, G. A., & Cavusgil, S. T. (2004). Innovation, organizational capabilities, and the born-global firm. *Journal of International Business Studies, 35*(2), 124–141.

Krueger, N. F., Jr., Reilly, M. D., & Carsrud, A. L. (2000). Competing models of entrepreneurial intentions. *Journal of Business Venturing, 15*(5–6), 411–432.

Laskovaia, A., Shirokova, G., & Morris, M. H. (2017). National culture, effectuation, and new venture performance: Global evidence from student entrepreneurs. *Small Business Economics, 49*(3), 687–709.

Lee, L. Y., & Sukoco, B. M. (2010). The effects of cultural intelligence on expatriate performance: The moderating effects of international experience. *The International Journal of Human Resource Management, 21*(7), 963–981.

Leung, A. K. Y., Maddux, W. W., Galinsky, A. D., & Chiu, C. Y. (2008). Multicultural experience enhances creativity: The when and how. *American Psychologist, 63*(3), 169.

Liao, Y., & Thomas, D. C. (2020). Conceptualizing cultural intelligence. In *Cultural intelligence in the world of work*. Springer.

Lopez, L. E., Kundu, S. K., & Ciravegna, L. (2009). Born global or born regional? Evidence from an exploratory study in the Costa Rican software industry. *Journal of International Business Studies, 40*(7), 1228–1238.

Lorenz, M. P., Ramsey, J. R., & Richey, R. G., Jr. (2018). Expatriates' international opportunity recognition and innovativeness: The role of metacognitive and cognitive cultural intelligence. *Journal of World Business, 53*(2), 222–236.

Lu, J. G., Hafenbrack, A. C., Eastwick, P. W., Wang, D. J., Maddux, W. W., & Galinsky, A. D. (2017a). "Going out" of the box: Close intercultural friendships and romantic relationships spark creativity, workplace innovation, and entrepreneurship. *Journal of Applied Psychology, 102*(7), 1091.

Lu, J. G., Quoidbach, J., Gino, F., Chakroff, A., Maddux, W. W., & Galinsky, A. D. (2017b). The dark side of going abroad: How broad foreign experiences increase immoral behavior. *Journal of Personality and Social Psychology, 112*(1), 1.

Lumpkin, G. T., & Dess, G. G. (1996). Clarifying the entrepreneurial orientation construct and linking it to performance. *Academy of Management Review, 21*(1), 135–172.

Lumpkin, G. T., & Pidduck, R. J. (2021). Global entrepreneurial orientation (GEO): An updated, multidimensional view of EO. In A. Corbett, P. Kreiser, L. Marino, & W. Wales (Eds.), *Advances in entrepreneurship, firm emergence, and growth, volume 22: Entrepreneurial orientation epistemological, theoretical, and empirical perspectives* (pp. 17–68). Emerald Publishing Group. https://doi.org/10.1108/S1074-754020210000022002

Maddux, W. W., Lu, J. G., Affinito, S. J., & Galinsky, A. D. (2020). Multicultural experiences: A systematic review and new theoretical framework. *Academy of Management Annals, 15*(2), 345–375.

Mainela, T., Puhakka, V., & Servais, P. (2014). The concept of international opportunity in international entrepreneurship: A review and a research agenda. *International Journal of Management Reviews, 16*(1), 105–129.

Marvel, M. R., Davis, J. L., & Sproul, C. R. (2016). Human capital and entrepreneurship research: A critical review and future directions. *Entrepreneurship Theory and Practice, 40*(3), 599–626.

McDougall, P. P., Jones, M. V., & Serapio, M. G. (2014). High-potential concepts, phenomena, and theories for the advancement of international entrepreneurship research. *Entrepreneurship Theory and Practice, 38*(1), 1–10.

McDougall, P. P., & Oviatt, B. M. (2000). International entrepreneurship: The intersection of two research paths. *Academy of Management Journal, 43*(5), 902–906.

McKeever, E., Anderson, A., & Jack, S. (2014). Entrepreneurship and mutuality: Social capital in processes and practices. *Entrepreneurship & Regional Development, 26*(5–6), 453–477.

McMullen, J. S. (2019). A wakeup call for the field of entrepreneurship and its evaluators. *Journal of Business Venturing, 34*(3), 413–417.

Minkov, M., Blagoev, V., & Hofstede, G. (2013). The boundaries of culture: Do questions about societal norms reveal cultural differences? *Journal of Cross-Cultural Psychology, 44*(7), 1094–1106.

Mollick, E., & Robb, A. (2016). Democratizing innovation and capital access: The role of crowdfunding. *California Management Review, 58*(2), 72–87.

Ng, R. (2013). Cultural intelligence. In *The encyclopedia of cross-cultural psychology* (pp. 310–313). Wiley-Blackwell.

Ng, K. Y., Van Dyne, L., & Ang, S. (2019). Speaking out and speaking up in multicultural settings: A two-study examination of cultural intelligence and voice behavior. *Organizational Behavior and Human Decision Processes, 151*, 150–159.

Nielsen, K., Nielsen, M. B., Ogbonnaya, C., Känsälä, M., Saari, E., & Isaksson, K. (2017). Workplace resources to improve both employee well-being and performance: A systematic review and meta-analysis. *Work & Stress, 31*(2), 101–120.

Oviatt, B. M., & McDougall, P. P. (1994). Toward a theory of international new ventures. *Journal of International Business Studies, 25*, 45–64.

Oviatt, B. M., & McDougall, P. P. (2005). The internationalization of entrepreneurship. *Journal of International Business Studies, 36*(1), 2–8.

Patel, P. C., & Fiet, J. O. (2009). Systematic search and its relationship to firm founding. *Entrepreneurship Theory and Practice, 33*(2), 501–526.

Peng, M. W. (2004). Identifying the big question in international business research. *Journal of International Business Studies, 35*(2), 99–108.

Pidduck, R. J. (2020). Cross-cultural rebels: How and when skillsets for seizing innovative opportunities emerge. In *Academy of Management Proceedings* (2020, 1, p. 10246). Academy of Management.

Pidduck, R. J. (2021). Entrepreneurial rule-breaking: Unpacking the emergence of a double-edged capability (SUMMARY). *Frontiers of Entrepreneurship Research, 41.*

Pidduck, R. J., & Clark, D. R. (2021). Transitional entrepreneurship: Elevating research into marginalized entrepreneurs. *Journal of Small Business Management.* https://doi.org/10.1080/00472778.2021.1928149

Pidduck, R. J., & Zhang, Y. (2022). Entrepreneurial sensing capabilities: The stimulating role of cross-cultural experience. *International Journal of Entrepreneurial Behavior & Research.* (Forthcoming).

Pidduck, R. J., Busenitz, L. W., Zhang, Y., & Moulick, A. G. (2020a). Oh, the places you'll go: A schema theory perspective on cross-cultural experience and entrepreneurship. *Journal of Business Venturing Insights, 14*, e00189.

Pidduck, R. J., Ghosh Moulick, A., & Busenitz, L. W. (2020b). Leveraging paradoxes for entrepreneurial cognition: A cultural tightness-looseness model (summary). *Frontiers of Entrepreneurship Research, 40.*

Pidduck, R. J., Shaffer, M. A., Zhang, Y., & Clark, D. R. (2020c). Unpacking the emergence of born global founders: A careers perspective. *Journal of Small Business Management.*

Pidduck, R. J., Clark, D. R., & Lumpkin, G. T. (2021). Entrepreneurial mindset: Dispositional beliefs, opportunity beliefs, and entrepreneurial behavior. *Journal of Small Business Management.* https://doi.org/10.1080/00472778.2021.1907582

Prashantham, S., & Dhanaraj, C. (2010). The dynamic influence of social capital on the international growth of new ventures. *Journal of Management Studies, 47*(6), 967–994.

Prashantham, S., & Floyd, S. W. (2019). Navigating liminality in new venture internationalization. *Journal of Business Venturing, 34*(3), 513–527.

Realo, A., Linnamägi, K., & Gelfand, M. J. (2015). The cultural dimension of tightness–looseness: An analysis of situational constraint in Estonia and Greece. *International Journal of Psychology, 50*(3), 193–204.

Reuber, A. R., Dimitratos, P., & Kuivalainen, O. (2017). Beyond categorization: New directions for theory development about entrepreneurial internationalization. *Journal of International Business Studies, 48*, 411–422.

Reuber, A. R., Knight, G. A., Liesch, P. W., & Zhou, L. (2018). International entrepreneurship: The pursuit of entrepreneurial opportunities across national borders. *Journal of International Business, 49*(1), 12. https://doi.org/10.1007/978-3-319-74228-1

Scheaf, D. J., Loignon, A. C., Webb, J. W., Heggestad, E. D., & Wood, M. S. (2020). Measuring opportunity evaluation: Conceptual synthesis and scale development. *Journal of Business Venturing, 35*(2).

Shane, S., & Venkataraman, S. (2000). The promise of entrepreneurship as a field of research. *Academy of Management Review, 25*(1), 217–226.

Shepherd, D. A., Wennberg, K., Suddaby, R., & Wiklund, J. (2019). What are we explaining? A review and agenda on initiating, engaging, performing, and contextualizing entrepreneurship. *Journal of Management, 45*(1), 159–196.

Shin, D., Hasse, V. C., & Schotter, A. P. (2017). Multinational enterprises within cultural space and place: Integrating cultural distance and tightness–looseness. *Academy of Management Journal, 60*(3), 904–921.

Spigel, B., & Harrison, R. (2018). Toward a process theory of entrepreneurial ecosystems. *Strategic Entrepreneurship Journal., 12*(1), 151–168.
Steensma, H. K., Marino, L., Weaver, K. M., & Dickson, P. H. (2000). The influence of national culture on the formation of technology alliances by entrepreneurial firms. *Academy of Management Journal, 43*(5), 951–973.
Stephan, U., & Uhlaner, L. M. (2010). Performance-based vs socially supportive culture: A cross-national study of descriptive norms and entrepreneurship. *Journal of International Business Studies, 41*(8), 1347–1364.
Stevenson, R. M., & Josefy, M. (2019). Knocking at the gate: The path to publication for entrepreneurship experiments through the lens of gatekeeping theory. *Journal of Business Venturing, 34*(2), 242–260.
Stevenson, R. M., Josefy, M. A., McMullen, J. S., & Shepherd, D. A. (2020). Organizational and management theorizing using experiment-based entrepreneurship research: Covered terrain and new frontiers. *Academy of Management Annals, 14*(2).
Tadmor, C. T., Galinsky, A. D., & Maddux, W. W. (2012). Getting the most out of living abroad: Biculturalism and integrative complexity as key drivers of creative and professional success. *Journal of Personality and Social Psychology, 103*(3), 520.
Tang, J., Kacmar, K. M. M., & Busenitz, L. (2012). Entrepreneurial alertness in the pursuit of new opportunities. *Journal of Business Venturing, 27*(1), 77–94.
Terjesen, S., Hessels, J., & Li, D. (2016). Comparative international entrepreneurship: A review and research agenda. *Journal of Management, 42*(1), 299–344.
Tiessen, J. H. (1997). Individualism, collectivism, and entrepreneurship: A framework for international comparative research. *Journal of Business Venturing, 12*(5), 367–384.
Vandor, P., & Franke, N. (2016). See Paris and… found a business? The impact of cross-cultural experience on opportunity recognition capabilities. *Journal of Business Venturing, 31*(4), 388–407.
Venkataraman, S. (1997). The distinctive domain of entrepreneurship research: An editor's perspective. In J. Katz & R. Brockhaus (Eds.), *Advances in entrepreneurship, firm emergence, and growth* (Vol. 3, pp. 119–138). JAI Press.
Verbeke, A., & Ciravegna, L. (2018). International entrepreneurship research versus international business research: A false dichotomy? *Journal of International Business Studies, 49*, 87–394.
Vora, D., Martin, L., Fitzsimmons, S. R., Pekerti, A. A., Lakshman, C., & Raheem, S. (2019). Multiculturalism within individuals: A review, critique, and agenda for future research. *Journal of International Business Studies, 50*(4), 499–524.
Ward, C., Bochner, S., & Furnham, A. (2020). *The psychology of culture shock.* Routledge.
Zahra, S. A., Korri, J. S., & Yu, J. (2005). Cognition and international entrepreneurship: Implications for research on international opportunity recognition and exploitation. *International Business Review, 14*(2), 129–146.
Zellmer-Bruhn, M., Caligiuri, P., & Thomas, D. C. (2016). From the editors: Experimental design in international business research. *Journal of International Business Studies, 47*(4), 399–407.

Robert J. Pidduck is an Assistant Professor at the Strome College of Business at Old Dominion University, Virginia. His research focuses on how, when, and why intercultural dynamics influence the ways entrepreneurs think and approach developing new ventures. His work has been published in outlets such as the Journal of Business Venturing, Journal of Small Business Management, Business Horizons, and Journal of Business Venturing Insights.

Daniel R. Clark is an Assistant Professor of Entrepreneurship at the Ivey Business School at Western University in Canada. His research focuses on how entrepreneurs and potential entrepreneurs make complex decisions, such as internationalization and founding a business, under uncertainty. His research has been published in the Journal of International Business Studies, Journal of Small Business Management, and the Canadian Medical Association Journal, among others.

Lowell W. Busenitz is an Emeritus Professor of Entrepreneurship at the University of Oklahoma in Norman. As an internationally renowned scholar in the field of entrepreneurship, Prof. Busenitz has served in many leadership positions and produced seminal articles that helped shape the domain of entrepreneurial cognition research. His work has been published in outlets such as the Academy of Management Journal, Journal of Management, Journal of Business Venturing, Entrepreneurship Theory and Practice, Strategic Entrepreneurship Journal, among many others.

Uncovering Entrepreneurial Belief Systems Through Cognitive Causal Mapping

Mauri Laukkanen and Francisco Liñán

Abstract This chapter discusses the grounds and methods of studying the knowledge structures (aka belief systems, cognitive maps, mental models) that underlie and guide entrepreneurs' and entrepreneurial actors' perceptions, intentions, decision-making and performance. Current entrepreneurial cognition research (ECR), largely emulating cognitive psychology, tends to emphasise individual cognitive processes, studying *how* entrepreneurs in general think and solve problems. This is important but underemphasises the also essential questions of *what* specific entrepreneurs know and think (or ignore); the contents, formation, relevance and consequences of their knowledge and beliefs. This chapter discusses some basic issues of cognition and the conditions of empirically studying knowledge or beliefs. It also presents an accessible and established method, cognitive comparative causal mapping (CCM), for revealing and analysing entrepreneurs' and entrepreneurial actors' belief systems, demonstrating it in the case of nascent micro entrepreneurs and small business advisors. In international entrepreneurship research, this approach facilitates, e.g., tracking the evolution of entrepreneurs' thinking during internationalisation or comparing their belief systems in different cross-cultural or cross-national contexts. Such research is supported by CMAP3, a CCM specific software, by enabling studies where the data, such as interviews, use different languages, the coding and reporting a standard language like English.

Keywords Comparative cognitive causal mapping · CMAP3 · Belief system · Cognitive map · Mental model · Nascent micro entrepreneurs · Small business advisors · Entrepreneurial cognition research · Cross-cultural/national research

---

M. Laukkanen (✉)
University of Eastern Finland, Business School, Kuopio Campus, Finland
e-mail: mauri.laukkanen@uef.fi

F. Liñán
Universidad de Sevilla, Facultad de CC, Económicas y Empresariales, Seville, Spain

A. Caputo et al. (eds.), *The International Dimension of Entrepreneurial Decision-Making*, Contributions to Management Science,
https://doi.org/10.1007/978-3-030-85950-3_3

1 Introduction

Entrepreneurial cognition research (ECR) has increased markedly in the 2000s (Baron, 2016; Grégoire et al., 2015). Its target phenomenon has been defined as the *knowledge structures* used, e.g., in venture creation, the central question as *how* entrepreneurs think by utilising those structures (Mitchell et al., 2007). As shown by recent reviews (Randolph-Seng et al., 2016), the subfield has so far in fact focused on *individual-level process* issues like biases, expertise, heuristics and problem-solving, largely emulating clinical-style cognitive psychology only migrated to entrepreneurial contexts. The orientation has produced important results such as the findings about causation and effectuation (Sarasvathy et al., 2007, 2015) or entrepreneurial scripts (Mitchell et al., 2009). The current emphasis has, however, also a downside.

First, the "how" orientation has meant largely overlooking content-related aspects of entrepreneurial knowledge, i.e., *what* do specific entrepreneurial actors know (or ignore), how accurate (or erroneous) their beliefs are and what impacts that has or how their knowledge evolves. The criticality of action knowledge is evident. For instance, expert entrepreneurs seem to develop a general problem-solving approach called *effectuation* for evaluating ventures (Sarasvathy et al., 2007). Such a decision-making and the actual ventures, however, occur in specific operative and strategic contexts of entities, states of affairs and their mechanisms. Founding a firm and managing it requires internalising and understanding at least that context's critical aspects by gradually developing and maintaining corresponding context-isomorphic, action-relevant knowledge or belief systems. This applies to all fields where individuals' or teams role is essential. Therefore, studying the beliefs of key actors has long been central, e.g., in political science and management and organisation cognition (MOC) (cf. Axelrod, 1976; Gary & Wood, 2011; Narayanan, 2005; Schraven et al., 2015; Walsh, 1995). Considering the similarities of cognitive demands placed by entrepreneurship and management, the same orientation seems relevant also in entrepreneurial contexts.

Second, the prevalent "how" orientation can breed misconceptions that ECR *always* requires the clinical-experimental methods of cognitive psychology (Baron & Ward, 2004; Evans, 1998; Gentner, 2004), verbal protocols of expertise studies (Chi, 2006; Grégoire & Lambert, 2015), even neuroscientific techniques (Fiske & Taylor, 2021; Morrison & Knowlton, 2012). Whilst appropriate in process-oriented studies, such methods are not accessible to many entrepreneurship researchers. Therefore, it is important to see that ECR can also be about what entrepreneurs think, i.e., *entrepreneurial knowledge and beliefs*. This means studying, e.g., what nascent, serial or successful or failed entrepreneurs or their stakeholders know or do not know about key issues or how certain events or interventions influence their thought patterns. Importantly, such research is practicable with normally accessible methods. This chapter aims to demonstrate this.

To do so, let us assume a study of finding out what nascent micro entrepreneurs and their counsellors in three European countries believe are the causes and consequences of individual entrepreneurship and of micro firms' success or failure. This raises two questions which this chapter can hopefully answer. First, why such studies? Theoretically, studying entrepreneurial actors' beliefs helps understand the so far largely neglected *cognitive* underpinnings of entrepreneurship and related mechanisms (Krueger, 2007; Liñán & Fayolle, 2015). This calls for more respective research in different contexts. In pragmatic and policy terms, the need of studying new venture counselling is evident, too. Whilst widespread (Rotger et al., 2012), such programmes' effectiveness is not obvious (Ratinho et al., 2020). For instance, some researchers emphasise the need for counsellors to empathise with their clients and to adapt the interventions to their beliefs (Nielsen & Klyver, 2020). That, however, requires understanding what the counsellors and their clients think about entrepreneurship and starting ventures. Furthermore, their beliefs reflect different national or cultural contexts (Welter, 2011). For instance, if it is common in a region to think that entrepreneurship is individually and socially rewarding, or conversely, that it is risky or something shunned by the dominant culture, that will be manifested in that region's level of entrepreneurship and economic and social well-being. Thus, this research can increase our understanding of counsellor-client relationships, perhaps especially in cross-cultural studies.

The second question is how to reveal someone's beliefs or theoretical notions like knowledge structures such as mental models? Different solutions have been discussed in the literature (cf., Chi, 2006; Evans, 1998; Gentner, 2004; Ifenthaler et al., 2011; Rouse & Morris, 1986). Their shared point of departure is that knowledge or beliefs cannot be observed directly nor elicited independent of the person. Neuroscientific techniques like functional magnetic resonance imaging (fMRi, Morrison & Knowlton, 2012) enable studying brain activities and related issues, which can be important also in entrepreneurship (Nicolaou et al., 2019). However, whilst such methods can show, e.g., that causal thinking engages the lateral prefrontal cortex, they cannot reveal exactly *what* the person knows or thinks about something (Khemlani et al., 2014). That must be *inferred* of *communications* usually in the form of documents, interview responses or questionnaires. This chapter discusses one such method, *comparative cognitive causal mapping* (CCM). Variants of cognitive mapping (Laukkanen & Wang, 2015) have been long used in fields like MOC and IT (Furnari, 2015; Narayanan, 2005), political science (Axelrod, 1976), environmental studies (Jones et al., 2011) and increasingly also in entrepreneurship (e.g. Laukkanen & Tornikoski, 2018; Lima & da Silva Müller, 2017; Schulte-Holthaus & Kuckertz, 2020; Tremml, 2020). We present two CCM studies, one of *nascent micro entrepreneurs* (NME), the other of *small business advisors* (SBAs). This facilitates assessing CCM's applicability for studying entrepreneurial actors' knowledge in general and in cross-cultural and cross-national contexts.

The chapter is structured as follows. We discuss next basic notions about human cognition and their methodological implications. The third section describes the study's context and methods. The fourth presents the findings about the SBAs' and NMEs' belief systems and discusses a survey conducted to test the method. The last section draws some methodological and research lessons for content-oriented ECR considering especially cross-cultural and cross-national contexts.

2 Conceptual and Methodological Underpinnings

2.1 Mental Models and Reasoning

Memory is a key aspect of cognitive functioning (Baddeley, 2010; Evans & Stanovich, 2013; Fiske & Taylor, 2021). It is usually conceptualised to consist of a long-term memory (LTM), a permanent information store with practically unlimited capacity, and a short-term or working memory (WM), a temporary information storage and conscious processing system. WM's capacity is limited, typically to 4–5 words/episodes and 5–7 numbers at a time.

Underlying the notions of *knowledge* and *belief*[1] is our ability of symbolic representation: the creation, acquisition and use of internal conceptions or models of our external reality. This notion is common in cognitive and social psychology and in fields like management and organisation cognition (MOC) and political science/psychology (Axelrod, 1976; Johnson-Laird, 2004, 2013; Markman & Gentner, 2001; Narayanan, 2005; Walsh, 1995). This is manifested in theoretical constructs that denote different hypothesised knowledge structures (schemas) (Fiske & Taylor, 2021). These include *scripts* (prototypical processes or event sequences) (Mitchell et al., 2009), *folk/naïve theories* (lay systems of belief) (Gelman & Legare, 2011) and *mental models* and/or *belief systems* (Bandura, 2001; Gentner, 2004; Johnson-Laird, 2010, 2013; Markman & Gentner, 2001). The latter terms refer to a person's more or less coherent interrelated beliefs/knowledge about a domain or issue, retained in LTM and augmented or generated in the WM using momentary reasoning and imagination. The term *cognitive map* denotes usually *spatial* objects' representations (Fiske & Taylor, 2021), sometimes also structures like mental models, but in applied studies also their overt representations like cause maps or most confusingly both aspects.

Mental models/belief systems are practically indispensable. When recalled or created *ad hoc* in WM, they enable the person discerning what exists in a given part of the world, comprehending how things function and running thought experiments using fast, mind's eye, "kinematic *simulation* of the world" (Hagmayer & Sloman, 2009; Johnson-Laird, 2013). This facilitates mentally intervening in perceived real or hypothetical situations by *if-then* inferences and thus flexible reasoning and comprehending about past, novel or even imaginary events and issues. This is also

[1] The terms knowledge and belief are used now interchangeably to refer to social actors' subjective knowledge, in practice propositions they hold and consider plausible enough to express as their views (Good & McDowell, 2015; cf. however, e.g., Churchland & Churchland, 2013).

a precondition of conceiving and planning of alternative courses of action, i.e., *subjectively reasoned* behaviour (Baumeister et al., 2011).

2.2 Origins of Knowledge and Beliefs

Understanding and influencing entrepreneurial knowledge requires understanding their origins. This involves first *experiential learning* based on observing and inferring events' co-occurrences and the consequences of one's own or others' behaviours (Cheng & Buehner, 2012; Holyoak & Cheng, 2011). Some beliefs result of intense experiences like growing in an entrepreneur family, leaving long-lasting beliefs about entrepreneurship as something rewarding or precarious. The other major source is *social transfer* by gradual cultural indoctrination, basic and professional education and working life knowledge transmission (Chi & Ohlsson, 2005; Wyer & Albarracín, 2005). Influential can be also the "common knowledge" conveyed by media and social arenas and the area-specific knowledge obtained of different guides and professional training and counselling (Forbes, 2014). Overall, social transfer typically explains most of people's active beliefs and knowledge (Chi & Ohlsson, 2005). Lastly, there are also cognitive processes whereby people unconsciously acquire higher level, often tacit knowledge (Chi & Ohlsson, 2005).

A different question is the *specific* knowledge/beliefs people acquire especially considering the huge amount of all potential knowledge. This and the largely automatic selection can be understood functionally. Knowledge people consider (or define) *relevant* to a task, situation or position, tends to be acquired, and conversely, bypassed if found unnecessary. Some knowledge will be generated and retained as a by-product of everyday problem-solving, some gets adopted resulting of strong evidence or social pressures. The outcome is that normal adults will possess large repositories (Chi & Ohlsson, 2005) of distinct items and systems of knowledge varying in terms of generality, veridicality and accessibility (tacit/explicit) concerning mainly things, issues and domains that are important to the individual. At social levels especially within organisations and professions, such processes can produce *communities of practice* (cf. Pyrko et al., 2017), characterised by unique belief systems. For example, the present SBAs who meet regularly and share training, information and experiences, probably form such a community.

Lastly, belief formation underlies *cognitive tendencies* and *biases*, although their impact in specific cases like the present respondents can be only surmised. An important common tendency is normal adults' in-built need to explain and to understand other people and the own world by finding plausible, not necessarily true causes or reasons for behaviour and events (Fiske & Taylor, 2021; Sloman & Lagnado, 2015). This is manifested in people's inherent or cultural (Bender et al., 2017) tendencies (Westmeyer, 2001) to explain behaviours and outcomes *teleologically* or *functionally* by referring to others' motives or to phenomena's functions, *tautologically* by assuming people have unique faculties, and *environmentally* by positing compelling conditions and factors. In the present case, such tendencies or perhaps explanatory heuristics could underlie especially beliefs (propositions) which the respondents express as tentative ideas. A second factor concerning especially the NMEs is our tendency to avoid *cognitive dissonance* (Fiske & Taylor, 2021; Sternberg & Sternberg, 2012). This is shown in resisting changing one's mind or in ignoring information that contradicts one's previous beliefs and decisions, in general in an inclination to believe what one wishes. Further, also presently probably relevant propensities include the *confirmation bias* to prioritise evidence that supports previous beliefs, an *illusion of control* and an optimistic bias (Baron, 2004).

2.3 Methodological Implications

The notion of mental models/belief systems implies that their key elements are *causal beliefs/propositions* that certain phenomena or states of affairs (A, B, C, etc.) exist and have some influence (or temporal) relationships (that A influences B, C follows B, etc.) (Sloman & Lagnado, 2015). Cause maps (see below) consist of *nodes* and *arrows* that correspond to the entities and relationships someone perceives in a domain. This makes causal mapping a highly useful formality for representing actors' phenomenological and causal beliefs and their systems, including conceived event sequences (scripts) (Ifenthaler et al., 2011; Jones et al., 2011).

Using causal maps underlies some constraints. First, as noted, knowledge/beliefs and their systems must be *externalised* in natural language or graphically before they can be analysed and interpreted (Evans, 1998; Ifenthaler et al., 2011; Rouse & Morris, 1986). Second, people have no *single* universal belief system/mental model, but *several* variously coherent and developed conceptualisations about *specific* issues or domains. This implies a researcher decision about which issues are relevant and focusing data elicitation accordingly. Third, belief systems cannot be expressed nor elicited as whole gestalts. When probed, people can express beliefs only as successive *binary propositions* (a → b, c → d, etc.), which correspond to what they recall and/or infer based on the recalled knowledge.

The construction of cause maps depends on the data. In *archival* CCM studies the data, causal propositions, are distilled from texts usually from among much irrelevant material (Axelrod, 1976). In the present case the original propositions had to be elicited by *semi-structured interviewing* (SSI) (Laukkanen & Wang, 2015). This has the additional benefit of acquiring mainly causal proposition and little redundant data. In cognitive terms, SSI probing activates the *declarative* LTM which contains retained facts and general notions like concepts, principles, ideas and theories (Baddeley, 2010; Chi & Ohlsson, 2005). Probing usually also triggers WM *reconstruction* using mental simulation, imagination and logical reasoning (Johnson-Laird, 2010, 2013). It follows that respondents may occasionally utter also things which do not exist in their LTM and might not occur to them when probed again. This must be observed in the study's instructions, uniform elicitation times and data interpretation.

As described below, in CCM, the original propositions are combined, after coding, first into individual cause maps (ICM), representing each respondent's belief systems. By intersecting the ICMs *aggregated cause maps* (ACM) can be constructed to represent the respondents' shared, *typical* belief patterns. Using ACMs also helps neutralise the impact of idiosyncrasies and random factors. It is, however, important not to overinterpret cause maps by assuming they are 1:1 replicas of mental models. This follows already of WM limitations (Leiser, 2001). However, when based on valid data elicited from properly instructed and sincere respondents, cause maps are very useful representations of actors' typical beliefs and reasoning patterns about the addressed domains at a given time.

2.4 Research Tasks and Expectations

Assessing the CCM approach involves a practical and a plausibility issue. The former varies by each researcher and study case. The latter means that the method and the findings make sense and conform to basic theory-based expectations.

Perhaps the first expectation is that both respondent groups do have more or less shared belief systems. This follows of belief systems' key role and formation logic as discussed above. A test of this expectation is whether plausible, coherent ACMs can be generated. That is not possible if the belief systems are so divergent that the elicited ICMs have only few shared notions and causal relationships.

Further expectations concern the respondents' belief systems' complexity and within-group congruence, manifested in a higher or smaller number of cause map nodes and causal relationships and more or less complex ACMs. In this respect, it can be assumed that the SBAs' belief systems and thus ACM will be more uniform and complex than those of the NMEs. This follows of the SBAs' business education, counselling experience and characteristics as a community of practice.

The NMEs' belief systems and ACM are more difficult to predict. Their educational and work-life backgrounds, personal situations and objectives vary. In general, it can be assumed that, as lay persons, their shared knowledge/beliefs will reflect, in addition to the above discussed cultural tendencies, also socially shared, common-sense ideas about entrepreneurship. On theoretical grounds (cognitive dissonance), their ideas about entrepreneurship should be sanguine, emphasising entrepreneurship's positive outcomes and feasibility. Otherwise, they would hardly be seeking counselling. A further factor is that the NMEs have no entrepreneurial experience, yet are seriously considering an entrepreneurial career. Thus, their belief systems about micro firms are less sophisticated and more divergent, suggesting simple ACMs. It is also likely that they have thought about entrepreneurship and sought related information. This suggests rudimentary but still diverse ideas about entrepreneurship and managing a business, also implying less uniform and simpler belief systems and thus a relatively simple ACM.

3 Context, Respondents, Method

3.1 Context and Participants

We present the CCM methodology using two recent study cases. In both, the context is *Finnish Entrepreneurship Agency* (FEA), the country's only nationwide provider of micro entrepreneur advisory services. Currently, there are 29 local agencies which employ some 90 SBAs, supported by voluntary local experts. In a typical year, FEA has around 15,000 clients and helps found 8000 firms, which corresponds to one half of Finland's early-stage entrepreneurs and one third of new firms. SBAs evaluate prospective entrepreneurs' business ideas and qualifications, offering no-cost advice whether and how to realise the project. They also provide contacts and endorsements about start-up allowances or loans. Currently only the start-up phase is covered.

The SBA sample ($N = 15$) was constructed by randomly selecting local FEA units and then inviting the manager SBA and one further SBA (if available) to participate. The sample includes 6 females and 9 males and was built stage-wise, observing active concepts' saturation (see below). The SBAs' mean age was 45.3 years (SD 8.76). They have worked long as SBAs (7.9 years SD 6.24). Most have an MSc and also several years' experience as owner-managers or in family business.

The NMEs are clients of two FEA agencies. As FEA cannot disclose client information, the participation had to be voluntary. The criterion was that they had not yet started the actual counselling so that the interviews would reflect their pre-founding beliefs. The NME sample too was based on tracking the saturation of their active concepts. The final sample ($N = 13$) included 8 female and 5 male participants. Their mean age was 44.1 years (SD 10.24) with a range of 27–57 years. Six NMEs have a university, five a polytechnic and two a trade school degree, a somewhat higher level compared with GEM studies' NMEs (Suomalainen et al., 2016).

3.2 Comparative Causal Mapping

The CCM method is discussed in Laukkanen (2018) and in detail in Laukkanen and Wang (2015). The main stages (Fig. 1) can be summarised as follows. The data, original causal propositions, were acquired using *semi-structured interviewing* (SSI) around two *anchor topics*: (1) Why does (or does not) someone become an entrepreneur and what follows? and (2) What are the causes and consequences of a micro firm's emergence and success or failure? As noted, a focusing of respondents' thinking and responses is necessary to elicit beliefs about the relevant domain, in this case, individual entrepreneurship and small firms' performance.

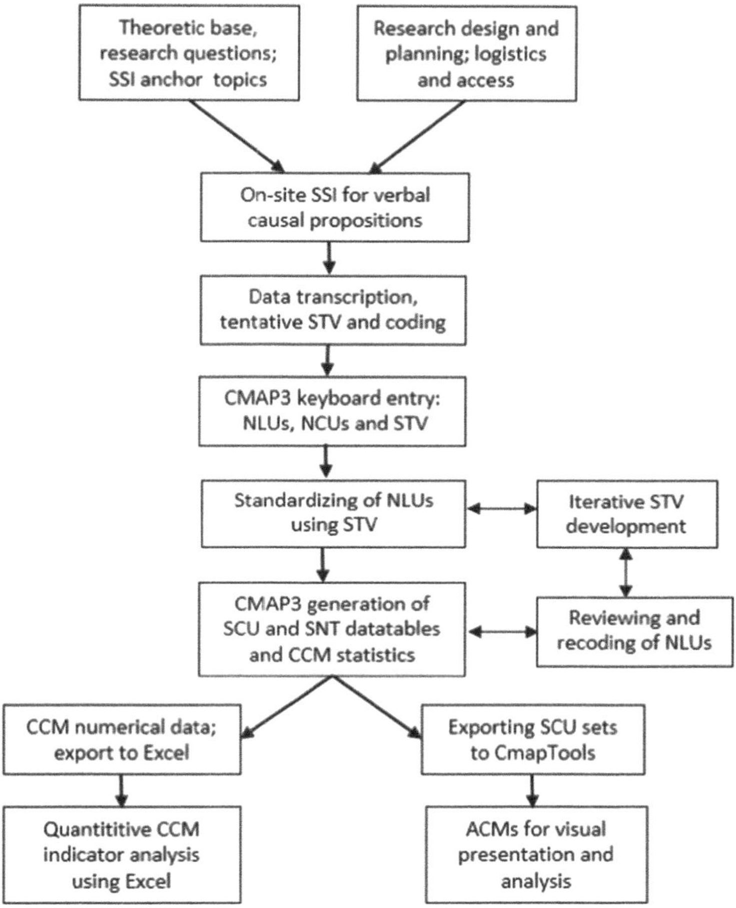

Fig. 1 Main stages of the CCM-SSI research process (For the abbreviations, please see the text)

Before starting, the SSI process was explained. It was emphasised that the respondents' own ideas, not "book wisdom", are sought and that no sensitive issues will be addressed. SSI started by asking first about the causes of the first anchor topic and then about its consequences. This produces a *first layer* of original notions and causal propositions, more familiar and easily recalled as the topic's proximate causes and effects. Then the *same format* was repeated using the elicited original concepts as *new anchors*. This generates a much larger *secondary layer* of concepts, causally more distant but still representing the respondents' retained beliefs and causal inferences. Because of the limited access time and the need to cover both domains consistently, the present SSI probed only about the antecedents of the primary causes and the consequents of the primary effects. When the first topic was covered and the respondent had not anything to add, the second anchor topic was addressed similarly. The allotted response times were kept uniform. The SBA interviews took a good hour ($M = 80.0$ min, SD = 16.9), the NMEs' duration was $M = 66.77$ min (SD = 13.99). The interviewer kept hand-written notes (see Laukkanen & Wang, 2015), backed by voice-activated recording (with permission).

As noted earlier, CCM-SSI data consist of causal propositions, i.e., concept pairs (a → b, b → c, etc.), where a notion, or rather its referent phenomenon, is stated to influence another notion or to be caused by it. The SBA data contained 1153 original concepts ($M = 76.87$, SD = 19.14 per respondent), called *natural language units* (NLU) and 1539 causal relationships, called, respectively, *natural causal units* (NCU) ($M = 102.60$, SD = 28.10 per respondent). NME data contained 923 NLUs ($M = 71.00$, SD = 16.49 per respondent) and 1312 NCUs ($M = 100.92$, SD = 21.69 per respondent).

The studies utilised a CCM specific application, CMAP3.[2] Natural language data, typical of SSI-CCM studies, makes this obligatory (cf. Haak et al., 2013). In practice, original data are keyboard entered into CMAP3, coded/standardised and processed to create the base for graphic cause maps and the numerical data which represent the respondents' belief systems and enable their visual and numerical analysis. The technical processes are explained in Laukkanen and Wang (2015) and in CMAP3 support documentation (Footnote 2).

A key step in CCM is *standardising* (coding) (Laukkanen & Wang, 2015). It converts the respondents' uttered concepts (now in Finnish) into standard terms (in English) which represent the underlying core meanings and referents. Usually, standard terms are developed iteratively by grouping and inferring of the original concepts and entered into a CMAP3 data table called *standard term vocabulary* (STV). In practice, standardising interprets the original concepts' meanings and defines them as *same-denoting* with an appropriate standard term. This also *compacts* data by identifying synonyms and homonyms and removing (presently) redundant details like polar states or attributes. Most importantly, standardising facilitates converting the NLUs into the STV's standard language and enables thus *comparing* the respondents' beliefs and defining their similarity or difference.

The present coding was at *low level*, where the standard terms are close to the original concepts. This simplifies coding and makes it more reliable compared with studies using higher-level standard terms. Because standardising influences the results of CCM, it must be done carefully ensuring its validity, e.g., by using external reviewers (see below).

A key feature of CMAP3 is that the NLUs and the STV reside in separate data tables and that the STV allows two parallel languages. This means that the original data and the STV can (but must not) be in *different* languages. This is important in cross-national studies (see Footnote 2) and generally in studies where the raw data

[2]CMAP3 installation file, the CCM/CMAP3 User Guide and support documents can be downloaded *without cost* at the University of Eastern Finland website: https://www3.uef.fi/fi/web/cmap. Setting up CMAP3 installs automatically two testable learning projects, the default project representing a fictional cross-national CCM study.

like interview responses and the reporting must use different languages. The technique facilitates also validating the individual standardising decisions using respondent feedback (Laukkanen & Wang, 2015).

After coding, the original data were processed by CMAP3 into *data tables*, one containing active *standard concepts* (SNT, standard node terms), the other standardised cause-effect links or pairs, called *standard causal units* (SCU). The process also determines which respondents own a given SNT and SCU; that is, had expressed the corresponding original concepts and causal propositions. The incidence information also enables distilling a respondent's or a group's active standard causal links, which can be then converted into pictorial ICMs or ACMs by exporting the SCU sets to a graphic application like *IHMC CmapTools*[3] or MS*PowerPoint* (Laukkanen & Wang, 2015). CMAP3 also calculates numerical indicators like densities and mutual distances of the ICMs. These as the above data tables can be exported to *MS Excel* for further analysis and printing.

3.3 Validity

In CCM—in qualitative studies generally—validity can be defined as the method's and the findings' *credibility* (Maxwell, 2013). In this case, at issue is did the SSI tap and do the emerging ACMs represent the respondents' typical beliefs and inference tendencies. Three aspects can be considered.

The first is data validity. Here it depends primarily on the respondents' *sincerity* (Axelrod, 1976): Did they say what they think and mean what they say? This can only be judged by examining the specific method and the context (Nicolini, 1999). The interviews were conducted in neutral, topic-relevant surroundings (FEA offices) following a standard protocol and allowing roughly equal response times. Importantly, the probing addressed general, not personal issues. The participants had also no obvious shared motives nor a practical possibility to collude so as to *systematically* bias, hide or fabricate what they *all* express. Thus, important indirect evidence of the studies' validity is that coherent, relatively detailed ACMs could be generated because this indicates *shared* belief systems. Otherwise, ACMs cannot emerge. In addition, ACMs reduce the impact of random errors and idiosyncratic biases. Overall, the present data can be assumed to reflect the participants' sincere, readily accessible knowledge and reasoning tendencies.

The second issue is coding. The ideal is reasonable *semantic validity* whereby the standard terms (in English) make sense in the context and the original concepts (here in Finnish) are consistently standardised and translated observing their original referents. To assess this, both studies' coding was reviewed by two experts, familiar with the method and the context (an SME professor, an experienced outsider SBA).

[3]IHMC CmapTools can be freely downloaded at: https://cmap.ihmc.us/cmaptools/cmaptools-download/

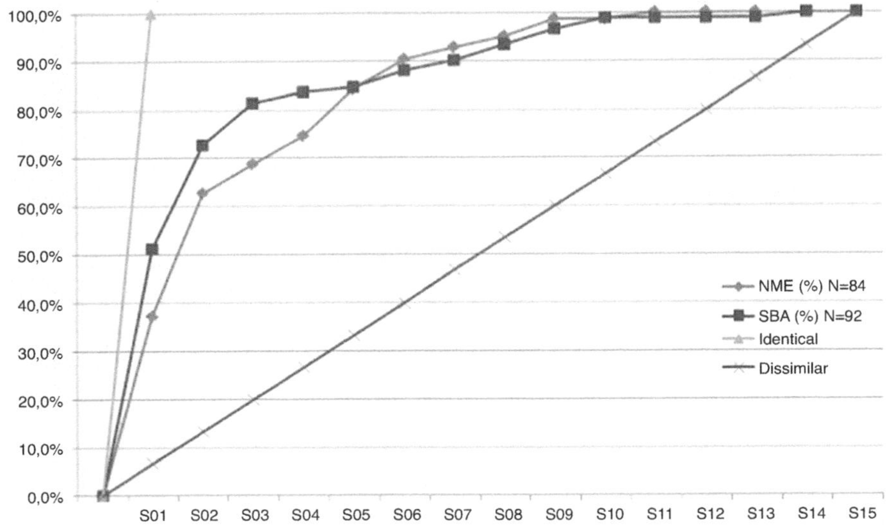

Fig. 2 Saturation of the SBAs' ($N = 15$) and the NMEs' ($N = 13$) active standard concepts

This led to some corrections, yet yielded a high inter-rater reliability (IRR) measured as average percent agreement (NME IRR = 99.42%, SBA IRR = 98.51%). This indicates essentially correct coding and high semantic validity.

Lastly, the credibility of causal maps (and mapping) implies reasonable *behavioural congruence* of the respondents' expressed beliefs and what they do (Axelrod, 1976). If so, cause maps correspond to and make understandable what the studied actors did or enable predicting their corresponding behaviours. When assessing this, the spheres (speech, overt action) must be comparable, i.e., at the same level of specificity and reasonably proximate in time. In this case, the broad congruence was tested by comparing the elicited core beliefs with what happens in NME/SBA counselling. The results are discussed below.

4 Findings

4.1 Examining Belief Systems' Sharedness

As noted, the first expectation concerned the studied groups' beliefs' homogeneity, indicated by the *saturation* of the respondents' concepts (Nelson et al., 2000). As shown in Fig. 2, the majority of their active concepts emerge already by the 7th respondent in both groups. After this, each additional participant contributes only 1 or 2 new concepts. As causal links follow the concepts, this indicates that the SBAs' and NMEs' belief systems concerning the inquired issues are relatively uniform.

The observed saturation serves also constructing the ACMs which represent the respondents' typical or core thought patterns. Technically, ACMs are intersections of ICMs and contain the standard nodes and causal relationships which a specific number of the group's members share. Causal mapping literature suggests a criterion of around 50% (Carley, 1997). In general, the threshold depends on how uniformly the groups think about the focal issue (Guest et al., 2006). In this case, the observed saturation pattern and the 50% rule both suggest cut-off points of $N \geq 6$ or $N \geq 7$. However, the ACMs must also present the participants' core thinking in a practical and comprehensible form. Using CMAP3, this could be tested by generating ACMs using different thresholds. This showed for both groups that $N = >6$ produces too dense, poorly readable ACMs, a high threshold ($N = >8$), respectively, simple ACMs, which risk excluding probably shared notions. $N \geq 7$ appeared a good compromise. This is also indicated by the high sharedness of ACMs' nodes (measured by their total frequency, TF, the number of respondents owning a standard concept). The SBA ACM's (Fig. 3) median TF = 8.0; the NME ACM (Fig. 4) median TF = 9.0.

4.2 SBA Belief System

The first ACM (Fig. 3) represents the SBAs' core belief systems about the causes and consequences of *nascent micro firms'* (NMF) emergence and success and failure. It contains 58 nodes and 114 causal links, some reciprocal. The nodes in bold are shared by nearly all SBAs.

This ACM is relatively complex, indicating sophisticated typical thinking. The left side displays the main factors of NMF success or failure as perceived by the SBAs. There are two primary mechanisms. One concerns the NMEs' business, manifested first in a business idea (BI) or a business plan (BP). The SBAs emphasise demand, "paying customers", the proposed business's competitiveness v. local competition, and the NMEs' resources' adequacy and their BPs' quality. In general, the factors SBAs observe are symmetrical and continuous, different states having a positive or negative impact on the outcome.

The second subsystem concerns NMEs' characteristics. The SBAs discern several background factors shown in the ACM. A specific one explaining especially failure is the standard notion *NMEs' negative attitudes/traits*. It summarises characteristics which the SBAs have encountered and consider problematic such as strong introversion, laziness, unconscientiousness and alcohol or moral problems.

Two further observations are noteworthy. First, the ACM indicates that the SBA emphasises the *negative* consequences of an entrepreneurial failure, suggesting an inherent tendency to avert risks as far as possible. Second, the SBAs emphasise the *positive* societal consequences of NMFs (and thus of midwifing them) but seem

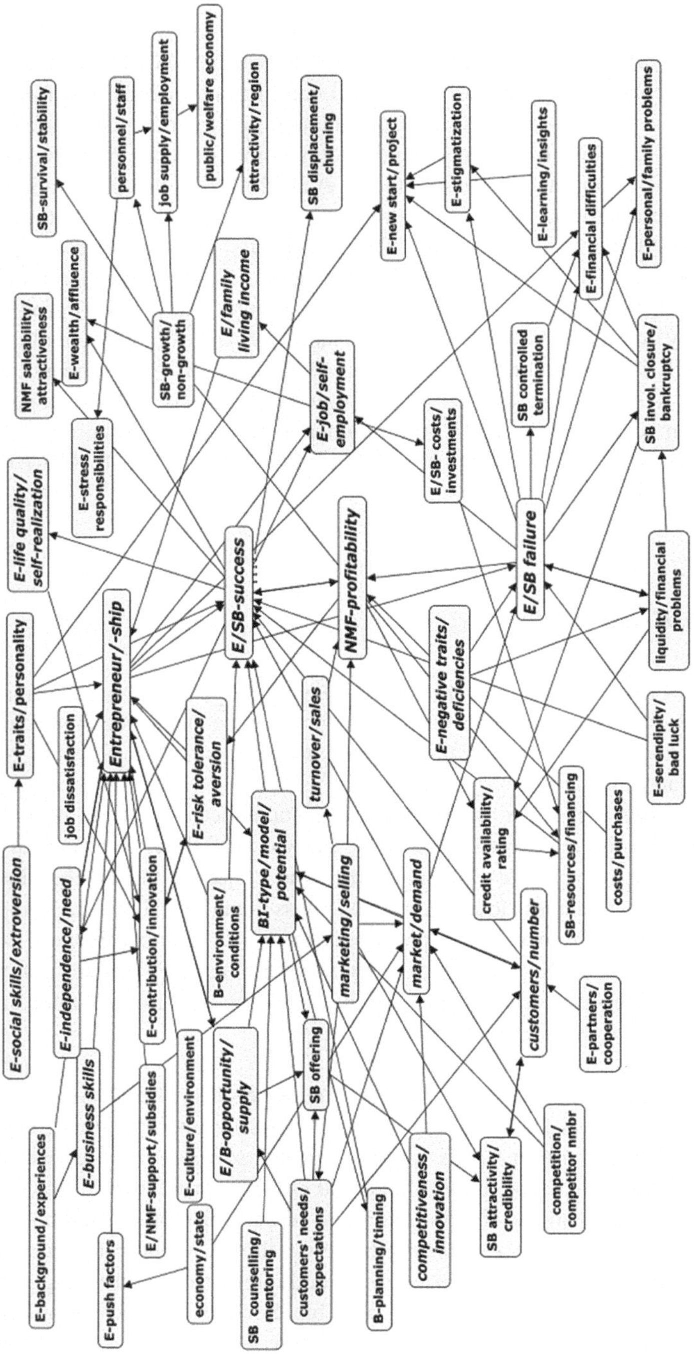

Fig. 3 The SBAs' aggregated cause map

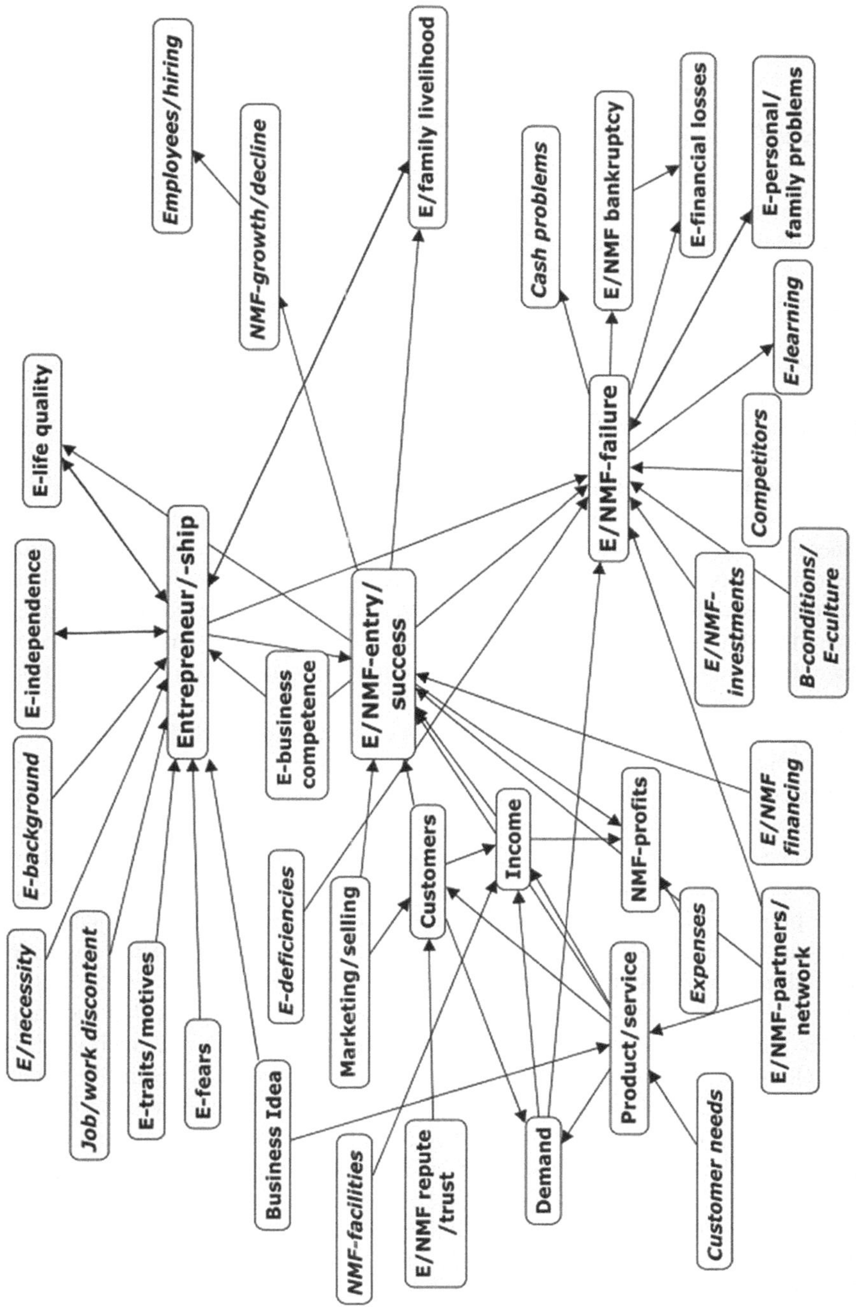

Fig. 4 The NMEs' aggregated cause map

unaware of their potential and common negative impacts like causing local firm and job churning (Bennett, 2014).

4.3 NME Belief System

The second ACM (Fig. 4) summarises the NME's entrepreneurship—and business-related beliefs. It contains 37 standard concepts and 56 relationships, some reciprocal, a concept appearing as a factor and an outcome. The concepts in bold are shared by all NMEs.

The ACM's upper part displays the NMEs' ideas about entrepreneurship. They explain it first by personal goals such as ensuring livelihood, independence and better life quality. Successful entrepreneurship realises those, which is why they appear as drivers and outcomes. The NMEs also believe that there are specific traits and motives that differentiate entrepreneurs from "normal" persons. Second, NMEs' have several beliefs concerning entrepreneurship's business aspects. They note that a Business Idea (BI), an accessible product or service or a detected need can trigger entrepreneurship, and that entrepreneurship requires certain competences about which their ideas, however, are hazier. Notably, to most NMEs *the* reason *preventing* entrepreneurship is *fears* of the consequences of a failure and of the uncertainty of being able to launch and run an NMF. Interestingly, this aspect did not come up in *any* SBA interview. Therefore, it is missing in the SBAs' ACM.

The ACM's middle part displays NMEs' core beliefs about NMF success. They explain it by an active, competent entrepreneur and a product/service which corresponds to customer needs, attracts customers and has partner network support. To influence customers, NMEs emphasise marketing, personal selling and reputation. As outcomes, ensuring livelihood and better life quality are mentioned again. More distant results include firm growth, hiring personnel and ability to provide jobs and support public welfare. Notably, stereotypic motives like wealth or social status do not appear in the ACM, only two NMEs noting them. Perhaps such things are perceived more hypothetical at this early stage.

The NME ACM's dense subsystem about NMF failure suggests that too they consider this a serious issue. They perceive several failure causes. Interestingly, nearly all NMEs believe that failure *always* means bankruptcy, leading to major losses and serious personal and family problems. The normal unforced termination seems unknown. However, the NMEs are remarkably euphoric: Failure can happen but not to one, but should it happen, one can return to a wage-earning job or restart having learned much. This may indicate the common avoidance of cognitive dissonance, here between intentions and perceived risks. At this stage, it is perhaps natural to diminish the dissonance by mentally minimising the latter.

4.4 Correspondence of Beliefs and Behaviours

To assess the congruence of the two groups' belief systems and respective behaviours, a brief SBA survey[4] ($N = 15$) was conducted to illuminate the foci and conduct of typical FEA counselling sessions. As evidence, this is asymmetric but unavoidable. The SBAs have counselling experience, the NMEs none. It seems, however, reasonable to assume that the NMEs' main concerns will be manifested in the SBAs' responses.

The ACM simply two, possibly three foci in typical counselling. The first concerns the NME's proposed business and personal goals. These are essential but largely neutral issues. For the NMEs, they mean entrepreneurship's preconditions; for the SBAs things they meet daily and which they are, by definition, prepared to handle. The other is NMEs' qualifications. Whilst the NMEs understand qualifications' significance, they can seldom assess their own capabilities relative to their projects. As for the SBAs, although they emphasise NME competence and characteristics, assessing them is difficult. The SBA belief system reflects this: the ACM contains things for which information is easily available and/or which concern observable characteristics like extraversion or consciousness, inferable (not necessarily accurately) from the NMEs' behaviours. The third but problematic issue is NMEs' fears, salient in the NME ACM but missing in the SBA ACM. The asymmetry suggests that NMEs' qualms are probably seldom actively tackled.

The survey broadly supports the above predictions. The SBAs emphasise the realism of proposed business, seeking evidence of a plausible business and revenue logic. They also examine NMEs' resources. As to NME capabilities, the SBAs emphasise personality, "a good E-type" with overt signs of motivation and drive, knowledge of the business and customers and appropriate skills. The NMEs' business plans are key tools of the SBAs. They facilitate concrete, numerical assessment and indicate the NMEs' communication, conscientiousness and mental capabilities.

The SBAs were specifically asked about NMEs' fears. The responses indicate that these issues come up rarely. The majority think that eventual qualms vanish automatically when the NMEs grasp their projects' practical realisability. Another approach, more typical of female SBAs, provides sympathetic listening, advice and encouragement. Two SBAs denied the existence of fears as "unentrepreneurial". Overall, it can be assumed that most SBAs would not refuse discussing a client's fears if the client wishes that and specifically expresses them. That, however, seems unusual in the present context. Why this is so and which counselling strategies make sense are interesting questions for further research.

---

[4]This SBA sample was randomly selected and invited to respond to an emailed open questionnaire. The sample followed a saturation logic, approaching new respondents till no essentially new notions emerged. This point was reached by $N = 15$. The SBAs' mean age was 54.50 (SD 7.82), average SBA-experience 17.08 years (SD 9.12) and business experience 20.69 years (SD 12.22). 10 had an MSc, 4 a Polytechnic (BBA) degree, 1 undefined.

5 Discussion

This section examines first the belief systems considering the theory-based expectations. It then discusses the CCM methodology and its variants and use in cross-cultural and cross-national studies. We conclude by some lessons of the study cases and suggest some directions for further CCM studies.

5.1 Evaluating the Findings

A first conclusion is that both respondent groups have *shared* beliefs systems as expected. This is indicated by the *congruence* of both groups' active concept bases and by the emergence of *coherent ACMs* when intersecting the respondents' ICMs. Second, the belief systems' overall *complexity* is also as predicted, the SBA ACM indicating clearly more sophisticated thinking about the probed issues compared with the NMEs. Such observations may seem now self-evident, but this is hindsight. At the outset they could be only surmised.

Second, the two groups' belief systems' contents provide persuasive evidence of the basic formation logic of practical knowledge. To behave intelligently, social actors must internalise and gradually develop their understanding of their external situations' structures and causal mechanisms. Thus, the SBA ACM indicates a rather detailed cognitive grip of things which are normally germane when counselling NMEs and assessing their projects, largely corresponding to established wisdom about small business and entrepreneurship. On the other hand, the SBAs seem to emphasise things of which information is readily available such as the NMEs' business plans. They may also overstress stereotypic ideas about the role of entrepreneurial personality and overt characteristics like extraversion or consciousness, found to predict entrepreneurial performance only moderately (Zhao et al., 2010). Furthermore, the SBA ACM indicates considerable risk aversion and also unawareness (or routine bypassing) of new micro firms' occasional negative consequences (Bennett, 2014). Such tendencies cannot but influence their inferences and recommendations. However, it should also be noted that the SBAs must prioritise the NMEs', not public, interests and that they have only few hours per client and must use mainly information the NMEs provide.

The NMEACM indicates surprisingly uniform and rather complex shared belief systems. This is unexpected considering that the respondents are lay persons with diverse and "non-entrepreneurial" backgrounds. The system of core beliefs can be assumed to reflect the cognitive impact of the similarities of their objectives and personal situations. It also probable that there has been some self-education using similar, readily available printed and digital materials, which reproduce received wisdom about small business and entrepreneurship. Thus, it is not surprising that the two groups' belief systems indeed partly overlap, which should facilitate constructive counselling. However, the NMEs' grasp of business terminology, processes and conditions is still embryonic, understandable at this stage.

To provide further evidence of the SSI-CCM approach, the SBA survey was conducted. The results indicate basic congruence of the respondents' counselling behaviours and their belief systems. The salient exception is NMEs' fears, prominent in their ACM but missing the SBA ACM. This could have reasons like unpreparedness to handle such problems or simply lack of time, but also cognitive, affective or cultural grounds like common stereotypic ideas about "proper" entrepreneurial behaviour. Methodologically, this observation emphasises that even strong beliefs are not always manifested in overt behaviours if the context or common cultural factors are against it. Reasoned action must observe and balance the actors' other beliefs and their subjective perceptions of the situation's demands.

5.2 Assessing the Methodology

According to Carley and Palmquist (1992: 605), "Cognitive mapping is perhaps the most useful means of exploring the nature of shared knowledge in social groups". The above studies demonstrate that CCM-SSI facilitates accessing, describing and analysing the typical belief systems of entrepreneurial actors like the SBAs and NMEs. The methodology is also applicable in different contexts, including settings involving different languages.

In practical terms, the cases show that CCM-SSI is similar to typical qualitative methods. It uses on-site acquisition of natural language data which require subjective interpretation and thus independent verification in some form. On the other hand, the method is not overly demanding in terms of technical know-how, resources and logistics. Importantly, the time per respondent required for data elicitation, processing and analysis is reasonable. For instance, the NME interviews took typically a good hour yet elicited rather detailed ICMs about two key domains. The downside is that systematic and transparent data processing is more or less requires using software like CMAP3. However, this also generates numerical data for "counting the countable", important in qualitative studies (Cassell & Symon, 1994; Maxwell, 2010). In addition, the data tables can be exported to Excel for advanced quantitative analysis and further, e.g., to SPSS for cluster analysis (Laukkanen & Wang, 2015).

What alternatives to present approach are there for *comparative* studies of belief systems? This depends on the question. The above studies' question is essentially: *What are group A's, B's, etc., beliefs about X?* This necessitates *uniform* acquisition of *original* causal propositions about the focal topics. That effectively eliminates using less controllable off-site elicitation and also structured approaches like the concept-pool method (Laukkanen & Wang, 2015; Markóczy, 2000), where the elicited concepts are researcher-defined. Conceivable on-site options for eliciting rich original data include text-writing tasks (Nadkarni & Narayanan, 2005) and low-structured interviewing (Nicolini, 1999). Their problem is that they require time or can tap only a restricted set of beliefs. Further issues can be ensuring uniformity and eliciting much redundant material in addition to relevant data.

The CCM approach can be modified. One way is to elicit uniform original data by video-conferencing, increasingly common because of the Covid-19 pandemic. Furthermore, the study can focus on exploring *specific beliefs*, e.g., the reasoning behind NMEs' fears or the role of social relationships. In this case, the probing would go deeper behind the antecedents of the causes, accessed in the above cases.

A very different possibility is to examine not belief systems' contents as here, but their *characteristics* such as differences of goal setting or simply relative complexity. That would allow using structured approaches like the above concept-pool method, permitting also larger samples and nomothetic studies. However, such studies should ensure that the pool instrument does represent the participants' natural thinking. CMAP3 supports also the concept-pool method.

5.3 Cross-cultural and Cross-national Studies

Culture has been defined as the set of values, beliefs and behavioural expectations or "... the collective programming of the mind that distinguishes the members of one group or category of people from others" (Hofstede, 2011: 3). This makes culture essentially a *cognitive* phenomenon, expressed and mediated through people's beliefs and causal reasoning (Bender et al., 2017; Oyserman & Lee, 2008), providing therefore an intuitive framework for explaining social behaviour. This also explains culture perspective's popularity in entrepreneurship studies (Engelen et al., 2009; Valliere, 2017) concerned, e.g., with national cultures' links with new firm emergence (Thurik & Dejardin, 2012) or with entrepreneurs' self-efficacy and fear of failure (Wennberg et al., 2013). Entrepreneurship studies commonly describe national cultures in terms of Hofstede's seminal dimensions power distance, individualism-collectivism, masculinity-femininity and uncertainty avoidance, later augmented with long-term-short term orientation and indulgence-restraint (Hofstede, 2001, 2011).

In the present context, cultures, especially national cultures, can be considered in two respects. First, they, rather their impacts, can be *research targets*. In this case the presently relevant issue is CCM's ability to detect valid manifestations of cultures and cultural dimensions. Although the above studies were not specifically "cultural", the findings enable roughly assessing CCM by examining the above ACMs' (Figs. 3 and 4) congruence with the Finnish culture in terms of Hofstede's dimensions. Thereby, particularly relevant observations of the ACMs concern the salience of individual, not societal benefits as entrepreneurship's goals, the prominence of NMEs' personal fears, and, in the SBAs' case, their shunning of failure and emphasis of formal plans. These aspects can be interpreted to indicate *individualism* and uncertainty *avoidance*, perhaps also short-*term normative orientation* and *indulgence*, all typical[5] characteristics of the Finnish national culture. Conversely, the ACMs show no traces of high *power distance* or *collectivity*, which are untypical of Finnish culture and should therefore be missing. The limited observations suggest that CCM enables exploring how cultures are manifested in actors' thought patterns. This may also provide one way of operationalising cultures, perhaps in particular cultures' specific aspects such as the prevalence of fears among nascent Finnish entrepreneurs.

Secondly, cultures are also research contexts that present distinctive problems, starting with the *availability* and *accessibility* of respondents; a precondition of data acquisition using methods like SSI. This is influenced by cultural factors like power distance, in practice varyingly rigid hierarchies and reachability of influential persons. Also, the esteem of academic research can vary, influencing accessibility but also how *open* the respondents are and thus data quality. A further condition of valid data is participants' *trust* in the researcher and the project (Maxwell, 2013; Nicolini, 1999). This too is a cultural issue, reflecting trusting or secretive societies (Welter & Alex, 2012), or professional and organisational silos. For instance, when studying professional elites of different cultures, not even necessarily different nationalities, the building of trust and rapport can take long and require repeated contacts and native members in the researcher team (Martinus & Hedgcock, 2015).

However, the issues should not be overstressed. First, the topics addressed in CCM studies are often neutral, not personal or controversial. Also framing the probing counts. For instance, when interviewing respondents like the NMEs, it may be better to ask what they think NMEs *in general* think, not what they personally think. For lay persons these tend to overlap. Secondly, especially with educated respondents more important than national cultural factors are often the findings' instrumental value and their personal values, even plain curiosity (Nelson et al., 2000). The authors' experience also suggests that simply feeling appreciated as informants and having, for once, an opportunity to "think aloud" and hear and be heard what one thinks, can be adequately motivating. For such reasons, CCM is, as a rule, probably more context-neutral than context-sensitive. Therefore, as shown above, CCM can, assuming appropriate probing, produce useful findings about cultures' manifestations in individual belief systems in different contexts.

Lastly, CCM studies can be also *cross-national*. This implies not only cultural differences but also problems of *translation* and *interpretation* if the respondents represent different language spheres. They may attach different meanings to the same words, problematic especially in the case of linguistically distant languages like Chinese v. English (Xian, 2008). The case is simpler when the parties share a language and/or in contexts like the EU where cross-national studies for practical and scientific purposes have become common (Birbili, 2000; Haak et al., 2013). However, the implications of cross-national settings are obvious. First, such CCM studies are ideally *joint projects*, native researchers handling data elicitation, translation and interpretation in each country, coordinated by a designated researcher/

[5] https://www.hofstede-insights.com/country-comparison/. See also Lindell and Sigfrids (2008).

team leader. Second, it is advisable to engage professional translators to ensure a valid translation of the original expressions into the project's standard and reporting language.

6 Conclusion

This chapter has discussed the CCM method applied to aspiring entrepreneurs and small business advisors. The findings show that the respondents' knowledge and understanding about starting and performance of new ventures differ markedly but logically. In research terms, this provides a new and deeper perspective to understanding entrepreneurial decision-making, in this case also counselling processes. Methodologically, the chapter shows that CCM, especially when computerised, facilitates an accessible and versatile approach to revealing and analysing entrepreneurial actors' subjective knowledge in different research contexts.

As for future CCM studies, one direction is to explore different *entrepreneur types'* belief patterns, e.g., solo v. team, first-time v. serial entrepreneurs, nascent entrepreneurs v. lay persons, educated vs. uneducated, nationals vs. immigrants, etc. Such studies are especially interesting in cross-cultural and/or cross-national settings. A second important application of CCM is to *track belief systems' evolution* resulting from interventions like counselling, critical events such as starting a firm, or when assessing the effectiveness of entrepreneurship education by examining the participants' mindsets' development (Nabi et al., 2017; Solesvik et al., 2013). Third, CCM can test or complement well-established theories. For instance, the widely used *theory of planned behaviour* (TPB) (Ajzen, 1991; Liñán & Fayolle, 2015) establishes how motivational antecedents determine individuals' entrepreneurial intentions. This, however, tells little (if anything) about the specific knowledge structures that drive persons to express favourable or unfavourable attitudes towards entrepreneurship, why they expect support from their reference people should they start up or what is the mental basis of their perceived control over the start-up process. Here, CCM can provide an essential complementing role. Lastly, representing an entirely different approach, CCM methods can help explore, using SSI data collected from persons who know a specific domain well, the structure and causal mechanisms of social or socio-technical *systems* for developing intervention methods or new theory (cf. Montibeller et al., 2008; Pyrko & Dörfler, 2018; Russell, 1999). We hope entrepreneurship researchers find this chapter interesting and inspiring to explore some of these avenues for future research.

References

Ajzen, I. (1991). The theory of planned behavior. *Organizational Behavior and Human Decision Processes, 50*(2), 179–211.

Axelrod, R. (Ed.). (1976). *Structure of decision: The cognitive maps of political elites*. Princeton University Press.

Baddeley, A. (2010). Working memory. *Current Biology, 20*(4), 136–140.

Bandura, A. (2001). Social cognitive theory: An agentic perspective. *Annual Review of Psychology, 52*, 1–26.

Baron, R. A. (2004). The cognitive perspective: A valuable tool for answering entrepreneurship's basic "why" questions. *Journal of Business Venturing, 19*, 221–239.

Baron, R. A. (2016). Thinking about cognition and its central role in entrepreneurship: Confessions of a 'reformed' behaviorist. In J. R. Mitchell, R. K. Mitchell, & B. Randolph-Seng (Eds.), *Handbook of entrepreneurial cognition* (pp. 62–85). Edward Elgar.

Baron, R. A., & Ward, T. B. (2004). Expanding entrepreneurial cognition's toolbox: Potential contributions from the field of cognitive science. *Entrepreneurship Theory & Practice, 2004*, 553–573.

Baumeister, R. F., Masicampo, E. J., & Vohs, K. D. (2011). Do conscious thoughts cause behavior? *Annual Review of Psychology, 62*, 331–361.

Bender, A., Beller, S., & Medin, D. L. (2017). Causal cognition and culture. In M. R. Waldmann (Ed.), *The oxford handbook of causal reasoning*. Online Publication. https://doi.org/10.1093/oxfordhb/9780199399550.013.34

Bennett, R. J. (2014). *Entrepreneurship, small business and public policy: Evolution and revolution*. Routledge.

Birbili, M. (2000). Translating from one language to another. *Social Research Update, 31*, 1–7. https://sru.soc.surrey.ac.uk/SRU31.html

Carley, K. (1997). Extracting team mental models through textual analysis. *Journal of Organizational Behavior, 18*, 533–558.

Carley, K., & Palmquist, M. (1992). Extracting, representing, and analyzing mental models. *Social Forces, 70*(3), 601–636.

Cassell, C., & Symon, G. (Eds.). (1994). *Qualitative methods in organizational research*. SAGE.

Cheng, P. W., & Buehner, M. J. (2012). Causal learning. In K. J. Holyoak & R. G. Morrison (Eds.), *The Oxford handbook of thinking and reasoning*. Oxford University Press.

Chi, M. T. H. (2006). Laboratory methods for assessing experts' and novices' knowledge. In K. A. Ericsson, N. Charness, P. J. Feltovich, & R. R. Hoffman (Eds.), *The Cambridge handbook of expertise and expert performance* (pp. 167–184). Cambridge University Press.

Chi, M. T. H., & Ohlsson, S. (2005). Complex declarative learning. In K. Holyoak & R. G. Morrison (Eds.), *The Cambridge handbook of thinking and reasoning* (pp. 371–399). Cambridge University Press.

Churchland, P. S., & Churchland, P. M. (2013). What are beliefs? In F. Krueger & J. Grafman (Eds.), *The neural basis of human belief systems, 2012* (pp. 1–19). Imprint Psychology Press.

Engelen, A., Heinemann, F., & Brettel, M. (2009). Cross-cultural entrepreneurship research: Current status and framework for future studies. *Journal of International Entrepreneurship, 2009*(7), 163–189.

Evans, J. S. B. T. (1998). The knowledge elicitation problem: A psychological perspective. *Behaviour and Information Technology, 7*(2), 111–130.

Evans, J. S. B. T., & Stanovich, K. E. (2013). Dual-process theories of higher cognition: Advancing the debate. *Perspectives on Psychological Science, 8*(3), 223–241.

Fiske, S., & Taylor, S. E. (2021). *Social cognition: From brains to culture* (4th ed.). SAGE.

Forbes, D. P. (2014). The infrastructure of entrepreneurial learning. In J. R. Mitchell, R. K. Mitchell, & B. Randolph-Seng (Eds.), *Handbook of entrepreneurial cognition* (pp. 364–382). Edward Elgar.

Furnari, S. (2015). A cognitive mapping approach to business models: Representing causal structures and mechanisms. In C. Baden-Fuller & V. Mangematin (Eds.), *Business models and modelling* (Vol. 33, pp. 207–239). Emerald.

Gary, M. S., & Wood, R. E. (2011). Mental models, decision rules, and performance heterogeneity. *Strategic Management Journal, 32*, 569–594.

Gelman, S. A., & Legare, C. H. (2011). Concepts and folk theories. *Annual Review of Anthropology, 40*, 379–398.
Gentner, D. (2004). The psychology of mental models. In N. J. Smelser & P. B. Bates (Eds.), *International encyclopedia of the social and behavioral sciences* (pp. 9683–9687). Elsevier.
Good, B., & McDowell, A. (2015). Anthropology of Belief. In J. D. Wright (Ed.), *International Encyclopedia of the Social and Behavioral Sciences* (Vol. 2, 2nd ed., pp. 493–497).
Grégoire, D. A., Cornelissen, J., Dimov, D., & van Burg, E. (2015). The mind in the middle: Taking stock of affect and cognition research in entrepreneurship. *International Journal of Management Reviews, 17*, 125–142.
Grégoire, D. A., & Lambert, L. S. (2015). Getting inside entrepreneurs' hearts and minds. In T. Baker & F. Welter (Eds.), *The Routledge companion to entrepreneurship* (pp. 450–465). Taylor and Francis, Kindle Edition.
Guest, G., Bunce, A., & Johnson, L. (2006). How many interviews are enough? An experiment with data saturation and variability. *Field Methods, 18*(1), 59–82.
Haak, M., Himmelsbach, I., Granbom, M., & Löfqvist, C. (2013). Cross-national and multi-language qualitative research: Challenges and recommendations. *British Journal of Occupational Therapy, 76*(7), 333–336.
Hagmayer, Y., & Sloman, S. A. (2009). Decision makers conceive of their choices as interventions. *Journal of Experimental Psychology, 138*(1), 22–38.
Hofstede, G. (2001). *Culture's consequences* (2nd ed.). SAGE.
Hofstede, G. (2011). Dimensionalizing cultures: The Hofstede model in context. *Online Readings in Psychology and Culture, 2*(1), 8. http://scholarworks.gvsu.edu/orpc/vol2/iss1/8
Holyoak, K. J., & Cheng, P. W. (2011). Causal learning and inference as a rational process: The new synthesis. *Annual Review of Psychology, 62*, 135–163.
Ifenthaler, D., Masduki, I., & Seel, N. M. (2011). The mystery of cognitive structure and how we can detect it: Tracking the development of cognitive structures over time. *Instructional Science, 39*, 41–61.
Johnson-Laird, P. N. (2004). The history of mental models. In K. Manktelow & M. Chung (Eds.), *Psychology of reasoning: Theoretical and historical perspectives* (pp. 179–212). Psychology Press.
Johnson-Laird, P. N. (2010). Mental models and human reasoning. *Proceedings of the National Academy of Sciences of the United States of America, 107*(43), 18243–18250. www.pnas.org/cgi/doi/10.1073/pnas.1012933107
Johnson-Laird, P. N. (2013). Mental models and cognitive change. *Journal of Cognitive Psychology, 25*(2), 131–138.
Jones, N. A., Ross, H., Lynam, T., Perez, P., & Leitch, A. (2011). Mental models: An interdisciplinary synthesis of theory and methods. *Ecology and Society, 16*(1), 46.
Khemlani, S. S., Barbey, A. J., & Johnson-Laird, P. N. (2014). Causal reasoning with mental models. *Frontiers in Human Neuroscience, 8(849)*, 1–15.
Krueger, N. F. (2007). What lies beneath? The experiential essence of entrepreneurial thinking. *Entrepreneurship Theory and Practice, 2007*, 123–138.
Laukkanen, M. (2018). Causal mapping in practice with CMAP3. In R. J. Galavan, K. J. Sund, & G. P. Hodgkinson (Eds.), *Methodological challenges and advances in managerial and organizational cognition* (Vol. 2018, pp. 147–174). Emerald Group Publishing.
Laukkanen, M., & Tornikoski, E. T. (2018). Causal mapping small business advisors' belief systems: A case of entrepreneurship policy research. *International Journal of Entrepreneurial Behavior & Research, 24*(2), 499–520.
Laukkanen, M., & Wang, M. (2015). *Comparative causal mapping: The CMAP3 method*. Gower Publishing.
Leiser, D. (2001). Scattered naive theories. *New Ideas in Psychology, 19*(2001), 175–202.
Lima, V. A., & da Silva Müller, C. A. (2017). Why do small businesses innovate? *RAI Revista de Administração e Inovação, 14*(2017), 290–300.

Liñán, F., & Fayolle, A. (2015). A systematic literature review on entrepreneurial intentions: Citation, thematic analyses, and research agenda. *International Entrepreneurship and Management Journal, 11*(4), 907–933.

Lindell, M., & Sigfrids, C. (2008). Culture and leadership in Finland. In J. S. Chhokar, F. C. Brodbeck, & R. J. House (Eds.), *Culture and leadership across the world: The GLOBE book of in-depth studies of 25 societies* (pp. 75–106). Erlbaum.

Markman, A. B., & Gentner, D. (2001). Thinking. *Annual Review of Psychology, 52*, 223–247.

Markóczy, L. (2000). National culture and strategic change in belief formation. *Journal of International Business Studies, 31*, 427–442.

Martinus, K., & Hedgcock, D. (2015). The methodological challenge of cross-national qualitative research. *Qualitative Research Journal, 15*(3), 373–386.

Maxwell, J. (2010). Using numbers in qualitative research. *Qualitative Inquiry, 16*(6), 475–482.

Maxwell, J. (2013). *Qualitative research design*. SAGE.

Mitchell, R. K., Busenitz, L., Bird, B., Gaglio, C. M., McMullen, J. S., Morse, E. A., & Brock Smith, J. (2007). The central question in entrepreneurial cognition research. *Entrepreneurship Theory and Practice, 31*(1), 1–27.

Mitchell, R. K., Mitchell, B. T., & Mitchell, J. R. (2009). Entrepreneurial scripts and entrepreneurial expertise: The information processing perspective. In A. L. Carsrud & M. Brännback (Eds.), *Understanding the entrepreneurial mind* (pp. 97–137). Springer.

Montibeller, G., Belton, V., Ackermann, F., & Ensslin, L. (2008). Reasoning maps for decision aid: An integrated approach for problem-structuring and multi-criteria evaluation. *Journal of the Operational Research Society, 59*, 575–589.

Morrison, R. G., & Knowlton, B. J. (2012). Neurocognitive methods in higher cognition. In K. J. Holyoak & R. G. Morrison (Eds.), *The Oxford handbook of thinking and reasoning* (pp. 67–89). Oxford University Press.

Nabi, G., Liñán, F., Fayolle, A., Krueger, N., & Walmsley, A. (2017). The impact of entrepreneurship education in higher education: A systematic review and research agenda. *Academy of Management Learning & Education, 16*(2), 277–299.

Nadkarni, S., & Narayanan, V. K. (2005). Validity of the structural properties of text-based causal maps: An empirical assessment. *Organizational Research Methods, 8*(9), 9–40.

Narayanan, V. K. (2005). Causal mapping: An historical overview. In V. K. Narayanan & D. J. Armstrong (Eds.), *Causal mapping for research in information technology* (pp. 1–19). Idea Group.

Nelson, K. M., Nadkarni, S., Narayanan, V. K., & Ghods, M. (2000). Understanding software operations support expertise: A revealed causal mapping approach. *MIS Quarterly, 24*(3), 475–507.

Nicolaou, N., Lockett, A., Ucbasaran, D., & Rees, G. (2019). Exploring the potential and limits of a neuroscientific approach to entrepreneurship. *International Small Business Journal: Researching Entrepreneurship, May, 2019*, 1–24.

Nicolini, D. (1999). Comparing methods for mapping organizational cognition. *Organization Studies, 20*(5), 833–860.

Nielsen, M. S., & Klyver, K. (2020). Meeting entrepreneurs' expectations: The importance of social skills in strong relationships. *Entrepreneurship & Regional Development, 32*(9–10), 737–756.

Oyserman, D., & Lee, S. W. S. (2008). Does culture influence what and how we think? Effects of priming individualism and collectivism. *Psychological Bulletin, 134*(2), 311–342.

Pyrko, I., & Dörfler, V. (2018). *Using causal mapping in the analysis of semi-structured interviews*. In: 78th Annual Meeting of the Academy of Management, August 14.

Pyrko, I., Dörfler, V., & Eden, C. (2017). Thinking together: What makes communities of practice work? *Human Relations, 70(4)*, 389–409.

Randolph-Seng, B., Mitchell, J. R., & Mitchell, R. K. (2016). Introduction: Historical context and future directions in entrepreneurial cognition research. In J. R. Mitchell, R. K. Mitchell, & B. Randolph-Seng (Eds.), *Handbook of entrepreneurial cognition* (pp. 1–60). Elgar.

Ratinho, T., Amezcua, A., Honig, B., & Zeng, Z. (2020). Supporting entrepreneurs: A systematic review of literature and an agenda for research. *Technological Forecasting and Social Change, 154*, 119956.
Rotger, G. P., Gørtz, M., & Storey, D. J. (2012). Assessing the effectiveness of guided preparation for new venture creation and performance: Theory and practice. *Journal of Business Venturing, 27*(4), 506–521.
Rouse, W. B., & Morris, N. M. (1986). On looking into the black box: Prospects and limits in the search for mental models. *Psychological Bulletin, 100*(3), 349–363.
Russell, R. D. (1999). Developing a process model of intrapreneurial systems: A cognitive mapping approach. *Entrepreneurship Theory and Practice, 23*(3), 65–84.
Sarasvathy, S. D., Dew, N., Read, S., & Wiltbank, R. (2007). *Effectual entrepreneurial expertise: Existence and bounds*. NPS Archive. http://hdl.handle.net/10945/41246
Sarasvathy, S. D., Ramesh, A., & Forster, W. (2015). The ordinary entrepreneur. In T. Baker & F. Welter (Eds.), *The Routledge companion to entrepreneurship* (pp. 227–243). Taylor and Francis. Kindle Edition.
Schraven, D. F. J., Hartmann, A., & Dewulf, G. P. M. R. (2015). Resuming an unfinished tale: Applying causal maps to analyze the dominant logics within an organization. *Organizational Research Methods, 18*(2), 326–349.
Schulte-Holthaus, S., & Kuckertz, A. (2020). Passion, performance and concordance in rock "n" roll entrepreneurship. *International Journal of Entrepreneurial Behavior & Research, 26*(6), 1335–1355. https://doi.org/10.1108/IJEBR-02-2020-0067
Sloman, S. A., & Lagnado, D. (2015). Causality in thought. *Annual Review of Psychology, 66*, 223–247.
Solesvik, M. Z., Westhead, P., Matlay, H., & Parsyak, V. N. (2013). Entrepreneurial assets and mindsets: Benefit from university entrepreneurship education investment. *Education+ Training, 55*(8–9), 748–762.
Sternberg, R. J., & Sternberg, K. (2012). *Cognition* (6th ed.). Wadsworth.
Suomalainen, S., Stenholm, P., Kovalainen, A., Heinonen, J., & Pukkinen, T. (2016). *Global entrepreneurship monitor Finnish 2015 report*. Research Reports, A 1/2016. Turku School of Economics, University of Turku.
Thurik, R., & Dejardin, M. (2012). Entrepreneurship and culture. In M. van Gelderen & E. Masurel (Eds.), *Entrepreneurship in context* (pp. 175–186). Routledge.
Tremml, T. (2020). Barriers to entrepreneurship in public enterprises: Boards contributing to inertia. *Public Management Review*, 1–26. https://doi.org/10.1080/14719037.2020.1775279
Valliere, D. (2017). Belief patterns of entrepreneurship: Exploring cross-cultural logics. *International Journal of Entrepreneurial Behavior & Research, 23*(2), 245–266.
Walsh, J. (1995). Managerial and organizational cognition: Notes from a trip down memory lane. *Organization Science, 6*, 280–321.
Welter, F. (2011). Contextualizing entrepreneurship: Conceptual challenges and ways forward. *Entrepreneurship Theory and Practice, 35*(1), 165–184.
Welter, F., & Alex, N. (2012). Researching trust in different cultures. In F. Lyon, G. Möllering, & M. N. K. Saunders (Eds.), *Handbook of research methods on trust* (pp. 50–60). Elgar.
Wennberg, K., Pathak, S., & Autio, E. (2013). How culture moulds the effects of self-efficacy and fear of failure on entrepreneurship. *Entrepreneurship & Regional Development, 25*(9–10), 756–780.

Westmeyer, H. (2001). Explanation: Conceptions in the social sciences. In N. J. Smelser & P. B. Bates (Eds.), *International encyclopedia of the social and behavioral sciences* (pp. 5154–5159). Elsevier.

Wyer, R. S., & Albarracín, D. (2005). Belief formation, organization, and change: Cognitive and motivational influences. In D. Albarracin, B. T. Johnson, & M. P. Zanna (Eds.), *The handbook of attitudes* (pp. 273–322). Lawrence Erlbaum.

Xian, H. (2008). Lost in translation? Language, culture and the roles of translator in cross-cultural management research. *Qualitative Research in Organizations and Management, 3*(3), 231–245.

Zhao, H., Seibert, S. E., & Lumpkin, G. T. (2010). The relationship of personality to entrepreneurial intentions and performance: A meta-analytic review. *Journal of Management, 36*(2), 381–404.

Mauri Laukkanen is professor emeritus, Department of Business, University of Eastern Finland, Kuopio Campus. After a family firm entrepreneur-manager career, he received his DBA at the Helsinki School of Economics in 1989. He served at the HSE (now Aalto University Business School) and the Universities of Vaasa and Jyväskylä before UEF, where he contributed to founding the present Department of Business, heading it in 1995–2002. His research interests include entrepreneurship and SB management, university-based entrepreneurship and venturing, local economic development, entrepreneurial and managerial cognition and cognitive research methods, especially comparative causal mapping. He has published several books and journal articles. Mauri Laukkanen lives in Lahti, Finland.

Francisco Liñán is a Full Professor (Catedrático) at Universidad de Sevilla, Spain. Researcher in the field of entrepreneurship, entrepreneurial intentions and entrepreneurship education. Author of several publications in international academic journals. Associate Editor at Entrepreneurship Education and Pedagogy. Editorial Board Member at Entrepreneurship Theory and Practice and International Entrepreneurship and Management Journal, among others. OECD specialist in inclusive entrepreneurship. Currently head of the research group PYMED (http://grupo.us.es/pymed/) and vice-dean for research and entrepreneurship at the Faculty of Economics and Business Sciences. Member of the coordination committee of ESU: European University Network on Entrepreneurship (www.esu-network.eu). Member of Spain's GEM and GUESSS teams.

International Entrepreneurial Ecosystem, Knowledge Exploitation and Innovation: Case of International Pharma-Biotech SME

Naïma Cherchem and Christian Keen

Abstract Although the literature has generally well defined the actors and their roles within international entrepreneurial ecosystems, more insight is needed on how SMEs fit into these networks and use them to broaden their knowledge exploitation frontiers and leverage their international innovation. This study draws upon knowledge-based theory and an international perspective on entrepreneurship and entrepreneurial ecosystems to examine how collaboration between actors within an international entrepreneurial ecosystem (IEE) stimulates knowledge exploitation and, consequently, the success of international SME innovation and commercialization. To this end, we examined an international *pharma-biotech* SME and collected primary data from in-depth interviews with its top management team and triangulated the interview data with secondary data. The study was initiated before the onset of the COVID-19 pandemic and continued 11 months after. Our research findings contribute to the theory that the diversity of an IEE's actors and the intensity of collaboration between them are fundamental to the dynamics of scientific, technological, market, and institutional knowledge exploitation and to international innovation success. Further, the dynamics of this knowledge exploitation can support the development of business agility, that is, adapting quickly and efficiently—and even gaining an advantage in pursuing new opportunities—in turbulent context such as the COVID-19 pandemic.

Keywords International entrepreneurial ecosystem · Knowledge exploitation · International innovation · Business agility · Covid-19 pandemic

---

N. Cherchem (✉)
Entrepreneurship & Strategy Department, Ted Rogers School of Management, Ryerson University, Toronto, ON, Canada
e-mail: naima.cherchem@ryerson.ca

C. Keen
Entrepreneurship and International Business, Faculty of Business Administration, Laval University, Québec, QC, Canada
e-mail: christian.keen@fsa.ulaval.ca

A. Caputo et al. (eds.), *The International Dimension of Entrepreneurial Decision-Making*, Contributions to Management Science,
https://doi.org/10.1007/978-3-030-85950-3_4

1 Introduction

Biopharmaceutical SMEs are entrepreneurial knowledge-based organizations (Gurău et al., 2010) that compete globally right from their inception (Gurău & Dana, 2020). One of their major challenges is their insistent need for highly complex and heterogeneous scientific and technological knowledge (Coradi et al., 2015) from a diversity of disciplines and functional areas of expertise. SMEs exploit knowledge from within their entrepreneurial ecosystem and seek to create and recombine this existing knowledge into knowledge inputs, which can then be used to lead innovation (Ghio et al., 2015).

Knowledge is considered as the most strategic resource when it comes to a firm's innovation capacity and internationalization (Scaringella, 2016). In fact, being part of abroad (i.e. cross-national) entrepreneurial ecosystem is a way for SMEs to maximize their access to key resources (Feld, 2020; Link & Sarala, 2019) such as knowledge bases. Their access to this type of international ecosystem also helps them establish various collaborations with different actors to innovate, co-create, and commercialize their products both locally and internationally (Awate et al., 2015; Theodoraki & Catanzaro, 2021) and even exploit their partners' resources (Vahlne & Johanson, 2020) as well as develop competencies and capabilities to support their internationalization (Morrish & Earl, 2020).

The few studies that have examined international knowledge-intensive SMEs have shown that establishing interactions with foreign partners allows these types of SMEs to take advantage of cross-cultural knowledge to enhance the quality of their innovation (Saridakis et al., 2019) and competitiveness (Naldi & Davidsson, 2014). These loosely interconnected interactions between different international partners are what form an *international entrepreneurial ecosystem*, or IEE. The entrepreneurship literature suggests that the different domestic and international actors within a given IEE are fundamental for the dynamic interplay between knowledge exploitation, knowledge absorptive capacity, innovation, and SMEs growth (Jafari-Sadeghi et al., 2019). Each of its actors has a specific role to play in adding value to the IEE (Machado et al., 2019). Both the value that a venture extracts from the IEE and the value it brings to it are valuable to the venture's innovation process and commercialization process (Feld, 2020). However, there is still very little insight in the literature about the role and function of the entrepreneurial ecosystem as it relates to supporting SMEs innovation and internationalization (Dabić et al., 2019).

Our research draws upon knowledge-based theory and an international perspective to entrepreneurship and entrepreneurial ecosystems to examine how collaboration between international entrepreneurial ecosystem (IEE) actors stimulates knowledge exploitation and thereby the success of international SME innovation and commercialization in the bio*pharmaceutical* industry. To this end, we examined an international *pharma-biotech* SME. This study collected primary data from in-depth interviews with its top management team and triangulated the interview data with secondary data.

This exploration aims to contribute to the field by: (1) answering the call made by Dabić et al. (2019) to expand our understanding of the role of SME knowledge exploitation in an industry characterized by fast-paced innovation, international reach, complexity of knowledge and operations, and interactions between multiple actors; (2) being one of the first to analyse the relationship between knowledge exploitation and the internationalization of innovation through IEEs in the context of the biotechnology industry; (3) showing that the diversity of IEE actors and the intensity of collaboration between them play an important role in knowledge exploitation efficiency and thus in the success of the development and commercialization of drugs in international markets; and (4) shed light on the exploitation dynamics and their role in developing business agility to overcome market turbulence and uncertainty such as caused by the COVID-19 pandemic, or other types of dynamic and turbulent international business environments (Caputo & Pellegrini, 2019).

This chapter is organized into four sections. The first discusses the importance of knowledge exploitation and IEEs in developing international innovation. The second outlines the empirical study description and research method. The third presents and discusses the empirical findings. Lastly, we conclude by outlining the research contributions and presenting them alongside the limitations and perspectives for future research.

2 Entrepreneurial Ecosystem: An International Approach

International science-based firms are driven by a constant need for knowledge to nurture their R&D activities and their innovation capacity. Those that lack this strategic resource, notably SMEs, need to rely on external sources (Jacobides et al., 2018). The majority of studies conclude that entrepreneurial ecosystems provide new SME ventures the knowledge needed to recognize, explore, and commercially exploit opportunities needed to start up and scale up (Bhawe & Zahra, 2019). However, much of the literature focuses on local and regional entrepreneurial ecosystems or otherwise examines the management of international R&D networks (Cantwell, 2017) or the patterns of global R&D internationalization (Awate et al., 2015). A newer approach supports the importance of studying entrepreneurial ecosystem from an international perspective where a firm fosters entrepreneurship abroad and strengthens international relational capital through the networks of an IEE (Theodoraki & Catanzaro, 2021).

As such, we adopt the definition of entrepreneurial ecosystem as developed by Mason and Brown (2014) and the international approach to state that IEE is a set of *international interconnected entrepreneurial actors, entrepreneurial organizations and institutions, and entrepreneurial processes which formally and informally interact, mediate, and govern business performance.*

Further, Bhawe and Zahra (2019) argued that resource exploitation within IEEs allows stakeholders to combine their resources, networks, and capabilities in a complementary manner cross-regionally and cross-nationally, and Al-Omoush et al. (2020) argued that knowledge access strategies have shifted from organizational knowledge creation to an inter-organizational network dynamic where sharing expertise and resources offers actors a competitive advantage, especially in high-pressure contexts. However, whereas the literature has generally well defined the actors and their roles within IEEs, more insight is needed on how SMEs fit into these networks and use them to broaden their knowledge frontiers and leverage their international innovation.

3 Knowledge Exploitation and Innovation Through International Entrepreneurial Ecosystems

Indeed, exploiting unique knowledge across cultural, institutional, geographical, and industrial contexts is an emerging area in entrepreneurship research (e.g. Belitski et al., 2019), notably as a tool to enhance the quality of innovation (Ramadani et al., 2017) and the level competitiveness (Naldi & Davidsson, 2014).

Zahra and George (2002: 190) define knowledge exploitation as a firm's ability "*to refine, extend, and leverage existing competencies or to create new ones by incorporating acquired and transformed knowledge into its operations*". As such, we can view knowledge exploitation as the deployment of internal and external knowledge (technological, market, institutional, experiential, etc.) to create a higher-performing organization.

Knowledge-based theory considers knowledge the most strategic resource for a firm's innovation capacity and internationalization (e.g. Scaringella, 2016). It is also a central aspect in international entrepreneurship research (Dana, 2017). Lange and Wagner (2019) show how biotechnology and pharmaceutical companies increase their innovation performance through external knowledge sourcing, and Gurău et al. (2010) show that biopharmaceutical SMEs require significant of resources to survive the main stages of their firm development process, taking advantage of their networking capabilities to use these resources in developing their intellectual property portfolio, as well as for production and commercialization. While we know that SMEs very much need both external and inter-organizational knowledge transfer, how SMEs exploit this knowledge is still poorly understood (Dabić et al., 2020).

The 2019 report of the digital accelerator Global Startup Ecosystem reiterates how knowledge is fundamental to efficiently functioning entrepreneurial ecosystems and can be seen as a combination of high-level creation of tangible intellectual property in the form of patents, research, and favourable policy environments. Dabić et al. (2020) make knowledge the key driver of internationalization and propose a major shift in the Uppsala firm internationalization model by suggesting that network-derived knowledge may influence knowledge bases, reduce uncertainty, and facilitate the development of new knowledge through exchanges in interconnected relationships. Bhawe and Zahra (2019) support this by seeing interactions between local and international actors within an IEE as stimulating and expediting a firm's internationally oriented capacity-building activities. In seeing the SME's ability to network and internationalize as a strategic capability, examining knowledge exploitation dynamics within IEEs is a critical next step and there is growing interest in how intra-IEE knowledge exploitation amplifies cross-border innovations and R&D activities (Ferraris et al., 2019). SMEs have recently started to internationalize their R&D activities by sourcing technical knowledge from different countries to improve their product, service, and process innovation performance outcomes (Awate et al., 2015; Ferraris et al., 2019). Ultimately, SME knowledge exploitation is a vehicle towards improving the effectiveness of international innovation implementation (Ferreira et al., 2017).

4 Methodology

4.1 Research Context

Gassmann and Keupp (2007) highlight the interests of studying the biotechnology sector because it is populated by many SMEs whose degree of internationalization differs considerably. This sector is also heavily regulated by authorities and governments controlling drug development and product safety to approve final products. Moreover, exports in this sector are restricted by different national and institutional standards and approval protocols. The work of pharmaceutical and biotechnology firms is based in intensive scientific, technological, commercial, and regulatory knowledge exploitation, which drive the success of their R&D activities and the development and commercialization of new drugs (e.g. Gassmann & Keupp, 2007; Gurău & Dana, 2020).

4.2 Method

We chose a comprehensive case study research (Dumez, 2016; Yin, 2002) of a medium pioneering French *pharma-biotech* SME that we will refer to as Alpha *pharma-biotech* for confidentiality reasons. The majority of case studies within this sector focus on large multinational firms but our interest here in a *pharma-biotech* SME is explained by the great contributions made by SMEs to the global economy while simultaneously suffering from resource constraints and—most notably for this exploration—from knowledge constraints, which hold them back from international pharmaceutical markets.

The choice of a single-case study is driven by our understanding of the importance of research contexts in extending theory. The use of single-case studies "*can enable the creation of more complicated theories than multiple cases, because single-case researchers can fit their theory exactly to the many details of a particular case*" (Eisenhardt & Graebner, 2007: 30). To build this study, we followed the entrepreneurial path of Alpha *pharma-biotech* including its collaborations with international partners to develop and commercialize new drugs in international markets. The study was initiated before the onset of the COVID-19 pandemic and continued 11 months after.

Alpha *pharma-biotech* was founded in 1982 by two doctors of pharmacy. While one spouse made her career in the pharmaceutical industry, the other continued doing academic research. Though uncommon at that time, they brought academic research and industrial pharmaceutical development together and founded Alpha *pharma-biotech* (hereinafter Alpha). Their objective was based on using novel fundamental research work to design and develop drugs that would be destined as leaders in a new therapeutic sector. A summary description of Alpha is presented in Table 1.

4.3 Data Collection and Analysis

We collected primary data through two in-depth interviews (approximately 90 minutes each), one with each of two senior management executives with extensive experience in the pharmaceutical and biotechnology industries at the operational, R&D, and strategic management levels. The first interview with the R&D department director was held face-to-face, while the second interview with Alpha's chief scientific officer was held by videoconference. We purposefully choose these two informants for their level of responsibility and involvement in R&D activities as well as in innovation and collaboration with Alpha's IEE partners, thereby meeting the standard criteria that informants be well informed of company strategic decisions and operations and experts in the research area (Marshall & Rossman, 2014). The two interviews were recorded and transcribed.

To ensure consistency and structure, we developed a semi-structured interview guide with open-ended questions. To ensure the validity of our study (Yin, 2002) and obtain an understanding of the overall data (Baxter & Jack, 2008), we triangulated the interview data with secondary data. In addition, the first author visited Alpha's research centre.

We adopted an inductive approach per Gurău and Dana (2020) to structure and analyse our data using an open-coding process through which each coauthor separately read, coded, and interpreted the collected data. We discussed differences in data interpretation and coding through successive feedback sessions, then extracted, enriched, modified, and refined the list of open codes until our respective coding reached a high degree of correlation. The major themes identified from the data were also analysed against findings from the literature review.

Ultimately, informants referred to an IEE as an "*international collaboration network*" and knowledge exploitation as "*collaboration*" to "*develop new patents and new intellectual property and run clinical tests*", "*communicate and publish scientific papers*", "*validate product in foreign markets*", and "*meeting international market policies and regulations*".

Table 1 Alpha *pharma-biotech*: firm summary

Key elements	Data
Year of foundation	1982
Ownership structure	100% family-owned and managed
Management structure	Two discrete entities: 1) *Alpha Biotech*—Created in 2001 with 45 employees managing the R&D department's four units: biochemistry/molecular biology, therapeutic chemistry, pharmacology, and pharmacokinetics. 2) 2) *Alpha Biotech Market*—Created in 1992 with 42 employees in charge of drug development and marketing.
Size	150 employees, two thirds of whom work in R&D (including subsidiaries in Europe and Tunisia) and two thirds of which have PhD or master's degree in science. The remaining one-third work in finance, marketing, HR, and regulatory affairs. Most functions unrelated to R&D (such as manufacturing and sales) are outsourced.
R&D department	The site covers over 12,845 m^2 of which nearly half is dedicated to laboratories equipped with cutting-edge scientific instruments. To meet regulatory requirements, operations are performed in strict compliance with good laboratory practices and are subject to periodic checks from the national French agency for the safety of health products.
Drug development and commercialization—Areas of research	*Leading research on molecules that are first in a given pharmacological class, and which constitute a therapeutic innovation in:* – Neurology – Immunology – Gastroenterology
Number of substances designed and studied each year	Over 1000 substances
Patents and new drugs developed	Average of three patents per year Average of two to three new drugs in clinical trials per year
Academic partners	INSERM, a public French scientific, technological, and biomedical research institute operating under the joint authority of the French ministries of health and research and dedicated to biomedical research in human health. Various medicinal chemistry university laboratories in Europe and the USA.
Expansion IEE partners	Belgium, the Netherlands, Luxembourg, Italy, Germany, the United Kingdom, Spain, the USA, Canada, China, Japan, and Tunisia.

5 Discussion

Our findings show that exploitation of external knowledge from different IEE partners speeds up the development of a new drug and speeds up its commercialization in international markets. In Alpha's case, external sources of knowledge include market sources, private R&D organizations, institutional sources, government, public research organizations, chambers of commerce, trade fairs, exhibitions and conferences, scientific journals, and trade/technical publications.

More specifically, Alpha exploits specialized types of knowledge:

- *Technological and scientific knowledge* (i.e. molecules, patents, academic publications, technological models for clinical tests);
- *Market knowledge* (i.e. customers, distributors, competitors);
- *Institutional knowledge* (regulatory standards and business laws).

We will now discuss the dynamics of knowledge exploitation as they pertain to Alpha and then conclude with how these dynamics allow Alpha to be performant and to develop the necessary business agility to overcome the challenges posed by the COVID-19 pandemic.

5.1 Scientific and Technological Knowledge Exploitation

Scientific and technological knowledge exploitation typically takes place during the pre-clinical phase of new drug development. Alpha acquires the rights to exploit a specific intellectual property from another partner (e.g. patent, technological model, protocol, or scientific paper) to access some complementary technological and scientific knowledge and conduct R&D activities in-house. This exploitation also includes the validation of a new drug in specific markets since some countries, such as Japan, require drug companies to run part of their clinical trials with their population because of the pharmaceutically relevant biological differences between Caucasian and Asian populations (e.g. absorption capacity for a given molecule, metabolism, and molecule elimination capacity).

> Because we are focusing on chronic diseases, we need to intensively exploit unique knowledge to create highly competitive drugs. [. . .] Our new drug for narcolepsy, a chronic sleep disorder, has a competitive advantage over other products that are made of stimulants. Our drug has no stimulants. For restless leg syndrome, we have three other molecules in clinical trials that were developed internally through collaborations with an American university research center and other universities in the UK, Spain, and Italy.

Our results confirm Gurau et al.'s (2010) study that posited that the organizational structure of R&D in many biotech-pharmaceutical SMEs is similar in some respects to the ones found in university research teams focused on special areas of research.

5.2 *International Market and Institutional Knowledge Exploitation*

In addition to technological and scientific knowledge exploitation, international market knowledge moderates the speed at which innovations are developed and commercialized internationally (Oviatt & McDougall, 2005). As our findings indicate, Alpha exploits international market knowledge to initiate its market research process, commercialize its drugs, and license its intellectual properties and patents in foreign markets. Alpha also exploits institutional knowledge to obtain approval from specialized governmental authorities governing the commercialization of drugs.

> While the regulations to access the European and North American markets are quite similar, regulations are different for China and Japan, which both require that clinical trials be done in their countries. So, if we do not include Japanese patients in our clinical trials, we are obliged to repeat them in Japan to demonstrate that there is an equivalence of our results in relation to Japanese patients versus Caucasian ones.

In the pharmaceutical industry, combined market and institutional knowledge is often vital to the commercialization of drugs as they contribute to the synchronization of science, business, and regulations. Our findings are in line with the research of Gurău et al. (2010) that demonstrated that biotech-pharmaceutical SMEs are often developed by successful scientists who seek to transform their innovations into commercial products yet must establish the scientific legitimacy and the safety of the innovation as well as the ethical aspects of the R&D activities. Alpha's IEE allowed them to do just this.

The extent of a firm's international market knowledge influences its commitment to the international market and its managers' perceptions of both risks and opportunities. Besides the dynamics of exploiting specialized knowledge, the diversity of collaborations with IEE partners was found to be another basis of Alpha's competitive advantage. This finding confirms those of Fuerst and Zettinig (2015) who state that in order to internationalize rapidly, firms require the type of knowledge developed from interactions with network partners. This is, moreover, supported by our findings that Alpha collaborates with two types of IEE partners: scientific and business.

Collaboration with scientific partners Alpha collaborates with academics and IEE expansion partners either in the early stage of discovery and R&D or in the finalization and production of its drugs

> Our motivation for these collaborations is to bring expertise that can complement what we have and develop more advanced projects and unique innovations.

> We have established scientific collaborations with both American and European partners at the early levels of our drug development process. The primary objective is to have access to scientific expertise and technological models that we do not have internally, such as the absorption mechanisms of molecules. We also leverage scientific collaborations during the development phase with contract research organizations which help us finalize clinical trials and synthesize the chemical molecules needed to support the pharmaceutical development of the drugs.

These scientific collaborations with scholars from universities in the USA, the UK, France, Spain, and Italy are in keeping with the company's values and its founders, that is, well rooted in academic research. Alpha's cofounder is 85 years old and still active in research with almost 800 published academic papers. His knowledge and expertise can initiate and facilitate contacts with international research centres. However, beyond this asset, what makes collaboration attractive is the nature of the project, the quality, and the importance of the developed molecule.

The international diversity of Alpha's knowledge exploitation process has strengthened its uniqueness in developing drugs that treat chronic diseases.

Collaboration with business partners at Alpha involves in the commercialization and marketing of its drugs. Their business partners (e.g. marketing, sales, and distribution partners and professional advisors) also help initiate negotiations with authorities towards acquiring product validation, such as from the United States Food and Drug Administration (a federal agency of the US Department of Health and Human Services) and the Ministry of Health in Japan.

> We don't have resources and staff in every country. [. . .] We have teams in our European subsidiaries that work with sales forces in the US, Japan, and China where we don't have sales forces but have business partners. We look for complementarity on a commercial level. As such, partners allow us to access resources and skills needed for our product's commercial and regulatory development.

> Our new narcolepsy drug is in the compliance phase with Health Canada for its commercialization thanks to a Canadian partner to whom we granted a license for the product [. . .] making it available for sale within a few months instead of years. The same product is now commercialized in the US and has a very important place in the market thanks to a business partner who worked with the FDA for its registration and commercialization.

Business partners embedded in a given ecosystem can co-evolve and co-develop through the process of commercial knowledge exploitation. Among the benefits of being embedded in a shared IEE is shortening the innovation phases and making products available to a wider customer base with the shortest time-to-market possible (Tolstoy & Agndal, 2010).

Our findings show that the diversity of IEE partners and their involvement in knowledge exploitation provide Alpha with unique resources and distinctive competencies for producing drugs for chronic diseases, reducing risks and foreign market uncertainty, reducing time-to-market, and increasing innovation performance. These findings support Cetindamar et al. (2020) that argue that innovative firms internationalize their collaborations to increase their competitive advantage through entrepreneurial networks that can exploit unique knowledge on a global scale.

In the same vein, knowledge exploitation can be a critical aspect of innovation's speed and quality. Studies show that the development and commercialization of a new drug can take from a year up to seven or more depending on the maturity of the intellectual property asset and the agreed length of time of co-development between partners (Patterson & Ambrosini, 2015). However, in Alpha's case, developing and commercializing a drug through knowledge exploitation-based collaborations occurs over a shorter time thanks to it having developed diverse collaborations with IEE partners to help successfully manage their innovation projects.

> Risk is a characteristic of the pharmaceutical industry [...] For decades, it was possible to commercialize products that were not innovative. Today only very innovative products can be successfully commercialized and our business adopts this approach. We work on products involving very risky innovation, important medical needs, and complicated indications, which are each important facet of the pharmaceutical industry.

Though a proven record of developing unique molecules is essential to gain legitimacy within the industry, the ability of a firm to successfully (and rapidly) bring such innovation to market is where a firm's IEE becomes so instrumental.

6 Knowledge-based Collaboration and Business Agility Development

Finally, as our key findings demonstrate the various dynamics through which Alpha exploits knowledge to develop new drugs and commercialize them in international markets, they also demonstrate how these dynamics contribute to the development of business agility that allows it to overcome the uncertainties of COVID-19 pandemic.

The competitive environment of the biopharmaceutical sector is in and of itself highly dynamic and unpredictable, especially for SMEs (Gurău et al., 2010). The context of COVID-19 crisis makes the overall business environment ever more uncertain. Our findings show how the diversity of IEE partners and the intensity of their shared knowledge exploitation appear to foster Alpha's business agility to efficiently adapt to this uncertainty.

> We closed our labs for 2 months during the first lockdown period, with some researchers continuing to work remotely while others were technically unemployed and compensated [...]. Then we opened up, and we went through a second lockdown period. However, this time we were well prepared to rapidly adapt our organization to continue working in an efficient way by switching to virtual networking, such as attending virtual conferences, effecting virtual collaborations and experimentation with different international partners, and undertaking virtual knowledge co-creation. Now we are pursuing new and very promising projects while saving on travel costs and time. We are adapting resources, processes, and technologies to meet the needs of the changing environment caused by this pandemic [...] thanks to the information and communication technologies platforms we have mobilized during this uncertain context.

This finding points to Alpha's significant agility capacity to quickly embrace the virtual working infrastructure and identify new ways of collaborating and operating with established partners. This organizational restructuring was quickly mobilized using an important set of IT capabilities that allowed them to respond to unexpected operating and management constraints, thus enabling continuous collaborative innovation and organizational learning with IEE partners despite the uncertainties. This agility enabled the firm to explore novel opportunities to work and operate in the volatile and uncertain context of the COVID-19 crisis. Our findings show that the established collaborative knowledge exploitation and rapid adoption of IT platforms played a significant role in developing new learning and achieving business agility to respond to the pandemic's constraints and uncertainties. The existing IEE allowed Alpha to recombine existing capabilities with new ones.

This finding falls neatly into prior research by Al-Omoush et al. (2020: 280) that defined business agility as "*a capability to rapidly discover innovative ways of doing business and proactively anticipate and respond to changes and discover new emerging opportunities*". We find that the speed at which a firm can perceive opportunities and obstacles, reorganize resources, and create innovations are all powerful drivers of organizational resilience and business agility, not least in turbulent environments.

7 Conclusion

Resource limitations prompt SMEs to seek out resources available in their networks and efficiently exploit them with a certain degree of complementarity to create distinctive innovations. Our study supports very recent research that argues that the close interaction between ecosystem members based abroad serves as sources of information, sources of opportunity, and sources of expertise. What is more, these interactions bring valuable international knowledge to regional ecosystems (Theodoraki & Catanzaro, 2021).

Our research offers an in-depth analysis of knowledge complementarity to explain the dynamics of knowledge-based collaboration and the interconnectedness of an IEE's actors. The case aptly shows the challenges and opportunities faced by most SMEs in global knowledge-intensive industries and how nurturing the R&D activities of international science-based ventures is driven by their need for continuous knowledge exploitation.

Collaborating with large firms, research centres, universities, and public institutions is key in fostering this SME's R&D capabilities and its access to patents and new technologies. It is also key in reducing risk in commercializing its products in international markets. Our research shows the importance of being part of an international entrepreneurial ecosystem that offers its SME members an opportunity to access, co-create, assimilate, transform, and deploy innovative knowledge in their development and commercialization of new products or services. Our exploration found that being part of an IEE was crucial at every stage of the value chain for this firm, from accessing new technologies, patents, and skills, which led to more R&D, to opening new international markets for their products. Different actors of international ecosystems play different roles depending on the SME's objective, the stage of its products, and its knowledge about the markets.

By approaching this topic in the context of the COVID-19 pandemic, we were also able to find that the development of knowledge exploitation combined with IT capabilities allows a business to develop a level of business agility that helps them adapt quickly and efficiently and even take advantage of new opportunities such turbulent contexts can offer. This business agility can provide managers with valuable insights into how best to manage the pressures of a crisis.

Alongside its original findings, our study's limitations nevertheless provide an impetus for further research. This study began before the onset of the pandemic and continued 11 months into it. As such, the research model of this study should be retested in further research, targeting larger samples from different sectors, business sizes, and countries in order to confirm our findings. It would also be interesting for future research to explore what types of resources can be leveraged from an IEE to increase the entrepreneurial productivity of each stage of an innovative SME's life cycle.

References

Al-Omoush, K. S., Simón-Moya, V., & Sendra-García, J. (2020). The impact of social capital and collaborative knowledge creation on e-business proactiveness and organizational agility in responding to the COVID-19 crisis. *Journal of Innovation & Knowledge, 5*(4), 279–288.

Awate, S., Larsen, M. M., & Mudambi, R. (2015). Accessing vs sourcing knowledge: a comparative study of R&D internationalization between emerging and advanced economy firms. *Journal of International Business Studies, 46*(1), 63–86.

Baxter, P., & Jack, S. (2008). Qualitative case study methodology: study design and implementation for novice researchers. *The Qualitative Report, 13*(4), 544–559.

Belitski, M., Caiazza, R., & Lehmann, E. E. (2019). Knowledge frontiers and boundaries in entrepreneurship research. *Small Business Economics, 56*, 521–531. https://doi.org/10.1007/s11187019001870

Bhawe, N., & Zahra, S. A. (2019). Inducing heterogeneity in local entrepreneurial ecosystems: the role of MNEs. *Small Business Economics, 52*(2), 437–454.

Cantwell, J. (2017). Innovation and international business. *Industry and Innovation, 24*(1), 41–60.

Caputo, A., & Pellegrini, M. M. (2019). An overview of the anatomy of entrepreneurial decisions. In *The anatomy of entrepreneurial decisions* (pp. 1–6). Springer.

Cetindamar, D., Lammers, T., & Zhang, Y. (2020). Exploring the knowledge spillovers of a technology in an entrepreneurial ecosystem—the case of artificial intelligence in Sydney. *Thunderbird International Business Review, 62*(5), 457–474.

Coradi, A., Heinzen, M., & Boutellier, R. (2015). Designing workspaces for cross-functional knowledge-sharing in R & D: the "co-location pilot" of Novartis. *Journal of Knowledge Management, 9*(2), 236–256.

Dabić, M., Lažnjak, J., Smallbone, D., & Švarc, J. (2019). Intellectual capital, organisational climate, innovation culture, and SME performance: evidence from Croatia. *Journal of Small Business and Enterprise Development, 26*(4), 522–544.

Dabić, M., Maley, J., Dana, L. P., Novak, I., Pellegrini, M. M., & Caputo, A. (2020). Pathways of SME internationalization: a bibliometric and systematic review. *Small Business Economics, 55*(3), 705–725.

Dana, L. P. (2017). International entrepreneurship research: how it evolved and directions for the future. *International Journal of Entrepreneurship and Small Business, 30*(4), 477–489.

Dumez, H. (2016). *Comprehensive research. A methodological and epistemological introduction to qualitative research.* Copenhagen Business School Press.

Eisenhardt, K. M., & Graebner, M. E. (2007). Theory building from cases: opportunities and challenges. *Academy of Management Journal, 50*(1), 25–32.

Feld, B. (2020). *Startup communities: building an entrepreneurial ecosystem in your city.* John Wiley & Sons.

Ferraris, A., Giachino, C., Ciampi, F., & Couturier, J. (2019). R&D internationalization in medium-sized firms: the moderating role of knowledge management in enhancing innovation performances. *Journal of Business Research, 128*, 711–718.

Ferreira, J. J., Ratten, V., & Dana, L. P. (2017). Knowledge spillover-based strategic entrepreneurship. *International Entrepreneurship and Management Journal, 13*(1), 161–167.

Fuerst, S., & Zettinig, P. (2015). Knowledge creation dynamics within the international new venture. *European Business Review, 27*(2), 182–213.

Gassmann, O., & Keupp, M. M. (2007). The competitive advantage of early and rapidly internationalising SMEs in the biotechnology industry: a knowledge-based view. *Journal of World Business, 42*(3), 350–366.

Ghio, N., Guerini, M., Lehmann, E. E., & Rossi-Lamastra, C. (2015). The emergence of the knowledge spillover theory of entrepreneurship. *Small Business Economics, 44*(1), 1–18.

Gurău, C., & Dana, L. P. (2020). Financing paths, firms' governance and corporate entrepreneurship: accessing and applying operant and operand resources in biotechnology firms. *Technological Forecasting and Social Change, 153*, 119935.

Gurău, C., Dana, L. P., & Lasch, F. (2010). Human capital for successful entrepreneurial ventures: the profile of the top management team (TMT) in UK biopharmaceutical SMEs. *International Journal of Entrepreneurship and Small Business, 11*(4), 436–454.

Jacobides, M. G., Cennamo, C., & Gawer, A. (2018). Towards a theory of ecosystems. *Strategic Management Journal, 39*(8), 2255–2276.

Jafari-Sadeghi, V., Nkongolo-Bakenda, J. M., Dana, L. P., Anderson, R. B., & Biancone, P. P. (2019). Home country institutional context and entrepreneurial internationalization: the significance of human capital attributes. *Journal of International Entrepreneurship, 18*, 165–195.

Lange & Wagner. (2019). The influence of exploratory versus exploitative acquisitions on innovation output in the biotechnology industry. *Small Business Economics, 56*, 1–22.

Link, A. N., & Sarala, R. M. (2019). Advancing conceptualisation of university entrepreneurial ecosystems: the role of knowledge-intensive entrepreneurial firms. *International Small Business Journal, 37*(3), 289–310.

Machado, D., Qu, Y., & Cervantes, M. (2019). *Innovation policies for sustainable development: low-carbon energy and smart-city initiatives*. OECD Science, Technology and Industry Policy Papers, n° 80, Éditions OCDE. https://doi.org/10.1787/6287ddb2-en

Marshall, C., & Rossman, G. B. (2014). *Designing qualitative research*. Sage.

Mason, C., & Brown, R. (2014). Entrepreneurial ecosystems and growth-oriented entrepreneurship. *Final Report to OECD, 30*(1), 77–102.

Morrish, S. C., & Earl, A. (2020). Networks, institutional environment and firm internationalization. *Journal of Business & Industrial Marketing*. https://doi.org/10.1108/JBIM-05-2019-0230

Naldi, L., & Davidsson, P. (2014). Entrepreneurial growth: the role of international knowledge acquisition as moderated by firm age. *Journal of Business Venturing, 29*(5), 687–703.

Oviatt, B. M., & McDougall, P. P. (2005). Defining international entrepreneurship and modeling the speed of internationalization. *Entrepreneurship Theory and Practice, 29*(5), 537–553.

Patterson, W., & Ambrosini, V. (2015). Configuring absorptive capacity as a key process for research intensive firms. *Technovation, 36*, 77–89.

Ramadani, V., Abazi-Alili, H., Dana, L. P., Rexhepi, G., & Ibraimi, S. (2017). The impact of knowledge spillovers and innovation on firm-performance: findings from the Balkans countries. *International Entrepreneurship and Management Journal, 13*(1), 299–325.

Saridakis, G., Idris, B., Hansen, J. M., & Dana, L. P. (2019). SMEs' internationalisation: when does innovation matter? *Journal of Business Research, 96*, 250–263.

Scaringella, L. (2016). Knowledge, knowledge dynamics, and innovation. *European Journal of Innovation Management, 19*(3), 337–361.

Theodoraki, C., & Catanzaro, A. (2021). Widening the borders of entrepreneurial ecosystem through the international lens, *The Journal of Technology Transfer*. https://doi.org/10.1007/s10961-021-09852-7

Tolstoy, D., & Agndal, H. (2010). Network resource combinations in the international venturing of small biotech firms. *Technovation, 30*(1), 24–36.

Vahlne, J. E., & Johanson, J. (2020). The Uppsala model: networks and micro-foundations. *Journal of International Business Studies, 51*(1), 4–10.

Yin, R. K. (2002). *Case study research. Design and methods*. Sage.

Zahra, S. A., & George, G. (2002). Absorptive capacity: a review, reconceptualization, and extension. *Academy of Management Review, 27*(2), 185–203.

Dr. Naïma Cherchem is an assistant professor in the Entrepreneurship and Strategy Department at Ted Rogers School of Management, Ryerson University. She is also an associate researcher at the Strategy and Society—Chair of Management at HEC Montréal. Her current research interests focus on strategic entrepreneurship, institutional entrepreneurship, cognition, entrepreneurial ecosystem, and internationalization.

Christian Keen, PhD, is an Assistant Professor at the Département de Management, Université Laval, Canada. Christian has an extensive research and working experience in Europe, Latin America, and North America. Before joining Université Laval, Dr. Keen was Director Graduate Program in Finance at Universidad ORT Uruguay and member of the Department of Marketing & Management at the University of Southern Denmark. His professional experience includes being member of several Board of Directors of private companies and NGOs. He teaches graduate and undergraduate courses in international entrepreneurship, entrepreneurship, and international business. His research interests are in the areas of international entrepreneurship, entrepreneurship, emerging economies, and rapidly growing firms. Christian is a member of the editorial board of the *International Journal of Entrepreneurship and Small Business, European Journal of Family Business, and associated editor at TIM Review.* He has presented his research in several international conferences such as Academy of International Business (AIB) and Academy of Management (AOM), and also published papers in those areas.

Ignorance and International Entrepreneurship. Two Sides of a Blade in the Decision to Enter a Foreign Market

Bob Bastian and Antonella Zucchella

Abstract The aim of this chapter is to further explore and understand the role of a topic seldom discussed so far in the decision to enter a foreign market for entrepreneurs, namely ignorance. Rather than providing an extensive literature review of the topic, we will explore why entrepreneurship scholars so far neglected the topic of how entrepreneurs, and their firms, "don't know." Specifically, this chapter will be focused on the entrepreneur as an individual when making the decision to enter a foreign market. Throughout this chapter, we shall analyze ignorance from different perspectives when foreign entry decisions on an individual level have to be made. We will discuss that widespread international knowledge may not naturally advance International Entrepreneurship opportunities, point out the idea that individual decisions are cognitively influenced by ignorance, and point to the relevance of knowing what you do not know in IE. Finally, the chapter calls for an integration of ignorance within the decision-making framework in IE.

Keywords Entrepreneurship cognition · Decision-making · Cognitive biases · International entrepreneurship · Foreign market entry

1 Introduction

> Perhaps all this talk about knowledge is a way of creating an appealing image of an economy going places in order to avoid discussing the darker prospects that haunt de-industrializing countries around the world. (Alvesson & Spicer, 2016, p. 30)

B. Bastian (✉)
University of Bergamo, Bergamo, Italy
e-mail: roland.bastian@unibg.it

A. Zucchella
University of Pavia, Pavia, Italy
e-mail: antonella.zucchella@unipv.it

A. Caputo et al. (eds.), *The International Dimension of Entrepreneurial Decision-Making*, Contributions to Management Science,
https://doi.org/10.1007/978-3-030-85950-3_5

Entering a foreign market is among the key decisions in a firm's management. In taking these decisions entrepreneurs are confronted with two apparently conflicting issues: on one side they want to pursue an opportunity for the growth of their firm, on the other side they fear the "liability of foreignness" (Zaheer & Mosakowski, 1997), which primarily consists of lack of "familiarity" with the foreign context. The literature in international business has been developed on the construct of the liability of foreignness and thus portrays internationalization as a process, in which firms need to acquire knowledge, either gradually via foreign operations, starting from less "unfamiliar" markets and from low commitment entry modes, as the original Uppsala model postulates (Johanson & Vahlne, 1977) or leveraging on foreign partnerships, as the revised Uppsala model suggests (Johanson & Vahlne, 2009). The latter substitutes the liability of foreignness with the liability of outsidership from networks. However, the "liability" read of the internationalization process persists. At the same time, the last thirty years have witnessed the surge of International Entrepreneurship studies, which have brought a new discourse about the international expansion of the firm. From the observation of cases of early and fast internationalization, the so-called international new ventures (Oviatt & McDougall, 2005a) and born global firms (Knight & Cavusgil, 2004), this new field of enquiry shifted the attention from the liabilities perspective to the pursuit of "cross border opportunities" (Oviatt & McDougall, 2005b). However, international entrepreneurship scholars have often explained the precocious and fast global growth through the role of business networks, thus somehow converging towards the later Uppsala model, or through the previous experience of the founders and their social capital.

Thus, both the liability and the opportunity interpretations seem to find a common ground on the key role of knowledge, either acquired via experience or through networks. But the empirical evidence about these processes of knowledge acquisition to explain international growth is elusive (Zucchella, 2021). Some firms start operations in foreign countries without any market-specific knowledge and—when young and with founders lacking previous experience in business—also with limited general knowledge (Nummela et al., 2020). Thus, knowledge and the decision to enter a foreign market reveal a possible gap in research.

Moreover, there is still little research in the field about entrepreneurial cognition in approaching international markets. The microfoundations in international business represent an underexplored area of inquiry (Zucchella, 2021), which calls for studies about the individual decision-makers, their cognition and their biases when facing decisions about foreign market entry. Research revealed that these decisions can be affected by cognitive shortcuts, but this is still an understudied area. Some of these biases do not necessarily imply a lack of general or market-specific knowledge about something, but rather a lack of cognitive awareness. "That is, firms can be overconfident at the beginning of the process because they do not understand what they do not know", which leads individuals to be partly ignorant in their decision-making process (Niittymies & Pajunen, 2019, p. 6). This implies that core decisions like entry into a foreign market are often affected by lack of knowledge, cognitive biases, or both.

Alvesson and Spicer (2012, p. 2) call for a more nuanced significance of knowledge because "researchers take it for granted that the foundation of industrial economies has shifted from natural resources to intellectual assets". Thus, firms that internationalize without relying on these sources of knowledge remain scarcely investigated.

Internationalization studies have confirmed that the cognitive perspective remains scarcely investigated (Aharoni et al., 2011; Maitland & Sammartino, 2015). This is a problematic issue since firms are recognized to follow heterogeneous paths, which can arguably be best understood by considering an individual's cognition as an antecedent of the decisions of the firm (Zahoor et al., 2020). The increased interest in understanding the role of the individual actor and her[1] cognitive strategy has—as mentioned above—lately been acknowledged to contribute to current microfoundations research gaps in IB and entrepreneurship (Buckley & Casson, 2020; Foss & Pedersen, 2019; Niittymies & Pajunen, 2019).

In this chapter, we provide arguments to answer these gaps and calls for studies, by pushing the field towards a better understanding of how cognitive aspects influence entrepreneurs in international settings (Dana, 2017). More specifically, we highlight the role of ignorance, which we define as *an inevitable widespread phenomenon that concerns a lack of information, knowledge, or awareness* (Roberts & Armitage, 2008; Shepherd et al., 2007). Ignorance as a topic is, despite its relevance, usually considered to be perpendicular to knowledge. While knowledge construction and knowledge formation processes are inevitably interwoven with entrepreneurship theories (e.g. entrepreneurs use knowledge structures when making judgements and decisions; internationalizing ventures aim at leveraging on their knowledge or their partners' knowledge), ignorance as a topic remains to be largely ignored (Ungar, 2008).

We argue that firms often find themselves with a lack of knowledge and information when facing internationalization decisions. These forms of ignorance impact the role of the bounded rational individual in her perception of the environment, and in her cognitive available tools to arrive at satisficing decisions (March & Simon, 1958). This chapter takes an unconventional perspective on entrepreneurship, namely, the existence of ignorance as a generic phenomenon. We elucidate this viewpoint by integrating the recently increased interest in understanding entrepreneurship cognition with internationalization studies. In doing so, shall we analyze the individual role in internationalization choices (Dabić et al., 2020) and discuss ignorance, heuristics and cognitive biases as affecting foreign market entry.

[1]Note that we use female pronouns when referring to the individual entrepreneur for readability reasons. Our theory is gender neutral.

2 The Concept of Ignorance

In this chapter, we define ignorance as *an inevitable widespread phenomenon that concerns a lack of information, knowledge, or (and) awareness* (Roberts & Armitage, 2008; Shepherd et al., 2007). The first assumption within our notion is that ignorance is *inevitable* because individuals in most cases do not have full knowledge or information about anything. Indeed, any sense of certainty produced by new knowledge automatically creates uncertainties about other matters. Choose one topic that had your interest in the last years and you will find yourself realizing that the more you read and learn, the more you became aware of how much you do did not know yet. An elegant example of this paradox is provided by Alvesson and Spicer (2012, p. 4), who use the example that "scientific inquiry into climate change has produced a sense of certainty about some issues (such as the long run increase in planetary heat in the last century), but also revealed new areas of ignorance (such as the precise causes of it) (Ungar, 2008)". This implies that new knowledge and information acquired by discoveries do not diminish ignorance. Thus, the basic idea is that ignorance is unavoidable and generic. Ignorance cannot be seen as the contrary of knowledge and is socially constructed. That is because "it is virtually impossible to speak intelligibly about ignorance without referring at least implicitly to a social standard of truth and falsehood, or irrelevance. Ignorance is made possible by the very nature of social interaction and language; and it is embedded in a variety of social norms, occasions, settings, roles, scripts, and identities" (Smithson, 1985, p. 168).

Although ignorance relates to everyone and clearly is a social issue, it is largely ignored by scholars. Among many explanations, we suggest that it may also depend on ignorance being most of the time unnoticed and is thus unproblematic (Ungar, 2008).

An example of an unproblematic but noteworthy case is Swatch. The Nicolas Hayek Swiss-founded firm entered a market in the early 1980s, when the Swiss industry was in turmoil, which resulted in decreases in exports and bankruptcies. It was the time when digital watches were expected to take over, and dominated by Japanese cheap mass production. The conventional approach for Swiss-based watch-makers was to focus on the luxury market. When Hayek recommended a merger in an attempt to save the two largest watch manufactures in Switzerland, he decided to radically move away from the traditional approach, ignoring the voices of many stakeholders. Some outraged suppliers refused to sell the necessary parts when hearing the plans. An investment bank replied: "This is not what consumers think of when they think of Switzerland. What the hell are you going to do with this piece of plastic against Japan and Hong Kong?" Hayek decided to proceed anyway. His solution? An inexpensive, plastic watch, using the Japanese dominated quartz technology, a Swiss brand with every possible colour of the rainbow, to be changed daily based on the mood and the clothing. The fact that in the years after Hayek's launch, Swatch sold close to 100 million watches worldwide, a successful born global case, illustrates the idea that acquiring knowledge from existing sources does not guarantee success (Mudambi, 2005; Taylor, 1993).

The example shows that there may be highly successful international entrepreneurs that make decisions based on what is, till then, unknown to thrive. Investors, customers, and suppliers might even be completely ignored for the better good. The case of Swatch elegantly illustrates that when individuals solely rely on existing knowledge, they may ignore contradictions, fail to reflect, overlook opportunities or pursue opportunities that many others are pursuing. In fact, "a fetishistic interest in knowledge and intelligence can in some cases drive ignorance and poor judgment" (Alvesson & Spicer, 2016, p. 40).

3 Being Aware When Deciding

The second assumption in our definition of ignorance is that it concerns a lack of information, knowledge, *or (and)* awareness. Knowledge involves information, facts, and skills acquired through education or experience (Roberts & Armitage, 2008). It refers to the cognitive structures that organize the perception of what people believe to be true, and the degree of confidence in that belief (Fischhoff et al., 1977; Fiske & Taylor, 1984). International entrepreneurs, however, often miss knowledge and experience because every foreign entry decision by definition has its own unique features with related context due to differences in terms of economic, political, and social-cultural conditions. It is often from the initial unknown features of a potential foreign market that firms eventually decrease their unfamiliarity over time. Later on, "they start to understand what they do not know and perceive their lack of knowledge. In the final stage of the process, they understand what they know and what there is to know about the foreign markets" (Niittymies & Pajunen, 2019). Through the process of obtaining experience, post hoc, someone may conclude to have made a reasonable successful decision under conditions of uncertainty (Langlois, 2007). A priori, however, judgements that should lead to sound decisions rely on many unknown factors within the mental model of the entrepreneur. Thus, to make rational decisions to enter a foreign market, it is important that ignorance such as a lack of information or knowledge is consciously acknowledged. This is an important issue for entrepreneurs because better decisions "follow from the increase of the level of awareness of one's mental processes and from the acquisition of more adequate knowledge about such processes" (Colombo et al., 2010, p. 446). Maintaining this constant level of awareness when decisions are made is, however, a difficult task. For example, research has shown that individuals often lack awareness of their sub-optimal decision-making processes, make faulty judgements and as a consequence, remain to be ignorant about what is not known to them (Dunning, 2011).

4 Degrees of Ignorance

> As we know, there are known knowns; there are things we know we know. We also know there are known unknowns; that is to say we know there are some things we do not know. But there are also unknown unknowns—the ones we don't know we don't know. (Donald Rumsfeld, former US Secretary of Defense)

Rumsfeld (2011), not notably well-known for his epistemological interests, once underscored a fundamental issue in the fields of entrepreneurship (Foss & Klein, 2012). Namely, the differences in decision-making between known and unknown issues, and the essential importance to consciously acknowledge and know the differences. Entrepreneurs act on a daily basis within such a complex international environment while relying on incomplete, non-objectively optimal decision-making processes under uncertain circumstances (e.g. Caputo & Pellegrini, 2019; Forbes, 2005; Packard et al., 2017; Townsend et al., 2018).

The awareness of these limitations in order to enter a foreign market is essential in identifying firstly the "known knowns"—information that entrepreneurs have and *know that they have*—and secondly the "known unknowns"—information that entrepreneurs do not have and *know that they lack* (Gross, 2007; Proctor & Schiebinger, 2008). There are also some elements that imply ignorance that is rather invisible to people. Those we call 'unknown unknowns'—information that is relevant to decisions but that entrepreneurs *do now know they lack* (Dunning, 2011). This is information that is not questioned because it lies outside a decision-maker's scope. Founders for instance may be unaware of data because they lack the skills to make sense to them, or because they are not brought to their attention (Hayward et al., 2006). "Unknown unknowns" may frequently refer to essential information such as potential problems, risks, actions, strategies, and lead to fatalities. Often, entrepreneurs and their firms do not know what to do with scenarios that represent unknown outcomes with the presence of forms of ignorance such as misinformation, complexity, volatility, uncertainty and ambiguity (Suarez & Montes, 2020). The Boeing 787 production issues (resulting in $10 billion additional costs) and the Fukushima crisis in Japan (forcing 100,000 to evacuate and $38 billion compensation costs) were novel, unknown, and thus unanticipated events that had massive consequences for the international economic environment (Kaplan et al., 2020). We follow Faulkner et al. (2017) in their distinctions that something "known" implies knowledge and "unknown" lack of knowledge, and that "known unknowns" suggest awareness while "unknown unknowns" suggest an absence of awareness. Unknown unknowns may go unrecognized until people got informed. Fischhoff et al. (1977) argued for example that people cannot critically evaluate and distinguish inferred knowledge when they are unaware of the nature of their perception.

This implies that a lack of awareness may need an external reference point to serve individuals becoming aware of their limitations. As a result, it is essential for entrepreneurs to reduce fatal "unknown unknowns" towards "known unknowns" and eventually "known knowns", by consciously searching and considering what might not be known yet. Ignorance is both socially constructed and socially de-constructed (Smithson, 1985). For example, Roberts (2015) suggested that unknown unknowns may be discovered a priori during moments of interaction with customers, competitors, and suppliers, or as a result of recruiting staff, because this would add new knowledge for the firm. We will briefly get back to ways to handle unknowns later on in this chapter.

5 The Role of Ignorance in International Entrepreneurship

When firms are involved with internationalization decisions, such as foreign market entry, they balance on a daily basis between their known, unknown, and unknowable knowledge (Chow & Sarin, 2002). That is because, taking any point in time, there are always some known matters and some unknown matters, to any individual (Faulkner et al., 2017). In economic theories, ignorance can represent a necessary part of the market process since it is described to be responsible for the creation of profitable opportunities (Kirzner, 1979). This disequilibrium is a consequence of market ignorance. "Thus, an understanding of ignorance, or limitation of knowledge, is crucial in Austrian thought" (Elias et al., 2020, p. 323).

In international business theories, internationalization is usually described as a process developed from knowledge and through which knowledge is further gradually acquired. However, this assumption overlooks alternative internationalization processes that rely on anything but knowledge. When international firms are in the process of discovering new markets, entrepreneurs often do not know what it is that they do not know. In some cases, they might not even deliberately be scanning or consciously searching (Mcmullen & Shepherd, 2006). The previous example of Swatch demonstrated that it is the process of discovering the unknown for entrepreneurs that often leads to success. It is not the awareness of what people know, but what people do not know, that leads to new insights and discoveries.

Additionally, internationalization studies have recently shown that foreign country entries do not necessarily elaborate on a slow and progressive process of acquiring knowledge, while more traditional entry forms like the Joint Venture point to the complementary role of knowledge (Buckley & Casson, 2009; Hennart, 1982; Hymer, 1960; Rugman & Verbeke, 2003). Instead, some firms that decided to enter a foreign market have been using an opposite approach. For instance, successful foreign entry strategies have been explained with the so-called in and out decisions, in which firms do not seem to build on knowledge (e.g. Melén & Nordman, 2009; Nummela et al., 2020). Galkina and Chetty (2015) and Nummela et al. (2020) illustrated this by documenting a serendipitous process in which the sequence of foreign country entries is basically random because it is the result of unsolicited orders and fortuitous contacts. These findings appear to confirm that it is the process of discovering the unknown for entrepreneurs that often leads to success.

After all, if the knowledge behind the decision was known to someone else, it would have been done before (Taleb, 2007). New knowledge however always leads to new perspectives of what is unknown. Entrepreneurs and their firms thus may never reach complete knowledge as long as new knowledge is discovered. In reality, "the unknown is not diminished by new discoveries. Quite the contrary: the realm of the unknown is magnified" (Gross & McGoey, 2015, p. 1). Nevertheless, entrepreneurship theories tend to be rather knowledge obsessed, but our theories about the knowledge intensive economy and knowledge-based organizations might not tell the complete story (Alvesson & Spicer, 2012).

The idea that some firms, with founders lacking previous experience, operate in foreign markets without any market-specific knowledge can imply that knowledge and experience may not unconditionally lead to the identification of new foreign markets or opportunities. In fact, the acquisition of new knowledge may in different situations lead to less positive results. That is because these information and knowledge processes have been suggested to create mental loops and contradictions. For example, Zahra et al. (2005) debated that widespread international experience may lead to overvaluing existing knowledge while ignoring or overlooking new information. That is because this kind of knowledge may result in an unhealthy, excessive degree of focus because "this experience may promote a rigid focus on familiar clues, causing new information to be ignored" (ibid., p. 139). This overestimation of solely previous knowledge may moreover move firms towards wrong decisions, because it causes entrepreneurs to ignore sensemaking and instead search for confirmation. Thus, entrepreneurs can fall prey to cognitive biases such as sunk-cost-fallacy (Arkes & Blumer, 1985; Weick, 1995), and become overly committed to the original choice when making a decision, "and then subsequently make decisions biased by psychological commitment" (McCarthy et al., 1993, p. 9).

6 Ignorance in Judgement and Decision-Making

So far, we have mostly analyzed ignorance as a lack of knowledge or information. Within the framework of international decision-making, however, we must not only consider decisions based on *limited knowledge or information,* but also based on *limited awareness*. Indeed, research has shown that we tend to underestimate the value of what we do not know while overvaluing what we do know, and as a result, ignore evidence that contradicts our preconceived ideas (Kahneman, 2011; Taleb, 2007). This leads us to propose that knowing what you do not know is a powerful tool to go ahead in today's society (Grant, 2021). Indeed, in every decision-makers best interest when entering a foreign market, it is probably optimal to confess her or his degree of ignorance. This, however, is a complicated skill to obtain and maintain. Research has shown that individuals often make inaccurate judgements and decisions while missing the insight of recognizing their shortcomings. The explanation for this statement can be found in the fact that the same knowledge that underlies the ability *to produce* correct judgement is also the knowledge that underlies the ability *to recognize* correct judgement (Kruger & Dunning, 1999, p. 1121). Both circumstances highlight the fact that people's insight into their deficits is imperfect and incomplete since they have been argued to be cognitively camouflaged in various ways (Dunning, 2011). We argue that, as one's environment becomes more complex and complicated, combined with an incomplete and uninformed mind due to novel, unknown circumstances, one's strategy to recognize ignorance becomes an essential part of a major decision such as entering a foreign market.

Decision-making is the "entire process of choosing a course of action" (Hastie, 2001, p. 657), usually preceded by an identification process which we know as judgement. Decisions such as foreign market entry rely on a dual-process mechanism when processing information. System 1 is known as the fast system of thought that works automatically. System 2 on the other hand involves effortful, slow, rational processing of information. Most of what individuals think and do happens in System 1. System 2 comes usually into play when System 1 runs into difficulty (Kahneman, 2011; Stanovich & West, 2000). Given the complexity and uncertainty of the entrepreneurial environment coupled with non-optimal information processing of the human mind, heuristics and biases may occasionally come into play (Caputo & Pellegrini, 2019; Grégoire et al., 2011; Packard et al., 2017). In fact, ignorance is believed to influence cognitive biases and heuristics in significant ways (Roy & Zeckhauser, 2015).

7 Heuristics and Cognitive Biases

Heuristics come into play when rather quick judgemental shortcuts must be made by entrepreneurs. They refer to simplifying fast and frugal mental shortcuts or principles that entrepreneurs use for information processing and problem-solving (Baron, 2007; Kahneman & Tversky, 1982). Heuristics additionally enable entrepreneurs to make sense of uncertain and complex situations more quickly (Mitchell et al., 2007). They represent "actionable simple rules that synthesize the entrepreneur's subjective knowledge, expectations, and vision, and for which optimal outcomes cannot be determined by mathematical methods" (Gilbert-Saad et al., 2018, p. 76). An example is Sarasvathy's research (2008) on effectuation that has been shown to support entrepreneurs in international settings and implies the existence of heuristics (Sarasvathy et al., 2014).

The field of IE has demonstrated that entrepreneurs are affected by these cognitive shortcuts in their decisions to enter a foreign market (Petersen et al., 2008). For example, Zahra et al. (2005) showed that entrepreneurs' cognition as a result may lead to more risky foreign activities, since it may lead to inaccurate opportunity evaluation. That is because System 1 thinking leads individuals to arrive at the first plausible-appearing explanations. Some scholars have suggested that heuristics interact in considerable means with ignorance because it "adds a dimension of the unknown beyond uncertainty. Thus, decision makers confronting it also suffer more from biases and heuristics than when faced merely with uncertainty" (Roy & Zeckhauser, 2017, p. 235). That is because some of the cognitive tools that often work out well tend to lean strongly towards what is known from previous experiences, or prior knowledge, when predicting the future, such as the availability heuristic (Tversky & Kahneman, 1973). For example, research has shown that availability leads economic forecasters to ignore crucial known information by solely judging *a moment*, and as a result overlooking well-known practices (Alvesson & Spicer, 2016; Lee et al., 2008).

The future, however, is mostly unknown. The cognitive ease that individuals apply to rely on their known past has little to say about judging a future world that is unpredictable and uncertain. A similar case occurs with the recognition heuristic. When individuals are presented two equal alternatives but only one of them is mentally recognized, it will automatically be valued higher. That is because people have a preference to bet on known probabilities (Ellsberg, 1961). Once individuals are confronted with an unknown situation, they tend to follow familiar clues and ignore unfamiliar contextual information. These heuristics imply that people overestimate what they know, and do little effort to find out what they might still be ignorant about. When decisions such as entering a foreign market are made, "crucial information is ignored, and the wrong lessons are drawn from experience", because people are not consciously aware of these heuristics (Alvesson & Spicer, 2016, p. 61).

Because heuristics simplify or ignore part of the information processing, they are associated with cognitive biases, systematic deviation from rationality or norms in judgement and decision-making (Gilovich et al., 2002; Kahneman & Tversky, 1982). Research on cognitive bias—systematic errors in decision-making (Kahneman, 2011)—has become an important area of study because it provides practical and empirical perspectives in entrepreneurial decision-making (e.g. Krueger, 2003; Zacharakis & Shepherd, 2001; Zahra et al., 2005). Most cognitive biases are undergone unconsciously, at least *a priori.*

Cognitive biases are known to make IE activities risky (Zahra et al., 2005), and ignorance plays a fundamental role. Some examples are overestimation, which leads entrepreneurs overvaluing previous market knowledge while ignoring novel information (Zahra et al., 2005), illusion of control, in which individuals overestimate their ability to control events while ignoring the base-rates, fundamental attribution error, where individuals tend to ignore contextual factors when entering a foreign market, halo effect, that may lead entrepreneurs to have a falsely positive image of a particular market without any previous experience, and confirmation bias, that inclines people to ignore solutions, such as leaving an unprofitable market, that contradict their primary judgement and as a result demonstrate cognitive dissonance. Similarly, when foreign entry decisions are made within a team of co-founders, the group think bias may cause entrepreneurs to "go with the crowd" and thus ignore arguments, contradictions, critique, doubts, and the consequences that follow from the decisions made.

While the above examples illustrate the unconscious character of biases with ignorance, that is not always the case. Some other biases may be perceived and operated consciously because a decision-maker believes the outcome will be favourable. For example, in the case of overconfidence (Busenitz, 1999; Gudmundsson & Lechner, 2013), entrepreneurs may be aware of the risks of entering unfamiliar foreign markets but simultaneously believe that they can beat the odds of breakdown, therefore ignoring the information and 'taking the risk for granted' (Hayward et al., 2006). Another example may be the sunk cost fallacy, where firms persist to invest in entering foreign markets that are clearly underperforming, hoping for a positive change and ignoring the less costly decision to abandon (Holland & Shepherd, 2013).

During the process of entering a market, additional cognitive biases may evolve, even when they are recognized. The status quo bias is one's tendency to hold on to pre-existing choices and is often triggered by loss aversion. That is because decision-makers are more affected by losses than by benefits. Research has demonstrated that firms keep investing in decisions that have been shown to not work, in order to win back their losses (Staw, 1981). Additionally, even when firms recognize their ignorance, they may fall prey to status quo bias because their awareness has not yet been overcome. For example, potential self-blame may affect decision-makers in "doing nothing or maintaining one's current or previous decision" (Samuelson & Zeckhauser, 1988, p. 7). This additionally shows the complex direction of cognitive biases, since, like with ignorance, one may lead to another. Ignorance may cause the emergence of biases, and these biases may additionally lead to new ignorance. A similar example is the indecision bias, which refers to inaction because of one's tendency to delay or play the game safe as a result of acknowledged ignorance, resulting decision-makers being paralyzed (e.g. Goldman, 1986; Mcmullen & Shepherd, 2006). Roy and Zeckhauser (2017, p. 237) note that indecisions facilitate individuals to "fail to recognize that choosing the unknown probability often offers valuable learning opportunities, opportunities that would otherwise be missed". Thus, cognitive biases that go well with ignorance do not only differ in degree of consciousness but may additionally emerge when acknowledged but not yet conquered.

8 Towards an Integration of Ignorance

So how do we move from here? Ignorance is a cognitive condition that affects all of us. That is not necessarily bad, as long as its presence is acknowledged. Rather than neutralizing ignorance, we propose that ignorance should be embraced by increasing one's awareness. In doing so, we see two directions to cope with ignorance.

Firstly, when analyzing the interaction of ignorance with heuristics and cognitive biases, entrepreneurs should tailor their decision-making processes through their dual-process theory (Kahneman, 2011; Stanovich & West, 2000). The type of ignorance that interacts with these processes is, as we have shown, often not beneficial for entrepreneurs when entering a foreign market. Thus, ignorance needs a neutralizing approach. Behavioural decision theorists have shown that situations where actors use counterfactual thinking (Baron, 2000) and search for feedback (Fischhoff, 1982) limit the functioning of cognitive biases, while Alvesson and Spicer (2012) pointed out that an inability or unwillingness to mobilize one's cognitive capacities is caused by a lack of critical thinking and reflexivity. The above

Table 1 Unmaking ignorance

		Situational point of view	
		From the individual	From an outsider
State of actors' or awareness of something	Conscious (Aware)	*Known knowns*: active relevant knowledge or competences at hand *Tool:* Leverage and develop further knowns by gaining knowledge and experience	*Known unknowns*: Perceived information and development needs *Tool:* Expose the unknown
	Unaware	*Unknown knowns*: Possessed, unknown or unutilized competence or knowledge *Tool:* Move to knowns with serendipitous processes	*Unknown unknowns*: Not perceived potential risks or failure factors *Tool:* Raise consciousness about the unknown

cases illustrate that obtaining an awareness of considering an alternative point of view in the decision-makers' thinking, either triggered by the self or by someone else, supports well-grounded decision-making. This could be done for instance by actively training metacognition, which refers to a conscious reflective process and helps individuals to organize their knowledge when making decisions (Flavell, 1979). Recognizing that a firm may cope with unknown unknowns and using scenario planning or foresight studies may help to transform them into known unknowns. Previous research has found these techniques beneficial to create several consistent scenarios to anticipate future possibilities (Loveridge, 2009). These processes may, as a result, help individuals in their decision-making process, because acknowledged ignorance by definition is less hurtful. Table 1[2] displays our adapted version of how different varieties of ignorance may be unmade best (Smithson, 2015). We separate the individual decision-maker from an outsider, suggesting that unknowns are better understood and comprehended when an outsider, such as with the help of feedback, exposes what is unknown.

Secondly, ignorance may also be beneficial. The Swatch example demonstrated that purposefully ignoring customers and investors may lead to new opportunities. Ignorance thus is not always unwanted and can even be used intentionally. Learning and discovering, for example, has been linked with consciously acknowledged and constructed ignorance. Similarly, tolerance of ignorance facilitates a creative entrepreneurial climate, and "not knowing" has benefits for knowledge creation and innovation in fast-changing markets (Roberts & Armitage, 2008). Having no complete access to full knowledge, or purposefully ignoring part of the information, surely may create benefits to firms. On many occasions, firms balance between known, unknown, and unknowable knowledge, applying in and out decision strategies, serendipity, or improvisation that rely on a lack or complete absence of knowledge. This may happen because the required knowledge is unavailable within

[2]We would like to acknowledge the role of the anonymous reviewer in our submission process, who generously provided us this table in order to better understand ways to unmake ignorance.

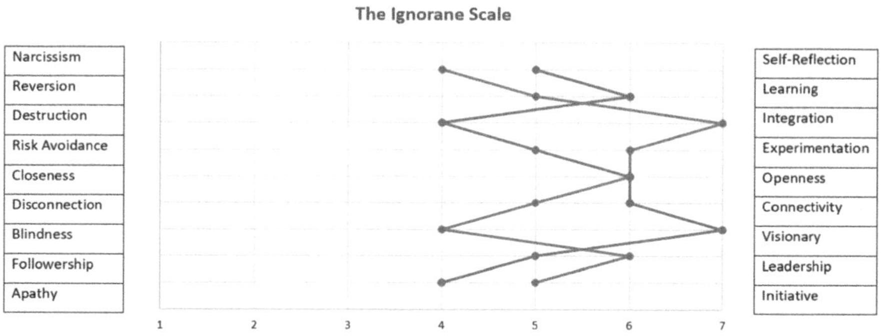

Fig. 1 The Ignorance Scale (Source: Adapted version from North & Kares, 2005)

the firm, or inaccessible because of the economic environment. Limited knowledge may eventually lead to action where full knowledge about a decision may lead a firm to be indecisive. The above cases illustrate that ignorance does not need a neutralizing approach as long as there are degrees of awareness about one's ignorance. Rather than eliminating one's ignorance, it may result in unexpected results that may be beneficial when entering a foreign market. Here, ignorance should be embraced as an advantage.

Finally, one of the main issues of studying ignorance is that it is hard to measure (Ungar, 2008). However, to understand ignorance better as a research topic, it has to be studied empirically eventually. An interesting approach to identify ignorance has been suggested by North and Kares (2005) who suggest ten disablers-enablers criteria of ignorance. The smaller the gap, the lower one's awareness of ignorance. A larger gap on the other hand increases the chance that someone is unaware of one's lack of knowledge or information in the decision-making process. We adapt this scale towards an entrepreneurial context in Fig. 1. The main goal of the scale is to lay out a gap analysis and can be filled in by entrepreneurs and their team members following a set of questions.

9 Conclusion

The aim of this chapter was to demonstrate the role of ignorance in International Entrepreneurship. We debated that scholars might have overemphasized the role of knowledge, while ignorance has been ignored. We have argued that firms who internationalize do not exclusively follow pre-defined knowledge strategies in order to find their most suitable foreign market. We have also demonstrated that following knowledge patterns, even if they exist, may not give satisfying results to firms, since it may result in overlooking opportunities and ignoring new important information.

Ignorance also plays an important role in entrepreneurial cognition and may cause, or be caused by, serious cognitive errors. The field of entrepreneurship,

International Entrepreneurship not excluded, has seen many fruitful contributions in the past two decades that highlighted the role of heuristics and biases in the decision-making process. Ignorance so far is a neglected topic in entrepreneurship. While uncertainty is "the favored child of behavioral decision, ignorance, in contrast, suffers neglect" (Roy & Zeckhauser, 2017, p. 232). We call for the inclusion of ignorance, because knowledge is power and knowing what you do not know is bliss (Grant, 2021). This chapter does not allow us for a full overview of ignorance, but we see promising future research contributions coming from scholars that focus on re-thinking and unlearning patterns, allowing us to analyze decision-makers not solely from a knowledge point of view. We also see potential contributions coming from studies aimed at reducing ignorance in entrepreneurial decision-making, perhaps by designing awareness training programmes for entrepreneurs. Future research contributions may also come from theoretical reviews, which would allow us to get a complete picture of the role of ignorance in the fields of entrepreneurship. Lastly, we see potential contributions coming from studies focused not only on the individual level but on the organizational level. For example, future studies might investigate how ignorance within organizations is created, strengthened and promoted (Alvesson & Spicer, 2016). Additionally, promising works could investigate how ignorance may be used strategically within organizations between employees or towards customers (Smithson, 1989). Finally, cognitive biases that relate to the organizational level of analysis, such as groupthink and halo effect, may become particularly interesting here. Recent calls have emphasized to "move one step further and show that ignorance needs to be understood and theorized as a regular feature of decision-making" (Gross & McGoey, 2015, p. 4). We make an effort to answer that request in this chapter. It is our hope that this contribution encourages our research community to embrace the topic as an existing, relevant concept.

Appendix

The questionnaire consists of 9 items that could be answered on a 7-point Likert Scale (1 = very low, 7 = very high) following the statement: *How would you rate entrepreneur's A capability to …*

… assess his/her willingness to recognize weaknesses, strengths and mistakes? (1)

… create awareness of the importance of knowing by learning and innovating? (2)

… stimulate a strong sense of the value of people by integration, networking, and communication? (3)

… be open for change, try new solutions, and permit errors? (4)

… see and integrate ideas, trends, and form open relationships and networking? (5)

… build and assess the value creation of networks and communities? (6)

… see and develop shared mental images of the future? (7)

... make transparent decisions toward a shared goal? (8)
... stimulate initiatives to mobilize and take actions? (9)

References

Aharoni, Y., Tihanyi, L., & Connelly, B. L. (2011). Managerial decision-making in international business: a forty-five-year retrospective. *Journal of World Business, 46*(2), 135–142.

Alvesson, M., & Spicer, A. (2012). A stupidity-based theory of organizations. *Journal of Management Studies, 49*(7), 1194–1220.

Alvesson, M., & Spicer, A. (2016). *The stupidity paradox*. Profile.

Arkes, H. R., & Blumer, C. (1985). The psychology of sunk cost. *Organizational Behavior and Human Decision Processes, 35*(1), 124–140.

Baron, R. A. (2000). Counterfactual thinking and venture formation: the potential effects of thinking about "what might have been". *Journal of Business Venturing, 15*, 79–92.

Baron, R. A. (2007). *Entrepreneurship: a process perspective*. In J. R. Baum, M. Frese, & R. A. Baron (Eds.), *The organizational frontiers. The psychology of entrepreneurship* (pp. 19–39). Psychology Press.

Buckley, P. J., & Casson, M. C. (2009). The internalization theory of the multinational enterprise: a review of the progress of a research agenda after 30 years. *Journal of International Business Studies, 40*(9), 1563–1580.

Buckley, P. J., & Casson, M. (2020). The internalization theory of the multinational enterprise: past, present and future. *British Journal of Management, 31*(2), 239–252.

Busenitz, L. W. (1999). Entrepreneurial risk and strategic decision making: it's a matter of perspective. *Journal of Applied Behavioral Science, 35*(3), 325–340.

Caputo, A., & Pellegrini, M. M. (2019). An overview of the anatomy of entrepreneurial decisions. In *The anatomy of entrepreneurial decisions* (pp. 1–6). Springer.

Chow, C., & Sarin, R. K. (2002). Known, unknown, and unknowable uncertainties. *Theory and Decision, 52*(2), 127–138.

Colombo, B., Iannello, P., & Antonietti, A. (2010). Metacognitive knowledge of decision-making: An explorative study. In A. Efklides & P. Misailidi (Eds.), *Trends and prospects in metacognition research* (pp. 445–472). Springer Science + Business Media.

Dabić, M., Maley, J., Dana, L. P., Novak, I., Pellegrini, M. M., & Caputo, A. (2020). Pathways of SME internationalization: a bibliometric and systematic review. *Small Business Economics, 55* (3), 705–725.

Dana, L. P. (2017). International entrepreneurship research: how it evolved and directions for the future. *International Journal of Entrepreneurship and Small Business, 30*(4), 477–489.

Dunning, D. (2011). The dunning-kruger effect: on being ignorant of one's own ignorance. In *Advances in experimental social psychology* (Vol. 44, 1st ed.). Elsevier Inc.

Elias, S., Chiles, T., Li, Q., & D'Andrea, F. (2020). Austrian economics and organizational entrepreneurship: a typology. *The Quarterly Journal of Austrian Economics, 23*(3–4), 313–354.

Ellsberg, D. (1961). Risk, ambiguity, and the savage axioms. *The Quarterly Journal of Economics, 75*(4), 643–669.

Faulkner, P., Feduzi, A., & Runde, J. (2017). Unknowns, black swans and the risk/uncertainty distinction. *Cambridge Journal of Economics, 41*(5), 1279–1302.

Fischhoff, B. (1982). Debiasing. In D. Kahneman, P. Slovic, & A. Tversky (Eds.), *Judgment under uncertainty: heuristics and biases*. Cambridge University Press.

Fischhoff, B., Slovic, P., & Lichtenstein, S. (1977). Knowing with certainty: the appropriateness of extreme confidence. *Judgment and Decision Making, 3*(4), 103–123.

Fiske, S. T., & Taylor, S. E. (1984). *Social cognition*. Addison-Wesley Pub. Co..

Flavell, J. H. (1979). Metacognition and cognitive monitoring a new area of cognitive—developmental inquiry. *American Psychologist, 34*(10), 906–911.

Forbes, D. P. (2005). Are some entrepreneurs more overconfident than others? *Journal of Business Venturing., 20*, 623–640.
Foss, N. J., & Klein, P. G. (2012). *Organizing entrepreneurial judgment*. Cambridge University Press.
Foss, N. J., & Pedersen, T. (2019). Microfoundations in international management research: the case of knowledge sharing in multinational corporations. *Journal of International Business Studies, 50*(9), 1594–1621.
Galkina, T., & Chetty, S. (2015). Effectuation and networking of internationalizing SMEs. *Management International Review, 55*(5), 647–676.
Gilbert-Saad, A., Siedlok, F., & McNaughton, R. B. (2018). Decision and design heuristics in the context of entrepreneurial uncertainties. *Journal of Business Venturing Insights, 9*, 75–80.
Gilovich, T., Griffin, D., & Kahneman, D. (2002). *Heuristics and biases: the psychology of intuitive judgment*. Cambridge University Press.
Goldman, A. I. (1986). *Epistemology and cognition*. Harvard University Press.
Grant, A. (2021). *Think again: the power of knowing what you don't know*. Penguin Publishing Group.
Grégoire, D. A., Corbett, A. C., & Mcmullen, J. S. (2011). The cognitive perspective in entrepreneurship: an agenda for future research. *Journal of Management Studies, 48*(6), 1443–1477.
Gross, M. (2007). The unknown in process: dynamic connections of ignorance, non-knowledge and related concepts. *Current Sociology, 55*(5), 742–759.
Gross, M., & McGoey, L. (2015). *Routledge international handbook of ignorance studies* (pp. 1–14). Routledge.
Gudmundsson, S., & Lechner, C. (2013). Cognitive biases, organization, and entrepreneurial firm survival. *European Management Journal, 31*(3), 278–294.
Hastie, R. (2001). Problems for judgment and decision making. *Annual Review of Psychology, 52*, 653–683.
Hayward, M. L. A., Shepherd, D. A., & Griffin, D. (2006). A hubris theory of entrepreneurship. *Management Science, 52*(2), 160–172.
Hennart, J. F. (1982). *A theory of the multinational enterprise*. University of Michigan Press.
Holland, D. V., & Shepherd, D. A. (2013). Deciding to persist: adversity, values, and entrepreneurs' decision policies. *Entrepreneurship: Theory and Practice, 37*(2), 331–358.
Hymer, S. (1960). *The international operations of national firms: a study of direct foreign investment*. The MIT Press.
Johanson, J., & Vahlne, J. E. (1977). The internationalization process of the firm—a model of knowledge development and increasing foreign market commitments. *Journal of International Business, 8*, 23–32.
Johanson, J., & Vahlne, J. E. (2009). The Uppsala internationalization process model revisited: from liability of foreignness to liability of outsidership. *Journal of International Business Studies, 40*(9), 1411–1431.
Kahneman, D. (2011). *Thinking fast and slow*. Straus & Giroux.
Kahneman, D., & Tversky, A. (1982). The psychology of preferences. *Scientific American, 246*(1), 160–173.
Kaplan, R. S., Leonard, H. B., & Mikes, A. (2020). The risks you can't forsee. *Harvard Business Review, 2020*, 40–46.
Kirzner, I. (1979). *Perception, opportunity and profit*. University of Chicago Press.
Knight, G. A., & Cavusgil, S. T. (2004). Innovation, organizational capabilities, and the born-global firm. *Journal of International Business Studies, 35*(2), 124–141.
Krueger, N. F. (2003). The cognitive psychology of entrepreneurship. In *Handbook of entrepreneurship research* (pp. 105–140). Kluwer.
Kruger, J., & Dunning, D. (1999). Unskilled and unaware of it: how difficulties in recognizing one's own incompetence lead to inflated self-assessments. *Journal of Personality and Social Psychology, 77*(6), 1121–1134.
Langlois, R. N. (2007). The entrepreneurial theory of the firm and the theory of the entrepreneurial firm. *Journal of Management Studies, 44*(7), 1107–1124.

Lee, B., O'Brien, J., & Sivaramakrishnan, K. (2008). An analysis of financial analysts' optimism in long-term growth forecasts. *Journal of Behavioral Finance, 9*(3), 171–184.

Loveridge, D. (2009). *Foresight: the art and science of anticipating the future*. Routledge.

Maitland, E., & Sammartino, A. (2015). Managerial cognition and internationalization. *Journal of International Business Studies, 46*(7), 733–760.

March, J. G., & Simon, H. A. (1958). *Organizations*. Wiley.

McCarthy, A. M., Schoorman, F. D., & Cooper, A. C. (1993). Reinvestment decisions by entrepreneurs: rational decision-making or escalation of commitment? *Journal of Business Venturing, 8*(1), 9–24.

Mcmullen, J. S., & Shepherd, D. A. (2006). Entrepreneurial action and the role of uncertainty in the theory of the entrepreneur. *Academy of Management Journal, 31*(1), 132–152.

Melén, S., & Nordman, E. R. (2009). The internationalisation modes of born globals: a longitudinal study. *European Management Journal, 27*(4), 243–254.

Mitchell, R. K., Busenitz, L. W., Morse, E. A., & Smith, J. B. (2007). The central question in entrepreneurial cognition research 2007. *Entrepreneurship: Theory and Practice, 806*, 1–27.

Mudambi, R. (2005). *Branding time: swatch and global brand management*. Temple University.

Niittymies, A., & Pajunen, K. (2019). Cognitive foundations of firm internationalization: a systematic review and agenda for future research. *International Business Review, 29*, 101654.

North, K., & Kares, S. (2005). Ragusa or how to measure ignorance: the ignorance meter. In *Intellectual capital for communities* (pp. 253–264). Elsevier.

Nummela, N., Vissak, T., & Francioni, B. (2020). The interplay of entrepreneurial and non-entrepreneurial internationalization: an illustrative case of an Italian SME. *International Entrepreneurship and Management Journal, 1*, 1–31.

Oviatt, B. M., & McDougall, P. P. (2005a). Toward a theory of international new ventures. *Journal of International Business Studies, 36*(1), 29–41.

Oviatt, B. M., & McDougall, P. P. (2005b). Defining international entrepreneurship and modeling the speed of internationalization. *Entrepreneurship: Theory and Practice, 29*(5), 537–554.

Packard, D., Clark, B. B., & Klein, P. G. (2017). Organization science uncertainty types and transitions in the entrepreneurial process. *Organization Science, 28*, 1–17.

Petersen, B., Pedersen, T., & Lyles, M. A. (2008). Closing knowledge gaps in foreign markets. *Journal of International Business Studies, 39*(7), 1097–1113.

Proctor, R. N., & Schiebinger, L. (2008). *Agnotology: the making and unmaking of ignorance*. Stanford University Press Stanford.

Roberts, J. (2015). Organizational ignorance. In *Routledge handbook of behavioral economics* (pp. 361–169). Routledge.

Roberts, J., & Armitage, J. (2008). The ignorance economy. *Prometheus: Critical Studies in Innovation, 24*(4), 335–354.

Roy, D., & Zeckhauser, R. (2015). The anatomy of ignorance: diagnoses from literature. In *Routledge international handbook of ignorance studies* (pp. 61–73). Routledge.

Roy, D., & Zeckhauser, R. (2017). Ignorance: literary light on decision's dark corner. In *Routledge handbook of behavioral economics* (pp. 230–249). Routledge.

Rugman, A. M., & Verbeke, A. (2003). Multinational enterprises and clusters: an organizing framework. *Governing Knowledge-Processes, 43*, 151–169.

Rumsfeld, D. (2011). *Known and unknown: a memoir*. Sentinel.

Samuelson, W., & Zeckhauser, R. (1988). Status quo bias in decision making. *Journal of Risk and Uncertainty, 1*, 7–59.

Sarasvathy, S. D. (2008). New horizons in entrepreneurship. In *Effectuation: elements of entrepreneurial expertise*. Edward Elgar Publishing.

Sarasvathy, S., Kumar, K., York, J. G., & Bhagavatula, S. (2014). An effectual approach to international entrepreneurship: overlaps, challenges, and provocative possibilities. *Entrepreneurship: Theory and Practice, 38*(1), 71–93.

Shepherd, D. A., Mcmullen, J. S., & Deveraux Jennings, P. (2007). The formation of opportunity beliefs: overcoming ignorance and reducing doubt. *Strategic Entrepreneurship Journal, 1*(1–2), 75–95.

Smithson, M. (1985). Toward a social theory of ignorance. *Journal for the Theory of Social Behaviour, 15*(2), 151–172.
Smithson, M. (1989). *Ignorance and uncertainty: Emerging paradigms*. Springer-Verlag.
Smithson, M. (2015). Afterword: ignorance studies. Interdisciplinary, multidisciplinary, and transdisciplinary. In *Routledge international handbook of ignorance studies* (pp. 61–73). Routledge.
Stanovich, K. E., & West, R. F. (2000). Individual differences in reasoning: implications for the rationality debate? *Behavioral and Brain Sciences, 23*(5), 645–665.
Staw, B. M. (1981). The escalation of commitment to a course of action. *Academy of Management Review, 6*(4), 577–587.
Suarez, F. F., & Montes, J. F. (2020). Building organizational resilience. *Harvard Business Review, 2020*, 47–52.
Taleb, N. N. (2007). *The black swan: the impact of the highly improbable*. Random House.
Taylor, B. (1993). *Message and muscle: an interview with Swatch Titan Nicolas Hayek*. Harvard Business Review.
Townsend, D. M., Hunt, R. A., McMullen, J. S., & Sarasvathy, S. D. (2018). Uncertainty, knowledge problems, and entrepreneurial action. *Academy of Management Annals, 12*(2), 659–687.
Tversky, A., & Kahneman, D. (1973). Availability: a heuristic for judging frequency and probability. *Cognitive Psychology, 5*(2), 207–232.
Ungar, S. (2008). Ignorance as an under-identified social problem. *British Journal of Sociology, 59*, 301–326.
Weick, K. E. (1995). *Sensemaking in organizations*. Sage Publication.
Zacharakis, A. L., & Shepherd, D. A. (2001). The nature of information and overconfidence on venture capitalists' decision making. *Journal of Business Venturing, 16*(4), 311–332.
Zaheer, S., & Mosakowski, E. (1997). The dynamics of the liability of foreignness: a global study of survival in financial services. *Strategic Management Journal, 18*(6), 439–463.
Zahoor, N., Al-Tabbaa, O., Khan, Z., & Wood, G. (2020). Collaboration and internationalization of SMEs: insights and recommendations from a systematic review. *International Journal of Management Reviews, 22*(4), 427–456.
Zahra, S. A., Korri, S. J., & Yu, J. (2005). Cognition and international entrepreneurship: implications for research on international opportunity recognition and exploitation. *International Business Review, 14*, 129–146.
Zucchella, A. (2021). International entrepreneurship and the internationalization phenomenon: taking stock, looking ahead. *International Business Review, 30*, 101800.

Bob Bastian is a PhD candidate at the universities of Bergamo and Pavia. He is also a teaching assistant in International Business, and Entrepreneurship, at the University of Pavia and at LUISS in Rome. Previously, Mr. Bastian was a visiting research fellow at the RUG in Groningen. He is also co-proponent for the EURAM entrepreneurship standing track "Entrepreneurial Decision Making and Behaviour". This year, he has been awarded the Manera research grant. His main research interests are focused on entrepreneurial cognition, emotions, and decision-making.

Antonella Zucchella is professor of Marketing and of Circular entrepreneurship at the University of Pavia in Italy. She has been visiting professor in various universities in Europe and the US and visiting researcher at Harvard Business School in 2019. Her research interests are in international entrepreneurship, small business management, sustainability and circular entrepreneurship. She published several articles in international journals and is also author of books on entrepreneurship. She has been awarded by International Business Review for the best article in 2018, she received the Emerald literati award for most outstanding paper in Multinational Business Review in 2017, twice awarded for the best paper in the International Business conference AIB. She has been keynote speaker in several international conferences.

Risk or Opportunity? Exploring the Relationship Between Entrepreneurial Decision and the Use of Equity Crowdfunding Campaigns in Less- and Well-Developed Regions in Italy

Simona Leonelli, Filippo Marchesani, and Francesca Masciarelli

Abstract Entrepreneurial decision-making is a complex area that impacts the creation and development of new ventures and is one of the main subjects of entrepreneurial research. Our study focuses on the impact of regional disparities on the entrepreneurial decision-making process regarding the adoption of alternative funding sources such as crowdfunding. Crowdfunding has recently garnered considerable interest because of its ability to "democratize" access to capital. Using a least-squares method (OLS) and inferential t-test statistics, we analyze how the entrepreneurial decision-making process differs across Italian regions on the adoption of equity crowdfunding campaigns as fundraising tools. Our results show that regional disparities matter in the entrepreneur's decision-making process, pushing it towards alternative tools such as crowdfunding. Overall, we provide evidence that crowdfunding has gained prominence in Italy in recent years and may be a viable option for entrepreneurs operating in less developed regions to bridge the traditional regional disparity gap.

Keywords Entrepreneurial decision-making · Entrepreneurship · Crowdfunding · Equity Crowdfunding · Regional Disparities

S. Leonelli (✉)
Department of Economics and Management, University of Padova, Padua, Italy
e-mail: simona.leonelli@unipd.it

F. Marchesani · F. Masciarelli
Department of Business Administration, University of "G. d'Annunzio" Chieti, Pescara, Italy
e-mail: filippo.marchesani@unich.it; francesca.masciarelli@unich.it

A. Caputo et al. (eds.), *The International Dimension of Entrepreneurial Decision-Making*, Contributions to Management Science,
https://doi.org/10.1007/978-3-030-85950-3_6

1 Introduction

Entrepreneurial decision-making is a complex area that holds an important position in entrepreneurship studies (Shepherd et al., 2015; Vermeulen & Curseuurseu, 2010). The decision-making process is critically important for firms and start-ups in terms of their survival and success. In fact, the entrepreneur's decision-making process influences the way to raise funds and the creation and the development of new ventures which are the main subjects of entrepreneurship research (Maine et al., 2015; Yang & Gabrielsson, 2017). The decision-making process has been analyzed from different perspectives, such as the characteristics of the entrepreneur (Horbach & Jacob, 2018; Neumann et al., 2019), market opportunities (Alam et al., 2020; Vissak et al., 2020) and also the geographical area (Clift et al., 2017; Jankowski, 2009), which will be the focus of our study.

Literature has dealt with the impact of geographic driving forces on entrepreneurial choice and firm development (Horváth & Rabetino, 2019; Sunny & Shu, 2019). The different economic development of the territory and the differences between regions of the same country affect the decision-making process and entrepreneurial strategies (Castelnovo et al., 2020; Horváth & Rabetino, 2019; Smith & Stevens, 2010). Regional disparities increase the distance between well- and less-developed geographical areas and consequently affect entrepreneurial choices. Entrepreneurs must therefore assess their strategies according to the geographic context.

In recent years, several studies have shown that the internationalization process and the increasing use of digital platforms have reduced regional disparities (Caputo et al., 2016). The internationalization process has also directly influenced the strategies of firms entering the global market (Gaur & Kumar, 2010) to find new market opportunities as well as other sources of financing (Smolarski & Kut, 2011). The entrepreneurs operating in a limited geographical context need to search for alternative online sources of financing such as crowdfunding (Belleflamme et al., 2014). According to Mollick's (2014) definition: "Crowdfunding allows founders of for-profit, artistic and cultural ventures to fund their efforts by drawing on relatively small contributions from a relatively large number of individuals using the internet, without standard financial intermediaries" (Mollick, 2014, p. 2). Crowdfunding is a concept that follows technological development and globalization which allows founders of for-profit, cultural, or social projects to request funding from many individuals, often in return for future products or equity. These allow local ecosystems, social-sustainable and start-ups to benefit from the growing trend of alternative funding sources. Thus, crowdfunding provides an environment for local eco-system and early-stage entrepreneurs where they can directly pitch their project to a community of online investors and be funded (Di Pietro, 2020).

We assume that the use of these alternative financial tools such as crowdfunding would allow entrepreneurs to break out of the traditional linkage between the SME and geographical area. In this context, we posit the following research question: Do regional disparities matter in the entrepreneurial decision-making process regarding the adoption of alternative financial sources such as crowdfunding?

The focus is on regional disparities among Italian regions, distinguished into less- and well-developed regions. They are characterized by different levels of uncertainty and high- and low-risk investments. Specifically, we analyze how the adoption of crowdfunding campaigns, in terms of alternative financial sources, differs across Italian regions as a fundraising tool.

Data was collected from the CrowdfoundMe and Mamacrowd platforms, which represent the leading equity crowdfunding marketplaces in Italy. We collected data on 621 projects over the period 2016–2020. By examining the different use of crowdfunding campaigns in well-developed and less developed Italian regions, we report the geographical distribution of crowdfunding projects to understand the impact of regional disparities on the entrepreneurial decision-making process in terms of the search for financial sources.

2 Theoretical Background

2.1 *Entrepreneurial Decision-Making Process in Firm Development*

Entrepreneurs' behaviour and decisions have an impact on Small and Medium-sized Enterprises' (SMEs) choices and performance, and this phenomenon has captured the interest of management scholars (Kollmann & Christofor, 2014; Zivdar et al., 2017). A large number of international studies tend to focus on firm-level characteristics to evaluate the entrepreneurial decision of SMEs in terms of management characteristics (Horbach & Jacob, 2018), innovation (Oliveira & Martins, 2010), financial structure (Akdal, 2011) and human capital investment (Onkelinx et al., 2016).

These characteristics affect entrepreneurial decisions at a different level and influence outcomes and ambitions throughout firm development (Perks & Hughes, 2008). This decision-making process is not only related to the characteristics of the company but also to the personal characteristics of the entrepreneur (Di Zhang & Bruning, 2011). There is a large group of studies that analyze the impact of the entrepreneur's aspects such as background (Tinkler et al., 2015), mindset (McGrath & MacMillan, 2000) and traits (Yan, 2010) on her decision-making process.

Furthermore, an additional element that influences the decision-making process is the impact of geographical area and urban dynamics on the business landscape (Castelnovo et al., 2020; Jankowski, 2009). Several direct factors have an effect on local entrepreneurial development, such as development policies (Malecki, 2009; Scott, 2006) and entrepreneurship promotion strategies (Bacq & Janssen, 2011). At the same time, the territory affects the decision-making process by offering opportunities and limits to the entrepreneur (Maroufkhani et al., 2018) and creating different scenarios and various conditions that enable the entrepreneur to choose the most impactful factors for the strategies and development of the firm (Vaillant & Lafuente, 2007). For example, there are many studies examining the weight that differences between countries and geographical areas have in the entrepreneur's decision-making process (García-Cabrera et al., 2016; Shepherd et al., 2015). However, only a few studies show the impact of location in explaining entrepreneurial decision-making, for example in fundraising and business strategies, especially in the context of regional disparities.

2.2 *The Role of Regional Disparities on SMEs' Choices*

Economic disparities between regions have been studied in different research fields such as employment (Filippetti et al., 2019), productivity (Castelnovo et al., 2020), human capital (Fonseca, 2017), and have grown significantly in the explanation and promotion of entrepreneurship (Muñoz & Kimmitt, 2019). Regional disparities also exist in well-developed countries and show differences in innovation and economic development at the regional level (Fratesi & Percoco, 2014). For example, in examining the Italian case, many differences have emerged in recent decades, related to innovation (Min et al., 2020), economic development (Gagliardi & Percoco, 2011) and employment (Ciriaci & Muscio, 2014).

Regional differences persist in a variety of contexts and are gaining importance for academic research and policymakers (Castelnovo et al., 2020; Filippetti et al., 2019; Fonseca, 2017). Regional disparities impact the region's own economy and local strategic enterprise development (Stuetzer et al., 2014). However, this difference is decreasing as a result of globalization and the world market. Recent studies have shown that SMEs' internationalization and digitalization can reduce regional disparities (Caputo et al., 2016). SMEs' digitalization and entrepreneurs' use of digital platforms can strongly impact firms' opportunity to operate in international markets (Neubert, 2018), expand the market (Gaur & Kumar, 2010) and find alternative financial sources (Smolarski & Kut, 2011). Therefore, entrepreneurs operating in a limited geographical context in terms of economic development, due to difficulties in raising capital may search for alternative online sources of financing such as crowdfunding (Belleflamme et al., 2014; Mollick, 2014).

2.3 *Crowdfunding as Entrepreneurial Financial Source*

Crowdfunding is "an online open call for financial resources either in the form of donation or in exchange for some form of reward and/or voting rights in order to support initiatives for specific purposes" (Schwienbacher & Larralde, 2010, p. 7).

The increasing development of crowdfunding is mainly related to the globalization process and to the need for start-ups and SMEs to get new credit and other funding sources (Langley & Leyshon, 2017). The main factor in the growth of crowdfunding is represented by the technological innovation of Web 2.0, which has allowed internet users to generate online content and share it with other users, making crowdfunding effectively viable (Kirby & Worner, 2014). In practice, crowdfunding can take different forms such as donation-based crowdfunding, rewards-based crowdfunding, debt-based crowdfunding and equity-based crowdfunding (Belleflamme et al., 2014). We focus on equity-based crowdfunding that represents the main form of a crowdfunding campaign in terms of capital and financing. As defined by Ahlers et al. (2015, p. 955): "Equity crowdfunding (ECF) is a form of financing in which entrepreneurs make an open call to sell a specified amount of equity or bond-like shares in a company on the Internet, hoping to attract a large group of investors". The open call and investments take place on an online platform (such as Mamacrowd, CrowdfundMe) that connects investors and entrepreneurs worldwide.

Over the years, crowdfunding has grown considerably due to its ability to bridge the gap between entrepreneurs and crowds and to democratize access to capital (Cumming et al., 2019; Troise & Tani, 2020). This has resulted in a viable option for entrepreneurs who face challenges in accessing traditional financing channels (Kim & Hann, 2013).

Over time, rapid technological development has reduced boundaries and distances and investors are now allocating far more risk financing via online equity crowdfunding platforms (Brown et al., 2020). Simultaneously, entrepreneurs have started to strategically approach ECF not only to raise funds but also as a marketing approach to engage the crowd by generating visibility, contract and feedback (Di Pietro et al., 2018).

We assume that crowdfunding allows us to move from the local context to the global marketplace. However, interesting relationships exist between territory and crowdfunding; a large stream of literature examines the impact of geographic position on campaign success, recognizing the importance of localization (Giudici et al., 2018; Josefy et al., 2017).

Previous studies suggest that although crowdfunding reduces the distance between local and global contexts (Ahlers et al., 2015), the geographical location also influences crowdfunding outcomes. The impact of the geographical proximity of crowdfunding campaigns to banks lies almost entirely in projects that are less attractive to the local population, whereas online projects are virtually immune to the competition between online crowdfunding and offline banks (Kim & Hann, 2013).

Localization effects also have an impact on successful campaigns due to local altruism or the promotion of projects sharing values with local communities (Josefy et al., 2017). For example, Giudici et al. (2018) show that the characteristics of the geographical area where entrepreneurs reside affect the success of the crowdfunding projects they propose. By analyzing reward-based entrepreneurial projects, they also note that the existence of social relationships between people residing in a specific geographical area increases the likelihood of success of the campaigns themselves.

Research on the relationship between crowdfunding and geographical area mainly focuses on investor decisions and campaign success factors (Ahlers et al.,

2015; Block et al., 2018; Lukkarinen et al., 2016; Nix-Stevenson, 2013; Vismara, 2018), while little is known about the reason why entrepreneurs decide to use alternative financial sources such as ECF campaigns in the context of regional disparities.

Most of the studies on crowdfunding have been developed in advanced economies that are relatively homogenous from an institutional, regulatory and cultural perspective (Bapna, 2019; Fornes & Cardoza, 2019; Giudici et al., 2013). However, even in the context of well-developed countries, there are internal disparities that can influence several aspects such as SMEs' strategies (Giudici & Rossi-Lamastra, 2018) and financial assets (Mollick, 2014).

Specifically, regional differences in market and economic structure can influence investments and crowdsourcing, which may either reinforce or offset the effects of geographical agglomeration (Filippetti et al., 2019). Firms are expected to operate more in the crowdfunding market when local markets are less responsive, which would generally be the case in economically less developed regions. At the same time, more economically and technologically developed regions are also more responsive to the use of financial and strategic instruments detached from traditional ones (Di Pietro & Butticè, 2020; Vassallo, 2016).

Therefore, we expect that the adoption of a tool such as crowdfunding in less developed regions to be less affected by regional disparities as a consequence of the 'democratizing' role that crowdfunding plays on the financial market (Kim & Hann, 2013). Aiming to evaluate the role of regional disparities in the entrepreneurial decision-making process in raising capitals, we posit:

Hypothesis: *Less developed regions are more likely to adopt alternative financing sources such as crowdfunding.*

3 Methodology

3.1 Sample and Data Collection

We collected data on 621 ECF campaigns launched on Mamacrowd and CrowdfundMe, two leading Italian ECF platforms, focusing on 20 Italian regions over a five-year period (from 2016 to 2020). We decided to focus on these platforms because they are respectively ranked first and second in the Italian ECF market in terms of transaction volume and number of campaigns. Both platforms are authorized by the Italian Securities Exchange Commission "Consob" and support innovative start-ups and SMEs by allowing the crowd to invest in ground-breaking Italian projects. Our data considered the adoption of ECF campaigns in the regions over the years.

In terms of regional information on economic development and innovation, we used the database of the Italian National Institute of Statistics (ISTAT) and the Chambers of Commerce. We employed ISTAT's database on "Territorial indicators for development policies" to evaluate economic indicators such as GDP and R&D

investment and the database of the Italian Chambers of Commerce to gain information about firm registration in each region over the years.

To distinguish between less developed and well-developed Italian regions, we considered the recent Italian Government and European Union ranking of regional development between 2014 and 2020. The European Union has used this division to allocate structural and investment funds and resources for economic, social, technological and territorial development. In the breakdown, less-developed regions are those with GDP per capita below 75% of the EU average, regions in transition are those with GDP per capita between 75% and 90%, and well-developed regions are those whose GDP per capita exceeds 90% of the EU average.

According to this ranking, the least developed regions are Basilicata, Calabria, Campania, Apulia and Sicily. The "transition" regions between less developed and well-developed ones are Abruzzo, Molise and Sardinia, while the others (i.e. Emilia-Romagna, Friuli-Venezia Giulia, Lazio, Liguria, Lombardy, Marche, Piemonte, Sardinia, Sicily, Tuscany, Trentino-South Tyrol, Umbria, Valle d'Aosta and Veneto), located mainly in central and northern Italy, are considered developed. We merged less developed and transition regions in our sample to oppose them to the developed ones and to highlight the different economic development between them, and we called the two sides less developed and well-developed regions.

3.2 *Operationalization of the Variable*

The dependent variable is called *CF_Campaign* and represents the total number of crowdfunding campaigns per Italian region. It is a continuous variable measured by the logarithm of the ratio of crowdfunding campaigns in each region to the total number of firms in the respective region. This variable is usually used to assess the adoption of crowdfunding campaigns and allows us to understand the adoption of these alternative financial tools in the local context (Lukkarinen et al., 2016; Piva & Rossi-Lamastra, 2018).

The independent variable in our model is called Total_Firms. Total_Firms is a continuous variable indicating the total number of companies listed in the Chamber of Commerce register. In the context of crowd-sourcing and regional development, the total number of firms operating in each region helps us to understand the current usage of crowdfunding campaigns based on possible users such as entrepreneurs and firms operating in each region. Total firms in the region as well as GDP per capita represent an economic indicator of each Italian region and a measure of the market value of regional economic development (Sternberg & Arndt, 2001; Yang et al., 2011).

In the regression model, we controlled for several factors at both the regional and crowdfunding level that can predict regional development. All variables are continuous variables, and the model specification includes the following indicator as a control variable. In Public R&D, we looked at each region's R&D expenditures relative to the population of the region itself. This variable is used to estimate the impact of public R&D in the technological and commercial value of regional innovation (Czarnitzki & Licht, 2006; Min et al., 2020). As for the development of start-up companies in each region, we considered the number of New Firms founded in a given year over the total of active companies by considering their registration with the Chamber of Commerce. The role of new firm birth is crucial to regional economic development efforts, since a high level of new firm creation significantly contributes to regional economic vitality and is a major sign of a dynamic economy (Lee et al., 2004). Finally, to have a better understanding of the role of crowdfunding development we also considered the investors' variable based on the total number of investors in ECF campaigns in each region. Most previous studies in this stream used the investors' variable to assess the quality of crowdfunding campaigns and their impact on the market (Bapna, 2019; Barbi & Mattioli, 2019; Cumming et al., 2019).

4 Results

The study was conducted using the ordinary least-squares method (OLS) and inferential t-test statistics to analyze the entrepreneurial decision-making process in the context of regional disparities.

We have a panel dataset consisting of 621 crowdfunding campaigns, including 47 campaigns from 2016, 109 campaigns from 2017, 124 campaigns from 2018, 155 campaigns from 2019 and 186 campaigns from 2020. Table 1 reports the descriptive statistics and inferential statistics of the t-test that were used to analyze the difference between less- and well-developed regions in our sample.

As we can see from Table 1, the difference between these two groups also emerges from a paired t-test. The results reveal significant differences between less- and well-developed Italian regions with respect to the use of crowdfunding campaigns ($p = 0.003$), the total number of firms in those areas ($p = 0.044$), the number of new firms' creation ($p = 0.034$), and the amount of R&D expenditure ($p = 0.036$). The values of these variables are slightly higher in well-developed regions than in less developed ones, although we had more observations in the well-developed sample.

Table 2 reports the correlation matrix of our model. We checked for possible multicollinearity issues. As we can see from Table 2, the variables public R&D display a correlation coefficient higher than 0.7, namely 0.788 and 0.867. We also ran the regressions excluding public R&D and all results were confirmed.

To assess potential multicollinearity, we computed the variance inflation factor (VIFs). For each model in Table 3, the mean and maximum VIF are well below the threshold of 3.2. We, therefore, concluded that multicollinearity is not a threat to the validity of our results.

Table 3 reports the empirical results of our model. In detail, column (1) reports our results for the total sample, while columns (2) and (3) are related to under- and

Table 1 Descriptive statistics and *t*-test

Variables	Obs.	Mean	Std. Dev.	95% Confidence interval for the difference		*p*
				Lower	Upper	
CF_Campaigns						
Total sample	100	6.370	13.542	4.191	8.548	
Less developed regions	40	2.500	10.981	1.739	3.056	
Well-developed regions	60	8.950	1.739	5.451	12.448	
Less vs well-developed regions	–	6.450	9.242	10.729	2.170	0.003***
Tot_Firms						
Total sample	100	266,646.728	256,528.112	221,301.214	311,992.265	
Less developed regions	40	210,426.147	228,531.214	157,276.922	263,575.348	
Well-developed regions	60	304,127.112	166,186.975	237,858.879	370,395.337	
Less- vs well-developed regions	–	93,700.970	62,344.239	184,829.258	2572.732	0.044*
Investors						
Total sample	100	187.340	431.861	118.167	2565.126	
Less-developed regions	40	97.325	348.614	61.558	133.091	
Well-developed regions	60	247.359	111.936	135.788	358.911	
Less- vs well-developed regions	–	15.025	236.378	288.736	11.313	0.061
New_Firms						
Total sample	100	16,438.633	2054.642	13,595.246	19,282.021	
Less-developed regions	40	13,467.981	14,330.035	9921.047	17,014.688	
Well-developed regions	60	18,419.071	1753.569	14,307.744	22,530.315	
Less- vs well-developed regions	–	4951.092	12,579.466	10,700.374	798.185	0.034*
Public R&D						
Total sample	100	244,214.212	267,494.243	195,289.345	293,138.739	
Less-developed regions	40	181,156.871	246,567.325	117,769.334	244,544.231	
Well-developed regions	60	286,252.633	198,200.236	217,151.398	355,353.718	
Less- vs well-developed regions	–	105,095.811	48,366.595	203,247.749	6943.897	0.036*

$^{*}p < 0.05$; $^{**}p < 0.01$; $^{***}p < 0.001$

Table 2 Correlation matrix

	Variable	[1]	[2]	[3]	[4]	[5]
[1]	CF_Campaign	1				
[2]	Tot_Firms	0.154	1			
[3]	Investors	0.385	−0.156	1		
[4]	New_Firms	−0.331	−0.690*	−0.340*	1	
[5]	PublicR&D	0.788	−0.043	0.193	−0.867*	−0.097

Notes: All variables are in logarithmic form

Table 3 Regression model

	(1) Total sample		(2) Under-developed		(3) Well-developed	
DV: CF_Campaigns	Model I	Model II	Model III	Model IV	Model V	Model VI
Tot_Firms		2.863*		6.034***		5.861*
		[1.687]		[1.854]		[2.398]
Investors	0.299***	0.339***	0.228**	0.284***	0.592**	0.493**
	[0.062]	[0.058]	[0.092]	[0.075]	[1.237]	[0.071]
New_Firms	0.053	2.705*	0.027	2.902*	0.411	4.891*
	[0.916]	[1.407]	[1.169]	[1.143]	[0.043]	[2.044]
PublicR&D	0.538	0.305***	0.138*	0.528***	0.337**	0.255***
	[0.216]	[0.073]	[0.122]	[0.059]	[0.411]	[0.071]
No. Of Observation	100	100	40	40	60	60
R-squared	0.821	0.683	0.812	0.764	0.456	0.752
Adj R-squared	0.698	0.578	0.788	0.712	0.409	0.671

Notes: DV = dependent variable. *$p < 0.050$; **$p < 0.010$; ***$p < 0.001$
All variables are in logarithmic form
Standard error in brackets

well-developed regions, respectively. Models I, III, and V only include the control variables, while Models II, IV, and VI add the independent variable.

Model II shows a positive and significant relationship between the total number of companies and the use of crowdfunding campaigns ($\beta = 2.863$, $p < 0.05$). This relationship is also significant in Model IV and Model VI. In detail, Model IV illustrates the positive and significant relationship between the total number of companies and the use of crowdfunding campaigns in less developed regions ($\beta = 6.034$, $p < 0.001$). Model VI shows the same relationship in well-developed regions ($\beta = 5.861$, $p < 0.05$). However, the relationship between the total number of companies and the use of crowdfunding campaigns is stronger in less developed regions than in well-developed ones, allowing us to accept Hypothesis 1, suggesting that firms located in less developed regions are more likely to adopt alternative financing sources such as crowdfunding.

5 Discussion and Conclusion

We examined the role of regional disparities in the entrepreneurial decision-making process and their impact on financing through ECF. We found that the entrepreneurial decision-making process over time was independent of regional disparities and economic development in the region itself. Until a few years ago, geographic distance mattered for small business lending; however, in recent years, technology has reduced the dependence of small businesses on local lenders (Alessandrini et al., 2009; Sun et al., 2019). Technological development has enabled SMEs as well as entrepreneurs and local projects to have national and international development following the internationalization process, which has also allowed local companies to enter a globally competitive environment for business strategies or fundraising (Kim & Hann, 2013; Agrawal et al., 2015).

Following this relationship, crowdfunding potentially changes the nature of geography and association in new ventures. To a certain extent at least, crowdfunding reduces the importance of traditional geographic constraints and regional disparities, although it potentially imposes new ones such as the technological gap. The innovative ability of online communities and the local area has been of increasing interest to scholars (Bodolica et al., 2019; Leckel et al., 2020; Williams & Cothrel, 2000), and crowdfunding represents a concrete way in which online communities can influence the creation of new ventures (Mollick, 2014). This fosters the "democratizing" power of crowdfunding in accessing credit, allowing us to overcome the traditional connection between entrepreneur and territory and expand into the national and international context.

Regarding the role of crowdfunding, the analysis of our case in Italy highlights two crucial findings. On the one hand, it confirms the growth in the use of ECF in Italy in recent years and its spreading to all regions of Italy. On the other hand, it appears that less developed regions, which offer fewer opportunities and fewer entrepreneurial choices (Khoury & Prasad, 2016; Naude et al., 2008), turn more to tools such as crowdfunding than more developed regions in proportion to the number of entrepreneurs and the number of companies.

Our paper contributes to the existing literature on crowdfunding and entrepreneurial decision-making as it confirms that crowdfunding diffusion across regions and countries also differs in terms of economic development and national institutional environments (Di Pietro & Butticè, 2020). These aspects have implications for future research but also suggest various limitations in terms of data and sample.

Less developed regions could promote the adoption of crowdfunding as a strategic and financial tool to support local development. This opportunity affects the entrepreneurial decision-making process in terms of crowdsourcing and firm development and helps to overcome the constraint of the local context by facilitating financing and stakeholder engagement (Langley & Leyshon, 2017). Thus, crowdfunding may help reduce regional disparities and open up new opportunities and perspectives to local firms. Future research could analyze this relationship by evaluating the measures and regional policies to support innovation and internationalization process in regions.

We conclude by pointing out the limits of the research. In terms of data, we could only refer to a 9-year period. To obtain more precise data, future research might extend the time frame over the years considered by also evaluating the influence of COVID-19. As regards our sample, we based our study on Italian regions. Future research might replicate this study in other countries, even those that are less economically developed than Italy, to provide a more comprehensive overview of the use of this tool in contexts of economic and social disparity.

References

Agrawal, A., Catalini, C., & Goldfarb, A. (2015). Crowdfunding: geography, social networks, and the timing of investment decisions. *Journal of Economics & Management Strategy, 24*(2), 253–274.

Ahlers, G. K., Cumming, D., Günther, C., & Schweizer, D. (2015). Signaling in equity crowdfunding. *Entrepreneurship Theory and Practice, 39*(4), 955–980.

Akdal, S. (2011). How do firm characteristics affect capital structure? Some UK evidence. *SSRN*. http://ssrn.com/abstract=1775706

Alam, M. N., Masroor, I., & Nabi, M. N. U. (2020). Does entrepreneurs' risk perception influence firm's rapidity in foreign market entry through moderation of entrepreneurial decision-making approach? *Review of International Business and Strategy., 30*(2), 225–243.

Alessandrini, P., Presbitero, A. F., & Zazzaro, A. (2009). Banks, distances and firms' financing constraints. *Review of Finance, 13*(2), 261–307.

Bacq, S., & Janssen, F. (2011). The multiple faces of social entrepreneurship: A review of definitional issues based on geographical and thematic criteria. *Entrepreneurship & Regional Development, 23*(5–6), 373–403.

Bapna, S. (2019). Complementarity of signals in early-stage equity investment decisions: Evidence from a randomized field experiment. *Management Science, 65*(2), 933–952.

Barbi, M., & Mattioli, S. (2019). Human capital, investor trust, and equity crowdfunding. *Research in International Business and Finance, 49*, 1–12.

Belleflamme, P., Lambert, T., & Schwienbacher, A. (2014). Crowdfunding: Tapping the right crowd. *Journal of Business Venturing, 29*(5), 585–609.

Block, J., Hornuf, L., & Moritz, A. (2018). Which updates during an equity crowdfunding campaign increase crowd participation? *Small Business Economics, 50*(1), 3–27.

Bodolica, V., Spraggon, M., & Soueid, M. A. (2019). Innovation drivers and trends in the retail industry: An application to emerging markets and the case of the Gulf region. *International Journal of Comparative Management, 2*(1), 51–66.

Brown, R., Rocha, A., & Cowling, M. (2020). <? covid19?> Financing entrepreneurship in times of crisis: Exploring the impact of COVID-19 on the market for entrepreneurial finance in the United Kingdom. *International Small Business Journal, 38*(5), 380–390.

Caputo, A., Pellegrini, M. M., Dabic, M., & Dana, L. P. (2016). Internationalisation of firms from Central and Eastern Europe: A systematic literature review. *European Business Review, 28*(6), 630–651.

Castelnovo, P., Morretta, V., & Vecchi, M. (2020). Regional disparities and industrial structure: Territorial capital and productivity in Italian firms. *Regional Studies, 54*(12), 1709–1723.

Ciriaci, D., & Muscio, A. (2014). University choice, research quality and graduates' employability: Evidence from Italian national survey data. *European Educational Research Journal, 13*(2), 199–219.

Clift, R., Sim, S., King, H., Chenoweth, J. L., Christie, I., Clavreul, J., Mueller, C., Posthuma, L., Boulay, A.-M., Chaplin-Kramer, R., Chatterton, J., DeClerck, F., Druckman, A., France, C., Franco, A., Gerten, D., Goedkoop, M., Hauschild, M. Z., Huijbregts, M. A. J., . . . Murphy, R. (2017). The challenges of applying planetary boundaries as a basis for strategic decision-making in companies with global supply chains. *Sustainability, 9*(2), 279.

Cumming, D., Deloof, M., Manigart, S., & Wright, M. (2019). New directions in entrepreneurial finance. *Journal of Banking & Finance, 100*, 252–260.

Czarnitzki, D., & Licht, G. (2006). Additionality of public R&D grants in a transition economy: The case of Eastern Germany. *The Economics of Transition, 14*(1), 101–131.

Di Pietro, F. (2020). *Crowdfunding for entrepreneurs: Developing strategic advantage through entrepreneurial finance*. Routledge.

Di Pietro, F., & Butticè, V. (2020). Institutional characteristics and the development of crowdfunding across countries. *International Review of Financial Analysis, 71*, 101543.

Di Pietro, F., Prencipe, A., & Majchrzak, A. (2018). Crowd equity investors: An underutilized asset for open innovation in startups. *California Management Review, 60*(2), 43–70.

Di Zhang, D., & Bruning, E. (2011). Personal characteristics and strategic orientation: Entrepreneurs in Canadian manufacturing companies. *International Journal of Entrepreneurial Behavior & Research, 17*(1), 82–103.

Filippetti, A., Guy, F., & Iammarino, S. (2019). Regional disparities in the effect of training on employment. *Regional Studies, 53*(2), 217–230.

Fonseca, M. (2017). Southern Europe at a glance: Regional disparities and human capital. In *Regional upgrading in Southern Europe* (pp. 19–54). Springer.

Fornes, G., & Cardoza, G. (2019). Internationalization of Chinese SMEs: The perception of disadvantages of foreignness. *Emerging Markets Finance and Trade, 55*(9), 2086–2105.

Fratesi, U., & Percoco, M. (2014). Selective migration, regional growth and convergence: Evidence from Italy. *Regional Studies, 48*(10), 1650–1668.

Gagliardi, L., & Percoco, M. (2011). Regional disparities in Italy over the long run: The role of human capital and trade policy. *Région et Développement, 33*, 81–105.

García-Cabrera, A. M., García-Soto, M. G., & Durán-Herrera, J. J. (2016). Opportunity motivation and SME internationalisation in emerging countries: Evidence from entrepreneurs' perception of institutions. *International Entrepreneurship and Management Journal, 12*(3), 879–910.

Gaur, A., & Kumar, V. (2010). Internationalization of emerging market firms: A case for theoretical extension. In *The past, present and future of international business & management (advances in international management, Vol. 23)* (pp. 603–627). Emerald Group Publishing Limited.

Giudici, G., Guerini, M., & Rossi Lamastra, C. (2013). Why crowdfunding projects can succeed: The role of proponents' individual and territorial social capital. SSRN working paper no. 2255944. Accessed January 13, 2020, from https://ssrn.com/abstract52255944

Giudici, G., Guerini, M., & Rossi-Lamastra, C. (2018). Reward-based crowdfunding of entrepreneurial projects: The effect of local altruism and localized social capital on proponents' success. *Small Business Economics, 50*(2), 307–324.

Giudici, G., & Rossi-Lamastra, C. (2018). *Crowdfunding of SMEs and startups: When open investing follows open innovation* (pp. 377–396). World Scientific Book Chapters.

Horbach, J., & Jacob, J. (2018). The relevance of personal characteristics and gender diversity for (eco-) innovation activities at the firm-level: Results from a linked employer–employee database in Germany. *Business Strategy and the Environment, 27*(7), 924–934.

Horváth, K., & Rabetino, R. (2019). Knowledge-intensive territorial servitization: Regional driving forces and the role of the entrepreneurial ecosystem. *Regional Studies, 53*(3), 330–340.

Jankowski, P. (2009). Towards participatory geographic information systems for community-based environmental decision making. *Journal of Environmental Management, 90*(6), 1966–1971.

Josefy, M., Dean, T. J., Albert, L. S., & Fitza, M. A. (2017). The role of community in crowdfunding success: Evidence on cultural attributes in funding campaigns to "save the local theater". *Entrepreneurship Theory and Practice, 41*(2), 161–182.

Khoury, T. A., & Prasad, A. (2016). Entrepreneurship amid concurrent institutional constraints in less developed countries. *Business & Society, 55*(7), 934–969.

Kim, K., & Hann, I. H. (2013). Does crowdfunding democratize access to capital? A geographical analysis. In *INFORMS conference on information systems and technology (CIST)*. Virginia.

Kirby, E., & Worner, S. (2014). *Crowd-funding: An infant industry growing fast*. IOSCO Research Department.

Kollmann, T., & Christofor, J. (2014). International entrepreneurship in the network economy: Internationalization propensity and the role of entrepreneurial orientation. *Journal of International Entrepreneurship, 12*(1), 43–66.

Langley, P., & Leyshon, A. (2017). Platform capitalism: The intermediation and capitalization of digital economic circulation. *Finance and society, 3*(1), 11–31.

Leckel, A., Veilleux, S., & Dana, L. P. (2020). Local open innovation: A means for public policy to increase collaboration for innovation in SMEs. *Technological Forecasting and Social Change, 153*, 119891.

Lee, S. Y., Florida, R., & Acs, Z. (2004). Creativity and entrepreneurship: A regional analysis of new firm formation. *Regional Studies, 38*(8), 879–891.

Lukkarinen, A., Teich, J. E., Wallenius, H., & Wallenius, J. (2016). Success drivers of online equity crowdfunding campaigns. *Decision Support Systems, 87*, 26–38.

Maine, E., Soh, P. H., & Dos Santos, N. (2015). The role of entrepreneurial decision-making in opportunity creation and recognition. *Technovation, 39*, 53–72.

Malecki, E. J. (2009). Geographical environments for entrepreneurship. *International Journal of Entrepreneurship and Small Business, 7*(2), 175–190.

Maroufkhani, P., Wagner, R., & Ismail, W. K. W. (2018). Entrepreneurial ecosystems: A systematic review. *Journal of Enterprising Communities: People and Places in the Global Economy, 12*(4), 545–564.

McGrath, R. G., & MacMillan, I. C. (2000). *The entrepreneurial mindset: Strategies for continuously creating opportunity in an age of uncertainty* (Vol. 284). Harvard Business Press.

Min, S., Kim, J., & Sawng, Y. W. (2020). The effect of innovation network size and public R&D investment on regional innovation efficiency. *Technological Forecasting and Social Change, 155*, 119998.

Mollick, E. (2014). The dynamics of crowdfunding: An exploratory study. *Journal of Business Venturing, 29*(1), 1–16.

Muñoz, P., & Kimmitt, J. (2019). Rural entrepreneurship in place: An integrated framework. *Entrepreneurship & Regional Development, 31*(9–10), 842–873.

Naude, W., Gries, T., Wood, E., & Meintjies, A. (2008). Regional determinants of entrepreneurial start-ups in a developing country. *Entrepreneurship and Regional Development, 20*(2), 111–124.

Neubert, M. (2018). The impact of digitalization on the speed of internationalization of lean global startups. *Technology Innovation Management Review, 8*(5), 44–54.

Neumann, O., Matt, C., Hitz-Gamper, B. S., Schmidthuber, L., & Stürmer, M. (2019). Joining forces for public value creation? Exploring collaborative innovation in smart city initiatives. *Government Information Quarterly, 36*(4), 101411.

Nix-Stevenson, D. (2013). Human response to natural disasters. *SAGE Open, 3*(3), 2158244013489684.

Oliveira, T., & Martins, M. F. (2010). Information technology adoption models at firm level: Review of literature. In *The European conference on information systems management* (p. 312). Academic Conferences International Limited.

Onkelinx, J., Manolova, T. S., & Edelman, L. F. (2016). The human factor: Investments in employee human capital, productivity, and SME internationalization. *Journal of International Management, 22*(4), 351–364.

Perks, K. J., & Hughes, M. (2008). Entrepreneurial decision-making in internationalization: Propositions from mid-size firms. *International Business Review, 17*(3), 310–330.

Piva, E., & Rossi-Lamastra, C. (2018). Human capital signals and entrepreneurs' success in equity crowdfunding. *Small Business Economics, 51*(3), 667–686.

Schwienbacher, A., & Larralde, B. (2010). *Crowdfunding of small entrepreneurial ventures. Handbook of entrepreneurial finance*. Oxford University Press.

Scott, A. J. (2006). Entrepreneurship, innovation and industrial development: Geography and the creative field revisited. *Small Business Economics, 26*(1), 1–24.

Shepherd, D. A., Williams, T. A., & Patzelt, H. (2015). Thinking about entrepreneurial decision making: Review and research agenda. *Journal of Management, 41*(1), 11–46.

Smith, B. R., & Stevens, C. E. (2010). Different types of social entrepreneurship: The role of geography and embeddedness on the measurement and scaling of social value. *Entrepreneurship and Regional Development, 22*(6), 575–598.

Smolarski, J., & Kut, C. (2011). The impact of venture capital financing method on SME performance and internationalization. *International Entrepreneurship and Management Journal, 7*(1), 39–55.

Sternberg, R., & Arndt, O. (2001). The firm or the region: What determines the innovation behavior of European firms? *Economic Geography, 77*(4), 364–382.

Stuetzer, M., Obschonka, M., Brixy, U., Sternberg, R., & Cantner, U. (2014). Regional characteristics, opportunity perception and entrepreneurial activities. *Small Business Economics, 42*(2), 221–244.

Sun, W., Li, Q., & Li, B. (2019). Does geographic distance have a significant impact on enterprise financing costs? *Journal of Geographical Sciences, 29*(12), 1965–1980.

Sunny, S. A., & Shu, C. (2019). Investments, incentives, and innovation: Geographical clustering dynamics as drivers of sustainable entrepreneurship. *Small Business Economics, 52*(4), 905–927.

Tinkler, J. E., Whittington, K. B., Ku, M. C., & Davies, A. R. (2015). Gender and venture capital decision-making: The effects of technical background and social capital on entrepreneurial evaluations. *Social Science Research, 51*, 1–16.

Troise, C., & Tani, M. (2020). *Exploring entrepreneurial characteristics, motivations and behaviours in equity crowdfunding: Some evidence from Italy*. Management Decision.

Vaillant, Y., & Lafuente, E. (2007). Do different institutional frameworks condition the influence of local fear of failure and entrepreneurial examples over entrepreneurial activity? *Entrepreneurship and Regional Development, 19*(4), 313–337.

Vassallo, W. (Ed.). (2016). Crowdfunding for sustainable entrepreneurship and innovation. IGI Global.

Vermeulen, P. A. M., & Curseuurseu, P. L. (Eds.). (2010). Entrepreneurial strategic decision-making: A cognitive perspective. Edward Elgar Publishing.

Vismara, S. (2018). Signaling to overcome inefficiencies in crowdfunding markets. In *The economics of crowdfunding* (pp. 29–56). Palgrave Macmillan.

Vissak, T., Francioni, B., & Freeman, S. (2020). Foreign market entries, exits and re-entries: The role of knowledge, network relationships and decision-making logic. *International Business Review, 29*(1), 101592.

Williams, R. L., & Cothrel, J. (2000). Four smart ways to run online communities. *MIT Sloan Management Review, 41*(4), 81–81.

Yan, J. (2010). The impact of entrepreneurial personality traits on perception of new venture opportunity. *New England Journal of Entrepreneurship, 13*(2), 21–35.

Yang, M., & Gabrielsson, P. (2017). Entrepreneurial marketing of international high-tech business-to-business new ventures: A decision-making process perspective. *Industrial Marketing Management, 64*, 147–160.

Yang, M. G. M., Hong, P., & Modi, S. B. (2011). Impact of lean manufacturing and environmental management on business performance: An empirical study of manufacturing firms. *International Journal of Production Economics, 129*(2), 251–261.

Zivdar, M., Imanipour, N., Talebi, K., & Hosseini, S. R. (2017). An explorative study of inputs for entrepreneurs' decision-making to create new venture in a high-tech context. *The International Journal of Entrepreneurship and Innovation, 18*(4), 243–255.

Simona Leonelli is Research Fellow at the University of Padova (Italy). Previously, she was Postdoctoral Research Fellow at the University G. d'Annunzio Chieti-Pescara (Italy) where she received her Ph.D. in Accounting, Management, and Finance in 2017. She was visiting researcher at Skema Business School (Nice—France). Her main research interest lies in the area of Entrepreneurship (i.e. personality traits, individual resilience, start-ups' innovation, entrepreneurial orientation), and Business Organization (i.e. organizational resilience and ambidexterity). She published in numerous journals including: Journal of Small Business and Entrepreneurship and Journal of Entrepreneurship and Small Business. She is the author of two books: "Entrepreneurial Personality and Small Business Management" (Edward Elgard Publishing), and "Sustainable entrepreneurship: How entrepreneurs create value from sustainable opportunities" (Emerald Publishing). She is an adjunct professor of Business Organization, Behavior in Organization, and Organization Design and Governance of Human Capital at the University of Padova.

Filippo Marchesani is a Ph.D. candidate in Accounting, Management and Business Economics and a teaching assistant in the Departments of Management and Business Administration at the University "G. d'Annunzio" of Chieti-Pescara. His research interests focus on Smart City development whit particular attention on the digitalization process, marketing strategies, knowledge spillover, human capital flow and crowdfunding. He has recently published these issues in International Marketing Review. Currently, he is a visiting researcher at the Department of Business Administration and Product Design at the University of Girona (Spain).

Francesca Masciarelli is Associate Professor at the University G. d'Annunzio. She received her Ph.D. from the University of Trento. She was visiting researcher at the Copenhagen Business School (DK) and at the University of Sussex (UK). Her research interests include social capital, management of innovation, and entrepreneurship. She has published on these issues on Organization Science, Journal of International Business Studies, Journal of Business Ethics, Regional Studies, Industry and Innovation, International Marketing Review, and Journal of Small Business and Entrepreneurship. She has also published two books with the Edward Elgard Publishing: "The strategic value of social capital: how firms capitalize on social assets" and "Entrepreneurial personality and small business management" a book with Emerald Publishing, "Sustainable entrepreneurship: How entrepreneurs create value from sustainable opportunities" and a book with Routledge, "Cultural Proximity and Organization: Managing Diversity and Innovation". She is a senior lecturer of Management and Entrepreneurship at the University G.d'Annunzio and LUISS University. She teaches Innovation in Corporate and University Master courses.

The Internationalization of Family SMEs: A Literature Review and Research Agenda

Franco Ernesto Rubino, Claudio Multari, and Giuseppe Valenza

Abstract The chapter intends to stimulate a debate on the internationalization processes of small and medium-sized family businesses (family SMEs), which is a specific topic that business literature has only recently deepened. Several research works are dealing with internationalization strategies, but only a few studies focus on SMEs' internationalization. The chapter aims to discuss the state of the art of the field, which seems to be increasingly explored by academics. Our focus was to identify the factors which can positively or negatively impact SMEs' internationalization processes. Moreover, we intend to fill the research gap in terms of literature review on the field. The methodology is based on a systematic literature review regarding 29 articles published in the last two decades, whilst most of them are written in more recent years. The study discusses background theories and key contributions of the field. A part of the findings unanimously suggests that there are factors that positively (or negatively) impact SMEs' degree of internationalization (DOI), instead, the effect of other determinants seems to be controversial, and should be better examined by future research works. Consequently, we then propose a research agenda to identify research gaps that should be explored.

Keywords Small family businesses · Small family firms · Family SMEs · Internationalization · Systematic literature review

---

F. E. Rubino
University of Calabria, Rende, Italy
e-mail: franco.rubino@unical.it

C. Multari
University 'Mediterranea' of Reggio Calabria, Reggio Calabria, Italy
e-mail: claudio.multari@unirc.it

G. Valenza (✉)
University of Palermo, Palermo, Italy
e-mail: giuseppe.valenza01@unipa.it

A. Caputo et al. (eds.), *The International Dimension of Entrepreneurial Decision-Making*, Contributions to Management Science,
https://doi.org/10.1007/978-3-030-85950-3_7

1 Introduction

Small and Medium-sized Enterprises (SMEs) represent two-thirds of all business economies worldwide (Family Firm Institute, 2014). European Commission defines an SME as a firm with less than 250 employees, and a turnover of fewer than 50 million euros or a balance sheet total not exceeding 43 million euros. In the EU and USA, the majority of SMEs (85%) are family businesses (FBs) (D'Angelo et al., 2016; Kontinen & Ojala, 2011a). As argued by some authors (Valenza et al., 2021; Caputo et al., 2019; Lambrecht & Naudts, 2008; Mandl, 2008), the main characteristics of a family business are: founder or family members, as head/s of the company; family members employed in the firm and/or involved in the decision-making process; non-family managers' decisions are influenced by the family group.

Furthermore, Lahiri et al. (2020) include as familiness' factors also the different risk-taking propensities, organizational goals and investment preferences, if compared to non-family firms (De Massis et al., 2018; Memili et al., 2015).

Globalization enhanced international opportunities even for familiar SMEs, which have always been considered less inclined to internationalize their business (Fernández & Nieto, 2005) for several factors: limited capital; leadership inflexibility and reluctance to change; disparate family goals, value and needs; conflict among family successors; lack of information about foreign market (Chittenden et al., 1996; Friedman & Friedman, 1994; Ward, 2004). Despite this, family businesses can experience remarkable performances in terms of financial results, at least when compared to non-family businesses (Nicolò & Valenza, 2019a).

Differences between FBs and non-FBs characteristics seem to be relevant to the internationalization process, as suggested by several studies (e.g. Scholes et al., 2016; Yang et al., 2020). Although management literature has broadly explored the internationalization process in general, only recently scholars have focused on family business strategy (e.g. P. Davis & Englis, 2000). Moreover, globalization and technology development have been constantly impacted the way to run a business, especially concerning internationalization strategies. This assumption leads to the imperative to pursue exploring internationalization processes (Caputo & Pellegrini, 2019), especially concerning family SMEs, which present differences if compared to non-family firms and larger companies.

Several SLRs dealt with the internationalization processes concerning firms from specific economic contexts (Alon et al., 2018; Caputo et al., 2016; Yaprak & Karademir, 2010), family firms (Arregle et al., 2017; Pukall & Calabrò, 2014) and SMEs (Dabic et al., 2020; Mejri & Umemoto, 2010), but there are no SLRs regarding the family SMEs' internationalization strategies. Hence, we found an existing literature research gap.

In light of the aforementioned premises, this study aims to explore the state of the art of the scientific literature on the internationalization of Family Small and Medium-sized Enterprises, proposing a systematic literature review.

The chapter is structured as follows: after this Introduction, we explain the methodology used to develop the study (Sect. 2). In Sect. 3, we analyze the extant literature on this topic by underlining prominent theories proposed by either older significant studies or more recent research papers. Then, we discuss and analyze remarkable findings of previous research, which in part are coherent with dominant theories, while others seem to be contrasting with older paradigms (Sect. 4). Finally, Sect. 5 (conclusion) presents a summary of the key finding of the work, suggesting future research directions.

2 Methodology

This study aims to provide a comprehensive depiction of the scientific knowledge that characterizes the research field of family SMEs and their internationalization processes. Therefore, a systematic literature review is proposed, which has been developed by adopting the systematic review protocol (Thorpe et al., 2005; Tranfield et al., 2003).

The systematic search was performed using the Scopus database, between October and December 2020. We could have considered other databases suitable for systematic searches, such as EBSCO or Web of Science. However, since the research field of family SMEs is a literature niche and a subpart of the family business literature that intersects with the Small and Medium-sized Enterprises field, Scopus provided a larger and more suitable database.

We used a search string to select those articles that included in their title, abstract or keywords, specific words related to the topic of family SMEs. To identify those articles closely related to business science and management, the search was limited to the subject area 'Business, Management and Accounting'. To assure reliability to the sample, we considered only articles published in peer-reviewed journals. The language was limited to 'English' to select only the mainstream contributions.

The final string, which was obtained after several attempts, is the following: TITLE-ABS-KEY (('small family' AND firm* OR venture* OR business* OR enterprise* OR compan*) OR ('family SME*') OR ('family small' AND firm* OR venture* OR business* OR enterprise* OR compan*) OR ('family*owned' AND small)) AND (LIMIT-TO (SRCTYPE, 'j')) AND (LIMIT-TO (DOCTYPE, 'ar')) AND (LIMIT-TO (SUBJAREA, 'BUSI')) AND (EXCLUDE (PUBYEAR, 2021)) AND (LIMIT-TO (LANGUAGE, 'English')). To validate the keywords to fully capture the phenomenon, we involved a panel of experts through whom we carried out an in-depth discussion on the validity of the keywords. Since the search was run between October and December 2020, we excluded publications in press included in 2021. The searching criteria used to select the articles of the dataset are resumed in Table 1.

Through these criteria, we obtained an initial sample of 324 documents. To ensure adherence to the research question, the authors carried out a filtering process consisting of independently reading abstracts of the documents in the sample (Caputo et al., 2016). When there was uncertainty, we read the entire papers for their inclusion or exclusion in the sample, via a panel discussion between the

Table 1 Dataset searching criteria

Search criteria	Parameters
Database	Scopus
Search keywords (Title, Abstract, Article's keywords)	Small family firm(s), small family venture(s), small family business(es), small family enterprise(s), small family company(ies), family SME(s), family small firm(s), family small venture(s), family small business(es), family small enterprise (s), family small company(ies), small family owned
Subject area	Business, Management and Accounting
Sources	Peer-reviewed journals
Language	English
Year excluded	2021

authors. The main goal of the panel discussion among the authors was to consider only those articles strictly connected to the research field of internationalization. First, we identified those articles that specifically focused on the topic of internationalization. Then, we excluded the documents less relevant to the research question. For example, papers on performance, succession, or organizational culture, were excluded when not strictly related to internationalization. We also excluded those articles which could not be considered research works (e.g. historical articles, educational case studies and industry reports).

The selection approach was therefore qualitative, critical and systematic. We could have put the keyword 'internationalization' in the string, but we wanted to adopt a qualitative approach to make sure not to miss relevant articles on internationalization, which is the core of this study.

Through these inclusive and exclusive criteria, we obtained a set of articles representing the state of the art of the research on the internationalization of family Small and Medium-sized family businesses, where the first bibliographic reference is dated 2002 (i.e. Poutziouris et al., 2002). No documents before 2002 matched the search criteria. In particular, the result was a final sample of 29 articles, published from 2002 to 2020, which formed the basis for the systematic literature review.

3 Internationalization of Family SMEs

In this section, we analyze the main theories used in the literature to study the internationalization processes of family SMEs. The section is divided into subsections, each of which focuses on a specific stream of research.

The review of the papers provided us information about the trend of scholars' interest in the family SMEs' internationalization process, which seems to be averagely increased in the last two decades, as evidenced by Graph 1.

This leads us to consider the internationalization process of the family SMEs as an emerging field in the business literature. It is possible to observe an increasing number of published articles, especially during the last year considered (2020).

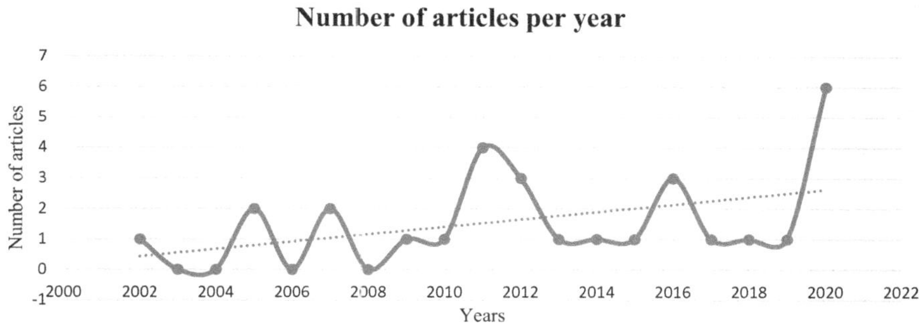

Graph 1 The trend of articles published on SMEs' internationalization process

Table 2 The most cited journals in the dataset

Journal name	Number of cited articles
International Business Review	3
Journal of Small Business and Enterprise Development	3
International Journal of Business and Globalisation	2
Journal of International Entrepreneurship	2
Journal of Small Business Management	2

Concerning the sources, 29 articles were published by 22 journals. Most of the journals in the dataset published only one article on family SMEs' internationalization, whilst some of them focused on this theme twice or three times over the years. Table 2 shows the journals with at least two articles published in the dataset. For each of the most cited journals, it is indicated the number of articles present in our sample.

International Business Review and *Journal of Small Business and Enterprise Development* published 3 articles, while *International Journal of Business and Globalisation*, *Journal of International Entrepreneurship* and *Journal of Small Business Management* published 2 articles for each. It is interesting to observe that no journals specialized in family firms, such as *Family Business Review* or *Journal of Family Business Strategy*, are included in the ranking shown in the table. Out of 22 journals, 1 is classified as 4 for the AJG ranking, 9 journals as 3, while 2 as 2.

By a systematic and critical review of the articles in the dataset, it arose several recurring topics about the family SMEs' internationalization process, as we resumed in Table 3.

The aforementioned topics represent the most important factors affecting the family SMEs' internationalization process, as argued by scholars. Hence, this led us to deepen and discuss them in the following paragraphs, to resume a framework of the most important dynamics that impact the phenomena.

Table 3 The most recurrent topics in the articles of the dataset

Topics	Numbers of articles
Capabilities and family involvement in Top Management Teams (TMT)	15
Social capital and its influence on internationalization	16
Influences of distance	7
Pathways of internationalization	7

3.1 Capabilities and Family Involvement in Top Management Teams

Top Management Team's (TMT's) capabilities and experience play an important role to plan, start and improve an internationalization strategy. Thus, based on the Resource-based View (RBV) (Grant, 1999), firm resources contribute to the development of dynamic capabilities which, 'in contrast to ordinary capabilities, that enable a firm to sell the *same* product to the *same* customers in the *same* market, support the firms to have *congruence with the environmental changes*' (Teece, 2012). Therefore, dynamic capabilities are essential to compete in the international market, which is characterized by broad differences in terms of culture, technology and customer preferences (Cavusgil et al., 1993; Charoensukmongkol, 2014; Dow, 2006; Lu et al., 2010).

Firm outcomes, as noted by the upper echelon theory, reflect the TMT's actions (Hambrick, 2007; Hambrick & Mason, 1984). Managers' decisions are influenced by their mental schemes, shaped by educational and functional backgrounds, experiences, perspectives, values and demographic characteristics (Hiebl, 2014; Tihanyi et al., 2000). Hence, TMT composition in terms of quality can broadly influence the degree of internationalization (DOI) of family SMEs, although it seems appropriate to specify that family SMEs in different countries may adopt a specific firm structure, shaped by culture, government and law systems, economic background and so on (Caputo et al., 2016; Dana et al., 2008; Koul et al., 2020; Poutziouris et al., 2002; Yu, 2009; Zapletalová, 2017).

As argued by Alayo et al. (2019), one of the main characteristics of FBs is the involvement of family members in the decision-making process, which represents an important determinant for internationalization. The percentage of family members inside TMT is defined as the 'family TMT ratio' (Calabrò et al., 2012). Often, in FBs, managers are chosen among family members (Mustakallio, 2002; Zarone et al., 2017), so they can lack the education and experience required to handle international strategies (Claver et al., 2009; Muñoz-Bullón & Sanchez-Bueno, 2012). Moreover, when all of TMT's members come from the same family, the interactions among members seem to be more direct and frequent, and this help information exchange and learning process (Gupta et al., 2006); but on the other hand, it conducts to a low level of diversity in terms of skills and knowledge (Alayo et al., 2019; Nicolò & Valenza, 2019b).

To solve the discussed issues, SMEs may decide to introduce non-family members in the TMT. External managers can apport 'extremely beneficial results' toward an internationalization strategy: they can apport (international) experience, capabilities, different visions, new ideas and their pre-existent social networks (Cruz & Nordqvist, 2011; Liang et al., 2013; Vandekerkhof et al., 2014). Furthermore, non-family managers can 'increase rationality and objectivity in the decision-making process, promoting change and innovation' (Alayo et al., 2019; Cruz & Nordqvist, 2011).

Another obstacle to the internationalization process can be represented by the presence of older generations, generally constituted by the founder generation, who seem to be more reluctant to change, less inclined to risk, and may present insufficient capabilities, knowledge and social networks to extend the business abroad (Basly, 2007; Fernández & Nieto, 2005; Shi et al., 2018; Yang et al., 2020). As argued by Basly (2007), conservatism can be discussed by three aspects: governance: the high-dependence of the firm to the owner-manager (Jenster & Malone, 1991); strategic: rigid devotion to a strategy (Gudmundson et al., 1999); cultural: independence from the environment and external culture (Donckels & Fröhlich, 1991).

The stagnation, as hypothesized by Alayo et al. (2019), can be overcome by the involvement of subsequent generations, which are generally better prepared, have upper-level education, and may have external experiences (Arzubiaga et al., 2019). Although they may lack specific firm experience like previous generations, the best way is represented by generational involvement in TMT, where the founder (or older) generation can provide firm and market experience and later generation can introduce creativity, innovation, diversity in TMT's capabilities and skills (Chirico et al., 2011; Sciascia et al., 2013).

Furthermore, family businesses are characterized by 'patient capital' (Sirmon & Hitt, 2003), which implies a long-term perspective that may enhance the adoption of choice of internationalization (Simon, 1996).

3.2 *Social Capital and Its Influence on Internationalization*

Social capital is an important resource, characteristic of FB, which can contribute to international strategies. While human capital is represented by the quality of every single firm member, social capital refers to the relationship existing among members (Lin et al., 2002). It can be defined as the 'actual or potential resources' (Bourdieu, 1986) that a firm can access and/or mobilize in purposive actions (Adler & Kwon, 2002).

Social capital is divided into internal and external: internal social capital refers to the relationship within the firm; external social capital consists of the social relationship that an organization has with external parties (Nahapiet & Ghoshal, 1998). Internal social capital constitutes an important resource, which improves the quality of TMT (and this, as argued, influences the internationalization process). We underline the existence of three main aspects of internal social capital related to the internationalization process: FCC (family commitment culture), SEW (socio-emotional wealth) perspective and stewardship orientation.

FCC is a distinguishing characteristic of FBs (Astrachan et al., 2002; Zahra et al., 2008) and can be defined as a 'consistent behaviour' (Becker, 1960), in which family and organizational values of a FB are fused in the culture of commitment (Segaro et al., 2014). For instance, FCC can be shaped by the employees' desire, need, and/or obligation to hold membership in the firm (Meyer & Allen, 1991; Riketta, 2002).

SEW perspective can be defined as 'the stock of affect-related value that a family derives from its controlling position in a particular firm' (Berrone et al., 2012). In general, the most relevant aspect of SEW is the importance of non-economic goals that family members seek in the business (Berrone et al., 2012).

As argued by some authors (Del Bosco & Bettinelli, 2020), SEW can be shaped in the following dimensions: family control and influence; family member's identification with the firm; binding social ties; emotional attachment; renewal of family bonds to the firm through dynastic succession (Berrone et al., 2012).

Scholes et al. (2016) discuss the positive and negative effects of SEW. On the one hand, SEW apports a longer-term view and this can conduct investments in terms of developing human resources, capabilities, network ties and financial reserve (patient capital). On the other hand, SEW may lead to the self-behaviour of family members, who can recruit incompetent employers or managers (based on family ties or personal friendly relationships), or inappropriately use the firm's resources.

The agency-based theory represents one of the main discussed paradigms in corporate governance literature (Eisenhardt, 1989). One of the focal points of the agency perspective deals with two problems caused by the divorce of ownership and control in a firm: moral hazard and adverse selection (Jensen & Meckling, 1976). Nevertheless, as argued by D'Angelo et al. (2016), in FBs, the relevant family influence often leads to a system where ownership and control are run (or influenced) by the same people. Hence, it is more appropriate to discuss stewardship orientation (Miller et al., 2007). This approach could be defined as an extension of SEW perspective, from family members to the whole firm. Indeed, in stewardship orientation, the executives (stewards) are motivated to act in the interests of principals (owners) (Davis et al., 1997; Donaldson & Davis, 1991). Stewards' behaviour is pro-organizational and collectivistic, and the most important qualities of a steward are trust, involvement, collectivism, commitment and long-term orientation (Davis et al., 1997). As proposed by Segaro et al. (2014), stewardship orientation may influence the level of internationalization of a FB in three ways: the unusual devotion to the continuity of the business, the emphasis placed on nurturing of employees and the seeking out of closer connections with customers.

External social capital improves the firm social network, which contributes to the firm's foreign expansion (Majocchi & Strange, 2012). As hypothesized by Basly (2007), social networking is important at least on two levels of internationalization activities: as a trigger of international expansion and, subsequently, for the decision about penetration and entry modes. Distributors, suppliers, customers, competitors, public administrations and non-profit organizations are some of several types of actors involved in a firm's social networks (Kontinen & Ojala, 2011c).

As suggested by Kontinen and Ojala (2011c), the ties of a firm can be analyzed by three aspects, as follow. *Types of ties*: formal, informal and intermediary. Formal ties refer to the link existing between individual business partners, which exchange goods or services (Adler & Kwon, 2002; Coviello & Munro, 1997). Informal ties are related to social relationships (i.e. with friends and family members), characterized by the lack of business transactions between the parties (Coviello, 2006; Larrson & Starr, 1993). In intermediary ties, as informal ties, there are no business transactions between the seller and the buyer but there is a third party (such as a promotion organization or an organizer of exhibitions), that facilitates the establishment of the network between the parties (Ojala, 2009). *Strength of ties*: strong or weak. Strong ties are limited and are based on closeness, trust, mutual respect and commitment (Kontinen & Ojala, 2011c). Weak ties are usually more than strong ties and are characterized by superficial relationships parties do not know well each other and there is no trust and emotional closeness (Söderqvist & Chetty, 2009). *Activeness*: active or passive. For active ties, the initiative of the formation of the tie is taken by the seller, while in passive ties, the initiative comes from the buyer (Johanson & Mattsson, 1987).

As argued by Kontinen and Ojala (2011c), an important way to create ties and improve SMEs' international opportunity recognition is to participate in professional forums (Ozgen & Baron, 2007) and trade exhibitions (McAuley, 1999; Meyer & Skak, 2002; Reid, 1984).

3.3 Influences of Distance

Although globalization and technology development has facilitated the internationalization process, studies have highlighted the importance of distance during the phases of entering and expanding a business in a foreign country (e.g. Del Bosco & Bettinelli, 2020; Kontinen & Ojala, 2010).

Del Bosco and Bettinelli (2020) analyzed three dimensions of distance (cultural, geographical and institutional) that affect family SMEs during the internationalization process.

Cultural distance is defined as the difference of cultural behaviours, social rules, between two national contexts (Hofstede, 1980; Sousa & Bradley, 2008). A pronounced cultural difference between a family SME and a target country may create difficulties in bridging social ties, misunderstandings, conflicts and may exist a lack of local environmental knowledge that can affect a firm's international business (Del Bosco & Bettinelli, 2020).

Geographic distance increases difficulties in activities' communication and coordination (Boeh & Beamish, 2012) and it raises transportation and communication costs (Ghemawat, 2001). It constitutes a barrier to information and knowledge exchange (Evenett & Keller, 2002; Storper & Leamer, 2001), which leads to information asymmetries (Ragozzino, 2009). Consequently, the sum of these factors can negatively affect the direct control of the firm over the foreign subsidiary (especially on employees) (Hennart, 2010).

Institutional distance refers to the distance between two countries' law systems, regulations, cognitive structures and social values (Kostova & Zaheer, 1999; Scott & Meyer, 1994). Wide institutional differences may increase difficulties in operating overseas (Kostova & Zaheer, 1999). The main risks associated with entering a foreign country with a weak formal institution structure are ambiguous regulations, low transparency, inefficiencies, corruption, political instability and terrorism (Chang et al., 2014).

Often distance is related to entry model choice, especially in the case of the establishment of a subsidiary overseas. Ownership decision (full ownership or shared with local partners) is frequently linked to distance (geographical, cultural and institutional) (Del Bosco & Bettinelli, 2020).

3.4 Pathways of Internationalization

The term 'pathways' refers to the different strategies that a firm can adopt in the internationalization process (Dabic et al., 2020; Kuivalainen & Saarenketo, 2012; Mathews & Zander, 2007). The entry choice in the international market influences multiple aspects, such as firms' revenue performances (Fernández Olmos et al., 2015). Based on the model proposed by Bell et al. (2003), there are three main internationalization pathways of SMEs: incremental way, born global firms and born-again global.

One of the most cited theories in literature on international business is the incremental model proposed by Johanson and Vahlne (1977). The Uppsala model describes internationalization as an incremental process in which firms expand their business abroad from closer countries to more distant countries. The paradigm consists of three stages: exportation, the involvement of agents and the founding of a foreign sales subsidiary. The building of an own production facility may follow the three stages.

The original Uppsala model highlights the relevance of distance and country specificity while his revision (Johanson & Vahlne, 2009) emphasizes the important role of networks and opportunity recognition in the internationalization process.

Born global represents the second pathway. These firms, less influenced by geographical distance, internationalize to several countries simultaneously and rapidly (Kontinen & Ojala, 2012b). As argued by Kuivalainen and Saarenketo (2012), born global firms commonly achieve foreign sales from two to five years from their founding, operate at least in five foreign countries, and have a minimum of 25% of their income from overseas sales. Born global firms usually develop products for the international market rather than for domestic market demand (Bell et al., 2004).

The third pathway is constituted by born-again global. Born-again global firms have previously focused on the domestic market but, after a critical event such as a takeover by another company or a change in ownership and/or TMT, these firms suddenly internationalize their business (Bell et al., 2003). New owners and/or managers can apport more financial resources, international market knowledge, managerial capability and they can bridge the acquired firm to their pre-existing networks.

4 Discussion

Most of the findings of the examined research papers seem to confirm the pre-existent literature theories but, in some cases, we found out discordance between the dominant theory assumptions and the outcomes of research works.

In general, family firms are less inclined to internationalize their business, if compared to non-family ventures, as confirmed by several research works (Davidkov & Yordanova, 2016; Fernández & Nieto, 2005). Moreover, the presence of external shareholders (Segaro, 2012) or foreign owners (Davidkov & Yordanova, 2016) significantly increases the chances to internationalize. Other studies found out no significant relationship between family control (Basly & Saunier, 2020) or the presence of a founder CEO (Yang et al., 2020) and DOI. Conversely, recent literature has examined the family features which can impact positively on internationalization, such as family commitment (if combined with strategic flexibility and/or stewardship orientation), patient capital and informal governance system (Calabrò & Mussolino, 2011; Segaro, 2012). Furthermore, Kontinen and Ojala (2010) found out that family SMEs' members, when entering foreign markets, are more motivated than non-FB to learn the culture and language of the target country to fill the lack of financial resources and managers and employers with international experience.

Regarding the composition of TMT in family SMEs, several empirical studies (Bika & Kalantaridis, 2017; Calabrò & Mussolino, 2011; Compagno et al., 2005; D'Angelo et al., 2016; Fernández & Nieto, 2005; Kontinen & Ojala, 2010; Segaro et al., 2014) have unanimously confirmed the positive relationship between the presence of non-family managers and the degree of internationalization. As suggested by Alayo et al. (2019), the presence of experienced external managers provides foreign market knowledge, experience, social networks transferred from past experiences and can help the SME's governance to solve conflicts in a more rational way. Moreover, Segaro (2012) found out that the presence of familial TMT is negatively related to internationalization, whilst parental TMT, if combined with stewardship orientation and behavioural integration, increases the DOI. Furthermore, D'Angelo et al. (2016) argue that external managers can exert their full potential if family control over the firm is less than 50% of shares. This is due to the conservatism and risk-aversion typically of family control. Bika and Kalantaridis (2017) concluded that non-family managers, in addition to network ties, provide organizational-social capital (managerial resources, learning processes, behavioural norms), which positively impacts the DOI. The presence of non-family members in

TMT, as found out by Compagno et al. (2005), seems to be more relevant in dynamic sectors than in stable sectors.

Recent FB literature has detected various factors that foster a firm's internationalization process. Among attitudes, it is opportune to cite international knowledge (generally provided by external managers) (Basly, 2007); international opportunity recognition, which is favoured by governance flexibility (Kontinen & Ojala, 2011b) and the presence of TMT members from different areas (Segaro et al., 2014); collectivistic culture (Zaefarian et al., 2020); TMT managerial capabilities and experience (Segaro, 2012); organizational social capital (Bika & Kalantaridis, 2017); and pro-active, risk-seeking and innovative entrepreneurial orientation (Davidkov & Yordanova, 2016). As displayed by Zaefarian et al. (2020), the presence of valuable, rare, imperfectly imitable, non-substitutability (VRIN) resources (Barney, 1991) is positively associated with internationalization.

The connection between generational succession and internationalization represents another common ground for family SMEs' studies. Indeed, some authors (Anand, 2013; Basly & Saunier, 2020; Fernández & Nieto, 2005; Segaro et al., 2014) found a positive relationship between the involvement of second and subsequent generations in TMT and firms' internationalization. Furthermore, concerning Japanese firms, Anand (2013) suggested the involvement of subsequent generations in the decision-making process to develop international strategies. Nevertheless, based on the research work by Yang et al. (2020) involving Chinese enterprises, generational succession provides significant results on export propensity, but marginal findings on export intensity.

Scholars have been paid great emphasis to the stewardship orientation, which seems to be more adequate than the agency theory to explain family SMEs' dynamics (Kontinen & Ojala, 2012a; Segaro, 2012; Segaro et al., 2014). For instance, Segaro (2012) suggested that the presence of stewardship, if combined with other factors (TMT managerial capabilities and experience, TMT behavioural integration) leads to a higher DOI. Moreover, stewardship orientation can mitigate the effects of family characters identified by dominant theory as a threat to internationalization, such as family ownership, family commitment, parental TMT and governance with particularism and personalism (Segaro, 2012).

Up-to-date literature seems to be increasingly concerned to SEW, which is considered one of the main characteristics of family control over the firm, thus its connection with international strategies could not be ignored by the scholars. Nevertheless, the results seem to be contrasting and it is not still clear how SEW perspective impacts on FBs' internationalization. Research studies (Lahiri et al., 2020; Scholes et al., 2016) found out equivocal the impact of socio-emotional goals on the DOI: on one side, current SEW can inhibit risk-seeking and the hiring of external employees, managers or shareholders to preserve total familiar control (Basly & Saunier, 2020; Yang et al., 2020); nonetheless, the pursuit of future SEW may generate patient capital to provide a more solid firm structure to future generations (Segaro, 2012).

Alayo et al. (2019) argued that the succession process can be complex for family firms. The model proposed by Shi et al. (2018) may mitigate the risks associated with generational succession by adopting the most adequate succession pattern. Based on the evidence from Chinese family businesses, these authors presented three main succession pattern models: evolutionary pattern (in which the founder remains in charge for a long time after succession, shaping the new generation), revolutionary pattern (no contact between old e subsequent generations), and co-evolutionary pattern (old family members guide the succession process by transferring firm-specific knowledge and network ties to ingoing generation). As suggested by Shi et al. (2018), the best way seem to be the co-evolutionary pattern, which can also generate accumulated experience through generations, and, in line with the outcome of Basly and Saunier (2020), this has a positive effect on family business essence, in addition to international firm-level.

Recent studies have broadly investigated the role of SMEs' networks concerning the choice to expand business overseas. Multiple studies found out the importance of international trade exhibitions as a driver to bridge new ties with international partners, which can introduce family SMEs to their home country (Kontinen & Ojala, 2011a, 2011b, 2011c; Scholes et al., 2016). Alliances have a positive impact on firms' internationalization (Fernández & Nieto, 2005) and social networking increases FB's international knowledge (Basly, 2007). Family SMEs are more likely to establish connections with only one network, and that could generate difficulties if discrepancies arise. As suggested by Kontinen and Ojala (2010, 2012a), it would be appropriate to bridge secondary networks to avoid the risk of quitting the internationalization strategy. Literature also focused on the different typologies of ties (weak and strong, formal and informal) and their impact on foreign strategies and international opportunity recognition, in addition to the role of activeness and reactiveness (Kontinen & Ojala, 2011c).

Scholars, over the years, have consistently investigated the pathways taken by FBs to internationalize their business (Johanson & Vahlne, 1977). A focal point related to the choice of the target country (or countries) is represented by the distance. Although physical distance constitutes the key point (even if globalization has downsized this aspect), recent literature has focused also on other categories of distance, such as cultural and institutional distance (Del Bosco & Bettinelli, 2020; Kontinen & Ojala, 2010). Del Bosco and Bettinelli (2020) found out that cultural distance is associated with full ownership choice of subsidiaries overseas, while high geographical distance leads to sharing ownership with foreign partners. Institutional distance must be considered from two points of view: if the institutional level of the foreign country is higher, firms may opt for full ownership; conversely, if the level is lower, the risks associated with entering a new market may lead to sharing subsidiary ownership with a local partner. These results seem to be confirmed by Kontinen and Ojala (2010).

5 Conclusions and Future Research Directions

Through a systematic literature review, our study aimed to discuss the state of art inherent family SMEs internationalization processes and to propose future research directions.

First of all, although the family SMEs' internationalization process seems to be a growing field in the business literature, we noticed that the most relevant journals specialized in the family business have mostly ignored the abovementioned subject.

As discussed in the previous sections, in family business literature there are features that positively (or negatively) impact SMEs' DOI. Some of these are accepted by most scholars, such as the presence of external managers with international capabilities and experience in TMT, the introduction of subsequential generations in the decision-making process, the presence of international opportunity recognition by the board and TMT members, governance dynamics shaped by stewardship orientation, social networking with foreign firms (which is lead, as argued above, firstly by the participation to international trade forums).

Instead, other findings seem to be controversial, for instance, the role of SEW in the internationalization process, which can be a threat because it may conduct to risk-avoiding by family members, but on the other hand, it generates patient social capital and the willingness to pass on future generation a more solid firm. For future studies, it would be interesting to better investigate the negative, but especially the positive role of SEW on international strategies.

Another controversial field is represented by family SMEs' external social capital, constituted by the ties that a firm bridges with third parties. As mentioned, social networking represents a driver to internationalize firms' business, but literature is not unanimously concordant about the types of ties that better impact internationalization (e.g. weak or strong, formal or informal). Future research works may better examine which forms of ties have a stronger influence on overseas expansion procedures.

Distance, when a FB decide to engage the international strategy, is still a determinant factor, particularly concerning the subsidiary ownership choice. Nevertheless, globalization and technological progress are transforming the concept of distance, year by year. In this regard, internationalization research cannot ignore these phenomena, so we suggest, for future studies, to research how progress impact the perceive of distance by the firms, and how they react to these persistent changes.

The ways throughout family SMEs undertake internationalization is one of the most discussed issues in internationalization FB literature. In this context, the more accepted theory is the incremental model (Uppsala). Despite most SMEs follow this way, phenomena such as born-global and born-again global firms are growing. Future research agenda may investigate these models to understand if they only constitute exceptions to the incremental model or are destined to deepen through the years.

Finally, based on the model proposed by Lahiri et al. (2020), we found interesting the tripartite division of features impacting firms' international strategy (resource-based, institution-based and industry-based). While resource-based determinants have been broadly discussed by scholars, institution-based and industry-based factors' results seem to be equivocal. In this regard, it would be appropriate to investigate deeply these aspects and to implement the tripod model in diverse business and geographical contexts.

References

Adler, P. S., & Kwon, S.-W. (2002). Social capital: Prospects for a new concept. *The Academy of Management Review, 27*(1), 17–40. https://doi.org/10.2307/4134367

Alayo, M., Maseda, A., Jainaga, T., & Arzubiaga, U. (2019). Internationalization and entrepreneurial orientation of family SMEs: The influence of the family character. *International Business Review, 28*, 48–59. https://doi.org/10.1016/j.ibusrev.2018.06.003

Alon, I., Anderson, J., Munim, Z. H., & Ho, A. (2018). A review of the internationalization of Chinese enterprises. *Asia Pacific Journal of Management, 35*(3), 573–605. https://doi.org/10.1007/s10490-018-9597-5

Anand, R. (2013). Internationalisation of the small and medium family firm in Japan. *International Journal of Business and Globalisation, 11*, 117–135. https://doi.org/10.1504/IJBG.2013.055598

Arregle, J., Duran, P., Hitt, M. A., & van Essen, M. (2017). Why is family firms' internationalization unique? A meta-analysis. *Entrepreneurship Theory and Practice, 41*(5), 801–831. https://doi.org/10.1111/etap.12246

Arzubiaga, U., Maseda, A., & Jainaga, T. (2019). Exploratory and exploitative innovation in family businesses: The moderating role of the family firm image and family involvement in top management. *Review of Managerial Science, 13*(5), 1–31. https://doi.org/10.1007/s11846-017-0239-y

Astrachan, J. H., Klein, S. B., & Smyrnios, K. X. (2002). The F-PEC scale of family influence: A proposal for solving the family business definition problem1. *Family Business Review, 15*(1), 45–58. https://doi.org/10.1111/j.1741-6248.2002.00045.x

Barney, J. (1991). Firm resources and sustained competitive advantage. *Journal of Management, 17*(1), 99–120. https://doi.org/10.1177/014920639101700108

Basly, S. (2007). The internationalization of family SME: An organizational learning and knowledge development perspective. *Baltic Journal of Management, 2*, 154–180.

Basly, S., & Saunier, P.-L. (2020). Familiness, socio-emotional goals and the internationalization of French family SMEs. *Journal of International Entrepreneurship, 18*(3), 270–311. https://doi.org/10.1007/s10843-019-00265-0

Becker, H. S. (1960). Notes on the concept of commitment. *American Journal of Sociology, 66*(1), 32–42.

Bell, J., Crick, D., & Young, S. (2004). Small firm internationalization and business strategy: An exploratory study of 'knowledge-intensive' and'traditional' manufacturing firms in the UK. *International Small Business Journal, 22*(1), 23–56. https://doi.org/10.1177/0266242604039479

Bell, J., McNaughton, R., Young, S., & Crick, D. (2003). Towards an integrative model of small firm internationalisation. *Journal of International Entrepreneurship, 1*, 339–362. https://doi.org/10.1023/A:1025629424041

Berrone, P., Cruz, C., & Gomez-Mejia, L. R. (2012). Socioemotional wealth in family firms: Theoretical dimensions, assessment approaches, and agenda for future research. *Family Business Review, 25*(3), 258–279. https://doi.org/10.1177/0894486511435355

Bika, Z., & Kalantaridis, C. (2017). Organizational-social-capital, time and international family SMEs: An empirical study from the East of England: International family SMEs. *European Management Review, 16*(3), 525–541. https://doi.org/10.1111/emre.12160

Boeh, K., & Beamish, P. (2012). Travel time and the liability of distance in foreign direct investment: Location choice and entry mode. *Journal of International Business Studies, 43*, 525–535. https://doi.org/10.1057/jibs.2012.10

Bourdieu, P. (1986). The forms of capital. In J. G. Richardson (Ed.), *Handbook of theory and research for the sociology of education* (pp. 241–258). Greenwood.

Calabrò, A., & Mussolino, D. (2011). How do boards of directors contribute to family SME export intensity? The role of formal and informal governance mechanisms. *SSRN Electronic Journal.* https://doi.org/10.2139/ssrn.1858925

Calabrò, A., Torchia, M., Pukall, T., & Mussolino, D. (2012). The influence of ownership structure and board strategic involvement on international sales: The moderating effect of family involvement. *International Business Review, 22*(3), 509–523. https://doi.org/10.1016/j.ibusrev.2012.07.002

Caputo, A., & Pellegrini, M. (2019). An overview of the anatomy of entrepreneurial decisions. In A. Caputo & M. Pellegrini (Eds.), *The anatomy of entrepreneurial decisions* (pp. 1–6). https://doi.org/10.1007/978-3-030-19685-1_1

Caputo, A., Pellegrini, M., Dabic, M., & Dana, L.-P. (2016). Internationalisation of firms from Central and Eastern Europe: A systematic literature review. *European Business Review, 28*(6), 630–651. https://doi.org/10.1108/EBR-01-2016-0004

Caputo, A., Pellegrini, M., Valenza, G., & Zarone, V. (2019). Conflicts and negotiations in the intergenerational succession of family firms: A literature review. In A. Caputo & M. Pellegrini (Eds.), *The anatomy of entrepreneurial decisions* (pp. 145–169). Springer. https://doi.org/10.1007/978-3-030-19685-1_7

Cavusgil, S., Zou, S., & Naidu, G. (1993). Product and promoting adaptation in export ventures: An empirical investigation. *Journal of International Business Studies, 24*, 479–506. https://doi.org/10.1057/palgrave.jibs.8490242

Chang, Y.-C., Kao, M.-S., & Kuo, A. (2014). The influences of governance quality on equity-based entry mode choice: The strengthening role of family control. *International Business Review, 23*(5), 1008–1020. https://doi.org/10.1016/j.ibusrev.2014.03.003

Charoensukmongkol, P. (2014). Cultural intelligence and export performance of small and medium enterprises in Thailand: Mediating roles of organizational capabilities. *International Small Business Journal, 34*(1), 1–18. https://doi.org/10.1177/0266242614539364

Chirico, F., Sirmon, D., Sciascia, S., & Mazzola, P. (2011). Resource orchestration in family firms: Investigating how entrepreneurial orientation, generational involvement, and participative strategy affect performance. *Strategic Entrepreneurship Journal, 5*(4), 307–326. https://doi.org/10.1002/sej.121

Chittenden, F., Hall, G., & Hutchinson, P. (1996). Small firm growth, access to capital markets and financial structure: Review of issues and an empirical investigation. *Small Business Economics, 8*(1), 59–67. https://doi.org/10.1007/BF00391976

Claver, E., Rienda, L., & Quer, D. (2009). Family firms' international commitment the influence of family-related factors. *Family Business Review, 22*(2), 125–135. https://doi.org/10.1177/0894486508330054

Compagno, C., Pittino, D., & Visintin, F. (2005). Corporate governance and advanced forms of internationalisation in Italian SMEs. *International Journal of Globalisation and Small Business, 1*(2), 168–182.

Coviello, N. (2006). The network dynamics of international new ventures. *Journal of International Business Studies, 37*, 713–731. https://doi.org/10.1057/palgrave.jibs.8400219

Coviello, N., & Munro, H. (1997). Network relationships and the internationalisation process of small software firms. *International Business Review, 6*(4), 361–386. https://doi.org/10.1016/S0969-5931(97)00010-3

Cruz, C., & Nordqvist, M. (2011). Entrepreneurial orientation in family firms: A generational perspective. *Small Business Economics, 38*, 33–49. https://doi.org/10.1007/s11187-010-9265-8
D'Angelo, A., Majocchi, A., & Buck, T. (2016). External managers, family ownership and the scope of SME internationalization. *Journal of World Business, 51*(4), 534–547. https://doi.org/10.1016/j.jwb.2016.01.004
Dabic, M., Maley, J., Dana, L.-P., Novak, I., Pellegrini, M., & Caputo, A. (2020). Pathways of SME internationalization: A bibliometric and systematic review. *Small Business Economics, 55*, 705–725. https://doi.org/10.1007/s11187-019-00181-6
Dana, L.-P., Hamilton, R., & Wick, K. (2008). Deciding to export: An exploratory study of Singaporean entrepreneurs. *Journal of International Entrepreneurship, 7*, 79–87. https://doi.org/10.1007/s10843-008-0032-8
Davidkov, T., & Yordanova, D. (2016). Exploring the Bulgarian family SMEs' reluctance to internationalise. *International Journal of Business and Globalisation, 17*(1), 123. https://doi.org/10.1504/IJBG.2016.077570
Davis, J., Schoorman, F., & Donaldson, L. (1997). Toward a stewardship theory of management. *The Academy of Management Review, 22*(1), 20–47. https://doi.org/10.2307/259223
Davis, P., & Englis, P. (2000). Internationalization and organizational growth: The impact of internet usage and technology involvement among entrepreneur-led family businesses. *Family Business Review, 13*, 107–120. https://doi.org/10.1111/j.1741-6248.2000.00107.x
De Massis, A., Frattini, F., Majocchi, A., & Piscitello, L. (2018). Family firms in the global economy: Toward a deeper understanding of internationalization determinants, processes, and outcomes. *Global Strategy Journal, 8*, 3–21. https://doi.org/10.1002/gsj.1199
Del Bosco, B., & Bettinelli, C. (2020). How do family SMEs control their investments abroad? The role of distance and family control. *Management International Review, 60*, 1–35. https://doi.org/10.1007/s11575-019-00406-6
Donaldson, L., & Davis, J. (1991). Stewardship theory or agency theory: CEO governance and shareholder returns. *Australian Journal of Management, 16*, 49–64. https://doi.org/10.1177/031289629101600103
Donckels, R., & Fröhlich, E. (1991). Are family businesses really different? European experiences from STRATOS. *Family Business Review, 4*(2), 149–160. https://doi.org/10.1111/j.1741-6248.1991.00149.x
Dow, D. (2006). Adaptation and performance in foreign markets: Evidence of systematic under-adaptation. *Journal of International Business Studies, 37*, 212–226. https://doi.org/10.1057/palgrave.jibs.8400189
Eisenhardt, K. (1989). Agency theory: An assessment and review. *Academy of Management Review, 14*, 57–74. https://doi.org/10.5465/AMR.1989.4279003
Evenett, S., & Keller, W. (2002). On theories explaining the success of the gravity equation. *Journal of Political Economy, 110*, 281–316. https://doi.org/10.1086/338746
Family Firm Institute. (2014). Global data point. Retrieved from https://www.ffi.org/
Fernández Olmos, M., Gargallo, A., & Giner-Bagües, E. (2015). Internationalisation and performance in Spanish family SMES: The W-curve. *BRQ Business Research Quarterly, 19*(2), 122–136. https://doi.org/10.1016/j.brq.2015.07.001
Fernández, Z., & Nieto, M. (2005). Internationalization strategy of small and medium-sized family businesses: Some influential factors. *Family Business Review, 18*, 77–89. https://doi.org/10.1111/j.1741-6248.2005.00031.x
Friedman, M., & Friedman, S. (1994). *How to run a family business*. Betterway Books.
Ghemawat, P. (2001). Distance still matters. The hard reality of global expansion. *Harvard Business Review, 79*, 137–140,142.
Giuseppe, V., Andrea, C., & Andrea, C. (2021) Is small and medium-sized beautiful? The structure and evolution of family SMEs research. *Journal of Family Business Management ahead-of-print(ahead-of-print)*. https://doi.org/10.1108/JFBM-03-2021-0024

Grant, R. (1999). The resource-based theory of competitive advantage: Implications for strategy formulation. *California Management Review, 33*, 3–23. https://doi.org/10.1016/B978-0-7506-7088-3.50004-8
Gudmundson, D., Hartman, E. A., & Tower, C. B. (1999). Strategic orientation: Differences between family and nonfamily firms. *Family Business Review, 12*(1), 27–39. https://doi.org/10.1111/j.1741-6248.1999.00027.x
Gupta, A. K., Smith, K. G., & Shalley, C. E. (2006). The interplay between exploration and exploitation. *Academy of Management Journal, 49*(4), 693–706. https://doi.org/10.5465/amj.2006.22083026
Hambrick, D. (2007). Upper echelons theory: An update. *Academy of Management Review, 32*, 334–343. https://doi.org/10.5465/AMR.2007.24345254
Hambrick, D. C., & Mason, P. A. (1984). Upper echelons: The organization as a reflection of its top managers. *The Academy of Management Review, 9*(2), 193–206. https://doi.org/10.2307/258434
Hennart, J.-F. (2010). Transaction cost theory and international business. *Journal of Retailing, 86*, 257–269. https://doi.org/10.1016/j.jretai.2010.07.009
Hiebl, M. (2014). Upper echelons theory in management accounting and control research. *Journal of Management Control, 24*, 223–240. https://doi.org/10.1007/s00187-013-0183-1
Hofstede, G. (1980). Culture's consequences: International differences in work related values. *Organization Studies, 4*(4), 390–391. https://doi.org/10.1177/017084068300400409
Jensen, M., & Meckling, W. (1976). Theory of the firm: Managerial behavior, agency costs and ownership structure. *Journal of Financial Economics, 3*, 305–360. https://doi.org/10.1016/0304-405X(76)90026-X
Jenster, P., & Malone, S. (1991). *Resting on your laurels: The plateauing of the owner-manager*. FBN Conference.
Johanson, J., & Mattsson, L.-G. (1987). Interorganizational relations in industrial systems: A network approach compared with the transaction-cost approach. *International Studies of Management and Organization, 18*, 34–48.
Johanson, J., & Vahlne, J.-E. (1977). The internationalization process of the firm: A model of knowledge development and increasing foreign market commitments. *Journal of International Business Studies, 8*, 23–32. https://doi.org/10.1057/palgrave.jibs.8490676
Johanson, J., & Vahlne, J.-E. (2009). The Uppsala internationalization process model revisited: From liability of foreignness to liability of outsidership. *Journal of International Business Studies, 40*, 1411–1431. https://doi.org/10.1057/jibs.2009.24
Kontinen, T., & Ojala, A. (2010). Internationalization pathways of family SMEs: Psychic distance as a focal point. *Journal of Small Business and Enterprise Development, 17*, 437–454. https://doi.org/10.1108/14626001011068725
Kontinen, T., & Ojala, A. (2011a). Social capital in relation to the foreign market entry and post-entry operations of family SMEs. *Journal of International Entrepreneurship, 9*, 133–151. https://doi.org/10.1007/s10843-010-0072-8
Kontinen, T., & Ojala, A. (2011b). International opportunity recognition among small and medium-sized family firms*. *Journal of Small Business Management, 49*, 490–514. https://doi.org/10.1111/j.1540-627X.2011.00326.x
Kontinen, T., & Ojala, A. (2011c). Network ties in the international opportunity recognition of family SMEs. *International Business Review, 20*, 440–453. https://doi.org/10.1016/j.ibusrev.2010.08.002
Kontinen, T., & Ojala, A. (2012a). Social capital in the international operations of family SMEs. *Journal of Small Business and Enterprise Development, 19*, 39–55. https://doi.org/10.1108/14626001211196398
Kontinen, T., & Ojala, A. (2012b). Internationalization pathways among family-owned SMEs. *International Marketing Review, 29*(5), 496–518. https://doi.org/10.1108/02651331211260359

Kostova, T., & Zaheer, S. (1999). Organizational legitimacy under conditions of complexity: The case of the multinational enterprise. *Academy of Management Review, 24*, 64–81. https://doi.org/10.2307/259037

Koul, S., Kumar, U., Kumar, V., & Singla, S. (2020). Internationalization: Case of an emerging home decor family business. *South Asian Journal of Business and Management Cases, 9*(3), 433–444. https://doi.org/10.1177/2277977920958083

Kuivalainen, O., & Saarenketo, S. (2012). International pathways of software born globals. In M. Gabrielsson & M. V. H. Kirpalani (Eds.), *Handbook of research on born globals* (pp. 263–284). Edward Elgar Publishing.

Lahiri, S., Mukherjee, D., & Peng, M. W. (2020). Behind the internationalization of family SMEs: A strategy tripod synthesis. *Global Strategy Journal, 10*(4), 813–838. https://doi.org/10.1002/gsj.1376

Lambrecht, J., & Naudts, W. (2008). *Overview of family business relevant issues*. Austrian Institute for SME Research on behalf of the European Commission.

Larrson, A., & Starr, J. A. (1993). A network model of organization formation. *Entrepreneurship Theory and Practice, 17*(2), 5–15. https://doi.org/10.1177/104225879301700201

Liang, X., Wang, L., & Cui, Z. (2013). Chinese private firms and internationalization: Effects of family involvement in management and family ownership. *Family Business Review, 27*, 126–141. https://doi.org/10.1177/0894486513480885

Lin, N., Cook, K., & Burt, R. (2002). Social capital: Theory and research. *Contemporary Sociology, 31*(1), 28–29. https://doi.org/10.2307/3089402

Lu, Y., Zhou, L., Bruton, G., & Weiwen, L. (2010). Capabilities as a mediator linking resources and the international performance of entrepreneurial firms in an emerging economy. *Journal of International Business Studies, 41*, 419–436. https://doi.org/10.1057/jibs.2009.73

Majocchi, A., & Strange, R. (2012). International diversification: The impact of ownership structure, the market for corporate control and board independence. *Management International Review, 52*, 879–900. https://doi.org/10.2307/41682290

Mandl, I. (2008). *Overview of family business relevant issues*. European Family Businesses.

Mathews, J., & Zander, I. (2007). The international entrepreneurial dynamics of accelerated internationalisation. *Journal of International Business Studies, 38*, 387–403. https://doi.org/10.1057/palgrave.jibs.8400271

McAuley, A. (1999). Entrepreneurial instant exporters in the Scottish arts and crafts sector. *Journal of International Marketing, 7*(4), 67–82. https://doi.org/10.1177/1069031X9900700405

Mejri, K., & Umemoto, K. (2010). Small- and medium-sized enterprise internationalization: Towards the knowledge-based model. *Journal of International Entrepreneurship, 8*, 156–167. https://doi.org/10.1007/s10843-010-0058-6

Memili, E., Fang, H., Chrisman, J. J., & De Massis, A. (2015). The impact of small- and medium-sized family firms on economic growth. *Small Business Economics, 45*(4), 771–785. https://doi.org/10.1007/s11187-015-9670-0

Meyer, J. P., & Allen, N. J. (1991). A three-component conceptualization of organizational commitment. *Human Resource Management Review, 1*(1), 61–89. https://doi.org/10.1016/1053-4822(91)90011-Z

Meyer, K., & Skak, A. (2002). Networks, serendipity and SME entry into Eastern Europe. *European Management Journal, 20*(2), 179–188. https://doi.org/10.1016/S0263-2373(02)00028-2

Miller, D., Le Breton-Miller, I., Lester, R., & Cannella, A. (2007). Are family firms really superior performers? *Journal of Corporate Finance, 13*, 829–858. https://doi.org/10.1016/j.jcorpfin.2007.03.004

Muñoz-Bullón, F., & Sanchez-Bueno, M. (2012). Do family ties shape the performance consequences of diversification? Evidence from the European Union. *Journal of World Business, 47*(3), 469–477. https://doi.org/10.1016/j.jwb.2011.05.013

Mustakallio, M. A. (2002). Contractual and relational governance in family firms: Effects on strategic decision-making quality and firm performance. *Dissertation for the degree of Doctor of Science in Technology to be presented with due permission of the Department of Industrial Engineering and Management for Public Examination and Debate in Auditorium Antin Sali at Institute of Design*, Lahti (Finland), 7th June 2002.

Nahapiet, J., & Ghoshal, S. (1998). Social capital, intellectual capital, and the organizational advantage. *The Academy of Management Review, 23*(2), 242–266. https://doi.org/10.2307/259373

Nicolò, D., & Valenza, G. (2019a). Il dinamismo e la competitività delle imprese italiane: le high-growth enterprises e le gazzelle familiari e non familiari. *Rivista Economica Del Mezzogiorno, 33*(3–4), 997–1019.

Nicolò, D., & Valenza, G. (2019b). The "start-up a business" strategy in the succession process planning. *China-USA Business Review, 18*(2), 1–12.

Ojala, A. (2009). Internationalization of knowledge-intensive smes: The role of network relationships in the entry to a psychically distant market. *International Business Review, 18*, 50–59. https://doi.org/10.1016/j.ibusrev.2008.10.002

Ozgen, E., & Baron, R. (2007). Social sources of information in opportunity recognition: Effects of mentors, industry networks, and professional forums. *Journal of Business Venturing, 22*, 174–192. https://doi.org/10.1016/j.jbusvent.2005.12.001

Poutziouris, P., Wang, Y., & Chan, S. (2002). Chinese entrepreneurship: The development of small family firms in China. *Journal of Small Business and Enterprise Development, 9*(4), 383–399. https://doi.org/10.1108/14626000210450568

Pukall, T. J., & Calabrò, A. (2014). The internationalization of family firms: A critical review and integrative model. *Family Business Review, 27*(2), 103–125. https://doi.org/10.1177/0894486513491423

Ragozzino, R. (2009). The effects of geographic distance on the foreign acquisition activity of U.S. firms. *Management International Review, 49*, 509–535. https://doi.org/10.1007/s11575-009-0006-7

Reid, S. (1984). Information acquisition and export entry decisions in small firms. *Journal of Business Research, 12*(2), 141–157.

Riketta, M. (2002). Attitudinal organizational commitment and job performance: A meta-analysis. *Journal of Organizational Behavior, 23*, 257–266. https://doi.org/10.1002/job.141

Scholes, L., Mustafa, M., & Chen, S. (2016). Internationalization of small family firms: The influence of family from a socioemotional wealth perspective. *Thunderbird International Business Review, 58*, 131–146. https://doi.org/10.1002/tie.21729

Sciascia, S., Mazzola, P., & Chirico, F. (2013). Generational involvement in the top management team of family firms: Exploring nonlinear effects on entrepreneurial orientation. *Entrepreneurship Theory and Practice, 37*(1), 69–85. https://doi.org/10.1111/j.1540-6520.2012.00528.x

Scott, W., & Meyer, J. (1994). *Institutional environments and organizations: Structural complexity and individualism*. Sage Publications.

Segaro, E. (2012). Internationalization of family SMEs: The impact of ownership, governance, and top management team. *Journal of Management and Governance, 16*, 147–169. https://doi.org/10.1007/s10997-010-9145-2

Segaro, E. L., Larimo, J., & Jones, M. V. (2014). Internationalisation of family small and medium sized enterprises: The role of stewardship orientation, family commitment culture and top management team. *International Business Review, 23*(2), 381–395. https://doi.org/10.1016/j.ibusrev.2013.06

Shi, H., Graves, C., & Barbera, F. (2018). Intergenerational succession and internationalisation strategy of family SMEs: Evidence from China. *Long Range Planning, 52*. https://doi.org/10.1016/j.lrp.2018.05.004

Simon, H. (1996). *Hidden champions*. Harvard Business School.

Sirmon, D. G., & Hitt, M. A. (2003). Managing resources: Linking unique resources, management, and wealth creation in family firms. *Entrepreneurship Theory and Practice, 27*(4), 339–358. https://doi.org/10.1111/1540-8520.t01-1-00013

Söderqvist, A. M., & Chetty, S. (2009). Strength of ties and their role in pre-founding, start-up and early internationalization. *12th McGill International Entrepreneurship Conference*.

Sousa, C., & Bradley, F. (2008). Cultural distance and psychic distance: Refinements in conceptualisation and measurement. *Journal of Marketing Management, 24*, 467–488. https://doi.org/10.1362/026725708X325959

Storper, M., & Leamer, E. (2001). The economic geography of the internet age. *Journal of International Business Studies, 32*, 641–665. https://doi.org/10.1057/palgrave.jibs.84909988

Teece, D. (2012). Dynamic capabilities: Routines versus entrepreneurial action. *Journal of Management Studies, 49*, 1395–1401. https://doi.org/10.1111/j.1467-6486.2012.01080.x

Thorpe, R., Holt, R., Macpherson, A., & Pittaway, L. (2005). Using knowledge within small and medium-sized firms: A systematic review of the evidence. *International Journal of Management Reviews, 7*(4), 257–281. https://doi.org/10.1111/j.1468-2370.2005.00116.x

Tihanyi, L., Ellstrand, A., Daily, C., & Dalton, D. (2000). Composition of the top management team and firm international diversification. *Journal of Management, 26*, 1157–1177. https://doi.org/10.1016/S0149-2063(00)00076-3

Tranfield, D., Denyer, D., & Smart, P. (2003). Towards a methodology for developing evidence-informed management knowledge by means of systematic review. *British Journal of Management, 14*(3), 207–222. https://doi.org/10.1111/1467-8551.00375

Vandekerkhof, P., Steijvers, T., Hendriks, W., & Voordeckers, W. (2014). The effect of organizational characteristics on the appointment of nonfamily managers in private family firms: The moderating role of socioemotional wealth. *Family Business Review, 28*, 104–122. https://doi.org/10.1177/0894486513514274

Ward, J. (2004). Growing the family business: Special challenges and best practices. *Family Business Review, 10*, 323–337. https://doi.org/10.1111/j.1741-6248.1997.00323.x

Yang, X., Li, J., Stanley, L., Kellermanns, F., & Li, X. (2020). How family firm characteristics affect internationalization of Chinese family SMEs. *Asia Pacific Journal of Management, 37*, 417–448. https://doi.org/10.1007/s10490-018-9579-7

Yaprak, A., & Karademir, B. (2010). The internationalization of emerging market business groups: An integrated literature review. *International Marketing Review, 27*(2), 245–262. https://doi.org/10.1108/02651331011037548

Yu, F.-L. (2009). Towards a structural model of a small family business in Taiwan. *Journal of Small Business & Entrepreneurship, 22*, 413–428. https://doi.org/10.1080/08276331.2009.10593463

Zaefarian, R., Tasavori, M., Eng, T.-Y., & Demirbag, M. (2020). Development of international market information in emerging economy family SMEs: The role of participative governance. *Journal of Small Business Management*. https://doi.org/10.1080/00472778.2020.1800337

Zahra, S. A., Hayton, J. C., Neubaum, D. O., Dibrell, C., & Craig, J. (2008). Culture of family commitment and strategic flexibility: The moderating effect of stewardship. *Entrepreneurship Theory and Practice, 32*(6), 1035–1054. https://doi.org/10.1111/j.1540-6520.2008.00271.x

Zapletalová, Š. (2017). International management of Czech family enterprises: Decisions on international entrepreneurial activities. *Central European Business Review, 6*, 51–61. https://doi.org/10.18267/j.cebr.186

Zarone, V., Valenza, G., & Caputo, A. (2017). Il fronteggiamento del rischio di conflittualità familiare. In N. Lattanzi (Ed.), *Le aziende familiari. Generazioni, società, mercato* (pp. 97–118). Giappichelli.

Franco Ernesto Rubino is a Full Professor in Business Administration at the University of Calabria (Italy). Former director of the Department of Business and Law Sciences, he's currently the head of the degree course of study in Business Administration and Management. His research is focused on business administration, public management, and accounting. He's the author of several research works published both in national and international journals and books.

Claudio Multari is a Ph.D. student in Law and Economics at the University "Mediterranea" of Reggio Calabria (Italy). His research is focused on business strategies, family business, and financial report analysis.

Giuseppe Valenza is an Assistant Professor in Business Administration at the University of Palermo (Italy). He received his Ph.D. in Law and Economics from the University 'Mediterranea' of Reggio Calabria, Italy. His research is mostly focused on family business, entrepreneurship, accounting history, and financial accounting. His research has been published in several international journals and presented at international conferences.

Internationalising HRM Framework for SMEs: Transcending High-Performance Organisation Theory's Economic Utilitarianism Towards Humanism

John Mendy

Abstract Previous Business and Management studies' decades-long focus on an economic utilitarian approach has neglected human-centric issues such as staff and management resilience building and socio-cultural competence capacity in addressing SMEs' performance-related challenges during internationalisation. Such prolonged omission in the debates has partially led to the wrong measures being adopted and SMEs' unsustainability when they trade across borders. By critiquing and applying High-Performance Organisation Theory's characteristics of management planning, commitment, productivity, compliance and collaboration onto SMEs' internationalisation, this chapter highlights the dual theory-practice gap of people-centric and economic barriers which have contributed to the fundamental management and staff performance challenges faced by SMEs. To contribute to both the SME internationalisation literature and resolve this gap, this chapter proposes an 'Internationalising HRM' framework consisting of four interdependent cardinal principles which highlight four aspects that are crucial in resolving SMEs' internationalisation challenges, namely competency, R & TD, social and resilience capacity. Each of these aspects highlights what the economic utilitarian approach of HPO Theory has missed over the years and develops a framework that can help SMEs' managers and decision-makers to address both the economic and human elements that are vital for a more sustainable SMEs' internationalisation. The chapter also contributes to facilitating a more resilient SME internationalisation culture as it shifts the focus from economics to people given the increasing need for smaller firms' member to develop sustainable resilience to perform in the longer term. This perspective is new and should be included in international HRM, Strategic HRM and SMEs' entrepreneurship. Implications of the study's findings, its framework and future research areas are highlighted.

Keywords High-Performance Organisation Theory · SMEs · International · HRM

J. Mendy (✉)
University of Lincoln, Lincoln International Business School, Lincoln, UK
e-mail: jmendy@lincoln.ac.uk

A. Caputo et al. (eds.), *The International Dimension of Entrepreneurial Decision-Making*, Contributions to Management Science,
https://doi.org/10.1007/978-3-030-85950-3_8

1 Introduction

This conceptual abstraction chapter focuses on examining the theoretical literature on High-Performance Organisation (HPO) to identify and fill the theoretical-practical gap of the dual economic and human-centric barriers to small and medium sized enterprises' (SMEs') internationalisation challenge. The research attention on SMEs has increased exponentially and internationally (Vrontis et al., 2016) mainly partly because of their practical financial contributions including employment generation despite resource constraints (Boxall & Purcell, 2003). However, recent scholarship from Paul et al. (2017) and Okpara and Kabongo (2010) has sought to highlight some of the practical exporting challenges/barriers faced by SMEs in the context of the movement of goods across the globe's borders or, what has been referred to in the literature as 'internationalisation'. Despite the practical benefits expounded by Boxall and colleagues, these scholars have also identified some theoretical gaps and signposted areas where future research directions may be helpful. One of these areas is in examining how a more international form of HRM may be helpful in addressing some, if not all, of the practical economic challenges faced by SMEs' internationalisation. Similarly, too, Dabić et al. (2019) have bibliometrically analysed 762 research articles in reputable journals between 1992 and 2018 and have highlighted subject specific aspects including knowledge transfer, Human Resource Development and the need to refocus geographical attention. These highlighted aspects point to the literature's emphasis on the urgent need to address SMEs' economic constraints but also a research requirement to rebalance the SME and internationalisation scholarship. This scholarship, they believe, had previously predominantly relied on Resource Based View of the firm theory (a predominantly economic-centric approach) and a quantitative methodological perspective on SMEs' internationalisation and research.

Whilst Dabić et al. have also recognised important human related aspects such as the development of regionally oriented entrepreneurial ecosystems, they championed talent management and knowledge transfer as part of a new shift aimed at addressing the previously under-developed human aspects in international HRM, SME and HRD scholarship. Whilst Paul and Shrivatava (2016) and Onkelinx et al. (2016) had earlier recognised human capital issue highlighted by Dabić et al., there seems to be an agreement that an examination of how HRM can contribute to SMEs' internationalisation is not only an important research area but the extent to which the HRM discipline may help in alleviating some of the practical challenges is also long overdue. Despite such recognition, the way in which such an examination can address the complexity of human capital and thereby show the practical value that SMEs' external knowledge acquisition, network building capacity and internationalisation facilitation can add to the internationalisation literature has not been attempted previously. The inclusion of these innovative measures and human-centric elements in the emerging scholarship (Ciabuschi et al., 2015; Dabić et al., 2019; Paul et al., 2017) signals a scholarly need to examine what else may be added to the HRM-oriented literature and, additionally, whether such an addition could be of some practical benefit for SMEs' internationalisation. Therefore, based on the literature on SMEs' internationalisation, there is both a theoretical *and* practical gap in the SME and internationalisation literatures that need to be filled. This chapter combines aspects from the SME, HRM and High-Performance Organisation literatures that have been treated separately previously to contribute to and fill the theory-practice gap, as identified. Whilst Paul et al. (2017) and Dabić et al. (2019) have recognised that people-related challenges lie at the core of SMEs' internationalisation problem, we do not know how combining the people management qualities can enhance SMEs' performance, productivity, efficiency and effectiveness despite recent attempts made by Lwango et al. (2017), Adomakou et al. (2018) and Edmondson and Harvey (2017). Even earlier attempts by Mendy and Rahman (2019) and Mendy (2020) had, respectively, contributed to either the theoretical or practical gap relating specifically to the people-centric and economic barriers to SMEs' internationalisation. However, even Mendy and his colleagues had missed the extent to which SMEs' sustainability within a highly competitive international environment can be maintained through a more human-centric approach. Therefore, the dual theoretical-practical gap in the HRM, SME and internationalisation literatures, whose resolution could help SMEs' survivability and sustainability internationally is the focus of this chapter.

Internationalisation is defined in this chapter as the growing set of business activities that relate to firms' trading across borders (Liesch et al., 2014). In practical terms, internationalisation is facilitated by teams (Edmondson & Harvey, 2017) in order to address the external competition faced by SMEs when they compete with larger firms in exporting goods (Grandinetti & Mason, 2012). However, adopting a team-centric approach has not fully resolved SMEs' practical internationalisation challenges despite repeated calls to further develop human capital (Shahzad et al., 2019) through additional perspectives such as employee motivation and voice other than the Resource Based View (Dabić et al., 2019; Ruzzier et al., 2007). Furthermore, the identification and examination of High-Performance Organisation's theoretical human capital-related aspects shows not only the combined people management areas that previous and emerging scholarship on SMEs, HRM and Internationalisation have separately tried to address but that their examination could resolve the on-going theory-practice gap in SMEs' internationalisation literature. HPO therefore forms this chapter's theoretical anchor as it addresses a gap by emphasising the importance of developing teams to improve both staff's and management's core competences. It is believed that doing so will also improve the performance of SMEs internationally despite their size (Balboni et al., 2013; Paul & Anantharaman, 2003). However, the fundamental foundations of teamwork, collaboration, competency development and task-centred productivity have been limited to examining the economic value of these aspects as a way to resolve the capital-centric challenges faced by SMEs (Naldi et al., 2007). The shortcomings of this economic-centric argument become even more apparent when one looks what have been referred to as innovative ways (Kim-Soon et al., 2017; Mamoghli et al., 2018) of addressing some of the international competitive pressures faced by SMEs (Conz et al., 2017; Hansen & Winther, 2014). However, these recent innovations have only sought to address one aspect of SMEs' inability to survive internationally, which is the economic aspect whilst negating humans.

By people-centrism, popularly referred to in traditional literature as Humanism, this chapter refers to the HRM practices that SMEs can utilise to address the longer term challenges relating to economic costs as well as other aspects faced by smaller firms when they internationalise their services and goods (Lindner et al., 2016; Ulrich & Dulebohn, 2015). As a philosophical concept, Humanism was initially propositioned by the educationist Niethammer in 1808 (see Graf, 2015) to refer to a new curriculum for German schools. The coined term found its way into the English language in 1836 and was popularised worldwide by German philologist Voigt from 1856. Voigt referred to Renaissance Humanism as part of a new philosophical movement in the revitalisation of classical thinking and learning. It is also noted in the literature that the actual concept may have been practised long before gaining entry into scholarly works. In addition to the Italian renaissance, many other nations across the globe also bought into some version of humanistic thought and values as was evident around 1765 with references to 'love of humanity' within the French Enlightenment movement. The eighteenth and nineteenth centuries witnessed more grassroots' level movements that sought to improve the human condition via human reasoning whilst creating and sharing knowledge through such a philosophical orientation. However, such an approach has been criticised for promoting humanity rather than an all supreme Being. As a philosophy, humanism promotes and focuses on the centrality of the human being as an agent to change the human condition. Although the different religious and non-religious movements have attributed a range of meanings to the notion, it is generally taken to highlight a sense of agency and the freedom to exercise choice over humanity's destiny. At its core lie human dignity and a belief on personal and collective freedom and equality.

To fill the theory-practice gap identified earlier, this chapter examines the combined theoretical frameworks of SME, HRM and High-Performance Organisation literatures to contribute to filling the theoretical *and* practical gap in SMEs' internationalisation literature. In Sect. 2, the major characteristics of High-Performance Organisation theory are examined. Furthermore, Sects. 2 and 3 challenge the material, economic-centric arguments propositioned by HPO scholars in the context of SMEs' internationalisation with a more humane and people-centric set of arguments. Section 4 examines the chapter's results and their implications and Sect. 5 concludes with a summary and the directions of future studies in internationalisation.

2 Literature Review: High-Performance Organisation (HPO) Theory

HPO Theory is a concept that has been adopted by organisations in the hope that it will bring about a sustainable and improved performance that can deal with the firms' economic challenges. This section examines some of the core HPO characteristics such as planning, teamwork, commitment, productivity and collaboration to see the extent to which its theory helps SMEs to resolve the performance-related challenges they face in internationalisation.

Attempts to define HPO Theory are polarised. Despite the definitional differences, there are a variety of terms/concepts used ranging from High-Performance Work Organisation, High-Performance Work Systems, Flexible, Agile, Resilient to Sustainable Organisation. These concepts seek to highlight the way a firm's structures, its procedures, processes, leadership and management capacity create an innovative and inclusive environment, which organisations such as SMEs can use to develop high levels of financial performance, productivity and engaged stakeholders (e.g., staff, management, community, clients). To ascertain the extent to which the HPO literature's key aspects help SMEs to address their performance-related challenges in a highly competitive international environment, it is necessary to further sub-categorise performance under financial and non-financial. The financial category highlights the importance for SMEs to have a return on investment or ROI. This involves the triple bottom line of socio-economic and environmental performance, higher outputs/productivity, growth and expansion. On the other hand, the non-financial category focuses on the extent to which customers, staff and other stakeholders are engaged with and committed to the organisation's vision, mission, objectives and values. Although the second category appears to have no financial linkages when compared to the first, its examination in this section's sub-sections shows the continuous emphasis of a financial aspect that dampens the people-related elements that it is supposed to emphasise. For the purpose of this chapter and on the basis of the available literature, HPO Theory is defined here as an organisation that achieves, maintains and sustains competitive advantage over its rivals by facilitating a financial and non-financial results' oriented set of activities, policies, procedures and processes towards that goal. This study focuses on SMEs as organisations that have not been examined using HPO Theory.

By attempting to draw from different theoretical and thematic insights on HPO Theory that highlight the key financial and non-financial aspects, which are expected to make SMEs internationally competitive (i.e., performing), the author critiques their underlying assumptions. This approach helps to highlight how each of the HPO categories/themes individually and collectively fosters a predominantly economic utilitarian perspective for SMEs whilst, at the same time, shows what has been lacking in HPO Theory. An alternative, more humanistic perspective referred to as 'Internationalising HRM', which highlights principal principles of Humanism serves as this chapter's contribution to HPO theorisation and the internationalisation of SMEs.

2.1 Strategic Management Planning

HPO Theory advocates that management planning can help SMEs become more financially viable (Sardi et al., 2020). However, the theory also assumes that this planning process can only be successful when undertaken in the longer term as this helps in creating additional (financial) value creation for SMEs' stakeholders, including staff, customers and the community (i.e., the extended team) that companies do business with (Katzenbach & Smith, 2015). Additionally, management is trained to help create reward systems that would keep staff satisfied such that financial viability and sustainability becomes achievable (Brown et al., 2010). However, this belief has prompted critique that it overlooks a much wider and more crucial staff development and knowledge management issue (Albassami et al., 2019; Cerchione et al., 2016) especially for SMEs that are resource constrained (Mendy & Rahman, 2019). HPO Theory also advocates value creation through the identification and facilitation of an on-going customer-organisational relational improvement. The theory also highlights that staff need to learn what customers want, understand their values and develop a more longer-term relational experience with customers. The theory goes further to highlight the need to develop networks and partnerships that span an SME's shareholders, client and general stakeholder networks in as doing so will improve an organisation's profitability and reputation within the wider society. HPO Theory also fosters management promotion and training from within and encourages every staff member to balance their individual short-term interests with those that can help sustain their organisations in the more strategic future. These aspects highlight how HPO Theory seeks to create a sense of job and psychological security whilst, at the same time, underscoring the need for strategic financial viability. However, such emphases fail to fully address the core human resource issues related to what staff regard as valuable, meaningful and sustainable in the longer term (Ali et al., 2020). There is also a lack of consensus in the literature on which specific HPO planning characteristic SMEs' management should specifically be focused on and adequately trained if overall financial and organisational performance is to be ensured in the longer-term (Higgs & Dulewicz, 2014). Therefore, the question remains whether such disagreement and lack of clarity in HPO Theory do not jeopardise the very SME viability the concept was designed to promote (Ali et al., 2020; Ogunyomi & Bruning, 2016). When Lampadarios et al. (2017) reviewed and synthesised empirical data from a range of SME successes from the 1990s to their study's publication, they sought to address this issue by highlighting the knowledge needed by both management and staff so as to facilitate SMEs' performance. The development of a conceptual framework of the necessary HPO characteristics, similar to the one provided by Bagorogoza and de Waal (2010) recognises the importance that knowledge creation, its sharing and utilisation may add to SMEs' members' value creation processes. However, it does not resolve the fragmentation of the knowledge that members may develop from the variety of partnerships and networks that SMEs engage with over time or even what counts as valuable knowledge to facilitate a much strategic higher performance for smaller firms. Similarly, Sidik (2012) had earlier identified barriers to SMEs' performance but whilst having produced a framework that expounds on and helps to resolve the apparent fragmentation of the linkages between the constituent entrepreneur's planning qualities and an SME's performance, fails to underscore how team working can help facilitate SMEs' performance capability through more innovative, market orientated and overall capacity development.

2.2 *Teamwork*

Sustaining an organisation's financial profitability also depends on having the right team that can bring about the types of improvements to firms' economic viability as highlighted in HPO Theory (Holbeche, 2005). Teamwork is expected to give SMEs competitive advantage over rivals that stick with more traditional methods. However, HPO Theory also recognises that continuous improvement is needed in an organisation's processes and procedures given the fact that the effective organisation of work and information dissemination still pose challenges to SMEs operating internationally. Additionally, the performance of individual teams is continuously monitored and measured to ascertain whether an SME's profitability and their strategic sustainability are being achieved. Such HPO orientations put both management and staff under constant pressure to perform financially and to secure their companies' financial viability especially in market environments that are always changing to meet customers', shareholders' and organisations' financial drives. Whilst HPO Theory advocates that team-members' skills need constant updating so as to match the development of new products and services in highly competitive and changing SME international environments, it fails to address whether the non-hierarchical nature of its team approach to product and service development actually resolves perennial customer-related performance problems in this aspect (Castagna et al., 2020). Likewise, we are none the wiser regarding how the human resources constraints in this area are resolved (Lin & Lin, 2016), given the theory's acknowledgement that management planning and competence development need to be improved further (Reinhardt et al., 2018). In attempts to resolve some of the improvements needed, Castka et al. (2001) examined characteristics that high performing teams or HPTs should have by producing and testing a case-study model on how HPTs successfully resolve overall team performance in UK SMEs. Similarly, Cocca and Alberti (2010) highlighted a 'good' set of performance management and produced a self-assessment tool that can address SMEs' performance objectives. However, these studies did not indicate the extent to which these resolutions can assist SMEs that seek to address their performance and financial viability within an internationalisation context.

2.3 Reinventing Staff and Management Commitment

SMEs also face the additional challenge of a wider staff commitment to performance (Asamany & Shaorong, 2018). Whilst HPO Theory seeks to resolve this by advocating combined management-staff development, it also highlights a deeper, more fundamental overall employment relations challenge in a wider internationalisation context. HPO Theory advocates that management should provide the working environment where values such as respect, commitment and engagement are supported/promoted. HPO Theory further highlights the need for all staff to work with management towards the achievement of their SMEs performance objectives, mission and goals. This can be done through the identification of appropriate measurement criteria. The latter are communicated to staff through an identified set of actions, activities, performances and rewards. Whilst employees are permitted to take risks and see mistakes as an opportunity to enhance their learning and improvement, HPO Theory does not specify how SMEs' management's values of independence, entrepreneurial leadership and drive can be balanced against the need to foster management-staff dialogue and the sharing of both financial and non-financial performance in the decision-making process. Whilst HPO Theory also allows experiments and mistakes, the constant pressure faced by SMEs and their management to stimulate change by continuously striving for renewal, the need to develop dynamic managerial capabilities and facilitate employees' flexibility do not indicate which staff and management competencies should be treated as core and which ones ought to be relegated to the skills' development scrapheap. HPO Theory has also not resolved the social aspects relating to which type of language can be jointly agreed upon between SMEs' management and staff as they seek to reinvent their commitment to value creation potential within an internationalisation context. Sardi et al. (2020) thought that a performance measurement system would help resolve this issue for four Europe-based SMEs. Whilst they showed the relevance of HRM in supporting, measuring and improving organisational performance, their conceptual frame did not specify how SMEs' performance measurement could enhance the quality of the performance outcomes internationally (Sousa & Aspinwall, 2010) and what HRM could contribute. Therefore, the identification of measurement tools and models do not necessarily guarantee strategic and higher performance standards for SMEs competing internationally (Simpson et al., 2012).

2.4 Task-Based Productivity

HPO Theory advocates for flexibility and diversity and proposes the recruitment and selection of creative, innovative and problem-solving staff and management to help SMEs overcome their performance constraints. It is believed that this strategy enhances task-orientation among staff, which leads to workplace productivity and performance. Corresponding notions such as High-Performance Work Practices (Combs et al., 2006) and High-Performance Work Systems (Becker & Huselid, 1998) have been used to draw our attention to the important role that HR practices relating to recruitment, performance measurement, management and appraisals can play in facilitating higher levels of firm performance outcomes/results. These practices also include aspects such as employee assistance programmes (or EAPs—Attridge, 2012), employee development (Dvir et al., 2002), lean production and management (Bonavia & Marin-Garcia, 2011) and effective performance measurement and monitoring (Gunasekaran et al., 2011). HPO's focus on continuous workforce skills' development interventions (Dutta & Sobel, 2016; Lepak & Snell, 1999) and the facilitation of the application of those competencies to work flexibly (Jasra et al., 2011) has been critiqued for not producing the creative problem-solving outcomes that have been anticipated (Pulakos et al., 2000; Guest, 2002) partly because of additional pressures from fluctuations in an external environment (Roza et al., 2011). When de Waal analysed 290 studies before 1995 and after 1995, he highlighted characteristics, including an organisation's structural design and its culture to achieve the higher performance that has eluded SMEs over the decades. Although this is a purely utilitarian and economic approach to managing human resources, the fact that Hiltrop (2005) highlighted the importance of applying the Organisation Capability model's structures to enhance a firm's ability to attract, retain and develop talented staff for higher performance draws our attention to the humanistic aspects that have been under-rated in HPO Theory for such a long time. By combining institutional, regulatory and socio-cultural aspects, Oseghale et al. (2019) highlighted the importance of the overlooked people-related aspects of HPO Theory. They even developed an ability, motivation and opportunity (AMO) model to show how staff can be developed to achieve the needed SME performance within a sub-Saharan African regional context. However, Kroon (2013) could not help but note the resource and decision-making constraints that SMEs continue to face when implementing practices associated with the high performance of 211 employees from 45 Dutch companies. Clearly, HPO Theory's assumptions and expectations of the aspects that could deliver higher levels of performance for SMEs within an internationalisation context have been exaggerated over the years principally because of its over-emphasis on the economic utilitarian perspective based on firm-level profitability. Some other alternative is needed.

2.5 Collaboration

To address the issue of what else might be needed to resolve SMEs' performance difficulty internationally, HPO Theory has turned to research and development and information dissemination as a platform that could facilitate collaboration between organisations and respective stakeholders. This is believed to enhance the longer-term sustainability of SMEs' performance. Through this, companies can develop their national and international networks of partnerships and alliances (Lepak &

Snell, 1999). Through such a resolution proposition, it has also been envisaged via HPO Theory that mergers and acquisitions could be enhanced internationally through the adoption of appropriate R&D practices. These resolution mechanisms will, in turn, help SMEs to overcome collaboration challenges through compliance, competition and productivity. Most companies have used ICT in trying to achieve such a performance boost (Kim-Soon et al., 2017). However, Soto-Acosta et al. (2016) have analysed how the fundamental use of technologies to facilitate financial performance sustainability has impacted adversely on Spain's manufacturing SMEs' ability to innovate and perform in the longer term. The ability of SMEs to combine knowledge dissemination and the appropriate utilisation of technology has shown how internet businesses' ability to perform could be largely affected by their effective usage of internal, technological capability. Such capability has been noted to be largely dependent on SMEs' international performance and their ability to collaborate with external partners and networks (Donbesuur et al., 2020; Mendy 2019). The level and scale of such collaboration is mainly dependent on a much-neglected aspect of HPO Theory, which is the extent to which the human aspects of performance can complement the traditional and predominant profit /economic-centric perspective of such theorisation.

3 Methodology

This chapter's methodology has been conducted based on and inspired by conceptual studies that have adopted a similar approach (Dabić et al., 2019; Ruzzier et al., 2006). A search of the literature included key search words such as High Performing Organisation, SMEs, internationalisation challenges and Human Resource Management, similar to the conceptual work by Liñán et al. (2019). These keywords led to the identification of critical literature on High-Performance Organisation and the extent to which they impacted on SMEs' ability to address performance-related challenges of internationalisation (Ruzzier et al., 2006). Secondly, the author also examined past conceptual studies from the Web of Science (WoS) database given its comprehensiveness and the interdisciplinarity of the performance-related issues that SMEs have been highlighted to address (Dar & Mishra, 2019). Thirdly, the author used an inclusion and exclusion criteria to determine which papers fitted the search criteria and, therefore, should be included in the theoretical review on HPO and which ones did not and were therefore omitted. Book reviews, conference proceedings and editorials were excluded as these did not serve the current chapter's purpose. Out of an initial total of over a hundred papers from the earlier search, these were compressed to just over seventy to form part of the theoretical review from a range of major journals on internationalisation, SMEs and High-Performance Organisation.

One of the foremost theory-based/bibliometric studies within recent internationalisation is Dabić et al. (2019). Having highlighted a variety of areas within SMEs' internationalisation, ranging from internationalisation strategies to the entrepreneurial capabilities required to be successful (Oviatt & McDougall, 1994) they also examined Resource Based View of the Firm (RBV) alongside other theoretical perspectives that shine an additional light on the predominantly economic dependency literature (Krishnan & Scullion, 2017). Commendable as the success factors needed to deal with the economic-centric difficulties (Caputo et al., 2016), the need to focus on how the core SME challenges within an internationalisation context have emerged was missed. Additionally, the use of a single HRM-based theory such as HPO to highlight the extent to which SMEs' internationalisation challenges were addressed was also missed. Therefore, this chapter's methodology and the selected literature on HPO were designed to analyse and address these fundamental omissions in the SME internationalisation literature. Although Dabić et al. (2019) highlighted Short and Palmer's (2008) recommendation of using human-scored systems, individual word count systems and computerised systems as part of a methodological process that may enhance data coding, content and data categorisation when undertaking a bibliometric analysis, the author used content analysis based on the fact that this chapter's main focus is to highlight the extent to which a specific theoretical perspective, which is HPO Theory, can be used to analyse how SMEs address their performance-related challenges when they internationalise their business. As a result, there was also no coding of the data but what has been done is a thematic presentation and analysis of the major themes that have been derived from the theoretical content examined here. The result of the analysis highlighted a critical need to internationalise HRM practices when SMEs venture outside their geographic boundaries. Additionally, the literature was also used to identify four major areas of how to enable SMEs' internationalisation of HRM practices. These include 'competency capacity', 'research and talent development', 'social capacity' and 'resilience capacity'. Each of these thematic aspects and their underpinning principles is presented in the results section of this chapter. The results of the analysis of HPO Theory's main areas, the extent to which they help to address SMEs' challenges and the resultant gaps in both theory and practice are presented next as a way of laying the grounds for the results of this study (see Table 1).

4 Results

The results follow a five-stage presentation consisting of an initial exposition of the main concept referred to here as 'Internationalising HRM' followed by four composite aspects of the developed concept, namely: (1) competency capacity; (2) R & TD capacity; (3) social capacity and (4) resilience capacity. There are also four underpinning principles for each of the four internationalising aspects to show what lies behind/informs each of the four core practical aspects of operationalising an Internationalising HRM Framework for SMEs. The concept and its aspects serve as contributions to what has been missing in HPO Theory regarding how SMEs deal with the challenges of performance related to their internationalisation efforts. These

Table 1 HPO and theory-practice gaps in SMEs' internationalisation challenges

HPO's major thematic areas	Relevance to SMEs challenges	Gaps to be resolved in SMEs internationalisation challenges
Strategic management planning	• Emphasis is on the management activities that can resolve the performance difficulty, • Little recognition of how HRM practices can help.	Theory: • Add information and knowledge acquisition, transfer, utilisation and evaluation into Internationalisation challenge literature Practice: • Using 'best HRM practices' to create added value in SMEs' processes
Teamwork	• Partnerships and network building are considered vital in performance resolution, • Social aspects are neglected.	Theory: • Deeper understanding of cultural variations and nuances • Socio-economic partnership networks Practice: • Navigating cultural complexities • Recognising new competences
Reinventing commitment	• Management's facilitation of management-staff development could resolve performance, • How it can be used to facilitate sustainability is neglected, • Sharing decision- making is not prioritised,	Theory: • Reconceptualising respect, commitment and engagement as resilience building Practice: • Nurturing a 'bounce back' mind set • Enhancing international partnerships by combining material and non-material capability
Task productivity	• A range of employment assistance programmes are thought useful, • The socio-cultural aspects that could boost performance are missed,	Theory: • Adding socio-cultural aspects in productivity and service delivery Practice: • Skills capacity to deal with resource trap • Legal compliance • Product value enhancement
Collaboration	• Technology can be used to facilitate information dissemination when performance in collaborative ventures is problematic, • Human aspects in boosting performance are downplayed,	Theory: • Greater understanding of what type (s) of knowledge is valuable for SMEs Practice: • Geographic skills awareness • Staff's creation of pragmatic knowledge sharing and transfer platforms • Social problem resolution

highlighted thematic areas also serve as contributions to Dabić et al.'s (2019) identification of the range of subject areas covered in the theoretical depictions on SMEs and internationalisation as well as to the variety of theories used to do so in the sense that there is a more focused attention here on what may have given rise to the SMEs' internationalisation performance-related challenge and how HPO Theory, which has been predominantly used to address such types of challenges, has been insufficient in doing so. The findings/results are conducted through thematic presentation and analysis of each theme derived from the theoretical content. This is done to ascertain not only the chapter's contribution but also what is needed for a shift from the economic utilitarianism to people-centric management used in HPO Theory to address the SME challenges to a much longer term need to highlight what the nature of the challenges are and how a different alternative to the economic-centric approach/perspective of HPO Theory could actually enhance smaller businesses' survivability in internationalisation.

4.1 Internationalising HRM Framework

The concept of 'Internationalising HRM' for SMEs was built from the shortcomings of earlier propositions in relation to how efficient and effective HPO Theory's aspects are in addressing the performance challenges faced by SMEs when they internationalise their business (Krishnan & Scullion, 2017). Despite Dar and Mishra (2019), Booltink and Saka-Helmhout and Mamoghli et al. (2018) pointing out the contributions of people practices in facilitating organisations' economic benefits we do not know how the people management practices highlighted in HPO Theory can be effectively used in combatting not only economic challenges as suggested by Ruzzier, Caputo et al. (2016) and Ardito et al. (2018) but also the overlooked socio-cultural aspects (Oseghale et al., 2019) which could potentially lead to the development of longer term individual and collective resilience for SMEs. Figure 1 below identifies the types of challenges that the development of an internationalising HRM perspective are intended to address when SMEs are confronted with similar issues highlighted in the introduction and the literature review sections as well as the missing aspects, following the tradition of Dabić et al. (2019) and Liñán et al. (2019). Additionally, this chapter highlights the underpinning principles of each of the aspects and how both serve as contributions to HPO Theory and the fields of Internationalisation and HRM. The implications for HRM and Internationalisation theory and practice are presented and discussed in the next sections.

4.2 Competency Capacity

4.2.1 Principle 1: Entrepreneurial Skill Capacity

The first principle entails developing the requisite skill for competency capacity within an 'Internationalising HRM' framework. This involves the need for HRM

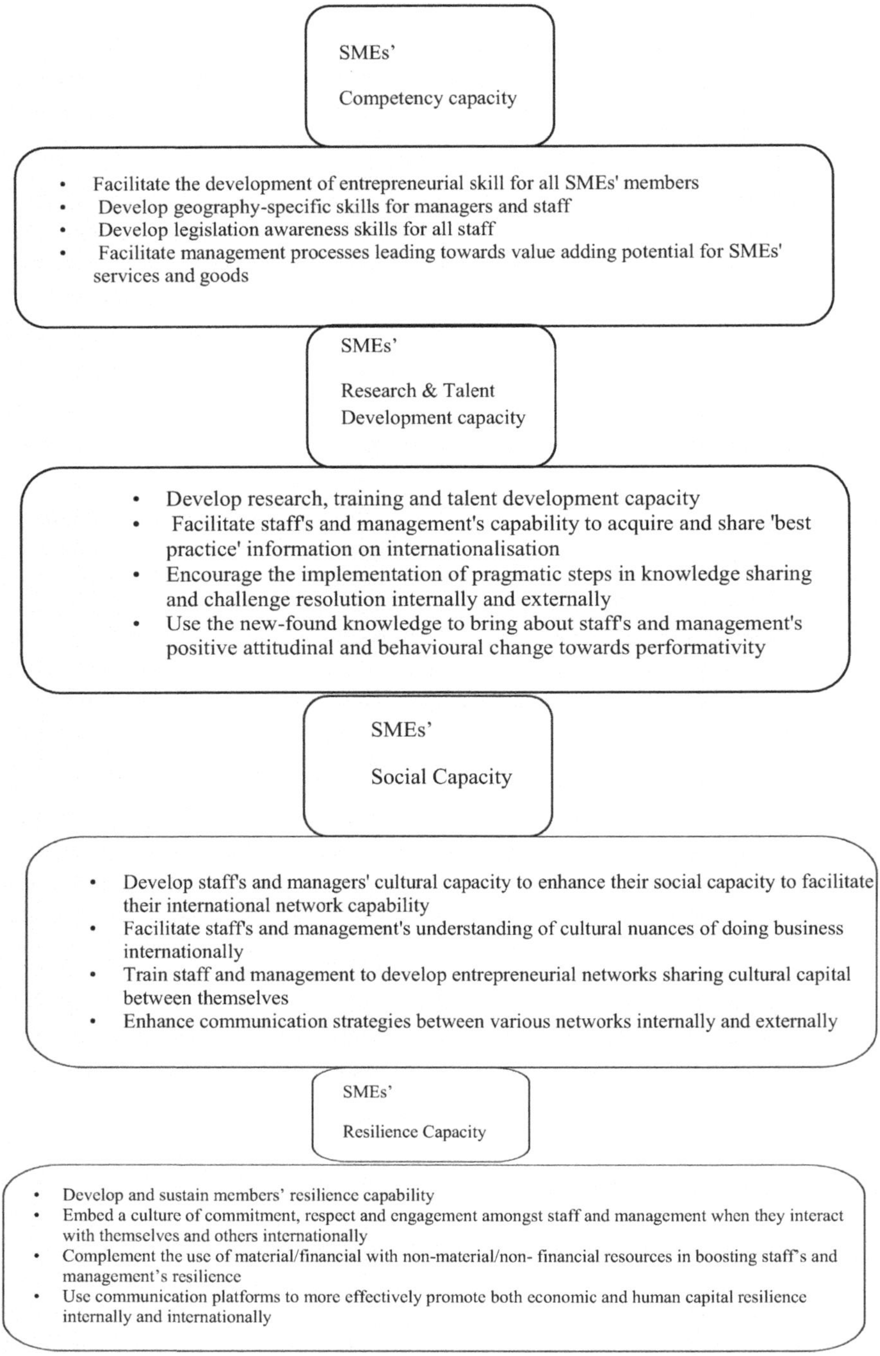

Fig. 1 Internationalising HRM Framework

specialists and practitioners to facilitate entrepreneurs and staff's capacity to develop and sustain entrepreneurial skill (Roza et al., 2011). This is critical as an earlier examination of the literature on HPO shows a lack of clarification and agreement on what specific skilled expertise is needed not only by management (Sardi et al., 2020) but also by other meaningful contributors such as staff. This clarification is crucial when SMEs internationalise their operations from one entrepreneurial geographic location to the next. We are also reminded that such a practice has a potentially adverse impact on SMEs' (Jasra et al., 2011) as it challenges their staff's and management's ability to share and manage the requisite knowledge needed (Albassami et al., 2019) for their performance (Dutta & Sobel, 2016). There is an additional challenge here, which includes the need for HRM to develop processes for the resolution of SME members capability to develop geography-specific skills to deal with the social problems that such geographic dislocation could cause to people (Dreher & Gassebner, 2013; Oseghale et al., 2019). It has also been highlighted in HPO Theory that SMEs need to comply with a country's legislation and related institutional frameworks when they internationalise their business. The proposal here to develop both management's and staff's entrepreneurial skill capacity helps in mitigating against the challenges caused to resource-strapped SMEs as they adapt their business processes to fit the new country's requirements. The development of such skill through the adoption of the appropriate HRM's facilitation of training processes helps SME members to actually enhance the value of their firm's products and services by making them not only legally compliant but also boosting staff's and management's competence to facilitate such a process. Although past and current theoretical postulations of HPO Theory, including those associated with Lepak and Snell (1999) have over-emphasised the economic utilitarian value of such a perspective and principle, there is an aspect which has been downplayed all along. This is how people management processes can contribute to such value production despite earlier attempts that have recognised the importance of doing so by Liñán et al. (2019) and Dvir et al. (2002). The development of entrepreneurial skill capacity emphasises on such an important but neglected aspect of people's skills in conjunction with their economic utilitarian contribution to SMEs' internationalisation (Mendy & Hack-Polay, 2018).

4.3 Research and Talent Development Capacity

4.3.1 Principle 2: Information and Knowledge Sharing Capacity

The second principle centres on developing research and training and development capacity within an 'Internationalising HRM' framework. It highlights the importance of HRM specialists to facilitate the development of staff's capability to not only acquire information about 'best practices' but also to share both tacit and explicit knowledge of how such practices are implemented pragmatically. This fills the HPO aspect regarding overlooked knowledge management (Lampadarios et al., 2017) and serves as recognition of Dabić et al.'s (2019) acknowledgement of how vital knowledge is in facilitating SMEs' internationalisation. To add to Dabić et al.'s (2019) work, HRM professionals should appropriately harness and use both tacit and explicit knowledge. This will add comprehensible value in ascertaining and resolving the customer relations problems that Castagna et al. (2020) or the collaboration bottlenecks that Mustapha and Yaakub or the financial performance issues highlighted by Donbeswuur et al. Filling these performance-related problems requires the identification areas where the obvious knowledge gaps may have been in SMEs' international operations and a deeper understanding of how that type of knowledge can effectively and efficiently be utilised by SMEs' international collaborators. Albassim et al.'s (2019), Lampadarios et al.'s (2017) and Soto-Acosta's identification of the technology as part of the knowledge management that had been overlooked in HPO Theory had not clarified the extent to which its transfer platforms go beyond resolving the economic/resource challenges faced by SMEs but also how sustainably innovative such transfer platforms (García-Lillo et al., 2017) can be to people. In essence, the human aspect that has been missed in addressing SMEs' performance challenges is what the combined information, knowledge-sharing and research and training and development aspects are expected to bridge. Although the literature recognises the importance of training and relationship building between management and staff to facilitate overall staff capability, we do not know how such a recognition can contribute to the human capital requirements of SMEs. Additionally, although it is also claimed by Barney (1991) that developing human potential can bring about not only behavioural change but also the vital economic-centric approach of HPO Theory, we do not know how the recognisable importance of such virtual knowledge management (Cerchione et al., 2016; Soto-Acosta et al., 2016) can enhance SMEs' performance practice. The literature also claims that research facilitates firms' productivity (Pisano, 1990) especially when companies try to gain competitive advantage internationally by enhancing their economic and resource-value through technical capability (Kim-Soon et al., 2017) without specifying how the vital people management processes could help. By combining research and talent development, the concept of 'Internationalising HRM' framework highlights the important nature of the interdependence of these aspects if SMEs are to successfully deal with their people-related internationalisation challenges.

4.4 Social Capacity

4.4.1 Principle 3: Cultural Competence Capacity

The third principle focuses on developing both staff's and managers' cultural competence capacity within an 'Internationalising HRM' framework. This involves HRM helping all SME members to identify the informal taken-for-granted cultural values around network creation, collegiality, 'can-do' spirit and 'being there' for one another as a set of valuable competences that could be used in a foreign/host country. The literature acknowledges that one of the fundamental resource constraints faced by SMEs' ability to internationalise their business into other markets has partly been caused by a cultural deficit (Dabić et al., 2019) as both staff and managers may not be aware of the institutional, regulatory and socio-cultural combinations that provide the cultural fabric within internationalisation contexts, the deeper understanding and navigation of which are crucial for international business success. However, apart from an identification of the potential benefits that the development of SMEs' capacities could have in enhancing a culture of innovation to ease some of the financial viability concerns (Sardi et al., 2020) of small firms (Gonzalez-Loureiro et al., 2017) understanding the cultural nuances and complexities of international collaboration networks is a missing, yet important human aspect in fostering firms' economic value. Evidently, there is a need to not only use cultural expertise to maintain external, economic business partnerships, but to also encourage members to adopt and integrate with foreign languages and customs. Therefore, an international HRM perspective should focus on facilitating HRM's capacity to develop such cultural know-how in SMEs' members to facilitate the social cohesiveness of entrepreneurial networks. This can additionally be done by developing more effective communication processes.

4.5 Resilience Capacity

4.5.1 Principle 4: Sustaining Bouncing Back Capacity

The fourth principle centres on developing SMEs' members' capacity not only to bounce back from the adversarial challenges but also to develop the wherewithal to sustain such a capability. This is a fundamental principle within an 'Internationalising HRM' framework as it helps SMEs, their owners and staff not only to recognise challenges as part of what they have to deal with in new geographic dispensations but also to nurture and learn key characteristics such as commitment, continuous engagement, the preparedness to challenge sub-standard performance, to learn from it and to bounce back when challenged. Resilience capacity consists of an organisation and individuals' recognition of social and cultural aspects that both parties need if they are to successfully deal with their commitment, productivity, compliance and collaboration problems internationally and what is needed to operationalise it. This aspect of internationalising HRM highlights aspects other than the economic utilitarianism of HPO Theory through the encouragement for SMEs to competently develop procedures enhancing skills development, flexible working, information sharing and value enhancing partnerships that have formed the crux of HPO Theory over the decades. Given the literature's recognition of the precarity of SMEs' sustainability as a result of their economic-resource dependency, the resilience capacity development combines both the material with the non-material resources that SMEs may have (e.g., social, cultural, aspirational and attitudinal) in an inextricably interdependent relationship so as to facilitate SMEs sustainability when they are challenged to operate internationally. This was absent in previous studies on how SMEs deal with their economic as well as people-related performance challenges. Resilience capacity now becomes a development issue for SME internationally within the new 'Internationalising HRM' framework as depicted below (Table 2).

4.6 Implications for HRM and Future Research

This section considers the chapter's findings', including the proposed 'Internationalising HRM' Framework's implications from a practical and research perspective.

The proposed framework serves as an extension of HPO Theory in terms of its practical benefits for managers in SMEs. The four aspects of 'Internationalising HRM' highlight areas that management need to prioritise when they are faced with and are intent on resolving not only the economic but also the people-related challenges/barriers that SMEs encounter in internationalisation. Each of the four aspects helps to facilitate managers' and entrepreneurs' decision-making competency and identifies the requisite need to develop appropriate mechanisms in the selection, skill, cultural and language training of both management and staff for international assignments. The literature on HPO Theory highlights the importance of management planning that focuses predominantly on boosting a firm's economic potential without much regard to how small companies' inadequate resources can be pragmatically harnessed to increase both the human and economic potential of all staff. Competency development, research and talent development, social and resilience capacity development indicate the very human-centric essentials that HPO Theory had neglected in previous Management and Business studies. By highlighting the important role that HRM professionals can play in redirecting SMEs' entrepreneurs' efforts towards greater humanism in their business practices, it is envisaged that smaller firms' managers can recognise the 'softer' socio-cultural and human behavioural aspects which need to be addressed urgently to forestall the economic-centric barriers that previous studies have sought to address. Bringing together the 'harder' economic-centric perspective in line with HRM implies that the triple-level coordination between a firm's need to be economically viable, the need to sustain people and the need to address environmental challenges are addressed simultaneously. There is an additional implication here, which is that HRM professionals need to rethink and re-design the way that people-centric procedures such as research, training, development and mentoring of staff are conducted. Such re-design and implementation will include a mix of financial performance, emotional and psycho-social wellbeing and cultural competency to facilitate greater chances of both management and staff performing successfully internationally. This fills the missing gaps in the social aspects needed in R & D collaborations across borders and

Table 2 Comparative analysis between HPO Theory's economic centrism and Internationalising HRM Framework's humanism

HPO Theory's economic-centric aspects	Internationalising HRM Framework's human-centric principles & aspects	Contributions of framework to SMEs & Internationalisation literature
• Management planning for financial viability • Reward staff for organisation's sustainability • Train staff to sustain organisation's profitability • Improve customer relations for profit • Develop networks to boost profits • value creation for stakeholders	• HRM to develop members' entrepreneurial skills to ease SMEs' resource constraints • HRM to develop staff's geography-specific skills to enhance their social integration	• New framework addresses SMEs' practical skills, resource and social integration constraints • New framework recognises competency development not only as an economic but also a social priority
• Team working to enhance organisation's competitivity • Monitor respective teams to ensure firm profitability • Update team-members' skills in line with product development	• Develop SMEs' members' awareness of international cultural nuances • HRM to develop members' ability to use cultural practices from different regions that work • Foster a climate of 'socio-cultural know-how'	• Team working has been broadened to include a deeper understanding of the cultural capital of international partners • 'Socio-cultural competence' is added to team working and overall organisational competitive capability
• Promote values of respect, engagement and commitment to enhance organisation's goals • Measure management's and staff's commitment • Identify actions and communicate measurement criteria	• HRM to develop a culture of resilience • HRM to develop procedures towards a culture of resilience building • HRM to facilitate a more sustainable staff as well as management commitment, engagement, productivity and flexible working as integral aspects of resilience development	• Values of respect, engagement and commitment are now fostered as part of a resilience-building culture for SMEs' survival
• Promote flexible working to boost productivity • Lean production is enhanced through performance monitoring • Direct skills' development interventions dampen staff creativity • Facilitate an organisation's capability through staff's skills' restructuring		
• Develop international networks through R & D	• HRM to develop research, training and development	• HRM now uses 'best practices' as an overall

(continued)

Table 2 (continued)

HPO Theory's economic-centric aspects	Internationalising HRM Framework's human-centric principles & aspects	Contributions of framework to SMEs & Internationalisation literature
• Overcome legal and productivity problems through partnership building • Use technology to build collaborations	using 'best practices' • HRM to help develop requisite knowledge acquisition and utilisation for SMEs • Use relationship building and knowledge transfer to boost SMEs' human capital • Use research and talent development to facilitate SMEs' members' behavioural change	international R & TD package to create human capital through knowledge acquisition, transfer and utilisation

the development of the requisite skilled expertise which had adversely impacted on HPO Theory's crucial aspects such as teamwork, commitment, task productivity and collaboration. Additionally, this new framework shows SMEs' managers, decision and policy makers what additional aspects need to be included in HPO Theory's management planning.

The second implication is related to research. Using HRM practices as a tool to train and develop staff as highly resilient performers highlights not only 'what' (i.e., the activities and actions required when doing business internationally) but also 'how' (i.e., ways of adapting to the myriad of personal, socio-cultural, emotional, performativity and economic challenges) to survive and be strategically sustainable. This study's results have exposed the fact that inasmuch as procedures are needed to implement HRM in diverse international SME environments HPO Theory and research should also consider 'how' to investigate and mitigate against other nuanced challenges of internationalisation beyond the economic-centric paradigm. By understanding the multi-facetted nature of the problem of performance-related challenges faced by SMEs and by appreciating the dual theory-practice gap that Business and Management scholarship has to deal with in SMEs' internationalisation, the implication is that current and potentially future studies could appreciate what types of new research are required to deal with this important set of issues. What this study has done is new in the sense that it successfully analysed HPO Theory, identified how an emphasis on the economic-centric paradigm had robbed prospective Business and Management research from focusing on the people/human-centric areas where improvements are actually needed to resolve SMEs' internationalisation. How to do so in research is suggested via an HRM pathway.

5 Conclusion

The chapter investigated HPO Theory to see how SMEs' performance-related challenges within internationalisation had been addressed in the theoretical debates and discussions. HPO Theory's five key themes have been analysed and the principal gap in their theorising highlights an over-emphasis on the economic utilitarian value of such an approach to work and organisations at the detriment of dealing with the fundamental human aspects. A deficit referred to here as the dual theory-practice gap in the HRM, SME and internationalisation literatures constituted the focus to this chapter. It was considered scholarly appropriate to pursue such an omission, whose resolution could help SMEs' survivability and sustainability internationally. Additionally, this deficit was used to develop an 'Internationalising HRM' framework, which highlights the humanism that needs to complement the economic argument of HPO Theory and therefore, serves as an alternative. Having shown the social, competency (i.e., skilled expertise), R & TD and resilience capacity development aspects where HPO Theory has been found wanting to address key people-related challenges faced in SMEs' internationalisation, an 'Internationalising HRM' perspective constituting such fundamental people-centric aspects has been developed. Its four underpinning principles were identified to guide SMEs' international decision makers and policy implementers. The four aspects and principles of the new framework suggest that it is high that HRM becomes central to SMEs' cross-border operations and that each of the aspects is used to help resolve the economic and people-related challenges faced by SMEs internationally. The results have highlighted areas of practical importance that decision makers ought to prioritise and how the interdisciplinarity between Business and HRM could be useful in sustaining SMEs' international ventures. The chapter has also highlighted the potential beneficial impact of using a range of information sources to develop and extend our knowledge and appreciation of challenges faced by SMEs and how these could be resolved not just economically but also humanistically.

Having successfully identified HPO Theory's shortcomings, the next thing was to see whether the economic utilitarian value perspective adopted by previous studies on internationalisation could be transcended to some other alternative view of conducting business. This additional objective proved slightly more challenging as previous studies and the literature had predominantly focused on either the challenges faced by MNEs or explored SMEs' economic utilitarianism. In order to resolve the study's dilemma, it was thought to explore theoretical aspects of HPO related theories with the aim of providing a way of dealing with the challenges as well as managing the complex international business interactions. The identification of lots of people and financial performance-related gaps prompted their inclusion in developing an 'Internationalising HRM' framework to add to SMEs' financial viability as envisaged by Sardi et al. (2020) whilst, at the same time, contributing to not only the identification of knowledge sources as anticipated by Albassami et al. (2019) but also how these can be managed through HRM development processes. The earlier theoretical works of Dabić et al. (2019) and Liñán et al. (2019) had signposted the need for additional investigative theoretical studies on SMEs and internationalisation challenges. This chapter addresses the way the challenges can be addressed via a development of an 'Internationalising HRM Framework', which fills earlier scholarship's research deficit. Previous studies stopped short of fulfilling this practice gap.

Future studies ought to build on the applicability of each of the 'Internationalising HRM' framework's aspects in a range of developing and developed economies' contexts with the view to comparing areas of convergence, divergence and complementarity/cross pollination of the HRM and business practices. Future theoretical developments on HPO Theory can also investigate and analyse a range of additional challenges and resolution mechanisms other than the social, competency, research and talent and resilience capacity development aspects propositioned in this chapter. By doing so it is anticipated that alternative research questions, methodologies and conceptual developments could be generated and used to address key emerging SME internationalisation challenges. It would also be interesting to see the extent to which the HRM discipline emerges as a more formidable systemic business partner especially in the context of SME. The work continues …

References

Adomakou, S., Opoku, R. A., & Frimpoong, K. (2018). Entrepreneurs' improvisational behaviour and new venture performance: Firm-level and institutional contingencies. *Journal of Business Research, 83*, 10–18.

Albassami, A. M., Hameed, W. U., Naveed, R. T., & Moshfegyan, M. (2019). Does knowledge management expedite SMEs performance through organizational innovation? An empirical evidence from small and medium-sized enterprises (SMEs). *Pacific Business Review International, 12*(1), 11–22.

Ali, Y., Younus, A., Khan, A. U., & Pervez, H. (2020). Impact of Lean, Six Sigma and environmental sustainability on the performance of SMEs. *International Journal of Productivity and Performance Management.*

Ardito, L., Besson, E., Petruzzelli, A. M., & Gregori, G. L. (2018). The influence of production, IT, and logistics process innovations on ambidexterity performance. *Business Process Management Journal, 24*(5), 1271–1284.

Asamany, A., & Shaorong, S. (2018). The ripple effects of performance management on employees? Perceptions and affective commitment among small and medium scale enterprises (SMEs). *International Journal of Business Administration, 9*(1), 55–63.

Attridge, M. (2012). Employee assistance programs: Evidence and current trends. In *Handbook of occupational health and wellness* (pp. 441–467). Springer.

Bagorogoza, J., & de Waal, A. (2010). The role of knowledge management in creating and sustaining high performance organisations: The case of financial institutions in Uganda. *World Journal of Entrepreneurship, Management and Sustainable Development, 6*(4), 307–324.

Balboni, B., Bortoluzzi, G., & Grandinetti, R. (2013). On the relationship between size, capabilities and internationalisation: An explorative analysis of Italian subcontracting SMEs. *International Journal of Globalisation and Small Business, 5*(1–2), 114–132.

Barney, J. B. (1991). Firm resources and sustained competitive advantage. *Journal of Management, 17*, 99–120.

Becker, B. E., & Huselid, M. A. (1998). High performance work systems and firm performance: A synthesis of research and managerial implications. *Research in Personnel and Human Resource Management, 16*, 53–101.

Bonavia, T., & Marin-Garcia, J. A. (2011). Integrating human resource management into lean production and their impact on organizational performance. *International Journal of Manpower, 32*(8), 923–938.

Boxall, P., & Purcell, J. (2003). *Strategy and human resource management*. Palgrave Macmillan.

Brown, M., Hyatt, D., & Benson, J. (2010). Consequences of the performance appraisal experience. *Personnel Review, 39*(3), 375–396.

Caputo, A., Marzi, G., & Pellegrini, M. M. (2016). The internet of things in manufacturing innovation processes: Development and application of a conceptual framework. *Business Process Management Journal, 22*(2), 383–402.

Castagna, F., Centobelli, P., Cerchione, R., Esposito, E., Oropallo, E., & Passaro, R. (2020). Customer knowledge management in SMEs facing digital transformation. *Sustainability, 12* (9), 3899.

Castka, P., Bamber, C. J., Sharp, J. M., & Belohoubek, P. (2001). Factors affecting successful implementation of high-performance teams. *Team Performance Management: An International Journal, 7*(7/8), 123–134.

Cerchione, R., Esposito, E., & Spadaro, M. R. (2016). A literature review on knowledge management in SMEs. *Knowledge Management Research & Practice, 14*(2), 169–177.

Ciabuschi, F., Forsgren, M., & Martín, O. M. (2015). Rationality vs ignorance: The role of MNE headquarters in subsidiaries' innovation processes. In *Knowledge, networks and power* (pp. 264–283). Palgrave Macmillan.

Cocca, P., & Alberti, M. (2010). A framework to assess performance measurement systems in SMEs. *International Journal of Productivity and Performance Management, 2*, 186–200.

Combs, J., Liu, Y., Hall, A., & Ketchen, D. (2006). How much do high-performance work practices matter? A meta-analysis of their effects on organizational performance. *Personnel Psychology, 59*(3), 501–528.

Conz, E., Denicolai, S., & Zucchella, A. (2017). The resilience strategies of SMEs in mature clusters. *Journal of Enterprising Communities: People and Places in the Global Economy, 11* (1), 186–210.

Dabić, M., Maley, J., Dana, L. P., Novak, I., Pellegrini, M. M., & Caputo, A. (2019). Pathways of SME internationalization: A bibliometric and systematic review. *Small Business Economics, 55*, 1–21.

Dar, I. A., & Mishra, M. (2019). Human capital and SMEs internationalization: Development and validation of a measurement scale. *Global Business Review, 15*, 1–17.

Donbesuur, F., Ampong, G. O. A., Owusu-Yirenkyi, D., & Chu, I. (2020). Technological innovation, organizational innovation and international performance of SMEs: The moderating role of domestic institutional environment. *Technological Forecasting and Social Change, 161*, 120252.

Dreher, A., & Gassebner, M. (2013). *Greasing the wheels? The impact of regulations and corruption on firm entry* (pp. 1–20). *Public Choice*.

Dutta, N., & Sobel, R. (2016). Does corruption ever help entrepreneurship? *Small Business Economics, 47*(1), 179–199.

Dvir, T., Eden, D., Avolio, B. J., & Shamir, B. (2002). Impact of transformational leadership on follower development and performance: A field experiment. *Academy of Management Journal, 45*(4), 735–744.

Edmondson, A. C., & Harvey, J. F. (2017). Cross-boundary teaming for innovation: Integrating research on teams and knowledge in organizations. *Human Resource Management Review, 28* (4), 347–360.

García-Lillo, F., Úbeda-García, M., & Marco-Lajara, B. (2017). The intellectual structure of human resource management research: A bibliometric study of the international journal of human

resource management, 2000–2012. *The International Journal of Human Resource Management, 28*(13), 1786–1815.
Gonzalez-Loureiro, M., Sousa, M. J., & Pinto, H. (2017). Culture and innovation in SMEs: The intellectual structure of research for further inquiry. *European Planning Studies, 0*(0), 1–24.
Graf, F. W. (2015). What is Humanism? My western response. In *Humanism in intercultural perspective* (pp. 111–118). transcript-Verlag.
Grandinetti, R., & Mason, M. C. (2012). Internationalization modes other than exporting. *European Business Review, 24*(3), 236–254.
Guest, D. E. (2002). Human resource management, corporate performance and employee wellbeing: Building the worker into HRM. *The Journal of Industrial Relations, 44*(3), 335–358.
Gunasekaran, A., Rai, B. K., & Griffin, M. (2011). Resilience and competitiveness of small and medium size enterprises: An empirical research. *International Journal of Production Research, 49*(18), 5489–5509.
Hansen, T., & Winther, L. (2014). Competitive low-tech manufacturing and challenges for regional policy in the European context – lessons from the Danish experience. *Cambridge Journal of Regions, Economy and Society, 7*, 449–470.
Higgs, M., & Dulewicz, V. (2014). Antecedents of well-being: a study to examine the extent to which personality and emotional intelligence contribute to well-being. *The International Journal of Human Resource Management, 25*(5), 718–735.
Hiltrop, J. M. (2005). Creating HR capability in high performance organizations. *Strategic Change, 14*(3), 121–131.
Holbeche, L. (2005). *The High-performance organization: Creating dynamic stability and sustainable success*. Routledge.
Jasra, M. J., Khan, M. A., Hunjra, A. I., Rehman, R. A. U., & Azam, R. I. (2011). Determinants of business success of small and medium enterprises. *International Journal of Business and Social Science, 2*(20), 274–280.
Katzenbach, J. R., & Smith, D. K. (2015). *The wisdom of teams: Creating the high-performance organization*. Harvard Business Review Press.
Kim-Soon, N., Ahmad, A. R., Kiat, C. W., & Sapry, H. R. M. (2017). SMEs are embracing innovation for business performance. *Journal of Innovation Management in Small and Medium Enterprises, 2017*, 1–17.
Krishnan, T. N., & Scullion, H. (2017). Talent management and dynamic view of talent in small and medium enterprises. *Human Resource Management Review, 27*(3), 431–441.
Kroon, B., Van De Voorde, K., & Timmers, J. (2013). High performance work practices in small firms: A resource-poverty and strategic decision-making perspective. *Small Business Economics, 41*(1), 71–91.
Lampadarios, E., Kyriakidou, N., & Smith, G. (2017). Towards a new framework for SMEs success: A literature review. *International Journal of Business and Globalisation, 18*(2), 194–232.
Lepak, D. P., & Snell, S. A. (1999). The human resource architecture: Toward a theory of human capital allocation and development. *Academy of Management Review, 24*(1), 31–48.
Liesch, P. W., Welch, L. S., & Buckley, P. J. (2014). Risk and uncertainty in internationalisation and international entrepreneurship studies. In *The multinational enterprise and the emergence of the global factory* (pp. 52–77). Palgrave Macmillan.
Lin, F. J., & Lin, Y. H. (2016). The effect of network relationship on the performance of SMEs. *Journal of Business Research, 69*(5), 1780–1784.
Liñán, F., Paul, J., & Fayolle, A. (2019). SMEs and entrepreneurship in the era of globalization: Advances and theoretical approaches. *Small Business Economics, 55*, 1–9.
Lindner, T., Muellner, J., & Puck, J. (2016). Cost of capital in an international context: Institutional distance, quality, and dynamics. *Journal of International Management, 22*(3), 234–248.
Lwango, A., Coeurderoy, R., & Giménez Roche, G. A. (2017). Family influence and SME performance under conditions of firm size and age. *Journal of Small Business and Enterprise Development, 24*(3), 629–648.

Mamoghli, S., Cassivi, L., & Trudel, S. (2018). Supporting business processes through human and IT factors: A maturity model. *Business Process Management Journal, 24*(4), 985–1006.
Mendy, J. (2019). Supporting creating shared value: Including local and global clusters of staff resistance to strategic SME restructuring. *Strategic Change, 28*(2), 157–161.
Mendy, J. (2020). Bouncing back from workplace stress: From HRD's individual employee's developmental focus to multi-facetted collective workforce resilience intervention. *Advances in Developing Human Resources, 22*(4), 353–369.
Mendy, J., & Hack-Polay, D. (2018). Learning from failure: A study of failed enterprises of self-employed African migrants in the UK. *Journal of Small Business and Enterprise Development, 25*(2), 330–343.
Mendy, J., & Rahman, M. (2019). Application of HRM's universal model: An examination of people vs institutions as barriers of internationalization for SMEs in a small developing country. *Thunderbird International Business Review, 61*(2), 363–374.
Naldi, L., Nordqvist, M., Sjöberg, K., & Wiklund, J. (2007). Entrepreneurial orientation, risk taking, and performance in family firms. *Family Business Review, 20*(1), 33–47.
Ogunyomi, P., & Bruning, N. S. (2016). Human resource management and organizational performance of small and medium enterprises (SMEs) in Nigeria. *The International Journal of Human Resource Management, 27*(6), 612–634.
Okpara, J., & Kabongo, J. (2010). Export barriers and internationalization: Evidence from SMEs in emergent African economy. *International Journal of Business and Globalization, 5*(2), 169–187.
Onkelinx, J., Manolova, T. S., & Edelman, L. F. (2016). Human capital and SME internationalization: Empirical evidence from Belgium. *International Small Business Journal, 34*(6), 818–837.
Oseghale, R. O., Nyuur, R. B., & Debrah, Y. A. (2019). Institutional factors and high-performance work organisations (HPWOs) in Sub-Saharan Africa (SSA). In *Management science* (pp. 199–218). Springer.
Oviatt, B. M., & McDougall, P. P. (1994). Toward a theory of international new ventures. *Journal of International Business Studies, 25*(1), 45–64.
Paul, A. K., & Anantharaman, R. N. (2003). Impact of people management practices on organizational performance. *International Journal of Human Resource Management, 14*, 1246–1266.
Paul, J., Parthasarathy, S., & Gupta, P. (2017). Exporting challenges of SMEs: A review and future research agenda. *Journal of World Business, 52*(3), 327–342.
Paul, J., & Shrivatava, A. (2016). Do young managers in a developing country have stronger entrepreneurial intentions? Theory and debate. *International Business Review, 25*(6), 1197–1210.
Pisano, G. P. (1990). The R&D boundaries of the firm: An empirical analysis. *Administrative Science Quarterly, 35*, 153–176.
Pulakos, E. D., Arad, S., Donovan, M. A., & Plamondon, K. E. (2000). Adaptability in the workplace: Development of a taxonomy of adaptive performance. *Journal of Applied Psychology, 85*(4), 612.
Reinhardt, R., Gurtner, S., & Griffin, A. (2018). Towards an adaptive framework of low-end innovation capability–A systematic review and multiple case study analysis. *Long Range Planning, 51*(5), 770–796.
Roza, M., Van den Bosch, F. A., & Volberda, H. W. (2011). Offshoring strategy: Motives, functions, locations, and governance modes of small, medium-sized and large firms. *International Business Review, 20*(3), 314–323.
Ruzzier, M., Antonci, C. B., Hisrich, R. D., & Konecnik, M. (2007). Human capital and SME internationalization: A structural equation modelling study. *Canadian Journal of Administrative Sciences/Revue Canadienne des Sciences de l'Administration, 24*(1), 15–29.
Ruzzier, M., Hisrich, R. D., & Antoncic, B. (2006). SME internationalization research: Past, present, and future. *Journal of Small Business and Enterprise Development, 13*(4), 476–497.

Sardi, A., Sorano, E., Garengo, P., & Ferraris, A. (2020). The role of HRM in the innovation of performance measurement and management systems: A multiple case study in SMEs. *Employee Relations: The International Journal, 43*, 589–606.
Shahzad, K., Arenius, P., Muller, A., Rasheed, M. A., & Bajwa, S. U. (2019). Unpacking the relationship between high-performance work systems and innovation performance in SMEs. *Personnel Review, 48*(4), 977–1000.
Short, J. C., & Palmer, T. B. (2008). The application of DICTION to content analysis research in strategic management. *Organizational Research Methods, 11*(4), 727–752.
Sidik, I. G. (2012). Conceptual framework of factors affecting SME development: Mediating factors on the relationship of entrepreneur traits and SME performance. *Procedia Economics and Finance, 4*, 373–383.
Simpson, M., Padmore, J., & Newman, N. (2012). Towards a new model of success and performance in SMEs. *International Journal of Entrepreneurial Behavior& Research, 18*(3), 264–285.
Soto-Acosta, P., Popa, S., & Palacios-Marqués, D. (2016). E-business, organizational innovation and firm performance in manufacturing SMEs: An empirical study in Spain. *Technological and Economic Development of Economy, 22*(6), 885–904.
Sousa, S., & Aspinwall, E. (2010). Development of a performance measurement framework for SMEs. *Total Quality Management, 21*(5), 475–501.
Ulrich, D., & Dulebohn, J. H. (2015). Are we there yet? What's next for HR? *Human Resource Management Review, 25*, 188–204.
Vrontis, D., Bresciani, S., & Giacosa, E. (2016). Tradition and innovation in Italian wine family businesses. *British Food Journal, 18*(8), 1883–1897.

Dr. John Mendy is Senior Lecturer and Programme Lead for MSc HRM based at the University of Lincoln, UK. He is interested in resilience research, the intersection between International HRM and International Business, Organisational Studies, Strategy, employment relationships, autism and employment/HRM policies and practices with specific foci on SMEs and MNEs in developed and emerging economies. John is a Senior Fellow of the Higher Education Academy (SFHEA, UK) and a Chartered Member of the CIPD (MCIPD, UK). John is the Chair of the Organisational Transformation, Change and Development Track at the British Academy of Management and has authored several peer-reviewed articles in respected journals. John has also won several awards, the most recent of which is the Best 2020 Special Issue on 'The Impact of Resilience in Developing Individual and Organizational Capacity to 'Bounce Back' from Challenges' in Advances in Developing Human Resources Journal. He also currently serves on the Editorial Boards of a number of journals, the exam boards of a couple of Higher Education institutions both in the UK and abroad and a Visiting Scholar.

Cross-cultural Tribes, Community and Indigenous Entrepreneurship

Paul Agu Igwe

Abstract This chapter distinguishes between "clan entrepreneurship", "kindred entrepreneurship", "tribal entrepreneurship", "community entrepreneurship" and nomadic entrepreneurship" within the broader theory of indigenous entrepreneurship. Using the case study of West African popular tribes of Igbo, Fulani, Hausa, and Yoruba, the unique cultural and indigenous elements of entrepreneurial behaviours have been examined and compared to advance indigenous entrepreneurship theories. The findings reveal that indigenous people have motives or drives for entrepreneurship, risk-taking, wealth-seeking and entrepreneurial learning that develop through indigenous cultures similar to modern entrepreneurship behaviours.

Keywords Indigenous entrepreneurship · Clan and Kindred entrepreneurship · Tribal entrepreneurship · Community entrepreneurship · Nomadic entrepreneurship

1 Introduction

This chapter evaluates the cultural and niche social elements of indigenous entrepreneurial behaviours. It examines "clan entrepreneurship", "kindred entrepreneurship", "tribal entrepreneurship", "community entrepreneurship" and nomadic entrepreneurship" within the broader theory of Indigenous entrepreneurship. Indigenous entrepreneurship is an emerging context in the field of management research. Hence, new studies focus on entrepreneurial identities, entrepreneurial attitudes and entrepreneurial behaviours which are influenced by Indigenous cultures (Bruton et al., 2018; Dana, 2015; Edwards, 2017; Greidanus & Sharpe, 2017). It has been stated that indigenous tribes are a minority—and a special type of minority (Dana, 2015). In the field of entrepreneurship, indigenous entrepreneurship is the "creation, management and development of new ventures by indigenous people for the benefit

P. A. Igwe (✉)
Lincoln International Business School, University of Lincoln, Lincoln, UK
e-mail: pigwe@lincoln.ac.uk

A. Caputo et al. (eds.), *The International Dimension of Entrepreneurial Decision-Making*, Contributions to Management Science,
https://doi.org/10.1007/978-3-030-85950-3_9

of indigenous people" (Dana & Anderson, 2007, p. 4). Cross-cultural entrepreneurship examines the management of entrepreneurship and businesses in different cultural and institutional settings (Engelen et al., 2009).

The literature reveals that the institutional and cultural environment determines the economic behaviours of Indigenous people but also for non-indigenous (Anggadwita et al., 2017; Igwe et al., 2020; Thornton et al., 2012). Cultural elements include the norms, values, family interaction and collaborative relationships (Anggadwita et al., 2017; Bruton et al., 2018; Igwe et al., 2020; Ratten, 2014). In this context, the phenomenon of "cross-cultural entrepreneurship" explains some of the diversity observable in the norms, customs, values and orientations of indigenous people and their economic behaviour. These norms and values differ from communities, tribes and ethnic groups. The neglect of roles indigenous tribes and communities may have impeded the development of entrepreneurship theories (Bruton et al., 2018; George et al., 2016). This article develops the theory of *"indigenousness"* defined as the unique inherent feature of *"cultural attributes"* inherent in the unique systems of customs, social values, collaborative relationships, economic orientations and behaviours.

Many indigenous people suffer oppression and deprivations of human rights, economic opportunities and political spaces (Igwe et al., 2018, 2020; Kouritzin & Nakagawa, 2018). Against the backdrop of neglect of indigenous people in management research, this chapter introduces indigenous entrepreneurship and sub-sets such as "clan entrepreneurship", "kindred entrepreneurship", "tribal entrepreneurship" and "community entrepreneurship". Although these concepts are embedded in the framework of the indigenous theory, there are variations in meaning. These concepts are explored in subsequent sections in this chapter. The case study method is the most widely used method by researchers for obtaining an in-depth assessment of an issue or event (Crowe et al., 2011; Rashid et al., 2019).

The preferred methodology is a case study. Case studies of popular West African tribes of Igbos, Fulani, Hausa, and Yoruba (Four major Nigerian ethnic groups) have been applied to explore the concept of indigenous entrepreneurship. Therefore, this chapter examines the culture and the niche social elements of the four indigenous tribes and their entrepreneurial behaviours. Next, there is a review of the literature and theoretical frames including indigenous theory, cultural theory, cross-cultural entrepreneurship (clan and kindred entrepreneurship, community, tribal and nomadic entrepreneurship), and institutional theories. These contexts are under-explored and under-represented in the literature. The last sections present the case studies of Igbo, Fulani, Hausa and Yoruba, followed by discussion and conclusions.

2 Literature Review and Theoretical Frames

2.1 *Indigenous Theory*

There are several definitions of indigenous (see, e.g., Peredo et al., 2004). The General Council of the International Labour Organisation (1991) convention provides a definition which states inter alia:

> People in independent countries who are regarded as indigenous on account of their descent from the populations which inhabited the country, or a geographical region to which the country belongs, at the time of conquest or colonisation or the establishment of present State boundaries and who, irrespective of their legal status, retain some or all of their own social, economic, cultural and political institutions. (cited in Peredo et al., 2004, p. 4)

In many regions, indigenous people share unique religious values, cultural and have a high entrepreneurial passion (Hubner et al., 2019). Also, Peredo et al. (2004) defined indigenous people as:

- Descent from populations inhabiting a region before later inhabitants
- Geographical, political, and/or economic domination by later inhabitants or immigrants
- Maintenance of some distinctive social-cultural norms and institutions

Although indigenous people are known for their entrepreneurial exploits in many regions by creating, managing and developing new ventures, they face several challenges. Several African and Asian indigenous tribes lack access to entrepreneurial resources, gender discrimination and misrepresentation in the national governance and economic system (see, for example, Igbo Indigenous people) (Igwe et al., 2018, 2020). Also, many indigenous populations are minority communities and disadvantaged groups (Hindle & Moroz, 2010) or discriminated (Marlow & McAdam, 2012). Turning problems into opportunities, there is a rise in entrepreneurship among indigenous such as the Aboriginals (Canada), Igbos, Yoruba, Hausa, Fulani (Nigeria), and Chagga, Kalenjin, Maasai (East Africa), Zulu, Xhosa, Ndebele, Venda, Khoisan (South Africa) Gonds, Bhils, Santhal, Andamanese, Khasi, Garo, Angami, Munda, Marwari (Indian), indigenous peoples of Maori (New Zealand) and indigenous people of Chinese.

2.2 *Cultural Theories and Pedagogies*

Culture represents the totality of a society's distinctive ideas, beliefs, values, and knowledge (Serrat, 2017), behaviours and artefacts that can be learned and transmitted between individuals (Creanza et al., 2017). Cultural studies on diverse societies often concentrate on how a particular phenomenon relates to matters of ideology, nationality, ethnicity, social class, and gender (Serrat, 2017). Schwartz (2006) presents seven cultural dimensions—Harmony (unity with nature & world at peace); Embeddedness (social order, obedience and respect for tradition); Hierarchy (authority & humble); Mastery (ambition & daring); Affective Autonomy (pleasure); Intellectual Autonomy (Broadmindedness & curiosity); and Egalitarianism (social justice & equality). Culture shapes entrepreneurial behaviours that are often examined against institutional practices and pedagogies. Schwartz (2006) goes on to link cultural theory to the three problems that confront all societies including embeddedness versus autonomy; hierarchy versus egalitarianism; and mastery versus harmony. In many indigenous communities, culture can be either a barrier to entrepreneurship or an entrepreneurial motivator.

The UNDP (2004) report states that:

> proponents of cultural determinism often label large parts of the world as simply "African" or "Islamic". But culture is not a homogeneous attribute. There are huge variations in language, religion, literature, art and living styles within the same cultural "group". (UNDP, 2004, cited in Telleria, 2015, p. 258)

Cultural Studies has been characterized by its willingness to democratize knowledge and challenge the frontiers of academic discipline (Richard, 2012). According to Richard (2012), cultural framework tends to fall into ambiguity and vagueness. It is important to examine the religion—and cultural dimensions of entrepreneurship. Telleria (2015) states that democratic culture is an essential factor to make political development thrive and states as follows:

> Cultural determinism—the idea that a group's culture explains economic performance and the advance of democracy—as an obstacle or a facilitator, has enormous intuitive appeal. But these theories are not supported by econometric analysis or history. (UNDP, 2004, p. 5, cited in Telleria, 2015, p. 259)

Schwartz (2006) provides examples of the cultural value orientations where egalitarianism and intellectual autonomy share the assumption that people can and should take individual responsibility for their actions and make decisions based on their understanding of situations. According to Schwartz (2006), embedded cultures emphasize maintaining the status quo and restraining actions that might disrupt in-group solidarity or the traditional order. He gives examples of the important values in such cultures as social order, respect for tradition, security, obedience, and wisdom. And high egalitarianism and intellectual autonomy usually appear together, as in Western Europe, while embeddedness and hierarchy are both high in the Southeast Asian cultures.

Within indigenous entrepreneurship literature, elements such as tribal life, ethnic identity, tribal attitudes, ethnic behaviours have been used to measure and evaluate the contributions of indigenous people to the field of entrepreneurship. Towards these notions, cultural theory defines traditional and modernistic practices in different regions (Light & Dana, 2013), the role and values of families and communities (Van Gils et al., 2014). Indigenous behaviours are influenced by culture, social norms and the rules which govern the conduct of economic activity and social interactions (Scott, 2008). Bonding is integral in the context of community entrepreneurship (Tubadji et al., 2014). Studies of entrepreneurial motivation tend to emphasize the role of internal factors like self-regulatory or affective constructs, for instance, entrepreneurial passion. Also, there is the influence of external elements like objectives or financial goals as drivers of entrepreneurial behaviour (Murnieks et al., 2019). Vivarelli (2012) emphasizes that the non-economic internal factors might have a more significant impact on entrepreneurial behaviours more than the external elements.

2.3 *Cross-Cultural Entrepreneurship*

Indigenous entrepreneurship is embedded in cultural norms and values that exist in society (Ratten & Ferreira, 2017). Globally, indigenous groups abound such as Maori in New Zealand (Frederick & Henry, 2004), Aborigines in Australia (Hindle & Lansdowne, 2005), Sámi Northern Europe (Dana & Remes, 2005), Native Americans in the United States (Pearson, 2005) and the Zulus in South Africa. Indigenous businesses have been making an impact across the globe and are at the forefront of change and innovations (Edwards, 2017), yet entrepreneurship scholars do not view indigenous entrepreneurship to be a distinctive research field (Hindle & Moroz, 2010). Out of curiosity, a search for Indigenous entrepreneurship produces limited results indicating that there are few previous studies on the concepts (Bruton et al., 2018; Greidanus & Sharpe, 2017; Hindle & Lansdowne, 2005; Hindle & Moroz, 2010).

Comparative cross-cultural research is required to examine different cultures and their outcomes (Engelen et al., 2009). Some cultures support or discourage entrepreneurial spirit (Boettke & Coyne, 2009) as well as become a vital resource for the creation, management and development of new ventures. Towards this direction, some studies focus on examining social structures and social relationships in entrepreneurship (Zellweger et al., 2019). It has been stated that Indigenous entrepreneurs and communities focus on developing community social capital (Greidanus & Sharpe, 2017; Kwon et al., 2013; Light & Dana, 2013).

2.4 *Clan and Kindred Entrepreneurship*

In the indigenous setting, extended family members form clan and kindred. Oxford dictionary definition of a clan is “a close-knit group of interrelated families”. In the context of entrepreneurship, “clan entrepreneurship” could be defined as the creation of business activities or extraction of value through a close-knit group of interrelated and extended families who share similar entrepreneurial orientation, intentions, and practices. Given the relatively recent turn to acknowledge the importance and roles of families and communities in entrepreneurship development clan entrepreneurship provide a platform for the future development of the field of indigenous management practices. Kindred in the indigenous setting defines a group of people connected or related through kinfolk, kin, tribe, or clan by birth, descent and sometimes by marriage. Kindred explores the dynamics and dilemmas of indigenous people from the sensibility and legacy of cultural orientations in contemporary society.

Also, kindreds within indigenous communities often have similar religious beliefs, norms, and values system that influence their entrepreneurial behaviour. Some scholars examined kindred issues like elemental, apocalyptic and archetypal about the events in the narrative (Crossley, 2004) and individualism-collectivism cultural dimensions (Gorodnichenko & Roland, 2011). African indigenous cultures highlight elements of communalism and collectivism where strong and able members of society are required to help the less able members to develop economic, social and entrepreneurship responsibility. In indigenous settings, families become a critical factor in the development of entrepreneurship and management orientation. For example, among the indigenous Igbos (Nigeria), the family is the most important element in their entrepreneurial drive, risk-taking and motivation (see, e.g., Igwe et al., 2018). Among Indian indigenous communities, "a closely-knit family relationship" provides greater labour resources and skills required for family enterprises (Dutta, 1997). Also, family identity and relationships reinforced trust that is required for business transactions (Dyer, 2012).

2.5 *Community and Tribal Entrepreneurship*

Some social sciences studies focus on understanding tribe and community by describing a tribe as a society and an ethnic group as a community (Godelier, 2010). The cultural values in indigenous communities emphasize trust and shared values and security within and between communities and unselfish behaviours and desire to live for others and focusing on what is good for others above what is good for oneself (Douwes et al., 2018). Trust and shared values become key entrepreneurial resource in indigenous communities. Also, Indigenous communities and tribes represent indigenous social groups who are tied together by families, clans or kinship relations, cultural values, shared resources and linkages (Cooney, 2008; Parwez, 2017). The notion of "community" has been used to represent a group with a consensual set of values, a group of people with shared values and a place-based understanding of identity (Rose, 1997).

Communities can develop an entrepreneurial culture that agents may engage to enable entrepreneurship (McKeever et al., 2015). Among indigenous Igbo people in Nigeria, their communities provide a positive platform, on which Igbo entrepreneurship thrives (Igwe et al., 2020). Also, the Marwari indigenous Indian business community is notable for its sustained entrepreneurial activity and success. From trading and money lending in the nineteenth century, the Marwaris own a majority of India's private industrial enterprise (Timberg, 2014).

2.6 *Indigenous Nomadic Entrepreneurship*

The practice of engaging in business activities involving working together and providing products and services through migratory behaviours that involve travelling from one location to another or country to another is regarded as indigenous nomadic entrepreneurship. The persons involved in these activities are referred to as nomad entrepreneurs. Indigenous Nomad entrepreneurs make necessary trips back and forth, as needed (Wien, 2016). Nomads have a special form of lifestyle entrepreneurship. Nomads are known to live a cheaper lifestyle, have cohesive family bonding and discover new cultures. They have freedom and can go anywhere within their limits of travel restrictions. In modern society, digital entrepreneurs are often called Nomad entrepreneurs referring to the freedom and migratory behaviours usually associated with Fulani Nomads.

2.7 *Institutional and Cultural Logics*

The institutional logics perspective in entrepreneurship research enables the examination of the reciprocal influence of social forces that influences entrepreneurial behaviours. An institutional logic is defined as "the socially constructed historical patterns of cultural symbols and material practices, including assumptions, values and beliefs, by which individuals and organizations provide meaning to their daily activity, organize time and space, and reproduce their lives and experiences" (Thornton et al., 2012, p. 2). Institutional forces (formal and informal) have three categories, the regulative pillar, and the normative and cognitive pillar (Scott, 2008). The regulative pillar involves rule setting, monitoring and sanctioning activities that may operate through formal processes such as courts or informal traditions. Both formal and informal regulations can influence indigenous entrepreneurial behaviours, innovations, and outcomes. Besides institutional factors, culture, family and community (Igwe et al., 2020) influence indigenous entrepreneurship that play a critical role in the creation, management and development of new indigenous ventures (Fig. 1).

Fig. 1 Determinants of indigenous entrepreneurship. Source: Author's framework

Families and communities provide the foundation for indigenous entrepreneurship by providing tangible and intangible resources, while culture determines entrepreneurial behaviours. Cultural theory explains that the normative pillar consists of norms and values that introduce how things should be done, and specialized values and norms are termed roles "conceptions of appropriate action for particular individuals or specified social positions" (Scott, 2008, p. 38). The process of entrepreneurship is shaped by the personal values of the entrepreneur, which depend on their culture, norms, location and other factors (Ratten, 2014). The notion of community explains the local cultural, social and legal context to the composition of the interinstitutional system (Marquis & Battilana, 2009). Actors or agents then internalize these norms and values to help establish further conformity at the organizational or societal level. The normative pillar defines "routines, beliefs, codes, roles, procedures, conventions, roles, strategies and organizational forms". Furthermore, Thornton et al. (2012) explain that the logics of the interinstitutional system include the institutional orders of formal and informal rules, family, community, norms, socio-cultural values, religion, state, market and corporation.

3 Methodology

The case study approach is the preferred method to enable the presentation and analysis of different indigenous tribal groups. This is method is best suited to generate an in-depth, multi-faceted understanding of a complex issue in its real-life context (Crowe et al., 2011). This approach enabled the analysis of four Indigenous tribes in Nigeria. Also, it enabled the analysis of the sub-set of Indigenous entrepreneurship including "clan entrepreneurship", "kindred entrepreneurship", "tribal entrepreneurship", "community entrepreneurship" and nomadic entrepreneurship". The objective is to provide foundational research from in-depth multiple case studies of Indigenous tribes. This article uses reports of past studies to explore and understand the similarities, differences, and commonalities between the cases. Although case studies enable an investigation of cases thoroughly and deeply, scholars can form a bias. Also, another weakness is the lack of primary data and validation.

4 Case Studies

4.1 Igbo Tribe

Igbos located in South-eastern Nigeria has a population of about 32 million (CIA World Factbook, 2016). They are enterprising and have a high entrepreneurial passion (Meagher, 2010; Madichie et al., 2008; Igwe et al., 2018). Also, Igbossh are a common language, traditions, institutions, family and kindred system, religion, customs, and lifestyles. Igbo societies are patriarchal and the males dominate authority, leadership, and political structures. Also, the family and extended family system is the most important element of Igbo societies and economic activities are usually based on family values, family capital or family participation. The Igbos have been described as suffering an institutional disadvantage compared to other Nigerian tribes (Igwe et al., 2018).

Igbo's motive or drive for entrepreneurship, risk-taking, wealth-seeking and learning process have indigenous and modern entrepreneurship elements. Igbos have been described as "naturally enterprising and ingenious" and can be found throughout Nigeria and West Africa" (Igwe et al., 2018, p. 34). For many decades, Igbos in the South-eastern region of Nigeria has practised Indigenous entrepreneurship system regarded as "stakeholder capitalism—a construct that businesses must elevate the interests of communities, workers, consumers, and the environment alongside those of shareholders" (Ekekwe, 2021, p. 1). Igbos practice individual and communal entrepreneurship. They are individualist when opportunity-seeking, profit-seeking and wealth-seeking. However, they are communal when building financial capital, social capital, human capital, and community development (Igwe et al., 2018, 2020). Also, family, kindred and clan are the important factors in Igbo entrepreneurship.

To overcome the disadvantage, Igbos take to business as a means of survival and wealth creation. An extended family system and an informal apprenticeship system (Nwa-boyi system) often regarded as the "Igbo Business School" system provide a safe environment for learning the business, starting the business, marketing, risk-taking, creativity and innovation (Igwe et al., 2020). Igbos have historically been migratory in habit trading outside their home regions and settling major cities in Nigeria, West African countries and the diaspora (Madichie et al., 2008). They dominate the private sector in West Africa, specializing in a wide range of businesses including exports and imports, trading, transportation, automotive spare parts, the movie industry (Nollywood), pharmaceuticals, hospitality, etc. (Igwe et al., 2018).

4.2 The Fulani

Like the Igbos, the Fulani tribe are migratory entrepreneurs. However, Fulani migration is regarded as nomadic. The Fulani are the largest nomadic group in the world and descend from both North Africa and sub-Saharan Africa (World Atlas, 2017). They were the first tribe in West Africa to convert to Islam and establish themselves not only as a religious group but also as a political and economic force in the West African region. The Fulani have therefore settled in the large plain areas of Nigeria, Senegal, Mauritania, Mali, Upper Volta, Niger, Guinea, Burkina Faso, and Chad and many other countries in Africa (Aderanti, 1998). The vast Fulani communities in the Western and Northern African countries are mostly very poor nomads, semi-nomads, and sedentary farmers (Marnham, 1979). The social system of Fulani culture is regulated by norms and value systems and males are heads of households (Usman, 2010).

Also, unlike the Igbos and Yoruba, Fulani entrepreneurship focus on livestock and trading. Fulani men and women are primarily nomadic herders and traders. Through their pastoralists and nomadic lifestyle, they established numerous trade routes in West Africa. They trade mainly in local markets and cattle is the most important livelihood asset. The Fulani are less entrepreneurial wealth-seeking and risk-taking compared with other Nigerian tribes. They hold to a strict caste system that includes mobility, merchants, crafts, blacksmiths, and descendants of slaves of wealthy Fulani. They produce and market locally handcrafted goods across North and West Africa. The social organization of nomadic Fulbe is based on patrilineal descent with gender stratification as the base of all social systems (Usman, 2010). Nomadic Fulbe girls engage in street hawking and other informal economic activities (Usman, 2010). These attributes make the Fulani an interesting group to study.

4.3 Hausa

Hausa Indigenous people in the northern part of Nigeria are predominantly Muslims, while a few are Christians. Hausa ethnic group is one of the largest and most popular ethnic groups in West Africa (Nigeria, Niger, Chad, Ghana, Cameroon, Benin and Mali). This ethnic group has about 24 million people in Nigeria and its traditions and culture are homogenized and people share similar beliefs and customs (Tersoo, 2018). Their main religion is Islam. Hausas were listed as one of the global middleman minority ethnic groups alongside such ethnic groups as the Jews of Europe, the Parsees of India and the Chinese of East Asia (Dandago, 2015). Hausa culture is replete with proverbs that negate the very essence of hardworking coupled with the influence of religion (Islam)which the people misinterpret as encouraging belief in destiny (Halliru, 2017). Since a majority of Hausas are Muslims, they do nothing that the Holy Quran forbids such as eating pork and alcohol consumption.

The entrepreneurial culture of the Hausa people is fascinating. Hausa Indigenous entrepreneurship involves production and labour activities relevant to their location and natural resources. The main sector the Hausa indigenous entrepreneurs dominate is agriculture and trade (Tersoo, 2018). Hausa people grow corn, millet, yams, different vegetables, cotton and peanuts, and breed horses, goats, and cattle (Tersoo, 2018). The Men hunt and go fish, while women are mostly involved in pottery, baskets, mats, knitting, among others (Tersoo, 2018). Also, Hausa entrepreneurs are famous for their cloth weaving and dyeing, cotton goods, leather sandals, metal locks, horse equipment and leather.

Leadership in the early Hausa states was based on ancestry and those who could trace their relations back to Bayajidda were considered royal. Hausa traditional marriage is mostly based on Islamic, and not expensive like the Igbo and Yoruba traditional marriage ceremonies. Hausas like the Fulani are regarded to have less entrepreneurial wealth-seeking and risk-taking ambition. Impliedly, entrepreneurs need not struggle nor worry about the competition from those who have developed superior strategies to guarantee success (Halliru, 2017). Women's economic development of the Hausa populace has remained at its lowest ebb, especially the Muslim group (Sabiu, 2018). The society, norms, beliefs, traditions of the society are believed to be significant in retarding the development and entrepreneurship progress of the Hausa people (Halliru, 2017). The underdevelopment has seriously affected the progress and advancement of Hausa society and the whole of Nigeria (Sabiu, 2018).

4.4 Yoruba

Yoruba group inhabits South-western Nigeria and other Africa countries of Benin, Ghana and Togo. Yoruba are Christians or Muslims (Hunwick, 1992). Yoruba were among the first ethnic groups in Africa to come into contact and trade with Europeans (Dandago, 2015). Ibadan and Lagos are the two major Yoruba cities and the largest city in the whole of Sub-Saharan Africa. Music and dance have always been an important part of their culture and Yoruba celebrate major events with colourful festivals such as Ayeye and the Eyo Olokun festival, celebrated by the people of Lagos (Lawal et al., 2009). The social, political, and economic civilization of the Yoruba nation started with the Oduduwa dynasty at Ile-Ife around 850 AD (Fadamiro & Adedeji, 2016). Evidence points to a powerful Yoruba kingdom in the eighth century in Ile-Ife (Ighobor, 2019). With the onset of the Atlantic slave trade, Yoruba people from Nigeria and Benin were forcibly transported to America as slaves.

Yoruba culture expanded across many borders to Trinidad, Cuba, Saint Lucia, Benin, Togo, Brazil, Guyana, Haiti, Jamaica, to name a few (Ighobor, 2019). "By being the last wave of mostly homogenous groupings of slaves to arrive in Salvador, they would leave one of the most visible and lasting cultural imprints on the growing Afro-Bahian community of Salvador, resulting in what Miguel Calmon called, "the brutal metamorphosis of Mangolas (Bantus) into Nagôs (Yoruba)" (Alonso, 2014, p. 33). The culture of a people has both geography and history as spatial and temporal entities, respectively, and the domains of space and time are essential to understanding the civilization of any group of people (Fadamiro & Adedeji, 2016).

Yoruba entrepreneurs are merchants, industrialists, traders or craftsmen (Britannica, 2014). Cultural landscapes are the material evidence of the interaction of the people with the environment, the repository of nature (Fadamiro & Adedeji, 2016). Yoruba traditional culture enables them to develop skills of craftsmen, blacksmithing, weaving, leatherworking, glassmaking, and ivory and wood carving, etc. Nowadays, many Yoruba entrepreneurs are popular in the banking sector, media, aviation, manufacturing, medicine and technology. Like the Igbos, the motive or drive for entrepreneurship, risk-taking, wealth-seeking and learning process was similar to indigenous and modern entrepreneurship (Ayinde, 2015).

5 Discussion

Indigenous people have the motive or drive for entrepreneurship, risk-taking, wealth-seeking and learning process that has both indigenous and modern entrepreneurship elements. Indigenous studies provide an opportunity to explore minority groups who are not often studied or researched in management and entrepreneurship. Cultural and family values are critical factors in the determination of entrepreneurial behaviours or outcomes of indigenous people. Understanding these elements will help to promote and support entrepreneurship growth and development. Among the four Nigerian indigenous groups—Igbos, Fulani, Hausa and Yoruba, Igbos are the most celebrated and successful indigenous entrepreneurs and innovators. All the indigenous groups are associated with uniquecultural orientations, religious norms, and values such as "collective family values" or community orientation, disadvantage, a sense of historical mistreatment or oppression. These indigenous groups desire to control their economic resources and to participate in their national economy. They have a "distinctive philosophy" oriented towards natural resources, family resources and capabilities.

Also, indigenous entrepreneurial behaviours are influenced by external elements like financial goals or non-economic internal factors such as lifestyle entrepreneurship (nomad entrepreneurs) or the entrepreneurial migratory tendency of Igbo people or cultural skills of the Yoruba and Hausa. All the indigenous groups are known to leverage community trust and communities create a unique social collaboration and network that is available to tap for entrepreneurial activities. Like among the Igbos, extended family trust, clan solidarity and kindred solidarity play an important role in entrepreneurial learning, social capital accumulation, reduction in transactions costs, reduction in information asymmetric and access to start-up capital required to develop indigenous enterprises. Therefore, the indigenous cultural and social environment provides a platform where the indigenous entrepreneurs feel confident and can develop roots, allocate resources to overcome institutional barriers and disadvantages. Challenges faced by indigenous entrepreneurs are overcome through different cultural collaborations (Igwe et al., 2020; Ratten, 2014).

Successful participation in the economic advancement by an Indigenous group is the manifestation of the evolving relationship between family orientations, institutional environment, and cultural orientations. Thus, the institutional logics perspective is often introduced as a "metatheoretical framework for analysing the interrelationships among individuals, and organizations in social systems" (Thornton et al., 2012, p. 2). "Institutions set bounds on rationality by restricting the opportunities and alternatives that people perceive (Barley & Tolbert, 1997). Therefore, the successes achieved by indigenous entrepreneurs are a manifestation of the "very specific articulation of indigenousness elements" such as family capital, community capital, cultural collaborations and initiatives.

6 Conclusion

Indigenous people have motives or drives for entrepreneurship that develop through indigenous cultures. Indigenous entrepreneurship is widely considered to be the most critical factor in the economic growth and innovations among cultural societies, minority groups and migrant groups. Igbos, Fulani, Hausa and Yoruba (four major Nigerian ethnic groups) have been analyzed to develop further understanding of the concept of indigenous entrepreneurship practices. This chapter makes several contributions. First, it contributes to research on new concepts in indigenous entrepreneurship such as clan, kindred and nomadic entrepreneurship. Second, this article supports the notion that indigenous entrepreneurship could be in response to disadvantage, towards overcoming institutional barriers or inherently family and community entrepreneurial orientations. Third, the neglect of indigenous management and business practices in the mainstream literature calls for more studies that integrate indigenous perspectives to the knowledge of broader entrepreneurship.

Understanding the inherently entrepreneurial and the historic economic activity of indigenous people could lead to the promotion of equality especially among minority groups, poverty reduction and economic growth. Discriminations and exclusions are high in many regions where indigenous people inhabit. They are excluded from education, public services, political representations, and decision-making authorities. Against the background of neglect or exclusion, indigenous people take into entrepreneurship to develop economic power, social and community development. These attributes make indigenous people located in many regions unique. The case study approach provides detailed (rich qualitative) information (McLeod, 2019). Although the case study lacks scientific rigour, this approach provided an opportunity for examining tribal groups and cultures which are underreported in the entrepreneurship literature. As a result, there is a lack of a coherent conceptual and analytical framework (Lam et al., 2019). Therefore, more studies are needed to explore indigenous entrepreneurial behaviours and indigenous business management practices.

References

Aderanti, A. (1998). Linkages between internal and international migration: The African situation. Africa -- emigration & immigration; social sciences; population geography; Migration. *International Social Science Journal, 50*(157), 387–396. http://www.iupui.edu/~anthkb/a104/kenya/african%20migration.htm

Alonso, M. C. (2014). The dispersal of the Yoruba people. In *The development of Yoruba candomble communities in Salvador, Bahia, 1835–1986. Afro-Latin@ Diasporas*. Palgrave Macmillan. https://doi.org/10.1057/9781137486431_3

Anggadwita, G., Ramadani, V., & Ratten, V. (2017). Sociocultural environments and emerging economy entrepreneurship women entrepreneurs in Indonesia. *Journal of Entrepreneurship in Emerging Economies, 9*(1), 85–96.

Ayinde, A. T. (2015). Indigenous and modern entrepreneurship practices among Yoruba people of West Africa: A theoretical perspective. *Journal of Demography and Social Statistics, 2*(1&2), 79–88.

Barley, S. R., & Tolbert, P. S. (1997). Institutionalization and structuration: Studying the links between action and institution. *Organization Studies, 18*, 93–117.

Boettke, P. J., & Coyne, C. J. (2009). Context matters: Institutions and entrepreneurship. *Foundations and Trends in Entrepreneurship, 5*(3), 135–209.

Britannica, T. (2014). *Editors of encyclopaedia (2014, June 30). Yoruba*. Encyclopedia Britannica. https://www.britannica.com/topic/Yoruba

Bruton, G. D., Zahra, S. A., & Cai, L. (2018). Examining entrepreneurship through indigenous lenses. *Entrepreneurship Theory and Practice, 42*(3), 351–361.

CIA World Factbook. (2016). *Eastern-Nigerian population*. Retrieved April 12, 2017, from www.cia.gov/library/publications/resources/the-world-factbook/geos/rp.html

Cooney, T. M. (2008). Why is community entrepreneurship worth debating? *Journal of Enterprising Communities: People and Places in the Global Economy, 2*(2), 1–16. https://doi.org/10.1108/jec.2008.32902baa.001

Creanza, N., Kolodny, O., & Feldman, M. W. (2017). Cultural evolutionary theory: How culture evolves and why it matters. *PNA, 114*(30), 7782–7789. www.pnas.org/cgi/doi/10.1073/pnas.1620732114

Crossley, R. (2004). Critical essay. In O. Butler (Ed.), *Kindred* (p. 279). Beacon.

Crowe, S., Cresswell, K., Robertson, A., Huby, G., Avery, A., & Sheikh, A. (2011). The case study approach. *BMC Medical Research Methodology, 11*(100), 1–17. https://doi.org/10.1186/1471-2288-11-100

Dana, L.-P. (2015). Indigenous entrepreneurship: An emerging field of research. *International Journal of Business and Globalisation, 14*(2), 158–169.

Dana, L.-P., & Anderson, R. B. (2007). *International handbook of research on indigenous entrepreneurship*. Edward Elgar.

Dana, T. E., & Remes, L. (2005). Entrepreneurship among the Sami people of Finland. *Journal of Small Business and Entrepreneurship, 18*(20), 189–200.

Dandago, K. I. (2015). Impact of culture on entrepreneurial attitude of Nigerians: A review of Hausa, Igbo and Yoruba cultures. *International Journal of Management Studies, Statistics & Applied Economics (IJMSAE), 5*(II), 29–40.

Douwes, R., Stuttaford, M., & London, L. (2018). Social solidarity, human rights, and collective action: Considerations in the implementation of the national health insurance in South Africa. *Health and Human Rights, 20*(2), 185–196.

Dutta, S. (1997). *Family business in India*. Response Books and Sage.

Dyer, W. G. (2012). How to create trust in family firms and rebuild it when it's lost: Implications for practice and research. In A. L. Carsrud & M. Brannback (Eds.), *Understanding family businesses: Undiscovered approaches, unique perspectives and neglected topics* (pp. 157–168). Springer.

Edwards, J. (2017, October 2). Indigenous entrepreneurship is all around us. *Guardian*. Retrieved from https://www.theguardian.com/commentisfree/2017/oct/02/indigenous-entrepreneurship-is-all-around-us

Ekekwe, N. (2021, May 29). A Nigerian model for stakeholder capitalism. *Harvard Business Review* [online]. Retrieved from https://hbr.org/2021/05/a-nigerian-model-for-stakeholder-capitalism

Engelen, A., Heinemann, F., & Brettel, M. (2009). Cross-cultural entrepreneurship research: Current status and framework for future studies. *Journal of International Entrepreneurship, 7*, 163–189. https://doi.org/10.1007/s10843-008-0035-5

Fadamiro, J. A., & Adedeji, J. A. (2016). Cultural landscapes of the Yoruba of South-Western Nigeria demystified as solidified time in space. *Space and Culture, 19*(1), 15–30. https://doi.org/10.1177/1206331215595751

Frederick, H. H., & Henry, E. (2004). Innovation and entrepreneurship among Pakeha and Maori in New Zealand. In K. Stiles & C. Galbraith (Eds.), *Ethnic entrepreneurship: Structure and process* (pp. 115–140). Elsevier Science.

George, G., Corbishley, C., Khayesi, J., Haas, M., & Tihanyi, L. (2016). Bringing Africa in promising directions for management research. *Academy of Management Journal, 59*(2), 377–393.

Godelier, M. (2010). Community, society, culture: Three keys to understanding today's conflicted identities. *Journal of the Royal Anthropological Institute, 16*, 1–11. https://doi.org/10.1111/j.1467-9655.2009.01593.x

Gorodnichenko, Y., & Roland, G. (2011). Which dimensions of culture matter for long-run growth? *American Economic Review Papers & Proceedings, 101*(3), 492–498.

Greidanus, N. S., & Sharpe, J. (2017). Indigenous entrepreneurship: International ventures in an intra-country context. *Academy of Management Proceedings, 2017*(1), 1–19. https://doi.org/10.5465/AMBPP.2017.16291abstract

Halliru, M. (2017). The effect of culture on the development of entrepreneurs among the Hausa Ethnic Group in Northern Nigeria. *Journal of Marketing and Management, 4*(1), 59–74.

Hindle, K., & Lansdowne, M. (2005). Brave spirits on new paths: Toward a globally relevant paradigm of indigenous entrepreneurship research. *Journal of Small Business and Entrepreneurship, 18*(20), 131–142.

Hindle, K., & Moroz, P. (2010). Indigenous entrepreneurship as a research field: Developing a definitional framework from the emerging canon. *International Entrepreneurship Management Journal, 6*, 357–372.

Hubner, S., Baum, M., & Frese, M. (2019). Contagion of entrepreneurial passion: Effects on employee outcomes. *Entrepreneurship Theory and Practice, 44*(6), 1112–1140. https://doi.org/10.1177/1042258719883995

Hunwick, J. O. (1992). *Religion and national integration in Africa: Islam, Christianity, and politics in the Sudan and Nigeria (series in Islam and society in Africa)* (p. 103). Northwestern University Press. isbn:978-0-8101-1037-3.

Ighobor, K. (2019). Bigger than Africa: Tales of the Yoruba people. Retrieved from https://www.un.org/africarenewal/magazine/december-2019-march-2020/bigger-africa-tales-yoruba-people

Igwe, P. A., Madichie, N. O., & Amoncar, N. (2020). Transgenerational business legacies and intergenerational succession among the Igbos (Nigeria). *Small Enterprise Research, 27*(2), 165–179. https://doi.org/10.1080/13215906.2020.1751692

Igwe, P. A., Newbery, R., Amoncar, N., White, G. R. T., & Madichie, N. O. (2018). Keeping it in the family: Exploring Igbo ethnic entrepreneurial behaviour in Nigeria. *International Journal of Entrepreneurial Behavior & Research, 26*(1), 34–53. https://doi.org/10.1108/IJEBR-12-2017-0492

International Labour Organisation. (1991). *Convention (No. 169) concerning indigenous and tribal peoples in independent countries*. University of Minnesota Human Rights Library.

Kouritzin, S., & Nakagawa, S. (2018). Toward a non-extractive research ethics for transcultural, translingual research: Perspectives from the coloniser and the colonised. *Journal of Multilingual and Multicultural Development, 39*(8), 675–687. https://doi.org/10.1080/01434632.2018.1427755

Kwon, S.-W., Heflin, C., & Ruef, M. (2013). Community social capital and entrepreneurship. *American Sociological Review, 78*(6), 980–1008.

Lam, W., Harris, P., & Yang, S. (2019). Understanding U.K. ethnic minority entrepreneurship from an enterprise culture perspective. *Journal of Public Affairs, 19*, 1–22. https://doi.org/10.1002/pa.1922

Lawal, N., Sadiku, M. N. O., & Dopamu, A. (2009). *Understanding Yoruba life and culture*. Africa World Press (the University of California). isbn:978-1-59221-025-1.

Light, I., & Dana, L.-P. (2013). Boundaries of social capital in entrepreneurship. *Entrepreneurship Theory and Practice, 37*(3), 603–624.

Madichie, N. O., Nkamnebe, A. D., & Idemobi, E. I. (2008). Cultural determinants of entrepreneurial emergence in a typical sub-Sahara African context. *Journal of Enterprising Communities: People and Places in the Global Economy, 2*(4), 285–299.

Marlow, S., & McAdam, M. (2012). Analyzing the influence of gender upon high -technology venturing within the context of business incubation. *Entrepreneurship Theory and Practice, 36* (4), 655–676.

Marnham, P. (1979). *Nomads of the Sahel. Report No. 33* (rev. ed.). Minority Rights Group.

Marquis, C., & Battilana, J. (2009). Acting globally but thinking locally? The enduring influence of local communities on organizations. *Research in Organizational Behavior, 29*, 283–302. https://doi.org/10.1016/j.riob.2009.06.001

McKeever, E., Jack, S., & Anderson, A. (2015). Embedded entrepreneurship in the creative reconstruction of place. *Journal of Business Venturing, 30*, 50–65. https://doi.org/10.1016/j.jbusvent.2014.07.002

McLeod, S. (2019). Case study method. Retrieved from https://www.simplypsychology.org/case-study.html

Meagher, K. (2010). *Identity economics: Social networks and the informal economy in Nigeria*. Textbook Published by Boydell & Brewer. Retrieved April 10, 2017, from http://eprints.lse.ac.uk/id/eprint/27379

Murnieks, C. Y., Klotz, A. C., & Shepherd, D. A. (2019). Entrepreneurial motivation: A review of the literature and an agenda for future research. *Journal of Organizational Behaviour, 41*(2), 115–143. Retrieved March 24, 2020, from https://onlinelibrary-wiley-com.proxy.library.lincoln.ac.uk/doi/pdfdirect/10.1002/job.2374

Parwez, S. (2017). Community-based entrepreneurship: Evidences from a retail case study. *Journal of Innovation in Entrepreneurship, 6*, 1–14. https://doi.org/10.1186/s13731-017-0074-z

Pearson, J. D. (2005). Native American teamsters. *Journal of Small Business and Entrepreneurship, 18*(20), 153–170.

Peredo, A. M., Anderson, R. B., Galbraith, C. S., HonIg, B., & Dana, L.-P. (2004). Towards a theory of indigenous entrepreneurship. *International Journal of Entrepreneurship and Small Business, 1*(1/2), 1–16.

Rashid, Y., Rashid, A., Warraich, M. A., Sabir, S. S., & Waseem, A. (2019). Case study method: A step-by-step guide for business researchers. *International Journal of Qualitative Methods, 18*, 1–13. https://doi.org/10.1177/1609406919862424

Ratten, V. (2014). Behavioral intentions to adopt technological innovations: The role of trust, innovation and performance. *International Journal of Enterprise Information Systems (IJEIS), 10*(3), 1–12.

Ratten, V., & Ferreira, J. J. (2017). Future research directions for cultural entrepreneurship and regional development. *International Journal of Entrepreneurship and Innovation Management, 21*(3), 163–169.

Richard, N. (2012). Humanities and social sciences in critical dialogues with cultural studies. *Cultural Studies, 26*(1), 166–177. https://doi.org/10.1080/09502386.2012.642608

Rose, G. (1997). Spatialities of 'community', power and change: The imagined geographies of community arts projects. *Cultural Studies, 11*(1), 1–16. https://doi.org/10.1080/09502389700490011

Sabiu, I. T. (2018). Hausa people of Northern Nigeria and their development. *Asian People Journal (APJ), 1*(1), 179–189. https://journal.unisza.edu.my/apj/index.php/apj/article/view/21

Schwartz, S. H. (2006). A theory of cultural value orientations: Explication and applications. *Comparative Sociology, 5*(2–3), 137–182.

Scott, W. R. (2008). *Institutions and organizations: Ideas and interests*. Sage Publications.

Serrat, O. (2017). Culture theory. In *Knowledge solutions*. Springer. https://doi.org/10.1007/978-981-10-0983-9_7

Telleria, J. (2015). What does culture mean for the UNDP? *Cultural Studies, 29*(2), 255–271. https://doi.org/10.1080/09502386.2014.900100

Tersoo, A. (2018). Hausa culture and traditions in Nigeria: Top facts to know. *Legit*. Retrieved from https://www.legit.ng/1147895-hausa-culture-traditions-nigeria-top-facts-know.html

Thornton, P. H., Ocasio, W., & Lounsbury, M. (2012). *The institutional logics perspective: A new approach to culture*. Oxford University Press.

Timberg, T. (2014). *The Marwaris: From Jagat Seth to the Birlas*. Penguin Books.

Tubadji, A., Kourtit, K., & Nijkamp, P. (2014). Social capital and local cultural milieu for successful migrant entrepreneurship. *Journal of Small Business & Entrepreneurship, 27*(3), 301–322.

UNDP. (2004). *Human development report. Cultural liberty in today's diverse world*. Oxford University Press.

Usman, L. M. (2010). Street hawking and socio-economic dynamics of nomadic girls of northern Nigeria. *International Journal of Social Economics, 37*(9), 717–734. https://doi.org/10.1108/03068291011062506

Van Gils, A., Dibrell, C., Neubaum, D. O., & Craig, J. B. (2014). Social issues in the family enterprise. *Family Business Review, 27*(3), 193–205.

Vivarelli, M. (2012). *Entrepreneurship in advanced and developing countries: A microeconomic perspective*. IZA DP No. 6513. Discussion paper series.

Wien, A. (2016, February 17). How I'm managing my business as a nomadic entrepreneur. *Forbes*. Retrieved from https://www.forbes.com/sites/andreawien/2016/02/17/how-im-managing-my-business-as-a-nomadic-entrepreneur/?sh=7c875d477673

World Atlas. (2017). Largest ethnic groups in Mali. Retrieved from http://www.worldatlas.com/articles/largest-ethnic-groups-in-mali.html

Zellweger, T. M., Chrisman, J. J., Chua, J. H., & Steier, L. P. (2019). Social structures, social relationships, and family firms. *Entrepreneurship Theory and Practice, 43*(2), 207–223.

Dr. Paul Agu Igwe is a Senior Lecturer and Programme Coordinator for BA Business & Enterprise Development at the Lincoln International Business School (LIBS), University of Lincoln, UK. He received his MSc and PhD in Business with Management from the University of Plymouth. Dr. Igwe is a member of the UNESCO Project on Sustainable Foresight. He is a fellow of the Chartered Institute of Management and Higher Education Academy. His research interest and expertise include Entrepreneurship, Small Businesses development, Business Strategy & Internationalization, Organizational analysis and educational issues. Dr. Igwe has published in many top-ranked ABS journals such as International Journal of Entrepreneurship & Innovation, International Journal of Entrepreneurial Behaviour Research, Studies in Higher Education, Politics & Policy, Innovations in Education and Teaching International, etc. He is a member of the editorial board of the International Journal of Public Sociology and Sociotherapy.

Sustainable Initiatives in International Markets

Aldo Alvarez-Risco and Shyla Del-Aguila-Arcentales

Abstract This chapter makes a novel contribution analyzing the necessary actions in education to generate professionals who can propose, implement and manage sustainability initiatives in companies for global markets. Likewise, various examples of industries that have been implementing initiatives that contribute to sustainable development are presented; thus, the actions that are being developed in the hospitality industry are presented, mentioning the research results and the examples of the most important hotels in the world regarding their sustainability reports. The initiatives in the supply chain management with a sustainable approach are also presented, mentioning its link with industry 4.0. Likewise, the components of sustainable transport were detailed, emphasizing sustainable ports and the use of electricity-based transport as an energy source. Finally, the sustainable plastic management strategies by some companies are mentioned.

Keywords Sustainable markets · International markets · International business · Green consumerism · Circularity · Sustainability · International trade

1 Introduction

Sustainability is an individual and collective development approach that is gaining more space in the world. From a business point of view, it has been observed that more companies adopt sustainable business models (Pizzi et al., 2021). However, little is known about these efforts in a concrete way, there being large initiatives from transnational companies, such as the hotel sector and even more it is necessary to

A. Alvarez-Risco (✉)
Universidad de Lima, Lima, Peru
e-mail: aralvare@ulima.edu.pe

S. Del-Aguila-Arcentales
Escuela Nacional de Marina Mercante "Almirante Miguel Grau", Callao, Peru

A. Caputo et al. (eds.), *The International Dimension of Entrepreneurial Decision-Making*, Contributions to Management Science,
https://doi.org/10.1007/978-3-030-85950-3_10

specify how education should be in universities to forge professionals who are 'born sustainable'. In other words, have a sustainable approach from day one as professionals.

The arrival of COVID-19 has increased the speed at which social changes are occurring. Thus, it has been possible to show that cities are urged to improve their living standards through the increasing use of technologies and digital resources, with the specific objective of having sustainable growth (Palumbo et al., 2021). Even though the interest of the rulers and even a certain group of citizens is to transition towards sustainable business models, this great step requires prior conditions, both in terms of infrastructure and the market. Likewise, there is a need for governance focused on technology and that the citizen, on the ecological side, be the centre of management activities. Measuring sustainability requires considering several factors that are influencing government, consumers, businesses and society at large (Pizzi et al., 2020). Thus, it will be possible to have a real approximation of the advance that can be had in an integral way. Students in universities should be trained with this multi-stakeholder vision and at the same time with an inclusive spirit.

2 Methodology

The research uses a documentary research method to the analysis of sustainable initiatives in international markets. For the collection of the information, we searched articles linked to terms: 'sustainable initiative+international market', 'sustainability+international market', 'sustainable+business model', 'sustainability +business model', 'sustainable+education'. It was used in the articles and indexed in Scopus and Web of Sciences. It was used in the articles with relevant information for the chapter.

We have established to answer the next question:

1. What should be taught in universities to have professionals with a sustainable approach?
2. What are the sustainable initiatives more relevant in international markets?

3 Results

3.1 Teaching in Universities to Have Professionals with Sustainable Approach

Education for sustainability has been a fundamental element in the training of business science students for a few years, since it gives them a global vision of the business, so that they can manage companies in an integral way, considering the elements of economic, environmental and mainly social sustainability so that companies can achieve important benefits and can contribute to a given social environment.

It is from this training based on sustainability that sustainable global managers can be achieved. On what should train in universities be based in order to have professionals with a sustainable approach? Education for Sustainability aims to build awareness and knowledge of sustainability issues but also to develop students and universities that are able to think disruptive, innovate and provide solutions towards more sustainable patterns of living around the world.

3.1.1 Deep and Constant Change

Education for global sustainability, one that can be applied to international markets, initially requires equipping the actors of the university education system (students, professors, university managers) with competencies, capacities and motivation to generate educational development plans based on the global demands of the market, considering the local reality and projecting it towards the world. This profound change needs to rethink what is being needed in companies at a global level and redesign the programs in their theoretical and practical components so that graduates can fit in the business needs of companies. This redesign must be carried out constantly due to the increasingly accelerated changes taking place in international markets.

3.1.2 Create Lifelong Learner

The current crisis has forced the markets to see great changes in a short time and that companies have had to modify their operations to be able to satisfy a new market in extreme conditions. This flexibility of constant learning and in a short time is an element that should be part of undergraduate and graduate university training, which not only provides content but also models professionals so that they know that more than ever they must continue learning because changes will be every more drastic and in a short time.

3.1.3 Multidisciplinary Teaching

Learning must be planned to bring together diverse business content for global business. Thus, health, economics, accounting, big data, finance, agriculture, among others, should be developed. The exchange with other professors and universities will contribute to the international component in the training; it should be noted that virtual exchanges have also started.

3.2 *Sustainable Initiatives and Their Impact on Worldwide Markets*

3.2.1 Hospitality Industry

The sustainability approach starts from professional training in universities (Hay & Eagle, 2020), in many cases placing greater attention on global business strategies to generate business and contribute to tackling climate change simultaneously (Shields, 2019). Likewise, these efforts must be developed by companies, motivating processes based on sustainability (Lorincová et al., 2019). Various efforts have been reported from the hospitality sector as was reported by Filimonau and De Coteau (2019) who reviewed the challenges in the classification, quantification and characterization of food waste in the hospitality industry, analyzed the opportunities and obstacles for its mitigation and based on examples of good commercial practices.

These sustainability initiatives were also reported by Wu et al. (2021) from 32 businesses located in Wales, UK. On the other hand, Filimonau et al. (2020b) evidenced the good practices in food management in UK and Netherlands restaurants and although it is true that it is not yet massively implemented, it is a great opportunity for companies to contribute with sustainable initiatives in global markets.

These sustainable initiatives have also been reported by Sakshi et al. (2020) who show the impact of environmental policy and training aspects in the hotels' sustainability practices, as well as the impact of these practices on their environmental and financial performance. After the survey of 312 managers, it was found that the hotels' environmental policy and training aspects have a positive statistical influence on sustainability practices. This data shows that more and more hotels are implementing sustainability initiatives in their business models and strategies. Another initiative that is growing is the hotel's offer of small rooms that allow optimizing waste management, making space more efficient and making a concrete contribution to Sustainable Development Goals (SDGs). Thus, you can see the report of Agyeiwaah (2020) that presents the results of small accommodation for the sustainable management of waste and that at the same time can reduce accommodation costs and at the same time generate a reduction in maintenance costs for the company.

Various hotels in the world are already using messages aimed at their consumers to ensure that they make a complete consumption of the food that is served daily since it is known that there are many foods that are prepared but not consumed. As reported by Kallbekken and Sælen (2013), a sign can be placed on the tables of the buffet breakfast at the hotel that allows guests to be warmly welcomed to serve more portions so that they can contribute to serving more portions and thereby reduce they heap up food. These same initiatives have been reported by Okumus et al. (2020). This global proposal for the management of food waste in the hospitality industry is also related to an increase in customer loyalty, as reported previously (Filimonau et al., 2020a; Kim & Hall, 2020).

There are many dogmas in the hotel industry. These dogmas do not allow the optimization of processes and should be eliminated soon in companies: 'the buffet is offered in hotels because there is no problem in food surcharges because that cost is already included in the customer's bill'. The implementation of this measure may seem easy but international markets are becoming more demanding and these sustainable initiatives need to be perfected to achieve the objective of waste management and at the same time ensure that consumers are able to be attracted and increase their intention to pay for the proposal of sustainable hospitality (Yetkin Özbük & Coşkun, 2020). The perspective of these sustainable initiatives for waste management will be increasingly demanded globally after the COVID-19 crisis (Filimonau, 2020).

Alvarez-Risco et al. (2020a) evaluated the most important hotel chains in the world about the offer in relation to sustainability on the same website. Preferred Hotels and Resorts, Hyatt Hotels and Hilton. However, there are other reports that may also be interesting to review, such as the one developed by Marriot (2020) which details the efforts to reduce carbon emissions by 30%, 50% food waste, achieve 30% renewable electricity, 250 adaptive reuse projects, among others.

3.2.2 Supply Chain Management

When the need to implement and develop sustainable initiatives arises, in the case of supply chain management it has been possible to identify some possible mechanisms (Cloutier et al., 2020):

a. Relationship management.
   Mechanism: Networking and training.
   Impact in sustainability: Voluntary projects and motivation.
b. Joint practices.
   Mechanism: Synchronizing activities and joint delivery scheduling.
   Impact in sustainability: Development of collaborative execution to reach the goal.
c. Digital activities, generation and exchange of information.
   Mechanism: Exchange of knowledge and information developed.
   Impact in sustainability: Enabling communication and collaboration.

When talking about related processes, Industry 4.0 has to be considered, which allows enhancing the industrial capability through digitally controlled manufacturing and thus contributes to sustainability which shows that there is a strong link between Industry 4.0 (Müller et al., 2018).

Successful supply chain experiences consider the coordination between the government, private investment focused on sustainability and the preferences of the companies that pay for the services (Zhang & Yousaf, 2020). A concrete example is the ports of Amsterdam (2021), Italy and Croatia through of SUSPORT programme (Italy-Croacia, 2021) and Antwerp (UN, 2021). These ports are essential because they generate a global commercial influence so that the international market moves towards sustainability since it is the only way in which products could pass through these ports. It is important to note that tools and technologies are required, as indicated Bjerkan and Seter (2019) to become a port in a sustainable: Management of environment and energy, concession agreements focus on sustainability, modal split, wind energy, solar energy, geothermal energy, electrification, biofuels, technological shift: trucks and drayage and others who can be established between big companies and the ports.

3.2.3 Sustainable Transportation

Globally, transport has been changing and currently a combination of forms of transport can be found that globally offers the market different options both in relation to price and its sustainable components. The sustainability of world trade is also based on electric cars which are increasingly available for individual use as well as at the company level. The life cycle process of plugin electric bus transportation is described by Alvarez-Risco et al. (2020b) (see Fig. 1).

Around the world, more ports are being achieved that use electricity as a source of energy such as Barcelona, Southern California.

3.2.4 Sustainable Management of Plastics

There are more sustainable initiatives that are shown in the international market such as those that are framed in the control of plastic (Alvarez-Risco et al., 2020c).

In relation to companies, some efforts can be described as Unilever (2021), Henkel (2021), Danone (2021), and Basf (2021). More and more industries are incorporating initiatives focused on sustainability so that they can offer international markets a product or service that allows them to be more efficient, generating less pollution, positive social impact and higher profits. However, in order to evaluate that companies can really implement plastic management, it is important to evaluate

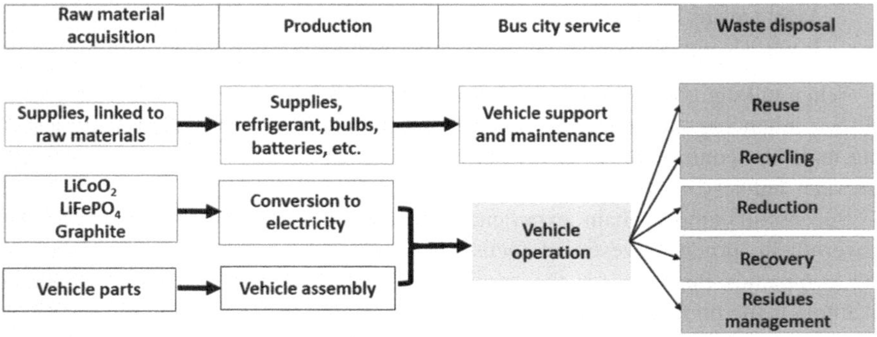

Fig. 1 Bus transportation life process of plug-in electric (PE)

what aspects are favouring and slowing down the change in purchasing, manufacturing, distribution, storage and other processes.

In that sense, Dijkstra et al. (2020) described in a systematic review the main facilitators for the development of competitive advantage. Another aspect that could also be recognized as a facilitator was the differentiation of products and services that provide strength for companies in order to achieve the implementation of plastic handling. Consumers also play a major role in demanding the company to offer a sustainable image based on its ecological management. It has also been possible to identify that the reduction in costs that is produced by the use of waste from production processes is a facilitator together with the alliance that companies can establish with institutions focused on research that allow the generation of technologies that help sustainability. The barriers to the implementation of plastic management are those that are linked to the high investment costs to acquire the necessary technologies as well as the training that must be carried out for sophisticated equipment, also taking into account the maintenance costs of said equipment; Likewise, it is possible that the consumer does not take this management of plastic as important or that these adjustments are not to the liking of consumers, with the probability of certain bottlenecks due to the limited inputs and that finally the market does not reward the investment of the company in this sustainable management.

One way in which barriers can be overcome is to gradually incorporate information on sustainability into the products and services that the company offers and evaluate the importance that customers give to such information so that some approximation can be obtained about the return on investment Alvarez-Risco and Del-Aguila-Arcentales (2021). What will be done; It should be noted that not all consumers will be impacted by this sustainable offer, but in those who do, it is necessary to know what additional aspect they would like to feel from the company's offer. Is it enough to say that they have environmental care policies? Will not it be very abstract? Is it better to say that we are saving 20% of the water consumption in the new containers or that we are collaborating with the planting of 1000 trees in a community?

The value that customers in international markets place on sustainability is evolving more and more and an example of this is what has been seen with the arrival of COVID-19. This pandemic has had negative impacts on health workers (Chen et al., 2020; Yañez et al., 2020; Zhang et al., 2020, 2021), people (Alvarez-Risco et al., 2020d, 2020e, 2021a, 2021b, 2021c, 2021d, 2021e; Quispe-Cañari et al., 2021) and companies (Apcho-Ccencho et al., 2021; Leiva-Martinez et al., 2021; Yan et al., 2021).

In this scenario, the question arises: What do customers value most in times of pandemic? What is the value that clients expect from multinationals?

In this sense, Bartolacci et al. (2020) have found that innovation and entrepreneurship, together with corporate social responsibility and green management, is an expected management to achieve that more SMEs are obtained with a sustainable business model. Sustainability will have a place in international markets to the extent that it can capture the sensitivity of customers in new, increasingly changing scenarios.

4 Conclusions

Companies and consumers increasingly demand sustainable products and services and multinationals must increasingly migrate to sustainable proposals for the manufacture, transport and waste management of the products and services they offer. What is described in this chapter can be used to propose multicentre research so that the level of conversion to sustainable practices can be known, its barriers and what the global market demands in the coming years.

References

Agyeiwaah, E. (2020). The contribution of small accommodation enterprises to sustainable solid waste management. *Journal of Hospitality and Tourism Management, 44*, 1–9. https://doi.org/10.1016/j.jhtm.2020.04.013

Alvarez-Risco, A., Estrada-Merino, A., & Perez-Luyo, R. (2020a). Sustainable development goals in hospitality management. In H. Ruël, A. Lombarts (Eds.) *Sustainable hospitality management. Advanced Series in Management* (Vol. 24, pp. 159–178). Emerald Publishing Limited, Bingley. https://doi.org/10.1108/S1877-636120200000024012

Alvarez-Risco, A., Del-Aguila-Arcentales, S., & Rosen, M. A. (2020b). Sustainable transportation in cities. *Building Sustainable Cities*. https://doi.org/10.1007/978-3-030-45533-0_12

Alvarez-Risco, A., Rosen, M. A., & Del-Aguila-Arcentales, S. (2020c). A new regulation for supporting a circular economy in the plastic industry: The case of Peru. *Journal of Landscape Ecology*, 13(1), 1–3.

Alvarez-Risco, A., Estrada-Merino, A., Anderson-Seminario, M. d. l. M., Mlodzianowska, S., García-Ibarra, V., Villagomez-Buele, C., & Carvache-Franco, M. (2020d). Multitasking behavior in online classrooms and academic performance: Case of university students in Ecuador during COVID-19 outbreak. *Interactive Technology and Smart Education*. (ahead-of-print). https://doi.org/10.1108/ITSE-08-2020-0160

Alvarez-Risco, A., Mejia, C. R., Delgado-Zegarra, J., Del-Aguila-Arcentales, S., Arce-Esquivel, A. A., Valladares-Garrido, M. J., Rosas del Portal, M., Villegas, L. F., Curioso, W. H., Sekar, M. C., & Yañez, J. A. (2020e). The Peru approach against the COVID-19 infodemic: Insights and strategies. *The American Journal of Tropical Medicine and Hygiene*, 103(2), 583–586. https://doi.org/10.4269/ajtmh.20-0536

Alvarez-Risco, A., & Del-Aguila-Arcentales, S. (2021). Crowdsourcing for sustainability: Case of sustainable development goals. In R. Lenart-Gansiniec, J Chen (Eds.), Crowdfunding in the public sector. *Contributions to finance and accounting*. Springer, Cham. https://doi.org/10.1007/978-3-030-77841-5_12

Alvarez-Risco, A., Del-Aguila-Arcentales, S., Yañez, J. A., Rosen, M. A., & Mejia, C. R. (2021a). Influence of technostress on academic performance of university medicine students in Peru during the COVID-19 Pandemic. *Sustainability*, 13(16), 8949. https://doi.org/10.3390/su13168949

Alvarez-Risco, A., Mlodzianowska, S., Zamora-Ramos, U., & Del-Aguila-Arcentales, S. (2021b). Factors of green entrepreneurship intention in international business university students: The case of Peru. *Entrepreneurial Business and Economics Review* (in press).

Alvarez-Risco, A., Mlodzianowska, S., García-Ibarra, V., Rosen, M. A., & Del-Aguila-Arcentales, S. (2021c). Factors affecting green entrepreneurship intentions in business university students in Covid-19 pandemic times: Case of Ecuador. *Sustainability*, 13(11), 6447. https://doi.org/10.3390/su13116447

Alvarez-Risco, A., Del-Aguila-Arcentales, S., & Yáñez, J. A. (2021d). Telemedicine in Peru as a result of the COVID-19 pandemic: Perspective from a country with limited internet access. *The American Journal of Tropical Medicine and Hygiene*. https://doi.org/10.4269/ajtmh.21-0255

Alvarez-Risco, A., Del-Aguila-Arcentales, S., Rosen, M. A., García-Ibarra, V., Maycotte-Felkel, S., & Martínez-Toro, G. M. (2021e). Expectations and interests of university students in COVID-19 times about sustainable development goals: Evidence from Colombia, Ecuador, Mexico, and Peru. *Sustainability*, 13(6), 3306. https://doi.org/10.3390/su13063306

Amsterdam, P. O. (2021). Sustainable ports. Retrieved from https://www.portofamsterdam.com/en/discover/sustainable-port

Apcho-Ccencho, L.-V., Cuya-Velásquez, B.-B., Rodríguez, D. A., Anderson-Seminario, M.d.l.M., Alvarez-Risco, A., Estrada-Merino, A., & Mlodzianowska, S. (2021). The Impact of international price on the technological industry in the United States and China during times of crisis: Commercial War and COVID-19. In K. D. Lawrence, R. K. Klimberg (Eds.), *Advances in business and management forecasting. Advances in Business and Management Forecasting* (Vol. 14, pp. 149–160). Emerald Publishing Limited, Bingley. https://doi.org/10.1108/S1477-407020210000014010

Bartolacci, F., Caputo, A., & Soverchia, M. (2020). Sustainability and financial performance of small and medium sized enterprises: A bibliometric and systematic literature review. *Business Strategy and the Environment, 29*(3), 1297–1309. https://doi.org/10.1002/bse.2434

Basf. (2021). Turning plastic waste into new chemical products. Retrieved from https://www.basf.com/global/en/who-we-are/sustainability/we-drive-sustainable-solutions/circular-economy/mass-balance-approach/chemcycling.html

Bjerkan, K. Y., & Seter, H. (2019). Reviewing tools and technologies for sustainable ports: Does research enable decision making in ports? *Transportation Research Part D: Transport and Environment, 72*, 243–260. https://doi.org/10.1016/j.trd.2019.05.003

Chen, X., Zhang, S. X., Jahanshahi, A. A., Alvarez-Risco, A., Dai, H., Li, J., & Ibarra, V. G. (2020). Belief in a COVID-19 conspiracy theory as a predictor of mental health and well-being of health care workers in Ecuador: Cross-sectional survey study. *JMIR Public Health and Surveillance, 6* (3), e20737. https://doi.org/10.2196/20737

Cloutier, C., Oktaei, P., & Lehoux, N. (2020). Collaborative mechanisms for sustainability-oriented supply chain initiatives: State of the art, role assessment and research opportunities. *International Journal of Production Research, 58*(19), 5836–5850. https://doi.org/10.1080/00207543.2019.1660821

Danone. (2021). Circular economy of packaging. Retrieved from https://www.danone.com/impact/planet/packaging-positive-circular-economy.html

Dijkstra, H., van Beukering, P., & Brouwer, R. (2020). Business models and sustainable plastic management: A systematic review of the literature. *Journal of Cleaner Production, 258*, 120967. https://doi.org/10.1016/j.jclepro.2020.120967

Filimonau, V. (2020). The prospects of waste management in the hospitality sector post COVID-19. *Resources, Conservation and Recycling, 168*, 105272. https://doi.org/10.1016/j.resconrec.2020.105272

Filimonau, V., & De Coteau, D. A. (2019). Food waste management in hospitality operations: A critical review. *Tourism Management, 71*, 234–245. https://doi.org/10.1016/j.tourman.2018.10.009

Filimonau, V., Matute, J., Kubal-Czerwińska, M., Krzesiwo, K., & Mika, M. (2020a). The determinants of consumer engagement in restaurant food waste mitigation in Poland: An exploratory study. *Journal of Cleaner Production, 247*, 119105. https://doi.org/10.1016/j.jclepro.2019.119105

Filimonau, V., Todorova, E., Mzembe, A., Sauer, L., & Yankholmes, A. (2020b). A comparative study of food waste management in full service restaurants of the United Kingdom and the Netherlands. *Journal of Cleaner Production, 258*, 120775. https://doi.org/10.1016/j.jclepro.2020.120775

Hay, R., & Eagle, L. (2020). Impact of integrated sustainability content into undergraduate business education. *International Journal of Sustainability in Higher Education, 21*(1), 131–143. https://doi.org/10.1108/IJSHE-05-2019-0174
Henkel. (2021). Circular economy. Retrieved from https://www.henkel.com/spotlight/features/circular-economy
Italy-Croacia, I. (2021). SUSPORT - SUSitanable PORTs. Retrieved from https://www.italy-croatia.eu/web/susport
Kallbekken, S., & Sælen, H. (2013). 'Nudging' hotel guests to reduce food waste as a win–win environmental measure. *Economics Letters, 119*(3), 325–327. https://doi.org/10.1016/j.econlet.2013.03.019
Kim, M. J., & Hall, C. M. (2020). Can sustainable restaurant practices enhance customer loyalty? The roles of value theory and environmental concerns. *Journal of Hospitality and Tourism Management, 43*, 127–138. https://doi.org/10.1016/j.jhtm.2020.03.004
Leiva-Martinez, M.-A., Anderson-Seminario, M.d.l.M., Alvarez-Risco, A., Estrada-Merino, A., & Mlodzianowska, S. (2021). Price variation in lower goods as of previous economic crisis and the contrast of the current price situation in the context of COVID-19 in Peru. In K. D. Lawrence, R. K. Klimberg (Eds.), *Advances in business and management forecasting. Advances in Business and Management Forecasting* (Vol. 14, pp. 161–166). Emerald Publishing Limited, Bingley. https://doi.org/10.1108/S1477-407020210000014011
Lorincová, S., Štarchoň, P., Weberová, D., Hitka, M., & Lipoldová, M. (2019). Employee motivation as a tool to achieve sustainability of business processes. *Sustainability, 11*(13), 3509. https://www.mdpi.com/2071-1050/11/13/3509
Marriot. (2020). 2020 serve 360 report. Retrieved from https://serve360.marriott.com/wp-content/uploads/2020/12/2020-Serve360-Report.pdf
Müller, J. M., Buliga, O., & Voigt, K.-I. (2018). Fortune favors the prepared: How SMEs approach business model innovations in industry 4.0. *Technological Forecasting and Social Change, 132*, 2–17. https://doi.org/10.1016/j.techfore.2017.12.019
Okumus, B., Taheri, B., Giritlioglu, I., & Gannon, M. J. (2020). Tackling food waste in all-inclusive resort hotels. *International Journal of Hospitality Management, 88*, 102543. https://doi.org/10.1016/j.ijhm.2020.102543
Palumbo, R., Manesh, M. F., Pellegrini, M. M., Caputo, A., & Flamini, G. (2021). Organizing a sustainable smart urban ecosystem: Perspectives and insights from a bibliometric analysis and literature review. *Journal of Cleaner Production, 297*, 126622. https://doi.org/10.1016/j.jclepro.2021.126622
Pizzi, S., Caputo, A., Corvino, A., & Venturelli, A. (2020). Management research and the UN sustainable development goals (SDGs): A bibliometric investigation and systematic review. *Journal of Cleaner Production, 276*, 124033. https://doi.org/10.1016/j.jclepro.2020.124033
Pizzi, S., Corbo, L., & Caputo, A. (2021). Fintech and SMEs sustainable business models: Reflections and considerations for a circular economy. *Journal of Cleaner Production, 281*, 125217. https://doi.org/10.1016/j.jclepro.2020.125217
Quispe-Cañari, J. F., Fidel-Rosales, E., Manrique, D., Mascaró-Zan, J., Huamán-Castillón, K. M., Chamorro–Espinoza, S. E., Garayar–Peceros, H., Ponce–López, V. L., Sifuentes-Rosales, J., Alvarez-Risco, A., Yáñez, J. A., & Mejia, C. R. (2021). Self-medication practices during the COVID-19 pandemic among the adult population in Peru: A cross-sectional survey. *Saudi Pharmaceutical Journal, 29*(1), 1–11. https://doi.org/10.1016/j.jsps.2020.12.001
Sakshi, S., Cerchione, R., & Bansal, H. (2020). Measuring the impact of sustainability policy and practices in tourism and hospitality industry. *Business Strategy and the Environment, 29*(3), 1109–1126. https://doi.org/10.1002/bse.2420
Shields, R. (2019). The sustainability of international higher education: Student mobility and global climate change. *Journal of Cleaner Production, 217*, 594–602. https://doi.org/10.1016/j.jclepro.2019.01.291
UN. (2021). Port of Antwerp: A pioneer among sustainable ports. Retrieved from https://www.un.org/en/coronavirus/port-antwerp-pioneer-among-sustainable-ports

Unilever. (2021). Rethinking plastic packaging – towards a circular economy. Retrieved from https://www.unilever.com/sustainable-living/reducing-environmental-impact/waste-and-packaging/rethinking-plastic-packaging/

Wu, Z., Mohammed, A., & Harris, I. (2021). Food waste management in the catering industry: Enablers and interrelationships. *Industrial Marketing Management, 94*, 1–18. https://doi.org/10.1016/j.indmarman.2021.01.019

Yan, J., Kim, S., Zhang, S. X., Foo, M.-D., Alvarez-Risco, A., Del-Aguila-Arcentales, S., & Yáñez, J. A. (2021). Hospitality workers' COVID-19 risk perception and depression: A contingent model based on transactional theory of stress model. *International Journal of Hospitality Management, 95*, 102935. https://doi.org/10.1016/j.ijhm.2021.102935

Yañez, J. A., Afshar Jahanshahi, A., Alvarez-Risco, A., Li, J., & Zhang, S. X. (2020). Anxiety, distress, and turnover intention of healthcare workers in Peru by their distance to the epicenter during the COVID-19 crisis. *The American Journal of Tropical Medicine and Hygiene, 103*(4), 1614–1620. https://doi.org/10.4269/ajtmh.20-0800

Yetkin Özbük, R. M., & Coşkun, A. (2020). Factors affecting food waste at the downstream entities of the supply chain: A critical review. *Journal of Cleaner Production, 244*, 118628. https://doi.org/10.1016/j.jclepro.2019.118628

Zhang, S. X., Chen, J., Afshar Jahanshahi, A., Alvarez-Risco, A., Dai, H., Li, J., & Patty-Tito, R. M. (2021). Succumbing to the COVID-19 pandemic—healthcare workers not satisfied and intend to leave their jobs. *International Journal of Mental Health and Addiction, 7*, 1–10. https://doi.org/10.1007/s11469-020-00418-6

Zhang, S. X., Sun, S., Afshar Jahanshahi, A., Alvarez-Risco, A., Ibarra, V. G., Li, J., & Patty-Tito, R. M. (2020). Developing and testing a measure of COVID-19 organizational support of healthcare workers – results from Peru, Ecuador, and Bolivia. *Psychiatry Research, 291*, 113174. https://doi.org/10.1016/j.psychres.2020.113174

Zhang, X., & Yousaf, H. M. A. U. (2020). Green supply chain coordination considering government intervention, green investment, and customer green preferences in the petroleum industry. *Journal of Cleaner Production, 246*, 118984. https://doi.org/10.1016/j.jclepro.2019.118984

Dr. Aldo Alvarez-Risco, PhD, is a full-time professor at Universidad de Lima in Perú in International Business Career. Also, he is a researcher member of the Global Business Research (GBR) group. He also holds PhD from Universidad Autónoma de Nuevo León, Doctorate in Pharmacy and Biochemistry, Master in Pharmacology and Pharmacist at the Universidad Nacional Mayor de San Marcos, and Master Pharmaceutical Care at Universidad de Granada. He is the coordinator of the South American Network of Pharmaceutical Care (REDSAF). He has been a speaker at academic events in 22 countries.

Prof. Shyla Del-Aguila-Arcentales is a researcher in the Sustainability area. She is a candidate for a Doctor degree and Master in Pharmaceutical Sciences at the Universidad Nacional Mayor de San Marcos and Pharmacist at Universidad Nacional de la Amazonia Peruana. She has experience in bio-business, circular economy, audit, environmental management and import-export management. It is linked to the ancestral knowledge of medicinal plants in the jungle regarding their traditional uses, and it is a solid academic networker.

Social Capital and the Morphogenesis of Actors: Lessons from International Social Entrepreneurs

Emilio Costales and Anica Zeyen

Abstract Social entrepreneurs tackle so far insufficiently addressed social and environmental challenges with the aim to create positive societal change. Numerous anecdotal and empirical cases underline the significant role played by personal or vicarious experience in identifying innovative ways of solving societal challenges. Against this background, international social entrepreneurs—social entrepreneurs who are foreigners in the country they set up their venture—pose an interesting conundrum that has so far not been sufficiently—if at all—addressed in the social entrepreneurship literature: how do social entrepreneurs navigate their new environment? By implementing morphogenetic and social capital theories, this chapter engages with illustrative examples from international social entrepreneurs operating in the Netherlands to develop a Social-Capital-Morphogenetic model, which serves to illuminate the role of social capital accumulation in navigating new environments. This chapter calls for greater emphasis on complexity and the systems level in further social entrepreneurship research to draw attention to the contextual complexities of social change and the implications of these complexities on the social entrepreneurship process.

Keywords Social Capital · Morphogenesis · Social Entrepreneurship · Social Innovation · Social Entrepreneurs · Social-Capital-Morphogenetic Model of Social Entrepreneurship

---

E. Costales (✉)
School of Business and Management, Royal Holloway University of London, Egham, UK
e-mail: emilio.costales@rhul.ac.uk

A. Zeyen
School of Business and Management, Royal Holloway University of London, Egham, UK

Department of Psychology, Faculty of Humanities, University of Johannesburg, Johannesburg, South Africa
e-mail: Anica.zeyen@rhul.ac.uk

A. Caputo et al. (eds.), *The International Dimension of Entrepreneurial Decision-Making*, Contributions to Management Science,
https://doi.org/10.1007/978-3-030-85950-3_11

1 Introduction

Social entrepreneurs tackle so far insufficiently addressed social and environmental challenges with the aim to create positive societal change through innovative approaches (Albert et al., 2016; Haugh & Talwar, 2016). Well-known examples are the Grameen Bank, the initiators of credit rings and the modern-day microcredit or Wikipedia, the world's first free encyclopaedia.

Extant research highlights that social entrepreneurs intend to overcome the roots, and not merely the symptoms, of a societal challenge (e.g., Dees, 1998), and thereby create system-level change. Thus, rather than merely providing shelter for the homeless, social entrepreneurs would aim to understand the cause of homelessness and identify ways of eradicating involuntary homelessness. As a result, for some, organisational redundancy is not only not feared but often desired and worked towards. To achieve this, social entrepreneurs require a detailed understanding of the various system components that led to the societal challenge. Moreover, they need to also understand current solutions and the reason for their (partial) inefficiency or ineffectiveness (Zeyen & Beckmann, 2019). Indeed, numerous anecdotal and empirical cases underline the significant role played by personal or in-depth vicarious experience in identifying more effective ways of solving a societal challenge (e.g., Zeyen & Beckmann, 2018; see Ashoka Fellows' profiles[1]).

Against this background, international social entrepreneurs—i.e., social entrepreneurs who are foreigners in the country they set up their venture—manifest an interesting conundrum that has so far not been sufficiently—if at all—addressed in the social entrepreneurship literature. As current research illustrates, in an international setting, entrepreneurial uncertainty is compounded by additional factors such as intercultural competence (e.g., Knowles et al., 2006) and lower endowment of regionally embedded social capital (e.g., Dahl & Sorenson, 2012). Due to the higher levels of social embeddedness of social entrepreneurs, we conjecture that the role of social capital will be even more crucial to social entrepreneurs than it is for commercial entrepreneurs (e.g., Praszkier et al., 2009). Put differently, our current understanding of social entrepreneurship would lead to the conclusion that international social entrepreneurs would be far less likely to succeed. However, there are numerous examples that seemingly contradict this assumption. Against this background, we raise the question: how do international social entrepreneurs navigate the social entrepreneurial process despite facing a potential lack of social capital?

In order to address this, we utilise both morphogenic (Archer, 1995) and social capital (Coleman, 1988) theory. Morphogenesis allows us to better perceive the influence of the structure-agency interaction on the social dimension, while social capital theory enables us to perceive the characteristics of social interaction that foster positive societal change. In combination, these insights help enhance our understanding of the nuances of societal configurations that inhibit inclusion of marginalised groups. We use these to conceptually develop a Social-Capital-

[1] https://www.ashoka.org/en-gb/ashoka-fellows

Morphogenetic model of social entrepreneurship. This framework enables understanding of how an initial lack and subsequent accumulation of social capital impacts the social entrepreneurial process of international social entrepreneurs. To demonstrate our conceptualisation, we make use of illustrative examples from international social entrepreneurs operating in the Netherlands. Our framework highlights how each stage of the entrepreneurial process may be affected as different types of social capital are accumulated. We show how the ability of international social entrepreneurs to create societal change strongly depends on the accumulation of social capital at each stage of the social entrepreneurial process.

The following subchapter will introduce the key concepts and theories used in this book chapter. We will start off by introducing the social innovation model of social entrepreneurship as this constitutes the basis for our conceptualisation. Following, we will introduce our two main theoretical lenses: Morphogenesis and social capital. In a third step, we then merge the notion of social entrepreneurship with the insights from both theories to develop our Social-Capital-Morphogenetic framework of social entrepreneurship. Throughout this conceptualisation, we will discuss how the international status of social entrepreneurs likely impacts the various stages. To illustrate these, we will use illustrative case examples from multiple international social entrepreneurs in the Netherlands. We conclude with some final remarks.

2 Social Entrepreneurship: A Social Innovation Perspective

This subchapter serves to introduce the concept of social entrepreneurship as we understand it for the purpose of this book chapter. In particular, we introduce a three-tiered social innovation model that will be the basis for our conceptualisations.

2.1 *Social Entrepreneurship: A Brief Introduction*

In his seminal work, Gregory Dees (1998) identified the pursuit of social betterment over profit as a distinguishing characteristic of the then nascent research field of social entrepreneurship. While scholars still disagree about the finer elements of its definition (Dacin et al., 2011; Short et al., 2009; Zeyen & Beckmann, 2019), they agree on a core social mission and inherent hybridity as fundamental core features of social entrepreneurship (Ebrahim et al., 2014).

The core social mission relates to the raison d'être of the entrepreneurial activity. Social entrepreneurs wish to create positive social change (Dacin et al., 2010). Therefore, social change is the objective of the endeavour rather than the means (Zeyen et al., 2014). This is what distinguishes social entrepreneurship from commercial entrepreneurship or corporate social responsibility (CSR). While both commercial entrepreneurship and CSR can create social value for society, it is not the reason for the organisation's existence. If we take, for example, Jeff Bezoz and

Amazon: the widespread availability of online shopping and door-step delivery is an innovative model. While this model creates accessibility to products for people who might otherwise not have access (e.g., disabled who cannot leave the house or during the COVID-19 lockdown), the organisation's purpose is profit. Similarly, if a company like Merlin Entertainment Group offers free entry to its theme parks such as LEGO®-Land for looked-after children, it constitutes a worthwhile CSR practice but does not constitute social entrepreneurship. It does not tackle the underlying societal problem which is a prerequisite for large-scale change that characterises social entrepreneurial behaviour.

Conversely, if we look at Muhammad Yunus and the Grameen Bank: the Grameen Bank provides microcredits to poor women in Bangladesh. This approach was innovative and earned Yunus and the Grameen Bank the Nobel Peace Prize in 2006. This model creates social value by helping those disenfranchised by the banking system and encouraging entrepreneurial behaviour. In contrast to the case of Amazon and Merlin, the Grameen Bank has social value creation as its organisational objective and therefore constitutes a social entrepreneurial example. Moreover, Yunus understood that one of the underlying systemic problems of poverty was the inaccessibility of capital in order to create opportunities for economic participation.

2.2 The Social Innovation Model of Social Entrepreneurship

In order to move beyond social value and affect social change, current research postulates that social innovation is crucial as it introduces new players by creating novel agential constellations. Social innovation's fundamental principles involve: (i) addressing needs neglected by the market or state, (ii) creating new institutional relations and (iii) empowering people to transform existing structures (Moulaert et al., 2013). The combination of these three principles enables the system-level change necessary to sustainably fulfil the intentions of the social entrepreneur. Enhancing understanding, cooperation and agential capacities are therefore key to meeting these principles (Moulaert & MacCallum, 2019).

Within the social entrepreneurship field, Nicholls' (2010) conceptualisation of the social innovation model of social entrepreneurship integrates the social innovation view firmly into the social entrepreneurship debate by contextualising the process of social entrepreneurship in a three-tiered framework with social change as the objective and social value creation as a necessary condition of this process. The creation of an enterprise and its longevity is of lesser concern against the backdrop of the social change objective. This model promotes the rationale that market failures are best addressed through systems reconfigurations (e.g., Mulgan, 2012; Nicholls, 2010).

For the purpose of this book chapter, we understand social entrepreneurship as conceptualised in the social innovation model of social entrepreneurship. Social entrepreneurship understood as such allows for the emergence of social innovation

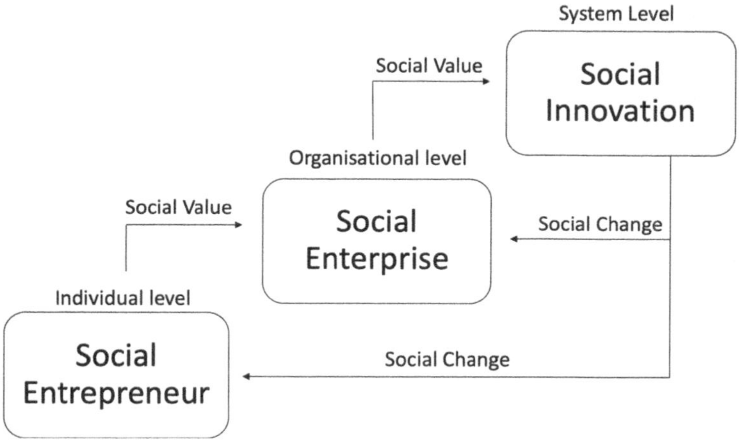

Fig. 1 Overview of the Social Innovation model, the strata under inspection and the strata of origination of social impacts

as both means and objective of social change. Indeed, *social innovation* as *means* appears by promoting mutual understanding of actors and coalescing towards mutually beneficial objectives (Moulaert & MacCallum, 2019). Yet, cooperation per se is not a sufficient condition for creating social change. While it can spur people into action and promote social value, social change requires institutional change (Hietschold et al., 2019) and behavioural change of other (corporate) actors (Schaltegger et al., 2016). *Social innovation* as *objective* emerges as a hybrid of existing elements crossing sectoral boundaries, institutional (re)creation and novel social relations between previously disparate and marginalised groups, which empowers people to transform existing structures and sets the stage for further innovation (Mulgan, 2007; Moulaert et al., 2013). Importantly, social entrepreneurship requires agency at all three societal levels—individual (micro), enterprise (meso) and societal (macro)—in order to create its objective of positive social change. Figure 1 illustrates this interplay.

If we go back to the example of Muhammad Yunus and the Grameen Bank, we can illustrate the potency of this way of understanding social entrepreneurship and the underlying social entrepreneurial process. Yunus recognised that those who could not afford collateral were disenfranchised by the traditional banking system (Yunus et al., 2010). The underlying formal and informal rules of the banking system inhibited what was considered high risk lending. Often the only option for the poor in the Global South would be to lend from the so-called loan sharks at interest rates that would often trap the individual in a vicious cycle of debt accumulation. Initially, Yunus used his own money to micro-lend to a small number of individuals. This experience combined with his expertise as an economics professor led to his realisation that entrepreneurial behaviour was not a rare quality (see Yunus et al.,

2010; London School of Economics, 2017). Consequently, the Grameen Bank enterprise emerged in 1976 to provide opportunities for entrepreneurship to the poor.

Going back to our three-tiered understanding of social entrepreneurship: the initial act of lending and realisation of the entrepreneurial potential of poor Bangladeshi communities represents the individual level. The founding of the Grameen Bank and the social value it provides represents the organisational level. In lieu of traditional collateral, the Grameen Bank provides group loans in order to leverage the social capital of loan recipients to ensure repayment (see London School of Economics, 2017). As a result, over 90% of loans provided by the Grameen Bank have been repaid.[2] Social innovation emerges as a means in this organisational stage through this use of peer lending (credit rings). On a systems level, the introduction of credit rings and micro-lending has changed the institutional landscape as the Grameen Bank showed that lending to the poor is indeed possible and also profitable. The introduction of micro-lending has since led to other innovations such as micro-saving or micro-insurance.

In short, social entrepreneurship aims to achieve positive societal change through social innovation as both a means and objective of the entrepreneurial process. To achieve this, social entrepreneurship requires linking the individual, organisational and system level together to not only change the moves we make within a given game but changing the rules of the game (cf. Beckmann, 2011). In the case of the Grameen bank, Muhammad Yunus, like most social entrepreneurs, was embedded in the sociocultural context of his venture as he is Bangladeshi himself. So how can such system-level change be achieved by individuals who are non-local? In order to conceptualise this, the following subchapter will introduce two theoretical frameworks that will serve as the basis for our conceptual framework for international social entrepreneurs.

3 Morphogenesis and Social Capital: Introducing Our Two Theory Lenses

This subchapter will introduce Morphogenesis and social capital as our two main lenses for gaining insights into how international social entrepreneurs deal with their lack of local embeddedness. In a first step, we will introduce morphogenesis and will then turn our attention to social capital.

[2] Grameen Bank's March 2021 monthly report (issued April 06, 2021) reveals 93% of cumulative lifetime dispersals have been repaid: https://grameenbank.org/data-and-report/monthly-report-2021-03-issue-495-in-usd/

3.1 *Morphogenesis and Social Entrepreneurship: Changing the Game*

The theory of Morphogenesis (Archer, 1995) examines the interplay between structure and agency and is adopted here to conceptualise how behaviour at the individual level affects structural change in a complex open system (Buckley, 1967). Morphogenesis is differentiated between similar theories (such as structuration theory) by the way structure and agency are seen as causally intertwinned adopting analytical dualism. Archer (2010) has been signposted as a means to offer an in-depth explanation. That is, relations between individual actors manifest from interactions between multiple collectivities. These collectivities exist on the basis of distributed material resources and ideational sources, which may result from past interactions between actors who are no longer living. These previous conditions form the bounded reality within which agency is enacted.

Agency refers to the capacity to act autonomously (e.g., Latour, 2005). Morphogenesis holds that structural and cultural antecedents maintain conditional influence upon agency, but do not determine agency. Rather, elaboration is mediated through agency. Actors are able to affect the capacities of their collectivities by articulating interests and organisational capability to impact consciousness and commitments of other actors within their groups. In the case of the social entrepreneur, causal powers manifest in the decision to exercise innovative articulation of existing deficiencies in the social dimension. Put differently, only by demonstrating how a collectivity is disadvantaged can organisations begin to address the disadvantage. For example, LGBTQ+ rights organisations could only emerge because members of the community raised awareness and demonstrated the systemic discrimination they faced.

Morphogenesis introduces a distinction between actors and agents to account for the individual decision-making processes among and between persons.[3] Such differences allow for their presence in multiple collectivities which elaborate their roles within the social dimension. Each morphogenetic cycle begins with stratified collectivities: the privileged and the underprivileged. These collectivities have varied vested interests, which will be simplified here to maintaining (their advantages) or improving (upon their disadvantages). The interaction between these collectivities then set the conditions for structural and cultural elaboration. These collectivities are divided into *primary agents* and *corporate agents* (Archer, 1995). *Primary agent* refers to those collectivities who are inarticulate in their demands and unorganised in pursuit of their vested interests. In contrast, *corporate agents* are articulate in their desires, have organisational capabilities and are party to negotiated societal transformation. Thus, *corporate agents* shape the context for all actors, while *primary agents* inhabit the context created, and, in doing so, reconstruct the environment corporate agents attempt to control.

[3] In addition to agents, actors are introduced as (i) individual persons filling their given roles and (ii) persons with both a personal and social self.

At any given point in time, a primary agent in one domain can be a corporate agent in another domain. For example, 'the poor' represents a collectivity structured by the capitalist system. However, within this collectivity sits multiple collectivities (e.g., unemployed, underpaid, disabled) which are each confronted with some form of barriers (such as racism, ageism, sexism) that leads them to be more concerned with their differences than their similarities. As a consequence, 'the poor' engage in decision-making processes to pursue their desires through special interest groups that address single issues rather than systematic and pluralistic vested interests of 'the poor' as a whole. In these instances, multiple corporate agents emerge in particular domains (e.g., trade union movement), while 'the poor' remain as primary agent. For the social entrepreneur, *social innovation* as *objective* cannot be obtained as a primary agent. Indeed, it requires them to move beyond inhabiting a context to shaping the context for all actors.

The dynamic nature of complex systems allows for the acquisition of new vested interests in accordance with novel social situations actors may occupy, as a consequence of role elaboration. Social entrepreneurs endeavour to articulate deficiencies in extant solutions in the social dimension and articulate the extent to which cooperation can ameliorate these deficiencies and move towards corporate agent status.

For the purpose of this chapter, a morphogenetic perspective on social entrepreneurship allows us to better understand the role of inter-person and intra- and inter-collectivity relationships and their crucial role in setting the context for the move from primary to corporate agent. Going back to our definition of international social entrepreneurs: morphogenesis helps facilitate a better understanding of how and why actors develop vested interest in new contexts and engage in changing the rules of the game.

3.2 Social Capital and Social Entrepreneurship: Playing the Game

In this subchapter, we briefly outline the role of (social) capital as it pertains to elaboration of agency and introduce three dimensions of social capital that we argue are necessary to affect social change.

Actors map the social context they belong to (Archer, 1995; Latour, 2005), therefore, a good starting point for conceptualising the social entrepreneurial process is the role of capital in mapping the environment. Capital refers to a unit of value that facilitates action (e.g., Light, 2004). Nineteenth century theorists recognised the role of financial and physical capital (e.g., Marx, 1867; Ricardo, 1817) and the twentieth century saw the rise in Human (e.g., Becker, 1962), Cultural (e.g., Bourdieu, 1979) and Social Capital (e.g., Coleman, 1988; Jacobs, 1961). The twenty-first century has witnessed the rise of the knowledge economy (e.g., Melachroinos & Spence, 2013) and with it a re-examination of social capital (e.g., Adler & Kwon, 2002; Lee, 2009).

Table 1 Brief overview of the forms of capital

Forms of capital	Definition
Financial	Most liquid capital in the form of available funds for investment (Light, 2004; Sowell, 1985)
Physical	Less liquid capital in the form of infrastructure (i.e., Land, Equipment and Technology (Light, 2004; Sowell, 1985)
Human	Less liquid capital in the form of training, knowledge and skills that increases productivity (Becker, 1962)
Cultural	Even less liquid capital in the form of 'cultural' knowledge that can be leveraged to the owner's socioeconomic advantage through identification of opportunity (Bourdieu, 1979; Light & Dana, 2013)
Social (a) Relational (b) Cognitive (c) Structural	Equally liquid (to cultural) capital in the form of social networks and their relationships and emerging norms. Uniquely accessible and consisting of multiple dimensions (Coleman, 1988; Lee et al., 2019; Light, 2004; Nahapiet & Ghoshal, 1998) (a) Trust, Obligations and expectations (Zheng, 2010) (b) Shared language and narratives (Lee, 2009) (c) Network affiliation (Nahapiet & Ghoshal, 1998)

Social capital is paradoxical in that it does not belong to a single individual, yet it is individuals who leverage and benefit from social capital (e.g., Waldstrøm & Svendsen, 2008). Differentiating between cognitive, relational and structural social capital enables us to examine why the outcomes of social capital accumulation are seldom unitary. *Cognitive* social capital refers to perceptual tools and communicative actions (e.g., Lee, 2009). It illustrates an individual's adoption of shared narratives and systems of codification. *Relational* social capital represents trust, reciprocity and expectations (Zheng, 2010), while *structural* social capital refers to personal or impersonal network ties (Nahapiet & Ghoshal, 1998). The beneficial outcomes associated with these dimensions are determined by the extent to which they ameliorate inefficiencies and access to resources (Coleman, 1988; Lee et al., 2019). As such, the dimensions of social capital need to be examined in their interdependency with one another, and the relationship between social and additional forms of capital (for overview see Table 1).

Fundamental to understanding the role of capital in all of its forms is their characteristic of mutual metamorphosis. That is, varying forms of capital metamorphose into one another (see Putnam et al., 2004). As a fuel of agency, the metamorphic process of capital is critical to conceptualising its role in the emergence of agency. For example, person A wants good x and metamorphoses their human capital into financial capital through their labour and purchases x. As a consequence of the metamorphic process, social and cultural capital represent the building blocks upon which agency is realised and informs the ways in which further capital is accumulated. Notwithstanding their intangibility, social and cultural capital have substantial implications for *how* resources are allocated and *why* decisions are made. In fact, the metamorphic process requires an initial stock of capital with which to initiate the process (Light, 2004).

Cultural capital (in our use) refers to the socioeconomic and cultural identities one is a part of. Individuals are born into both but can only 'easily' change one: socioeconomic identity (cf. Lin, 1999). Cultural capital draws from a unique intergenerational archive that is itself the result of past structure–agency interactions, which influences agency (cf. Wekker, 2016) and shapes the mental models and bounded reality within which decisions are made (Light & Dana, 2013). For example, as it pertains to the cultural identity, we might expect those individuals whose culture promotes a certain type of economic activity to undertake those activities (see Light & Dana, 2013). In regard to the socio-economic status, Putnam et al. (2004) note that an individual's cultural capital often reflects the affluence one is born into. For example, they use the concept of knowing how to dress for success and the sartorial knowledge associated with it to a higher socio-economic status.

In sum, both morphogenesis and social capital theory highlight the importance of social embeddedness and understanding the institutional setting for successfully identifying and implementing a viable and effective solution to a societal challenge.

4 The Social-Capital-Morphogenetic Model of (International) Social Entrepreneurship

In the previous subchapters, we outlined our understanding of social entrepreneurship and provided an introduction to both Morphogenesis and social capital. We will now develop and illustrate the Social-Capital-Morphogenetic model of social entrepreneurship. Throughout our conceptualisation, we will discuss how the international status of social entrepreneurs impacts the social entrepreneurial process. We will illustrate these with the use of examples from case studies we conducted in the Netherlands.[4] In line with our understanding of social entrepreneurship from a social innovation perspective, we will proceed in three steps. First, we will look at the individual level. Second, we will analyse the organisational level and will end with the system level.

4.1 Morphogenesis, Social Capital and International Social Entrepreneurship

There are different notions of what constitutes an international social entrepreneur. For one, it refers to social entrepreneurs who internationalise from their home country to another country, e.g., through export (cf. Saridakis et al., 2019). On the

[4]Please note that these case studies are only supposed to be illustrative of our conceptual argument. It is not our intention to use them for purposes of induction or abduction. To protect the identity and to keep confidentiality, we anonymised our case studies.

other hand—and as we understand it for the purpose of this book chapter—it refers to immigrants conducting social entrepreneurship in a country that is not their country of origin. To be clear, this does not refer to social entrepreneurs who might have started their venture in their home country and are now expanding to another country, but to individuals who moved to a new country of residence and then decide to start a social venture in that country. Our two theoretical lenses allow us to carve out the challenges that these international social entrepreneurs face.

The initial endowment of cultural capital can be a reflection of the collectivities one is a part of. For example, we might expect an individual from an Eastern culture to have a stronger stock of social capital than one from a Western culture as a consequence of the relatedness within Eastern culture (Snitker, 2010). Similarly, we might expect the 'quality' of social capital to be higher for those born into a higher socio-economic status as they are likely more connected to other individuals with influence or decision-making power. While this cultural capital endowment might increase over time for international social entrepreneurs, we conjecture that it is nonetheless low.

The social embeddedness of social entrepreneurs requires that they leverage the transmutative properties of different forms of capital in innovative ways. Often, entrepreneurial behaviour begins in areas where social entrepreneurs have knowledge of the existing institutional framework, a higher stock of social capital or lower uncertainty in regard to resource acquisition (e.g., Dahl & Sorenson, 2012). For international social entrepreneurs, we would expect an absence of this knowledge and greater uncertainty. The relational and cognitive dimensions of social capital enable social entrepreneurs to penetrate the institutional framework of a new setting by familiarising themselves with the collectivities they aim to engage with, and the deficiencies facing these collectivities. For example, investing in relational and cognitive social capital may reveal that individuals with autism spectrum disorder (ASD) are uniquely competent at processing numbers, yet the current system does not actively promote employment of individuals with ASD. A social entrepreneur may then provide an opportunity for employing people with autism for work heavily reliant on number processing.[5]

If we combine the insights from both Morphogenesis and social capital, we can see that social entrepreneurship is an innovative translation of the ideational oversights which lead to marginalised collectivities, by making issues palatable within existing structures. As a consequence of the translation process, social entrepreneurs invest in local knowledge which affects their ability to enhance the capacity of the collectivities they are involved with (cf. North, 1993; Archer, 1995). Social innovation enables social entrepreneurs to overcome the counter intuitiveness of positive-sum potential within social interactions (Beschorner & Kolmar, 2016) by accumulating and operationalising social capital. Indeed, social capital is a vital resource that facilitates access to additional material and non-material resources by affecting actors' perceived quality of life and ability to act (Coleman, 1988). The

---

[5] See the case of Spcialisterne for more information.

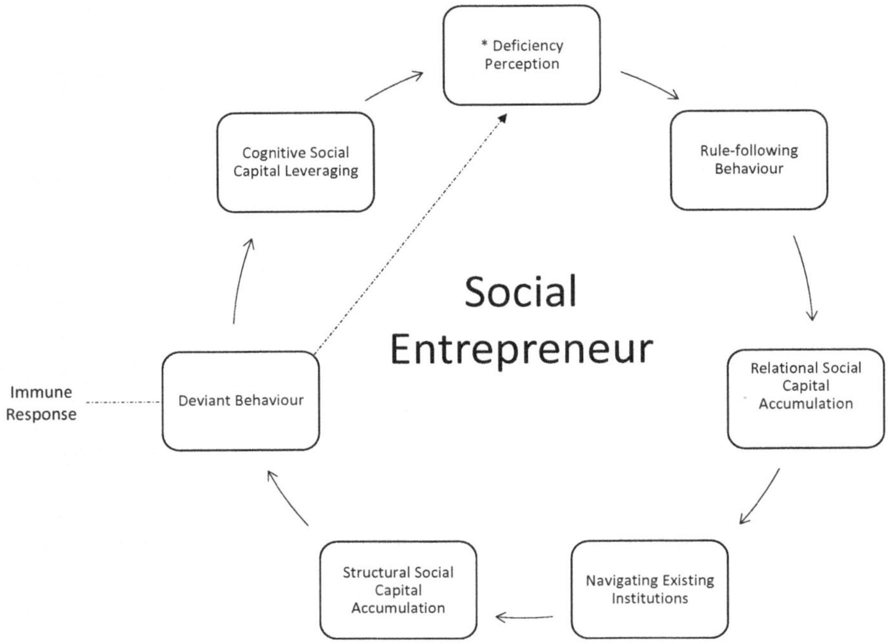

Fig. 2 Social entrepreneur cycle within the Social-Capital-Morphogenetic model

social innovation model of social entrepreneurship framework presents a lens to understand how social capital is accumulated and leveraged to engage in social innovation. However, we require further conceptualisations to understand how international social entrepreneurs are successful in identifying and implementing social innovations despite the challenges they face.

4.2 Individual Level: The Social Entrepreneur

Social entrepreneurs act in response to a perceived deficiency in the system and thus *deficiency perception* sits at the top of the cycle. Following morphogenetic theory, we assume that at that point it might not yet be feasible to fully articulate this deficiency. Thus, the social entrepreneur may (unknowingly) adhere to the rules that give rise to the deficiency in question. We call this the *rule-following behaviour* stage (see Fig. 2 for visualisation). For example, a social entrepreneur who wishes to address problems caused by inequalities will, for the time being, adhere to the rules that caused it in the first place. In following these rules, relational social capital (sc) begins to build. That is, obligation and expectations are formed.

As relational sc develops, *questioning and navigating the existing institutions* begins. Coleman (1988) notes that social capital is significant in an individual's perceived quality of life and, by extension, of those around them. It is therefore possible that the social entrepreneur has a sufficiently high stock of relational sc and is therefore able to fully articulate this deficiency and can thus bypass the *rule-following* stage and begin navigation.

Once a social entrepreneur starts *navigating existing institutions*, i.e., works with and around existing rules, they *accumulate structural sc* due to their interactions with other individuals, and organisations that safeguard or work within the given set of rules. As the social entrepreneur's aim is not to perpetuate the status quo but rather to change the way challenges are addressed, we conjecture that we will be able to observe the emergence of *deviant behaviour*. Here, deviance results from the ineffectiveness of the norms underpinning existing ways of solving the societal problem at hand. While the term deviance sometimes has a negative connotation, in the context of morphogenesis it is meant in a neutral sense and therefore has the potential to benefit (Merton, 1968) disadvantaged collectivities. For example, a workshop may be developed, which promotes active participation of a previously unincluded group (e.g., boxing for youth offenders).

In response to this deviant behaviour, social entrepreneurs are likely to face an *immune response* by the system. Analogous to biological systems like the human body, changes to the status quo of a social system usually inadvertently lead to (negative) immune responses. In other words, the context in which the social entrepreneur operates is more likely to reject the idea and might even go as far as actively fight against it. If we go back to our example of boxing workshops for youth offenders, such projects are likely to create a controversy. Many members of the public will be opposed to teaching young adults with criminal records how to box due to a perception that this will only increase their ability to impose harm on others and in turn make things worse for society. Thus, a potential immune response at the micro level would be that the social entrepreneur receives many negative comments, family and friends expressing doubts or even receiving hate messages via social media.[6]

We argue that the extent to which the social entrepreneur is negatively or positively impacted by these immune responses depends on their pre-existing stock of social capital and especially the quality of the structural sc accumulated during their journey. This is because immune responses are likely to trigger feedback loops. Positive feedback loops amplify the status quo, while negative feedback loops counter the status quo and act as a regulator. For example, in pursuit of support, a social entrepreneur may fail to receive it because they were unable to appropriately express how their vision is applicable or desirable to the supporter in question. We can expect a negative feedback loop to present itself and allow for regulation to the way the entrepreneur expresses their vision in future attempts. Accumulation of cognitive sc accelerates in response to these feedback loops. The *cognitive sc leveraging* stage emerges at the point where a positive feedback loop manifests

[6]Immune responses occur at all levels and at various stages of the social entrepreneurial process.

and an enterprise begins trading. The tangibility of this leveraging can be seen in the development of business acumen (e.g., adoption of business language).

If we now consider a social entrepreneur who was not born in the country they start their venture in, we can see how their process could be impacted at this stage. Internationals will enter the social entrepreneurial process with a far lower level of social capital than their local counterparts. While we assume a general low level of social capital for international social entrepreneurs at the start of their journey, differentiating between the three types of social capital is crucial as they impact the social entrepreneurial process in different ways. *Structural sc*—i.e., personal and impersonal networks—is lower due to lack of opportunity to build up these networks during school, university, vocational training and family and friend interactions. Not having the access to the same networks as locals will likely increase time and energy spent by the individual social entrepreneur and will make it harder to navigate existing institutions. Low levels of *cognitive sc* will impede their ability to engage in certain types of deviant behaviour. Constructive deviance often necessitates a grasp of existing narratives in order to circumvent or reshape them. Therefore, low levels of cognitive social capital can lead to ineffective deviant behaviour. It could also lead to a misinterpretation of immune responses as certain narrative models are not understood. While negative feedback loops as argued above would usually lead to changes in approaches, we argue that this feedback loop mechanism is somewhat distorted for international social entrepreneurs. Low *relational* sc is likely to increase time and energy spent on building trust and to decode expectations.

To illustrate, we use the example of Anna, a Dutch-American social entrepreneur operating in Amsterdam, who talks about her lack of social capital and the struggles she faces

> I've been trying to get to know the impact community here, because what I found is I was really starting from scratch and in [my hometown in the USA], having graduated from [the local university], I already had a pretty thick network within [my home town in the USA] with start-ups, and it was pretty easy to find work and jobs. Because once you're in a startup hub, for example, people get to know you and then your resume gets sent out and that's sort of it [. . .] I got involved with the impact hub hoping to get to know about more resources.

The frustration that Anna describes reflects her struggle with comparing a situation in which she had a good level of endowment of social capital and the situation she faced in Amsterdam as someone who had just moved there from the USA. When Anna initially arrived in the Netherlands, she spent a year "getting used to the Netherlands". She realised that she would not be able to just start a social venture but had to learn how the business system in the Netherlands worked. This clearly highlights how Anna tried to build up cognitive social capital. She started working in cafes and other places to further develop her understanding of the Netherlands and to start building relational social capital. Anna's example shows how much time it took her to accumulate a base—albeit still lower—level of social capital before she could progress further in her social entrepreneurial process. These activities needed to take place prior to the ideation stage.

Anna's case also highlights the granularity of cognitive social capital and the consequent (in)ability to engage effectively with feedback loops. Anna is Dutch by

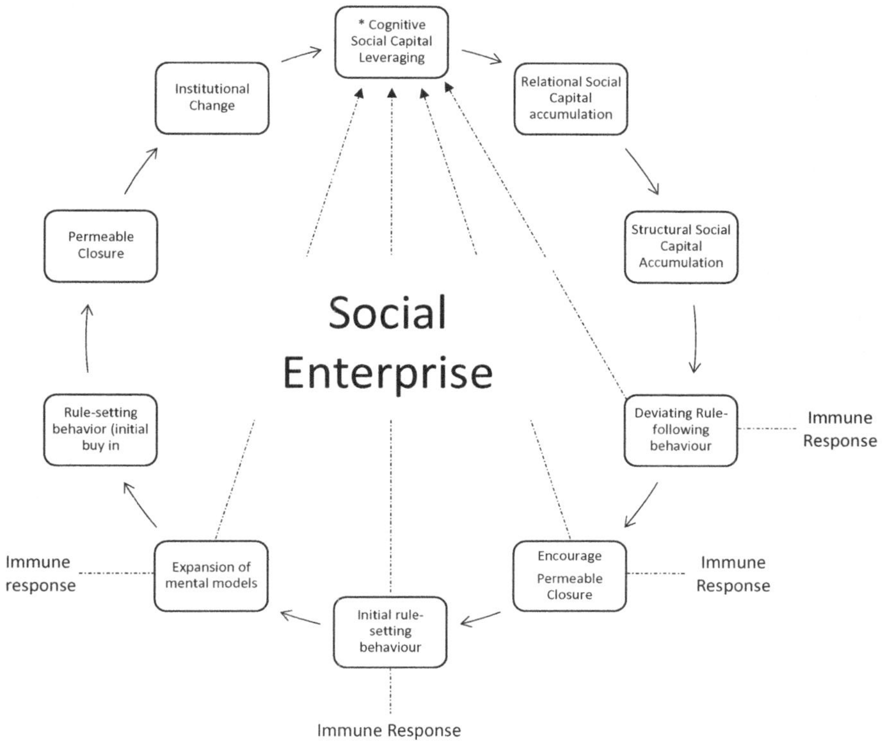

Fig. 3 Social enterprise cycle within the Social-Capital-Morphogenetic model

citizenship but was raised outside the Netherlands. As a consequence, while she speaks Dutch, she is not familiar with certain more colloquial expressions which sometimes lead to misunderstandings. Similarly, she is unfamiliar with certain nuances in day-to-day interactions. These seemingly little things will restrict her ability to leverage cognitive social capital as certain feedback loop nudges would not be recognised or be misinterpreted by her.

4.3 Organisational Level: The Social Enterprise

At the enterprise level, shown in Fig. 3, the first point of operationalisation builds off of the *leveraging of cognitive sc*. The business acumen developed encourages further development of relational sc as it increases trusts by others and allows the social entrepreneur to better understand obligations and expectations.

When the enterprise's values are identified, the social entrepreneur accumulates further structural sc as their values resonate with others (Nahapiet & Ghoshal, 1998).

As structural sc increases and facilitates meaningful social interaction, acquisition of non-material resources such as innovation and knowledge is enhanced (Anderson et al., 2007). If the accumulated structural sc is sufficiently in depth, *deviating rule-following behaviour* begins to emerge. That is, through engagement with their network (be that an accelerator, incubator, multipurpose space, or a digital space or industry networks) the enterprise adopts similar behaviour to that of other organisations within their network. Yet, while the enterprise mimics certain behaviour, it deviates from it to the extent that rule-following would detract from the social entrepreneur's values. For example, an enterprise may operate as an incubator—which are often apolitical and tend to focus on a business logic—but deviate in that they adopt politics because it may view political and economic narratives as too interconnected to only focus on one.

At this juncture, the enterprise faces an immune response. That is, potential stakeholders may be less inclined to engage with, what they may perceive as, a political incubator. A feedback loop emerges as a consequence of this immune response. In fact, Ullmann-Margalit (1977) notes that change to taken-for-granted rules requires the imposition of negative external effects for those who do not follow the rules. As a consequence, closure is a necessary condition for preventing negative deviance within an organisation and ensuring trustworthiness within the enterprise. This imposition often emerges as a by-product of adopted doctrine (e.g., employment contract). However, equally important are informal constraints on behaviour (e.g., adherence to the core social mission of the social venture). It is important to highlight that this organisational closure can stifle positive innovative deviancy (Coleman, 1988). The social enterprise, thus, needs to allow for *permeable closure*. That is, deviance that leverages and aligns with the relational sc that has been accumulated, but does not, on the surface, seem to align. For example, if an enterprise has embraced its political inclination (which itself is an act of deviance), we would expect that the political inclination throughout the enterprise would be similar or otherwise non-divisive, lest it lead to a form of infighting, which Archer (1995) identifies as barriers to organisation. Permeable closure allows for avoidance of the stifling implication of groupthink by promoting diverging politics to the extent that it informs the deep-rooted values of the enterprise.

As a consequence, the enterprise is confronted with an internal and external immune response. For example, if an enterprise and its actors embrace potentially unpopular views, it risks alienating its external supporters. Similarly, if actors within the enterprise have significantly divergent views, how then is the enterprise to impose reasonable negative effects without alienating a particular group of actors. The resulting balancing act represents another feedback loop. This allows for an initial stage of rule-setting behaviour by the entrepreneur. For example, to ameliorate internal alienation, a rule may be implemented stating that a deviant idea should be evaluated by articulating the benefit to the enterprise. Such a methodological articulation of these implications has the potential to promote win-win semantics. Subsequently, through the external behaviour of the enterprise, this methodological articulation can reach external stakeholders. Indeed, this promotes the expansion of mental models that morphogenesis holds elaborates the role of actors.

The inherent difficulty of promoting permeable closure is compounded by the perceived distance between the international social entrepreneur and their stakeholders—we can expect that this distance would pose a barrier to the legitimacy of their deviant rule-following behaviour and attempts towards permeable closure. To illustrate, we use the example of Laura, a German social entrepreneur operating in Amsterdam.

> I think what I find the most challenging is that I don't speak Dutch. And I think if you are leading an organization that is inherently political, because I think unlike many other spaces, we are political and we're not afraid to discuss politics in any shape or form. I feel like I sometimes lack the cultural and historical knowledge to really position [the business] correctly. So I would really like for more Dutch speaking people to be on the board.

Interestingly, Laura herself puts down her challenges to not speaking Dutch. While we concede that this is in fact a problem, we would suggest that it merely exacerbates the underlying challenge. We would argue that even if Laura were to speak Dutch or had more board members that are Dutch speaking, she would still face similar challenges. As Anna's case highlighted merely speaking the language is not sufficient. So rather than having more Dutch-speaking individuals within the enterprise, Laura would probably be better advised in having more people born and raised in the Netherlands on her board that could help the organisation navigate given structures and mental models.

Laura's social enterprise openly engages in political discussions that address the root of the social enterprise's social mission. Due to this political nature, it is important for the organisation to permeably close. They intend to do so by engaging people from various backgrounds to acquire relevant expertise. However, for her social enterprise this is proving challenging as she herself reflects that many members are from a privileged background. We conjecture that diversifying her organisation will be made even more difficult due to her status as an international social entrepreneur. She is surrounded by other foreigners and therefore less likely to have access to people with other socioeconomic backgrounds. Moreover, her approach to ensure permeable closure is based on her grasp of cognitive social capital, which in turn is based more strongly on a German than a Dutch context.

As actors' roles begin to elaborate and deficiencies of the status quo and potential remedies are increasingly articulated, we would expect to see an *initial buy-in to the rule-setting behaviour* of the social enterprise. In Laura's case, if methodical self-reflection and deconstruction of one's own position in society is repeatedly undertaken, it can be expected that such behaviour would be adopted in facets of actors' lives that extend beyond the boundaries of the enterprise. The increased adoption of the win-win articulation and innovative deviance enables the solidification of *permeable closure*. Indeed, closure is necessary to monitor and guide behaviour and facilitate external articulation that extends the enterprise's reach and influence and promoting institutional change.

4.4 System Level: Society at Large

As discussed previously the achievement of social innovation as objective requires institutional creation, novel social relations between disparate groups, and empowerment of marginalised groups beyond sectoral boundaries. Figure 4 illustrates how the impacts of social and human capital synthesise at the systems level.

Diffusion of institutional change sits at the top of the system cycle and is promoted by the enterprise through its external behaviour in two ways: the social enterprise's organisational remit and the diffusion of new rule behaviour by the enterprise's actors within their respective collectivities. Indeed, morphogenesis of agency holds that members of collectivities maintain the ability to elaborate the capabilities of other actors within their collectivity. We can therefore expect *new rule acceptance* to emerge from this dual promulgation—from the enterprise and its actors.

Thus, new rule acceptance invokes an immune response that emerges from the interaction between entrenched interests and developing rules. In fact, large-scale social change can emerge more seamlessly if it is accepted by entrenched interest groups (cf. North, 1995). This feedback loop allows the enterprise to identify the narratives required to create acceptance for their suggested system change. *Mitigated Immune Response* emerges when the entrenched interests are placated, at which

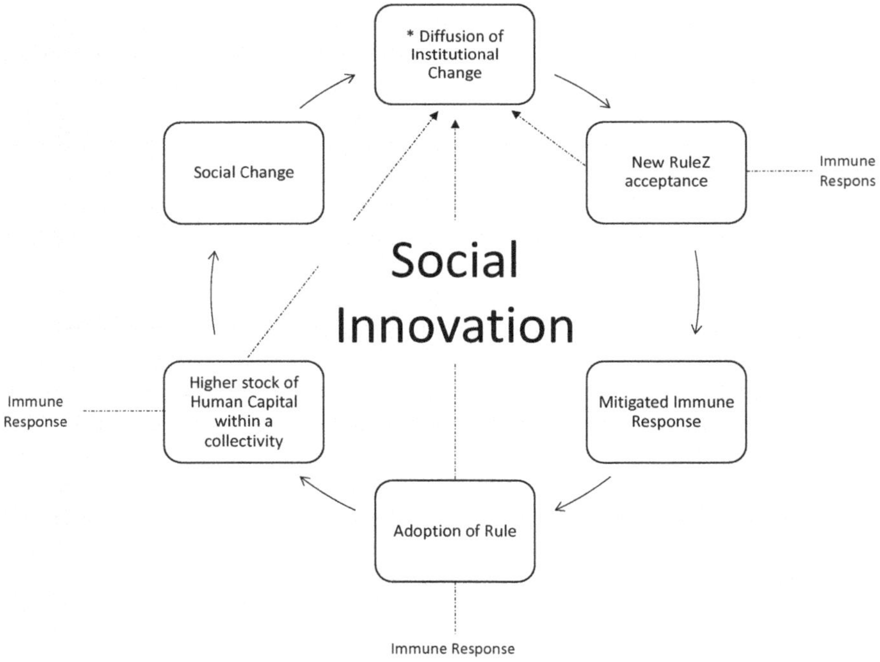

Fig. 4 Social innovation cycle within the Social-Capital-Morphogenetic model

point *adoption of rule* begins. The features of system change necessitate a shift in the perception of those who act upon these perceptions. Thus, adoption of a new rule begins small and slow and is a consequence of the new rule's interaction with the existing institutional frame that comprises an individual's context (cf. North, 1993).

This process will arguably be more challenging for international social entrepreneurs. They might find it more difficult to initiate rule changes that fit within the local context and would therefore enable others to start following it. Here, arguments are similar to those already expressed at the individual and organisational level and are linked to all three types of social capital.

At the same time, being situated more on the outside of a given system might enable an international social entrepreneur to better recognise voids in the institutional framework that can be exploited to create social change. Thus, the lack of local social capital can be advantageous under certain conditions. To illustrate, we use the example of Walter, an Irish social entrepreneur operating in Amsterdam.

Walter experiences significant challenges in creating change at the system level due to his lack of social embeddedness:

> It's very hard for us to survive here. There's actually not a culture here for buying food ingredients and cooking it, and that was something I never thought about before. I never prepared for. And so it's actually quite difficult to convince people here as to why we're doing what we're doing.

Walter expresses his frustration about the challenges in creating "mental shifts" as his organisation's approach requires completely different behaviours by customers to what they are used to. As such, Walter and his social enterprise need to translate their mission and its relevance to the system (that is the Netherlands) in a way that is easily understood in given narratives. However, as a foreigner himself, this is less feasible due to a lack of relevant cognitive social capital.

Walter responded to this negative feedback loop by moving to accumulate relational and structural social capital concurrently, by collaborating with local artisanal producers that share his values. In doing so, he builds his network while also building the trust of that network. By working with local Dutch partners, Walter aims to overcome his low endowment of social capital by tapping into the social capital of others. While it might be harder for him to build up relational social capital and in particular trust, he can use the relational social capital that local producers and partners already possess. Analogously, by combing forces with locals who share his vision, he can acquire cognitive social capital for himself while at the same time utilising that of others.

Relational sc accumulation emerges, not just for Walter and his business, but also for the wider community.

> A lot of customers started to feel very sorry for us. They'd be looking at me and they'd be saying, 'this guy works really hard and he's doing something that we all believe in.' So I would be providing kind of service to these people to help them change their lives. And so they very much appreciate what we're doing. And over the course of the last six months, we've had an army of volunteers coming in and say to us, how can we help you guys? What can we do? They see that we're actually serving the community and doing something that satisfies a need in them.

In Walter's case, as adoption of the new rule gains traction, human capital accumulates in previously uninvolved collectivities as more members of the community engage. Indeed, human capital is created by the changes within actors that increase their ability to act in new ways (Coleman, 1988). As the stock of human capital increases, so do the roles actors take on and their ability to mobilise additional actors within their collectivity. A feedback loop emerges at this juncture from an immune response arising in the way human capital is synthesised and promulgated. Taking Walter's case as example, in the instance that the win-win environment potential of his venture idea is not accurately distilled among a new collectivity, it may serve to alienate the collectivity in question. In such an instance, the resultant feedback loop allows the enterprise and its actors to reimagine and articulate their message more accessibly.

At such a time that the social enterprise's remit becomes accessible (i.e., Walter's vision and rule-setting are disseminated), we can expect *incremental progressive system change* to result from an increased shift in mental models and the beginning of a new cycle, leading to further diffusion of system change. This system-level diffusion and adoption is what makes the social enterprise (and by extension the social entrepreneur) a corporate agent. A social enterprise remains in the primary agent category if their remit and message is not adequately diffused through and adopted by the system. Morphogenesis holds that primary or corporate agent status is perpetually fluctuating as a consequence of the dynamic nature of complex systems. Figure 5 illustrates the interactions between the social entrepreneur, enterprise and innovation cycles.

5 Discussion

In an entrepreneurial context, knowledge and subsequent agency emerges from a mixture of lived experience, network interactions and learning from others (Aldrich & Kim, 2007). Traditional economic theories, such as Rational Choice theory (e.g., Smith, 1776), presuppose that decision makers have full knowledge, yet recent literature (see Pellegrini et al., 2020) points to an invisible interworking of tangible and intangible dimensions which contribute a sense of belonging and may foster collaborative relational configurations. The authors demonstrate the complexity of these interworkings by illustrating the variability of development trajectories despite similar contextual conditions. We may conjecture that higher levels of uncertainty facing international social entrepreneurs compounds this complexity and highlights the reality of partial knowledge and the role social capital plays in accumulating knowledge and informing the social entrepreneurial process.

Lejarraga and Pindard-Lejarraga (2020) note that boundedly rational agents tend to be more effective in environments with high uncertainty and few learning opportunities. Thus, our Social-Capital-Morphogenetic model of social entrepreneurship demonstrates how social capital accumulation may enable international social entrepreneurs to tap into existing relational configurations in pursuit of

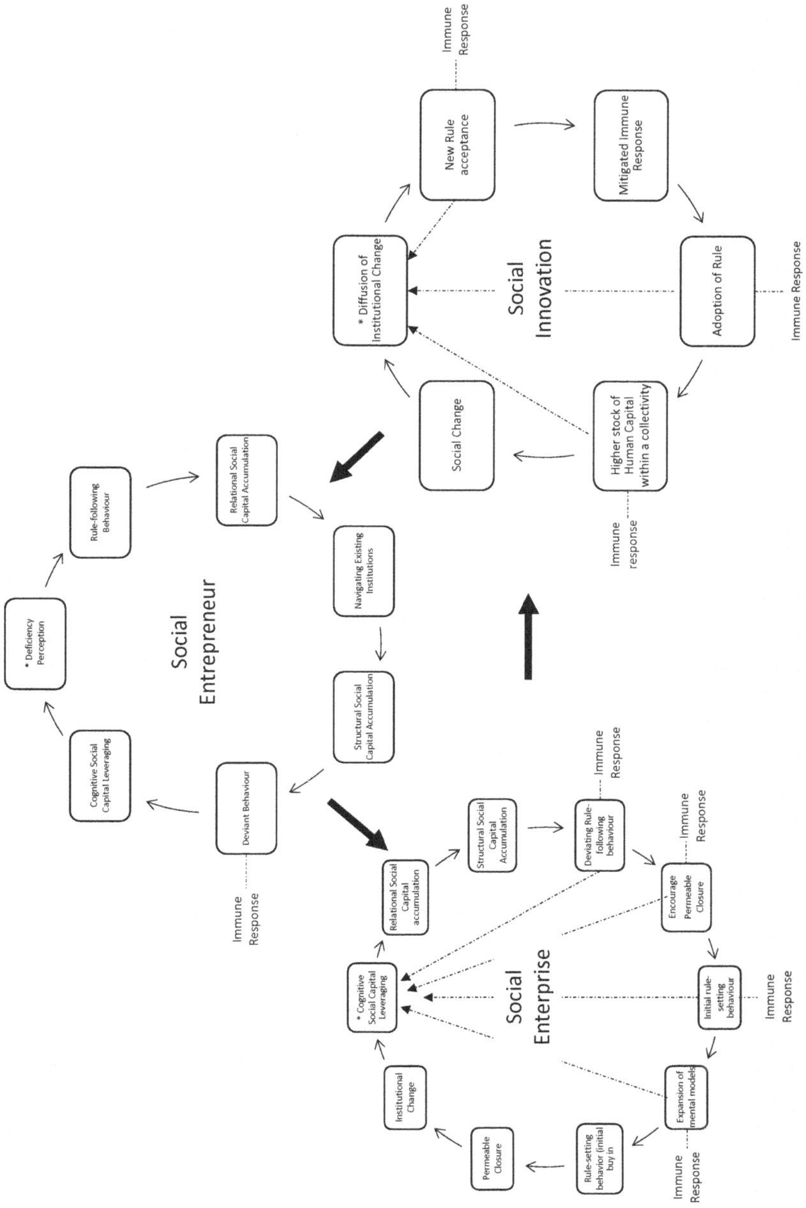

Fig. 5 Completed framework of the Social-Capital-Morphogenetic model

objectives such as increased legitimacy or access to resources. Similarly, our model illustrates the extent to which relational and cognitive social capital promote learning from network interactions and enhance the quality of network relations to engage in rule-setting behaviour and systems level change.

5.1 Social Capital and Effectual and Causal Logics

Our conceptualisation and illustrative cases suggest that an underlying objective (or effect) of social capital accumulation is to offset the inherent uncertainty of being an international social entrepreneur. Indeed, we insinuate that social entrepreneurs and international social entrepreneurs in particular adopt a partial patchwork quilt approach (Sarasvathy, 2009). That is, on the one hand, their actions reflect effectual logics, whereby they rearrange traditional relationships between individuals and their environment to create new opportunities for change. On the other hand, they adopt causal logics to the extent that their stock of social capital provides a level of predictability and reduced uncertainty surrounding their decision-making process.

5.1.1 Social Capital and Effectual Logics

Effectual logics refers to an internal framework with which entrepreneurs conceptualise problems and formulate solutions or opportunities for change. Effectual reasoning draws novel connections between ideas, means and action, thereby endogenously creating opportunities for social change. The effectuation process involves operating with a given set of means and selecting possible effects from these means (Sarasvathy, 2001). To put it simply, effectuation is like making dinner based on what is available in the fridge.

In the context of social entrepreneurship, effectuation emerges as part of creating value that goes beyond economic value. That is, economic value is of concern to the social entrepreneur principally because economic value is a translation which fits seamlessly with the existing system. Thus, ideas and the ability to articulate these ideas is part of the social entrepreneur's given set of means. Similarly, the reality of the social entrepreneur's collectivities and subsequent stock of (social) capital comprises these given means to the extent that they shape the social entrepreneur's ideas, ability and method of articulation.

We have discussed that social capital has a unique characteristic of accessibility. Indeed, the gregariousness of human beings encourages agential interactions, with each interaction having the potential to enable access to utilisable resources, a new collectivity or an expansion of agency. Effectuation logics hold that the opportunity presented by each interaction is the direct result of what the social entrepreneur makes of it, while the opportunity potential is a direct result of the similarities between those involved (cf. Sarasvathy et al., 2003). For international social entrepreneurs, the initial othering of them diminishes their opportunity potential. Indeed,

Anna, Laura and Walter demonstrate decisions to accumulate social capital for ameliorating this othering.

5.1.2 Social Capital and Causal Logics

In contrast to effectual logics, causal logics adopt a point of departure whereby one views a predictable and subsequently controllable future (Sarasvathy, 2001). That is, a causal process involves operating with a desired effect and choosing means to achieve it. Going back to our cooking example, causation is picking a certain dish to cook and then going to the shops to get ingredients. Additionally, causation involves developing new means to meet these selected ends. Traditional economic theories suggest that decisions involve a given goal, knowability of the results of a decision, and knowability of means emerging from the results of previous decisions. The extreme uncertainty of engaging in international social entrepreneurship presents a significant barrier to the causal process. Similarly, while international social entrepreneurs would be able to identify an end they wish to achieve, they might struggle to identify the most effective means due to the challenges linked to low social capital endowment as outlined in our Social-Capital-Morphogenic model of social entrepreneurship.

Despite the perception of a wider deficiency, we see that the contextual conditions of the new institutional framework within which our international social entrepreneurs find themselves requires a re-examination of the deficiency in question. Indeed, knowledge of the environment is antecedent to predictability. The mission of the international social entrepreneur necessitates a holistic understanding of the system and thus understanding may become an objective. Cognitive social capital allows for this holistic understanding by elucidating the meanings of language in a given context—it highlights how the social entrepreneur can articulate the deficiencies they perceive in relation to the insufficiency of the current solutions. Relational social capital promotes this understanding by creating a conduit of legitimacy between the social entrepreneur and their stakeholders. That is, there is cohesion between the social entrepreneur's rhetoric and action. Structural social capital represents the extent to which the social innovation diffuses through the system. That is, structural social capital enables predictability through widespread involvement and subsequent understanding of the behaviour in the new environment.

5.2 Feedback Loops and Rule Setting Behaviour

Feedback loops emerge at multiple stages within the social entrepreneurial process in response to the behaviour of the social entrepreneur and the enterprise. Each cycle is initiated through an effectual process. That is, entrepreneurs make decisions based on available means with an eye towards acceptable risk rather than know ability of the future. Central to the effectual logics is the emphasis on achieving the goal rather than avoiding failure.

The initial othering of international social entrepreneurs leads them to engage in the accumulation of different types of social capital, particularly relational and cognitive social capital. Investment in social capital sits well within the threshold of risk acceptability as a consequence of social capital's accessibility relative to the learning potential of deep agential interaction. That is, the time investment in interaction is worth the mapping of the institutional environment that these interactions provide. As a consequence of these interactions, the means and tools of the international social entrepreneur expand.

The implications for deviance and rule-setting behaviour are that the feedback loop cycle introduces a portfolio of disconnection between the social entrepreneur and the system that the international social entrepreneur is able to learn from. This portfolio enables relative predictability because it encompasses lived experiences and accumulated knowledge which a (partial) causation process is adept at leveraging. That is, as the international social entrepreneur continues this stumble-and-learn cycle, we would expect a level of pattern recognition which serves to better exploit contingencies as they arise. This is not to be confused with predicting; however, it enables the international social entrepreneur to distinguish between natural phenomena and human agential phenomena.

The distinction between what is made by nature and what is human-made within a system is critical to invoke system change. In order for international social entrepreneurs to fulfil their overarching aim of social change, they need to first be able to articulate and organise towards deficiencies within the dominant structure. If this is achieved, international social entrepreneurship can then represent an effective translation of deficiencies into narratives around which organisation is possible. In order to engage in rule-setting behaviour, the international social entrepreneur needs to engender an environment of trust in their actions and reciprocity amongst the communities they endeavour to create. For the international social entrepreneur, social capital provides the resources to do this.

6 Concluding Remarks

We set out to introduce a framework for examining the social entrepreneurial process of social entrepreneurs and apply it to individuals who were not born in the country they start their ventures in. We find that the initial paucity of social capital has significant implications for how international social entrepreneurship is undertaken. By infusing social capital and morphogenetic theories with the social innovation model of social entrepreneurship, our framework highlights how the social entrepreneurial process is affected as each type of social capital is accumulated. In a new environment, the given means of international social entrepreneurs to pursue their general vision are ideas and articulation. The accessibility of social capital complements these means and is crucial to their social entrepreneurial mission.

Our model (Fig. 5) suggests that the role of social capital in the international process is ordered between the three dimensions. That is, the relational and cognitive social capital seem to be primary in that they present a conduit of access for mapping the new environment, which enables the social entrepreneur to engage in quality bridge building. Structural social capital emerges in two ways: (i) surface structural social capital, which refers to the introductory stage (this can occur by simply joining a meet-up group and involves 'knowing' who is in the network) and can precede relational and cognitive social capital, (ii) deep structural social capital, which refers to the diffusion throughout a network as a direct consequence of the quality of interaction (this requires trust and similar ideational resources and leads to knowledge about the system) and cannot precede the relational and cognitive dimensions.

Insofar as international social entrepreneurs adopt a patchwork quilt approach, effectual logics push international social entrepreneurs towards accumulating relational and cognitive social capital to create opportunity for social change. Relational and cognitive social capital enables ideational navigation of the international social entrepreneur's new landscape, while structural social capital enables a physical navigation of the new landscape. That is, relational and cognitive social capital offer endogenous resources for the international social entrepreneur, while structural social capital is an exogenous resource—both of which are necessary for rule-setting behaviour and altering the system.

As a consequence, our model has implications for teaching, policy-making and future research. It calls for greater emphasis on complexity and the systems level in social entrepreneurship education. Particularly, we suggest an emphasis on teaching an ambivalence perspective of social entrepreneurship (see Zeyen & Beckmann, 2018) to equip students with the necessary knowledge and skills to recognise the contextual complexities of social change. The ambivalence view on social entrepreneurship postulates that most means used and ends addressed in the social entrepreneurial process are ambivalent, i.e., can be both 'good' and 'bad'. In the context of international social entrepreneurship, this view can help students understand the ambivalent nature of social capital endowment (or lack thereof) as well as lead to fruitful discussions about the potency (or lack thereof) of international social entrepreneurship in comparison with domestic social entrepreneurship. Our model further allows students to analyse in more depth the activities of social entrepreneurs within a given system and to thus evaluate their ability to create system change.

From a policy-making perspective, our framework suggests that interventions should focus on agent-based models (See Paarlberg & Bielefeld, 2009) and enhance communication between social entrepreneurs and their stakeholders.[7] Such interventions could manifest through liminal municipal partnerships with a social venture. For example, offering short-term use of public spaces for an empowerment

[7] We refer here to a Luhmann theory of communication which sees communication as the interpretation of and distinction between information and the method by which the information is conveyed, whereby meaning of the communication is determined by the receiver (see Leyesdorff 1996 for a brief overview of Luhmann's theory of communication).

workshop or social venture expo may serve to kick-start the process of social capital accumulation and familiarisation with the environment. Existing literature (e.g., Pellegrini et al., 2019) demonstrates the value of multiple interactions for disseminating and recombining knowledge. Indeed, there are significant second order impacts of knowledge sharing when networks are expansive, which encourages a morphogenetic elaboration of knowledge within and between actors. As we have shown, this could be particularly beneficial for international social entrepreneurs. Further, interventions which bring local and international change makers together hold the potential of developing endogenous and exogenous resources for the actors involved.

Our Social-Capital-Morphogenetic model centres around the synthesis of morphogenetic theory, social capital theory and a social innovation model conceptualisation of social entrepreneurship. Throughout our conceptualisation, we used illustrative cases that are based on somewhat homogeneous cases of international social entrepreneurs in the Netherlands. Future research should empirically validate the relations within our model. Particularly, further research would benefit from building on our conceptualisation to incorporate how domestic social entrepreneurs accumulate social capital to provide a within data comparison. Such comparison may serve to further highlight the impact of each dimension of social capital in the social entrepreneurial process. Moreover, future research could generate further insights into the relationship between different types of social capital (endowment) within both domestic and international social entrepreneurship. Similarly, quantitative analysis could be introduced which endeavours to better understand and potentially quantify what we have called 'immune response' as a function of a place's propensity of (social) entrepreneurship (see the Global Entrepreneurship Index[8]).

In conclusion, our model provides insights on the (international) social entrepreneurial process in at least three ways: firstly, our model serves to introduce social innovation as both a means and objective within a multi-tiered process. In so doing, we delineate the morphogenetic implications of social entrepreneurial behaviour. Indeed, by incorporating morphogenetic theory we illustrate how social entrepreneurship develops and is developed by interactions between and among various actors. Secondly, our framework demonstrates the role of feedback loops and their relation with causal and effectual logics. Thirdly, we draw attention to the role of endogenous (e.g., initial stock of social capital) and exogenous (e.g., accumulated portfolio of local knowledge) contextual factors on the social entrepreneurial process.

---

[8] https://thegedi.org/global-entrepreneurship-and-development-index/

References

Adler, P. S., & Kwon, S. W. (2002). Social capital: Prospects for a new concept. *Academy of Management Review, 27*(1), 17–40.

Albert, L. S., Dean, T. J., & Baron, R. A. (2016). From social value to social cognition: How social ventures obtain the resources they need for social transformation. *Journal of Social Entrepreneurship, 7*(3), 289–311. https://doi.org/10.1080/19420676.2016.1188323

Aldrich, H. E., & Kim, P. H. (2007). Small worlds, infinite possibilities? How social networks affect entrepreneurial team formation and search. *Strategic Entrepreneurship Journal, 1*(1–2), 147–165.

Anderson, A., Park, J., & Jack, S. (2007). Entrepreneurial social capital: Conceptualizing social capital in new high- tech firms. *International Small Business Journal, 25*(3), 245–272. https://doi.org/10.1177/0266242607076526

Archer, M. S. (1995). *Realist social theory: The morphogenetic approach*. Cambridge university press.

Archer, M. S. (2010). Morphogenesis versus structuration: On combining structure and action. *British Journal of Sociology, 61*, 225–252.

Becker, G. S. (1962). Investment in human capital: A theoretical analysis' some activities primarily affect. *Journal of Political Economy, 70*, 9–49. https://doi.org/10.1086/258724

Beckmann, M. (2011). The social case as a business case: Making sense of social entrepreneurship from an ordonomic perspective. In *Corporate citizenship and new governance* (pp. 91–115). Springer.

Beschorner, T., & Kolmar, M. (2016). Locating ordonomics. *zfwu Zeitschrift für Wirtschafts-und Unternehmensethik, 17*(3), 446–458.

Bourdieu, P. (1979). Les trois états du capital culturel. *Actes de La Recherche En Sciences Sociales, 30*, 3–6. https://doi.org/10.3406/arss.1979.2654

Buckley, W. (1967). *Sociology and modern systems theory*. Englewood Cliffs.

Coleman, J. S. (1988). Social capital in the creation of human capital. *American Journal of Sociology, 94*, S95–S120.

Dacin, M. T., Dacin, P. A., & Tracey, P. (2011). Social entrepreneurship: A critique and future directions. *Organization Science, 22*(5), 1203–1213. https://doi.org/10.1287/orsc.1100.0620

Dacin, P. A., Dacin, M. T., & Matear, M. (2010). Social entrepreneurship: Why we don't need a new theory and how we move forward from here. *Academy of Management Perspectives, 24*(3), 37–58.

Dahl, M. S., & Sorenson, O. (2012). Home sweet home: Entrepreneurs' location choices and the performance of their ventures. *Management Science, 58*(6), 1059–1071. https://doi.org/10.1287/mnsc.1110.1476

Dees, J. G. (1998). *The meaning of "social entrepreneurship"*. CASE.

Ebrahim, A., Battilana, J., & Mair, J. (2014). The governance of social enterprises: Mission drift and accountability challenges in hybrid organizations. *Research in Organizational Behavior, 34*, 81–100. https://doi.org/10.1016/j.riob.2014.09.001

Haugh, H. M., & Talwar, A. (2016). Linking social entrepreneurship and social change: The mediating role of empowerment. *Journal of Business Ethics, 133*(4), 643–658. https://doi.org/10.1007/s10551-014-2449-4

Hietschold, N., Voegtlin, C., Scherer, A.G. & Gehman, J. (2019). What we know and don't know about social innovation: A multi-level review and research agenda. In Academy of management proceedings (2019, 1, p. 12332). Academy of Management.

Jacobs, J. (1961). The uses of city neighborhoods. In *The death and life of great American cities* (pp. 112–140). Random House.

Knowles, D., Mughan, T., & Lloyd-Reason, L. (2006). Foreign language use among decision-makers of successfully internationalised SMEs: Questioning the language-training paradigm. *Journal of Small Business and Enterprise Development, 13*(4), 620–641.

Latour, B. (2005). *Reassembling the social. An introduction to actor-network-theory*. Oxford University Press.
Lee, R. (2009). Social capital and business and management: Setting a research agenda. *International Journal of Management Reviews, 11*(3), 247–273.
Lee, R., Tuselmann, H., Jayawarna, D., & Rouse, J. (2019). Effects of structural, relational and cognitive social capital on resource acquisition: A study of entrepreneurs residing in multiply deprived areas. *Entrepreneurship & Regional Development, 31*(5–6), 534–554.
Lejarraga, J., & Pindard-Lejarraga, M. (2020). Bounded rationality: Cognitive limitations or adaptation to the environment? The implications of ecological rationality for management learning. *Academy of Management Learning & Education, 19*, 289–306.
Leydesdorff, L. (1996). Luhmann's sociological theory: Its operationalization and future perspectives. *Social Science Information, 35*(2), 283–306.
Light, I. (2004). Social capital's unique accessibility. *Journal of the American Planning Association, 70*(2), 145–151.
Light, I., & Dana, L. P. (2013). Boundaries of social capital in entrepreneurship. *Entrepreneurship: Theory and Practice, 34*, 1003–1019. https://doi.org/10.1111/etap.12016
Lin, N. (1999). Social networks and status attainment. *Annual Review of Sociology, 25*(1), 467–487.
London School of Economics. (2017). *A world of three zeroes: The new economics of zero poverty, zero unemployment, and zero carbon emissions*. Retrieved September 5, 2018, from https://www.lse.ac.uk/Events/2017/11/20171110t1830vOT/A-World-of-Three-Zeroes
Marx, K. (1867). *1976. Capital: A critique of political economy*. Verlag von Otto Meisner.
Melachroinos, K. A., & Spence, N. (2013). The territorial impact of the knowledge economy: Intangibles and regional inequality in Great Britain. *European Planning Studies, 21*(10), 1491–1508.
Merton, R. K. (1968). *Social theory and social structure*. Simon and Schuster.
Moulaert, F., & MacCallum, D. (2019). *Advanced introduction to social innovation*. Edward Elgar Publishing.
Moulaert, F., MacCallum, D., & Hillier, J. (2013). Social innovation: Intuition, precept, concept. In *The international handbook on social innovation: Collective action, social learning and transdisciplinary research* (pp. 13–24). Edward Elgar Publishing.
Mulgan, G. (2007). *Social innovation what it is, why it matters and how it can be accelerated* (Vol. 22). Skoll Centre For Social Entrepreneurship. https://doi.org/10.1515/zna-1967-1247
Mulgan, G. (2012). The theoretical foundations of social innovation. In *Social innovation* (pp. 33–65). Palgrave Macmillan.
Nahapiet, J., & Ghoshal, S. (1998). Social capital, intellectual capital, and the organizational advantage. *Academy of Management Review, 23*, 242–266. https://doi.org/10.5465/amr.1998.533225
Nicholls, A. (2010). The legitimacy of social entrepreneurship: Reflexive isomorphism in a pre–paradigmatic field. *Entrepreneurship Theory and Practice, 34*(4), 611–633.
North, D. C. (1993). Institutions and credible commitment. *Journal of Institutional and Theoretical Economics (JITE)/Zeitschrift für die gesamte Staatswissenschaft, 149*, 11–23. https://doi.org/10.1017/cbo9780511808678
North, D. C. (1995). Five propositions about institutional change. In *Explaining social institutions* (pp. 15–26). University of Michigan Press.
Paarlberg, L. E., & Bielefeld, W. (2009). Complexity science—an alternative framework for understanding strategic management in public serving organizations. *International Public Management Journal, 12*(2), 236–260.
Pellegrini, M. M., Caputo, A., Ciappei, C., & Dana, L. P. (2020). Evolving differently from the same set of pre-conditions: A qualitative longitudinal study of entrepreneurship and genius loci. In *The entrepreneurial behaviour: Unveiling the cognitive and emotional aspect of entrepreneurship*. Emerald Publishing Limited.

Pellegrini, M. M., Caputo, A., & Matthews, L. (2019). Knowledge transfer within relationship portfolios: The creation of knowledge recombination rents. *Business Process Management Journal, 25*(1), 202–218. https://doi.org/10.1108/BPMJ-06-2017-0171

Praszkier, R., Nowak, A., & Zablocka-Bursa, A. (2009). Social capital built by social entrepreneurs and the specific personality traits that facilitate the process. *Social Psychology [Psychologia Spoleczna], 4*(10–12), 42–54.

Putnam, R., Light, I., de Souza Briggs, X., Rohe, W. M., Vidal, A. C., Hutchinson, J., Gress, J., & Woolcock, M. (2004). Using social capital to help integrate planning theory, research, and practice: Preface. *Journal of the American Planning Association, 70*(2), 142–192.

Ricardo, D. (1817). *On the principles of political economy and taxation*. John Murray.

Sarasvathy, S. D. (2001). Causation and effectuation: Toward a theoretical shift from economic inevitability to entrepreneurial contingency. *Academy of Management Review, 26*(2), 243–263.

Sarasvathy, S. D. (2009). *Effectuation: Elements of entrepreneurial expertise*. Edward Elgar Publishing.

Sarasvathy, S. D., Dew, N., Velamuri, S. R., & Venkataraman, S. (2003). Three views of entrepreneurial opportunity. In *Handbook of entrepreneurship research* (pp. 141–160). Springer.

Saridakis, G., Idris, B., Hansen, J. M., & Dana, L. P. (2019). SMEs' internationalisation: When does innovation matter? *Journal of Business Research, 96*, 250–263.

Schaltegger, S., Hansen, E. G., & Lüdeke-Freund, F. (2016). *Business models for sustainability: Origins, present research, and future avenues*. SAGE.

Short, J. C., Moss, T. W., & Lumpkin, G. T. (2009). Research in social entrepreneurship: Past contributions and future opportunities. *Strategic Entrepreneurship Journal, 3*(2), 161–194. https://doi.org/10.1002/sej.69

Smith, A. (1776). *An inquiry into the nature and causes of the wealth of nations: Volume one*. W. Strahan and T. Cadell.

Snitker, T. V. (2010). The impact of culture on user research. In *Handbook of global user research* (pp. 257–277). Morgan Kaufmann.

Sowell, T. (1985). *Marxism: Philosophy and economics*. Allen & Unwin. Print.

Ullmann-Margalit, E. (1977). *The emergence of norms*. Clarendon.

Waldstrøm, C., & Svendsen, G. L. H. (2008). On the capitalization and cultivation of social capital: Towards a neo-capital general science? *The Journal of Socio-Economics, 37*(4), 1495–1514.

Wekker, G. (2016). *White innocence*. Duke University Press. https://doi.org/10.1215/9780822374565

Yunus, M., Moingeon, B., & Lehmann-Ortega, L. (2010). Building social business models: Lessons from the Grameen experience. *Long Range Planning, 43*(2–3), 308–325.

Zeyen, A., & Beckmann, M. (2018). *Social entrepreneurship and business ethics: Understanding the contribution and normative ambivalence of purpose-driven venturing*. Routledge.

Zeyen, A., & Beckmann, M. (2019). Narratives, hagiographies, and future perspectives. In *Social entrepreneurship and business ethics: Understanding the contribution and normative ambivalence of purpose-driven venturing* (pp. 240–249). Routledge.

Zeyen, A., Beckmann, M., & Akhavan, R. (2014). Social entrepreneurship business models: Managing innovation for social and economic value creation. In *Managementperspektiven für die Zivilgesellschaft des 21. Jahrhunderts* (pp. 107–132). Springer Gabler.

Zheng, W. (2010). A social capital perspective of innovation from individuals to nations: Where is empirical literature directing us? *International Journal of Management Reviews, 12*(2), 151–183.

Emilio Costales is a PhD researcher at the School of Business and Management at Royal Holloway University of London and a member of the Centre for Research into Sustainability and Digital Organisation and Society Research Centres. Emilio's research is focused on the role of Social Entrepreneurs in the development of Human-Centric Smart Cities.

Dr. Anica Zeyen is a Senior Lecturer in Entrepreneurship and Sustainability at the School of Business and Management at Royal Holloway University of London and a Research Associate at the Department of Psychology at the University of Johannesburg. She received her PhD on social entrepreneurship from Leuphana University Lueneburg. Anica's research links disability-related topics with (social) entrepreneurship and inclusive organising. Anica volunteers as a disability advocate.

Determinants of the Internationalisation Process of Colombian Firms

Vanessa Pertuz, Luis Francisco Miranda, Arturo Charris-Fontanilla, and Javier Viloria Escobar

Abstract Internationalisation is recognised as a fundamental strategy for the sustainability of firms in an increasingly globalised environment. However, this is a complex process that requires to develop internal capabilities. Despite its importance, evidence of internationalisation processes in emerging countries is scarce. In that sense, the objective of this study is to analyse the determinants of the internationalisation process in Colombia. For the purposes of this study, the sample is made up of Colombians who responded to the 2015 GEM Adult Population Survey (APS). Our results indicate that the decision to internationalise is associated with ease of doing business, reference models and public media about successful new businesses.

Keywords Internationalisation · GEM · Colombian firms · Innovation

1 Introduction

Both economic integration and globalisation promote the internationalisation of firms (Olmos, 2011; Pawęta & Zbierowski, 2015; Song & Lee, 2020). In addition, the rapid development of technology has made internationalisation strategies more accessible to companies (Dabić et al., 2020). In this context, internationalisation is

V. Pertuz
Universidad Nacional Abierta y a Distancia, Escuela de Ciencias Básicas, Tecnología e Ingeniería, Grupo de Investigación Gestindustriales EOCA, Atlántico, Colombia
e-mail: vanessa.pertuz@unad.edu.co

L. F. Miranda (✉)
Innovscience Research Group—IVS, Santa Marta, Colombia
e-mail: lmiranda@innovscience.co

A. Charris-Fontanilla · J. V. Escobar
Instituto Nacional de Formación Técnica Profesional Humberto Velásquez García, Ciénaga, Colombia

A. Caputo et al. (eds.), *The International Dimension of Entrepreneurial Decision-Making*, Contributions to Management Science,
https://doi.org/10.1007/978-3-030-85950-3_12

set up as a business growth strategy (Ciravegna et al., 2018; Denicolai et al., 2021; Pinho et al., 2018; Rahman et al., 2020) and an indispensable condition for business survival (Olmos, 2011). Indeed, many countries promote business internationalisation processes of the firms (Pinho et al., 2018).

Internalisation is conceived as a gradual process that generates dynamics of change into the organisations (Pawęta & Zbierowski, 2015). This process also involves a number of difficulties (Li, 2019), complex interactions (Ciravegna et al., 2018), uncertainty, and risks associated with validating a value proposition in international markets (Orero-Blat et al., 2020) characterised by a high heterogeneity and complexity (Hilmersson & Johanson, 2020).

Academic interest in the internationalisation process of firms began in the late 1960s (Brandão et al., 2019; Pawęta & Zbierowski, 2015). As a result of the global financial crisis of 2008 and 2009, researchers are interested in analysing internationalisation processes in emerging economies (Chen et al., 2016). However, empirical evidence of internationalisation processes in Latin America is scarce (Chen et al., 2016), despite the fact that firms in Latin American countries began to internationalise as of the 1970s (Chen et al., 2016).

Each firm's internationalisation decision is driven by an underlying reason, dependent on the company's context (Ahsan et al., 2020). Furthermore, the international expansion of a firm is affected by the internationalisation strategies of other companies in the same sector (Song & Lee, 2020). Indeed, the degree, diversification and speed of internationalisation stem from motivations from the organisation's environment (Song & Lee, 2020). Thus, companies increase the speed of internationalisation if they perceive competitors to speed up the process (Song & Lee, 2020). Additionally, foreign competition has a positive effect on the rate of internationalisation of companies (Chen et al., 2020).

In this sense, increasing competition and the lack of opportunities in national markets make companies identify market opportunities abroad (Pinho et al., 2018). Similarly, severe competition, market saturation and market regulations drive companies to look for opportunities to internationalise (Song & Lee, 2020). In addition, internationalisation is conceived as a strategy to differentiate itself from competitors (Hsieh et al., 2019) or to prevent competitors from gaining a dominant position in the market (Ciravegna et al., 2018).

Literature also recognises innovation as an element generating competitive advantages (Arredondo Trapero et al., 2016; Kato-Vidal, 2019; Pamplona & Penha, 2019; Pino Soto, 2018; Pulgarin-Molina et al., 2017). Innovation, understood as a process involving a broad set of factors with complex interrelationships (Speldekamp et al., 2020), has become a need for organisations to react to changes in the current globalised environment (Lii & Kuo, 2016).

One of the most addressed topics in the field of international business is, for instance, the globalisation of innovation activities by companies (Perri & Andersson, 2014). This globalisation has taken place thanks to the increasing internationalisation of R&D by large corporations, causing subsidiaries to start playing a leading role in the development of these activities (De Beule & Van Beveren, 2019). The literature on foreign R&D investment has noted that companies internationalise R&D activities to improve the way existing assets are used and the way they become competitive in the external market. But they also do so to create completely new technology assets through foreign-based R&D (Narula & Zanfei, 2009).

For example, while innovation activities would be expected to take place mainly in the country of origin, the globalisation of innovation has enabled subsidiaries to develop R&D activities themselves (De Beule & Van Beveren, 2019), because sources of competitive advantage do not reside in a single country but in many countries, suggesting that new ideas or products may arise in different countries and then be exploited on a global scale (Narula & Zanfei, 2009). On this way, subsidiaries can facilitate local adaptation of the multinational's products or services and acquire global technology for the rest of the corporation (De Beule & Van Beveren, 2019).

At the same time, the internalisation decision stimulates innovation and the development of new skills in the organisation (Lam-González et al., 2019; Rodriguez-Giron & Vanneste, 2018). Innovation is recognised as a significant predictor of companies' intention to internationalise (Pinho et al., 2018). In this sense, internationalisation allows companies to increase their capacity for innovation, through the learning acquired (Javadian & Richards, 2020).

Technological capabilities also create competitive advantages for companies, which favour their internalisation processes (Amorós et al., 2016). In this sense, innovative technology increases the company's likelihood of international expansion (Amorós et al., 2016). Thus, technology has a significant relationship with the international entrepreneurial spirit (Amorós et al., 2016), considering that increasing the level of use of information technologies improves the company's internationalisation capacity (Lecerf & Omrani, 2020). In this respect, the literature highlights the impact of digital technologies on the success of the internationalisation process, specifically in the context of small and medium-sized enterprises (Hervé et al., 2020). This impact is maximised when technologies are integrated into organisational processes and supported by organisational innovation processes (Cassetta et al., 2020).

The literature validates the link between the availability of financial resources and the internationalisation of companies (Rahman et al., 2020). Specifically, effective financial management includes aspects associated with planning actions according to objectives, carrying out the budget based on planning, controlling actions, and evaluating the success of the plan's execution (Villegas, 2015). In addition, clarity in the organisational structure (Villegas, 2015) and the orientation of the system towards the strategic objectives of the company (Savina & Kuzmina-Merlino, 2015) significantly influence the planning and effectiveness of financial management.

From this perspective, financial management is aimed at guaranteeing the resources required to achieve organisational objectives in highly changing environments (Kuzmina-Merlino & Savina, 2015). On the other hand, the financial risk management policy constitutes a central axis of the current commercial strategy, because exchange rate risk has been identified as a threat to international financial management and the creation of value of companies (Vivel-Búa & Lado-Sestayo,

2018). In sum, there is a positive relationship between financial resources and the realisation of international expansion processes (Li, 2019).

The successful search for international activities generates significant benefits for the company, associated with improving profitability and competitiveness (Pinho et al., 2018). Similarly, external knowledge is recognised as an important mechanism for promoting internationalisation (Wu & Liu, 2018). In this sense, organisational ambidexterity is positively associated with internationalisation (Lee et al., 2020; Wu & Liu, 2018) and improves the overall performance of firms (Lee et al., 2020). From this perspective, the orientation towards the recognition of business opportunities is a significant predictor of the internationalisation of firms (Hsieh et al., 2019; Pinho et al., 2018). The identification of opportunities impacts the internationalisation process of firms (Pinho et al., 2018).

Internationalisation processes require also a variety of organisational capabilities (Uner et al., 2020) since company-specific factors such as executive demographic characteristics and knowledge resources affect the decision to internationalise (Song & Lee, 2020). In this regard, the literature of international business also highlights that the acquisition of knowledge accelerates the development of the capacities of firms to internationalise (Hilmersson & Johanson, 2020) and affects the propensity to internationalise (Feng et al., 2020). Thus, the internationalisation process requires developing routines involving various sources of knowledge (Hilmersson & Johanson, 2020). In addition, dynamic capabilities have a direct effect on the export performance of companies (Saputra et al., 2020), self-efficacy, as a trait of an entrepreneurial personality, has a positive impact on the degree of internationalisation (Yang et al., 2020).

Also, despite the growing number of research on the subject, there is little emphasis on literature on the determinants of internationalisation in companies (Li, 2019), and little consensus on the impact of the explanatory variables on the export behaviour of companies (Olmos, 2011). Additionally, a gap is identified in the literature associated with the classification of the different reasons for internationalisation and the business characteristics that make up these reasons (Ahsan et al., 2020).

Although many studies take a macro perspective to analyse the likelihood of internationalisation, we adopt, following previous studies such as Li (2019), a micro perspective since individuals' resources are fundamental factors in explaining international entrepreneurship. In this sense, this study is mainly oriented from the theoretical perspective of resources and capacities, an approach that suggests that there is a positive relationship between the resources of entrepreneurs and their international business activities (Li, 2019).

These resources can be human capital, social capital and cognitive factors. According to previous studies, entrepreneurs' resources increase their ability to recognise and capture business opportunities and increase their intention to explore international markets (Li, 2019). In words of Evald et al. (2011), the human capital of the owner or founder of a company is essential to decide whether or not his/her company should open up to international markets. At the same time, they argue that an optimistic perception of the business environment makes the internationalisation process less uncertain. Entrepreneurs always are trying to identify opportunities. Entrepreneurial opportunities "are those situations in which new goods, services, raw materials, and organizing methods can be introduced and sold at greater than their cost of production" (Casson, 1982 cited by Shane & Venkataraman, 2000, p. 220). For Evald et al. (2011) cognitive factors and the entrepreneur's contact networks are also factors that affect the horizon of their decisions and the level of risk willing to accept, as in the case of a process as uncertain and risky as internationalisation.

Human capital is one of the most important factors for the economic growth of the countries (Kwon, 2009). It refers "to the stock of knowledge and skills possessed by individuals" (Becker 1964 cited by Jones et al., 2010, p. 653). The Theory of Human Capital "indicates that people possess varying skills, knowledge, and experience that have economic value" (Marvel, 2013, p. 404). Becker (1994) distinguishes two types of human capital: general and specific. General human capital alludes to "generic knowledge and skill, not specific to a task or a company, usually accumulated through working experiences and education" (Kwon, 2009, p. 5), while specific human capital "refers to skills or knowledge that is useful to a particular setting or industry, whereas general human capital, such as literacy or formal education, is useful to a great variety of employers" (Wiklund & Shepherd, 2003 cited by Marvel, 2013, p. 404). In that sense, not all people are able to identify entrepreneurial opportunities. It depends on prior knowledge and capabilities (Ko, 2012).

Capabilities refer to specific abilities regarding to entrepreneurial, managerial and technical functions (Ucbasaran et al., 2008). Capabilities help to reinforce the self-efficacy belief for entrepreneurial activity. There are many indicators of entrepreneurial capabilities, as perceived entrepreneurial capabilities. It refers to the fact that an individual can recognise that he/she has the required knowledge and abilities to start a new business.

How individuals recognise opportunities (as the opportunity to export) is a key question in the entrepreneurship field. Moreover, researchers suggest that the opportunity identification process and the entrepreneurs' human capital have a relationship that requires additional research attention (Ucbasaran et al., 2008). Previous studies suggest that human capital can help to understand why some individuals, and not others, can recognise business opportunities in the place where they live. For example, individuals with higher human capital inputs inform superior outputs. In the specific case of entrepreneurship, those outputs are related to identification, pursuit and exploitation of opportunities (Shane, 2003, cited by Ucbasaran et al., 2008, 155).

Over the past few decades academics have proposed a large number of models to analyse the determinants of internationalisation (Li, 2018), few studies have investigated how individual factors affect entrepreneurs' intention to search international markets for their products. In this sense, our study aims to analyse how individual factors such as human capital, social capital and cognitive factors affect an entrepreneur's likelihood of opting for international markets or not, given that so far most studies in the field of international business have focused on macro factors and company-level factors (Pawęta & Zbierowski, 2015). Considering the above, this article addresses the determinants of the internationalisation process in Colombian firms, based on data from the Global Entrepreneurship Monitor (GEM).

2 Methodology

2.1 Research Design

This is a study that adopts a cross-sectional design, since it analyses data from variables collected over a determined-do time period over a predefined sample population or subset (Saunders & Lewis, 2012). This cross-sectional study is based on a publicly available dataset in which data is collected employing a survey strategy.

2.2 Sample and Database

The information that will be analysed in this study is secondary, since it uses data systematically collected by the Global Entrepreneurship Monitor—GEM, in its Adult Population Survey (APS). The GEM is the most prestigious and extensive study on the state of entrepreneurship worldwide, and its main objective is to measure the level of entrepreneurship in countries and analyse their relationship with local economic development (Acheampong & Tweneboah-Koduah, 2018; Pinho & Thompson, 2017; Simmons et al., 2014).

The APS explores the role of the individual in the life cycle of the business process. The focus is not only on the characteristics of the company, but also on the motivation of people to start a company, the actions taken to start and manage a company, as well as the attitudes related to the spirit business. The APS is administered to a minimum of 2000 adults in each economy, ensuring that it is nationally representative (GEM Colombia, 2019).

For the purposes of this study, the sample is made up of Colombians who responded to the 2015 GEM Adult Population Survey (APS), that is, 3.686 individuals.

2.3 Data Analysis Technique

We applied a logistic regression to analyse the relationship between the variables of our study. A logistic regression is especially useful when the dependent variable is dichotomous.

A logistic model explains the probability of success in any situation.

Table 1 Variables description

Variable	Measures
Export	What proportion of your customers will normally live outside the country?
Easy_business	In my country, it is easy to start a business.
Product_novelty	Will all, some or none of your potential customers consider this product or service new and unfamiliar?
Competence	Right now, are there many, few or no other businesses offering the same products or services to your potential customers?
Technology	How long have the technologies or procedures required for this product or service been available?
Financial_inst	Banks or other financial institutions (Received or expect to receive money from. . .?)
Reference_model	Do you know someone personally who started a business in the past 2 years?
Opportunity	In the next six months, will there be good opportunities for starting a business in the area where you live?
Skills	Do you have the knowledge, skill and experience required to start a new business?
Public_media	In my country, you will often see stories in the public media and/or Internet about successful new businesses.

Source: own elaboration

$$y = \begin{cases} 1 \; with \; probability \; p \\ 0 \; with \; probability \; 1 - p \end{cases}$$

In our case, the explanatory variable adopts 1 when in a business the proportion of clients who live outside the country is equal to or greater than 25% (GEM Colombia, 2019), and 0 otherwise. The explanatory variables are also dichotomic in nature (Table 1).

3 Results and Discussion

According to Table 2, the decision to internationalise is associated with ease of doing business, reference models and public media about successful new businesses. Internationalisation is also associated with the product novelty. In that sense, the importance of the innovation in the process of internationalising firms has been addressed in the literature (Santoro et al., 2019). In this sense, a study carried out in Colombia highlights that knowledge-intensive business services (KIBS) firms are highly effective to increase the propensity to export (Moreno-Gómez et al., 2021). Also, the literature highlight that integrated companies achieve better performance in innovation (Luo & Triulzi, 2018). Indeed, the processes of interaction and collaboration between actors are the key to generating innovations (Pamplona & Penha, 2019). Thus, literature recognises the relationship between innovation and competitiveness (Kato-Vidal, 2019). In this scenario the integration of the company's

Table 2 Regression output

	Model A	Model B	Model C
Export Easy_business	0.388* (2.03)	0.386* (2.02)	0.394* (2.11)
Product_novelty	1.099*** (4.76)	1.130*** (4.90)	1.132*** (4.91)
Competence	1.137*** (5.56)	1.169*** (5.71)	1.168*** (5.70)
Technology	0.473 (1.80)		
Financial_inst	1.467*** (7.09)	1.496*** (7.20)	1.499*** (7.25)
Reference_model	0.371 (1.96)	0.368 (1.94)	0.373* (2.00)
Opportunity	0.0329 (0.17)	0.0367 (0.19)	
Skills	0.220 (0.97)	0.224 (0.99)	0.227 (1.00)
Public_media	0.483* (2.19)	0.494* (2.24)	0.500* (2.30)
Constant	−4.996*** (−17.73)	−4.985*** (−17.74)	−4.979*** (−17.84)
Observations	3686	3686	3686
Pseudo R-squared	0.207	0.204	0.204

t statistics in parentheses
$^{*}p < 0.05$, $^{**}p < 0.01$, $^{***}p < 0.001$

processes or their relationship with other actors has a fundamental role, considering that innovation requires new behaviours and interactions with stakeholders (Neutzling et al., 2018).

Additionally, the competition of the firm influences the decision of the companies to internationalise. Indeed, companies in economies in transition are more vulnerable than those in fully developed countries in internationalisation processes, and face greater risks of competition (Caputo et al., 2016). Also, emerging market internationalising firms increase their entrepreneurial orientation through internationalisation (Purkayastha et al., 2021). In this sense, the performance of organisations is determined by their resources and capabilities to use the accumulated knowledge (Andreeva & Kianto, 2012). Knowledge currently corresponds to a strategic resource for business decision-making, through the implementation of technological surveillance and competitive intelligence processes (Pinto & Malcón, 2018). From this perspective, knowledge management aims to identify and leverage the knowledge available in the organisation to achieve the improvement of processes (Andreeva & Kianto, 2012) and the acquisition of a strategic advantage (Talamante-Lugo et al., 2019).

Knowledge also facilitates innovation, improves process quality and promotes a culture based on learning, to maintain high-level human talent (Andreeva & Kianto, 2012). In this sense, knowledge management corresponds to one of the main strategies to innovate and consolidate a sustainable competitive advantage in companies (Alzubi, 2018; Andreeva & Kianto, 2012; Pino Soto, 2018; Sanchez-Gutierrez et al., 2016; Talamante-Lugo et al., 2019).

Finally, access to banks or other financial institutions is a significant variable in the decision of internationalisation of firms. In this way, the availability of resources runs to a fundamental element to obtain and maximise business competitiveness (Lii & Kuo, 2016). In this regard, literature considers different approaches. The first highlights that companies with strong internal resources achieve better performance in their environment (McCan & Folta, 2011). The second approach highlights the importance of acquiring external resources required for the development of the organisation, through exchange related to other companies (Lii & Kuo, 2016) or through clusters (Speldekamp et al., 2020). A third approach, it conceives organisations as open systems, with structures that involve the relationship with their environment (Aldana-Bernal & Bernal-Torres, 2018).

4 Conclusions

This study analyses the determinants of the internationalisation process in Colombian firms, based on data from the Global Entrepreneurship Monitor (GEM). We found that factors such as facility of doing business, reference models and public media about successful new businesses have a positive and significant relationship with the propensity of entrepreneurs to export.

This study is very important because of the context in which it is addressed. Colombia is one of the countries with the highest rate of entrepreneurial intent worldwide. However, although the quality of life of Colombians "has improved substantially over the last decade with rising incomes and declining poverty. Nevertheless, Colombia remains one of the most unequal countries in terms of income distribution compared to the OECD and much of Latin America" (de la Maisonneuve, 2017, p. 5).

We suggest that future studies address the process of internationalisation of entrepreneurs, considering in addition to individual resources, how informal institutions would influence the extent of internationalisation. Finally, the main limitation of this study is that it has been raised from a cross-section design. Future research should analyse this same phenomenon from a longitudinal perspective.

References

Acheampong, G., & Tweneboah-Koduah, E. Y. (2018). Does past failure inhibit future entrepreneurial intent? Evidence from Ghana. *Journal of Small Business and Enterprise Development, 25*, 849–863. https://doi.org/10.1108/JSBED-03-2017-0128

Ahsan, F. M., Sinha, A., & Srinivasan, R. (2020). Exploring firm-level antecedents that drive motives of internationalization: A study of knowledge intensive Indian firms. *Management and Organization Review, 16*, 867–906. https://doi.org/10.1017/mor.2020.3

Aldana-Bernal, J. C., & Bernal-Torres, C. A. (2018). Soft factors in the management of integration supply chains and/or networks: Approximation to a conceptual model [Factores blandos en la gestión de integración de las cadenas y/o redes de abastecimiento: Aproximación a un modelo conceptual]. *Information Technology, 29*, 103–114. https://doi.org/10.4067/S0718-07642018000200010

Alzubi, Y. (2018). Knowledge transfer for sustainability: The role of knowledge enablers in the construction industries in Jordan. *World Journal of Science Technology and Sustainable Development, 15*, 325–337. https://doi.org/10.1108/wjstsd-04-2018-0023

Amorós, J. E., Basco, R., & Romaní, G. (2016). Determinants of early internationalization of new firms: The case of Chile. *The International Entrepreneurship and Management Journal, 12*, 283–307. https://doi.org/10.1007/s11365-014-0343-2

Andreeva, T., & Kianto, A. (2012). Does knowledge management really matter? Linking knowledge management practices, competitiveness and economic performance. *Journal of Knowledge Management, 16*, 617–636. https://doi.org/10.1108/13673271211246185

Arredondo Trapero, F., Vázquez Parra, J. C., & de la Garza, J. (2016). Factores de innovación para la competitividad en la Alianza del Pacífico. Una aproximación desde el Foro Económico Mundial. *Estud Gerenciales, 32*, 299–308. https://doi.org/10.1016/j.estger.2016.06.003

Becker, G. S. (1994). Human capital revisited. In *Human capital: A theoretical and empirical analysis with special reference to education* (3rd ed., pp. 15–28). The University of Chicago Press.

Brandão, F., Breda, Z., & Costa, C. (2019). Innovation and internationalization as development strategies for coastal tourism destinations: The role of organizational networks. *Journal of Hospitality and Tourism Management, 41*, 219–230. https://doi.org/10.1016/j.jhtm.2019.10.004

Caputo, A., Matteo Pellegrini, M., Dabic, M., & Dana, L. P. (2016). Internationalisation of firms from Central and Eastern Europe: A systematic literature review. *European Business Review, 28*, 630–651. https://doi.org/10.1108/EBR-01-2016-0004

Cassetta, E., Monarca, U., Dileo, I., Di Berardino, C., & Pini, M. (2020). The relationship between digital technologies and internationalisation. Evidence from Italian SMEs. *Industry and Innovation, 27*, 311–339. https://doi.org/10.1080/13662716.2019.1696182

Chen, H., Zeng, S., Wu, C., & Fu, H. (2020). The dual effect of foreign competition on emerging market firms' internationalization. *Management Decision*. https://doi.org/10.1108/MD-11-2019-1525

Chen, J., Saarenketo, S., & Puumalainen, K. (2016). Internationalization and value orientation of entrepreneurial ventures—a Latin American perspective. *Journal of International Entrepreneurship, 14*, 32–51. https://doi.org/10.1007/s10843-016-0169-9

Ciravegna, L., Kuivalainen, O., Kundu, S. K., & Lopez, L. E. (2018). The antecedents of early internationalization: A configurational perspective. *International Business Review, 27*, 1200–1212. https://doi.org/10.1016/j.ibusrev.2018.05.002

de la Maisonneuve, C. (2017). Towards more inclusive growth in Colombia. *OECD economics department working papers, no. 1423*, OECD Publishing, Paris. https://doi.org/10.1787/334902e0-en

Dabić, M., Maley, J., Dana, L. P., Novak, I., Pellegrini, M. M., & Caputo, A. (2020). Pathways of SME internationalization: A bibliometric and systematic review. *Small Business Economics, 55*, 705–725. https://doi.org/10.1007/s11187-019-00181-6

De Beule, F., & Van Beveren, I. (2019). Sources of open innovation in foreign subsidiaries: An enriched typology. *International Business Review, 28*, 135–147. https://doi.org/10.1016/j.ibusrev.2018.08.005

Denicolai, S., Zucchella, A., & Magnani, G. (2021). Internationalization, digitalization, and sustainability: Are SMEs ready? A survey on synergies and substituting effects among growth paths. *Technological Forecasting and Social Change, 166*, 120650. https://doi.org/10.1016/j.techfore.2021.120650

Evald, M. R., Klyver, K., & Christensen, P. R. (2011). The effect of human capital, social capital, and perceptual values on nascent entrepreneurs' export intentions. *Journal of International Entrepreneurship, 9*, 1–19. https://doi.org/10.1007/s10843-010-0069-3

Feng, X., Ma, X., Shi, Z., & Peng, X. (2020). How knowledge search affects the performance of reverse internationalization enterprises: The co-moderating role of causation and effectuation.

Journal of Knowledge Management, 25, 1105–1127. https://doi.org/10.1108/JKM-05-2020-0393
GEM Colombia. (2019). *Dinámica de la Actividad Empresarial en Colombia*. Universidad ICESI.
Hervé, A., Schmitt, C., & Baldegger, R. (2020). Internationalization and digitalization: Applying digital technologies to the internationalization process of small and medium-sized enterprises. *Technology Innovation and Management Review, 10*, 28–40. https://doi.org/10.22215/timreview/1373
Hilmersson, M., & Johanson, M. (2020). Knowledge acquisition strategy, speed of capability development and speed of SME internationalisation. *International Small Business Journal of Research Entrepreneurship, 38*, 536–556. https://doi.org/10.1177/0266242620909029
Hsieh, L., Child, J., Narooz, R., et al. (2019). A multidimensional perspective of SME internationalization speed: The influence of entrepreneurial characteristics. *International Business Review, 28*, 268–283. https://doi.org/10.1016/j.ibusrev.2018.09.004
Javadian, G., & Richards, D. (2020). Examining gendered variations in the internationalisation of businesses. *International Journal of Management and Enterprise Development, 19*, 126–148. https://doi.org/10.1504/IJMED.2020.107399
Jones, O., Macpherson, A., & Thorpe, R. (2010). Learning in owner-managed small firms: Mediating artefacts and strategic space. *Entrepreneurship and Regional Development, 22* (7–8), 649–673.
Kato-Vidal, E. L. (2019). Productividad e innovación en pequeñas y medianas empresas. *Estud Gerenciales, 35*, 38–46.
Ko, S. (2012). Entrepreneurial opportunity identification: A motivation-based cognitive approach. *Journal of Applied Management and Entrepreneurship, 17*(2), 23–37.
Kuzmina-Merlino, I., & Savina, S. (2015). Assessing the effectiveness of improved financial management system using the expertise-oriented approach. *Procedia Social and Behavioral Sciences, 207*, 833–842. https://doi.org/10.1016/j.sbspro.2015.10.174
Kwon, D. B. (2009). Human capital and its measurement. In *The 3rd OECD world forum on "statistics, knowledge and policy" charting progress, building visions, improving life* (pp. 27–30). OECD World Forum.
Lam-González, Y. E., Suárez-Rojas, C., & León, C. J. (2019). Factors constraining international growth in nautical tourism firms. *Sustainability, 11*, 6846. https://doi.org/10.3390/su11236846
Lecerf, M., & Omrani, N. (2020). SME internationalization: The impact of information technology and innovation. *Journal of the Knowledge Economy, 11*, 805–824. https://doi.org/10.1007/s13132-018-0576-3
Lee, J. Y., Yang, Y. S., & Park, B. I. (2020). Interplay between dual dimensions of knowledge sharing within globalized chaebols: The moderating effects of organization size and global environmental munificence. *International Business Review, 29*. https://doi.org/10.1016/j.ibusrev.2019.101637
Li, T. (2018). Internationalisation and its determinants: A hierarchical approach. *International Business Review, 27*, 867–876. https://doi.org/10.1016/j.ibusrev.2018.01.009
Li, T. (2019). Engagement in international entrepreneurship: Interactive effects of resource-based factors and institutional environments. *Journal of Global Entrepreneurship Research, 9*, 1–17. https://doi.org/10.1186/s40497-019-0185-z
Lii, P., & Kuo, F. I. (2016). Innovation-oriented supply chain integration for combined competitiveness and firm performance. *International Journal of Production Economics, 174*, 142–155. https://doi.org/10.1016/j.ijpe.2016.01.018
Luo, J., & Triulzi, G. (2018). Cyclic dependence, vertical integration, and innovation: The case of Japanese electronics sector in the 1990s. *Technological Forecasting and Social Change, 132*, 46–55. https://doi.org/10.1016/j.techfore.2017.12.009
Marvel, M. R. (2013). Human capital and search–based discovery: A study of high–tech entrepreneurship. *Entrepreneurship Theory and Practice, 37*(2), 403–419.
McCan, B. T., & Folta, T. B. (2011). Performance differentials within geographic clusters. *Journal of Business Venturing, 26*, 104–123.

Moreno-Gómez, J., Escandón-Charris, D., Moreno-Charris, A., & Zapata-Upegui, L. (2021). Analysis of the role of process innovation on export propensity in KIBS and non-KIBS firms in Colombia. *Competitiveness Review An International Business Journal, 31*, 497–512. https://doi.org/10.1108/CR-12-2019-0154

Narula, R., & Zanfei, A. (2009). *Globalization of innovation: The role of multinational enterprises*. The Oxford Handbook of Innovation.

Neutzling, D. M., Land, A., Seuring, S., & Nascimento, L. F. M. d. (2018). Linking sustainability-oriented innovation to supply chain relationship integration. *Journal of Cleaner Production, 172*, 3448–3458. https://doi.org/10.1016/j.jclepro.2017.11.091

Olmos, M. F. (2011). The determinants of internationalization: Evidence from the wine industry. *Applied Economic Perspectives and Policy, 33*, 384–401. https://doi.org/10.1093/aepp/ppr017

Orero-Blat, M., Palacios-Marqués, D., & Garzón, D. (2020). Knowledge assets for internationalization strategy proposal. *Journal of Innovation and Knowledge*. https://doi.org/10.1016/j.jik.2020.08.002

Pamplona, J. B., & Penha, A. C. (2019). Innovation policy for the mining sector in Brazil: A comparative analysis with Sweden centered on the interactions of involved agents. *Cad EBAPEBR, 17*, 959–974. https://doi.org/10.1590/1679-395174445x

Pawęta, E., & Zbierowski, P. (2015). Individual-level determinants of international orientation of a firm: A study based on global entrepreneurship monitor data. *Journal of Intercultural Management, 7*, 43–58. https://doi.org/10.1515/joim-2015-0003

Perri, A., & Andersson, U. (2014). Knowledge outflows from foreign subsidiaries and the tension between knowledge creation and knowledge protection: Evidence from the semiconductor industry. *International Business Review, 23*, 63–75. https://doi.org/10.1016/j.ibusrev.2013.08.007

Pinho, J. C. M., Martins, L., & Soares, A. M. (2018). Small businesses' internationalization: International readiness in the context of Asian countries. *Asia-Pacific Journal of Business Administration, 10*, 50–63. https://doi.org/10.1108/APJBA-05-2017-0043

Pinho, J. C. M., & Thompson, D. (2017). Institutional-driven dimensions and the capacity to start a business. *International Marketing Review, 34*, 787–813. https://doi.org/10.1108/imr-12-2015-0279

Pino Soto, C. G. (2018). Innovation and internationalization on the competitiveness of exporting firms: Lessons from South American emerging economies. *Academia Revista Latinoamericana de Administración, 31*, 651–662. https://doi.org/10.1108/ARLA-12-2016-0336

Pinto, I., & Malcón, C. (2018). Inteligencia de negocios e inteligencia competitiva como elementos detonadores para la toma de decisión informada: Un análisis bibliométrico. *Revista Internacional de Investigación e Innovación Tecnológica, 6*, 1–9.

Pulgarin-Molina, S. A., Castro, A. M., Ballesteros, A., & Barrera, J. M. (2017). Innovation and the development of exportable supply in non-traditional goods: A longitudinal study in a Latin American economy. *International Journal of Innovation Science, 9*, 265–282. https://doi.org/10.1108/IJIS-10-2016-0036

Purkayastha, A., Kumar, V., & Gupta, V. K. (2021). Emerging market internationalizing firms: Learning through internationalization to achieve entrepreneurial orientation. *Journal of World Business, 56*, 101207. https://doi.org/10.1016/j.jwb.2021.101207

Rahman, M., Akter, M., Odunukan, K., & Haque, S. E. (2020). Examining economic and technology-related barriers of small- and medium-sized enterprises internationalisation: An emerging economy context. *Business Strategy and the Environment, 3*, 16–27. https://doi.org/10.1002/bsd2.71

Rodriguez-Giron, S., & Vanneste, D. (2018). Determinants for tourist destinations' international markets access: The case of Southern Ecuador and Germany. *Tourism, 66*, 282–301.

Sanchez-Gutierrez, J., Mejia-Trejo, J., Vargas-Barraza, J. A., & Vazquez-Avila, G. (2016). Intellectual capital, impact factor on competitiveness: Manufacturing industry SMEs in Mexico. *Measuring Business Excellence, 20*, 1–11. https://doi.org/10.1108/MBE-12-2015-0059

Santoro, G., Mazzoleni, A., Quaglia, R., & Solima, L. (2019). Does age matter? The impact of SMEs age on the relationship between knowledge sourcing strategy and internationalization. *Journal of Business Research, 128*, 779–787. https://doi.org/10.1016/j.jbusres.2019.05.021
Saputra, D., Abdurachman, E., Kuncoro, E. A., et al. (2020). The mediating effect of the internationalization process on knowledge management and export towards smes export performance. *International Journal of Innovation, Creativity and Change, 11*, 550–562.
Saunders, M. N., & Lewis, P. (2012). *Doing research in business and management*. Pearson.
Savina, S., & Kuzmina-Merlino, I. (2015). Improving financial management system for multi-business companies. *Procedia Social and Behavioral Sciences, 210*, 136–145. https://doi.org/10.1016/j.sbspro.2015.11.352
Shane, S., & Venkataraman, S. (2000). The promise of entrepreneurship as a field of research. *The Academy of Management Review, 25*(1), 217–226.
Simmons, S. A., Wiklund, J., & Levie, J. (2014). Stigma and business failure: Implications for entrepreneurs' career choices. *Small Business Economics, 42*, 485–505. https://doi.org/10.1007/s11187-013-9519-3
Song, S., & Lee, S. (2020). Motivation of internationalization and a moderating role of environmental conditions in the hospitality industry. *Tourism Management, 78*, 10450. https://doi.org/10.1016/j.tourman.2019.104050
Speldekamp, D., Knoben, J., & Saka-Helmhout, A. (2020). Clusters and firm-level innovation: A configurational analysis of agglomeration, network and institutional advantages in European aerospace. *Research Policy, 49*, 103921. https://doi.org/10.1016/j.respol.2020.103921
Talamante-Lugo, E., Felix-Moreno, J. L., Feuchter-Leyva, C. I., Sanchez-Schmitz, G., Hernández, J. L. O., & Romero, L. F. (2019). Use of storage technologies to select knowledge management tools and strategies for m-smes. *Ingeniare, 27*, 421–430. https://doi.org/10.4067/S0718-33052019000300421
Ucbasaran, D., Westhead, P., & Wright, M. (2008). Opportunity identification and pursuit: Does an entrepreneur's human capital matter? *Small Business Economics, 30*(2), 153–173.
Uner, M. M., Cetin, B., & Cavusgil, S. T. (2020). On the internationalization of Turkish hospital chains: A dynamic capabilities perspective. *International Business Review, 29*, 101693. https://doi.org/10.1016/j.ibusrev.2020.101693
Villegas, B. S. (2015). Factors influencing administrators' empowerment and financial management effectiveness. *Procedia Social and Behavioral Sciences, 176*, 466–475. https://doi.org/10.1016/j.sbspro.2015.01.498
Vivel-Búa, M. M., & Lado-Sestayo, R. (2018). Foreign exchange exposure in Latin America: Evidence for Spanish firms. *Academia Revista Latinoamericana de Administración, 31*, 212–238. https://doi.org/10.1108/ARLA-04-2017-0130
Wu, H., & Liu, Y. (2018). Balancing local and international knowledge search for internationalization of emerging economy multinationals: Evidence from China. *Chinese Management Studies, 12*, 701–719. https://doi.org/10.1108/CMS-09-2017-0254
Yang, M. M., Li, T., & Wang, Y. (2020). What explains the degree of internationalization of early-stage entrepreneurial firms? A multilevel study on the joint effects of entrepreneurial self-efficacy, opportunity-motivated entrepreneurship, and home-country institutions. *Journal of World Business, 55*, 101114. https://doi.org/10.1016/j.jwb.2020.101114

Vanessa Pertuz PhD in Management. Master in Research and Development Project Management. Professor at Universidad Nacional Abierta y a Distancia-UNAD, Colombia. She is an Associate Researcher recognised by the Ministry of Science, Technology and Innovation of Colombia (MINCIENCIAS).

Luis Francisco Miranda Ph.D. student in Business at the Universitat de Barcelona. Master in Business Research. His research is focused on open and collaborative innovation, environmental management, sustainability-oriented innovation, and entrepreneurship.

Arturo Charris-Fontanilla Dean of the Faculty of Administrative, Economic and Accounting Sciences of Instituto Nacional de Formación Técnica Profesional Humberto Velásquez García, Ciénaga, Colombia. His research is focused on entrepreneurship, competitiveness, and strategy.

Javier Viloria Escobar PhD candidate in Educational Sciences of Universidad del Magdalena, Colombia. Business Administrator. Professor of Instituto Nacional de Formación Técnica Profesional Humberto Velásquez García, Ciénaga, Colombia. Active member of the Research Group on Management of Organisations-GIGO.

The manufacturer's authorised representative in the EU is Springer Nature Customer Service Centre GmbH, Europaplatz 3, 69115 Heidelberg, Germany. If you have any concerns regarding our products, please contact ProductSafety@springernature.com

Printed and bound by CPI Group (UK) Ltd, Croydon, CR0 4YY
30/09/2026
02225650-0006